IN F
WE T

IN FED
WE TRUST

BEN BERNANKE'S WAR
ON THE GREAT PANIC

DAVID WESSEL

THREE RIVERS PRESS
NEW YORK

To Morris and Irm Wessel, my parents,
who showed me the way

CONTENTS

PREFACE

April 2010

In the year that has passed since this book was first published, a few things have become clearer. The United States did not suffer another Great Depression, and the economy—though far from healthy—came out of intensive care. The actions of the Federal Reserve, the Congress, and the Bush and Obama administrations stabilized the banking system. The stock market rebounded, and credit markets moved toward something resembling normal. With some hesitation, the U.S. Senate confirmed Ben Bernanke for a second four-year term as Fed chairman. This edition includes a new epilogue that carries the story through these developments.

New details about pivotal moments continue to emerge in e-mails, congressional hearings, and memoirs. New explanations of the root causes of the crisis are being fashioned in academic seminars and journals. A new global financial regulatory regime is being crafted in an attempt to prevent a recurrence of the Great Panic. But the basic story remains the same: The United States found itself at the edge of the abyss and was pulled back in large measure through the efforts of the Federal Reserve.

DRAMATIS PERSONAE

In the Government

BEN BERNANKE
Chairman, Federal Reserve Board (2006–)

DONALD KOHN
Vice Chairman, Federal Reserve Board (2006–)
Member, Federal Reserve Board (2002–2006)

KEVIN WARSH
Member, Federal Reserve Board (2006–)

TIMOTHY GEITHNER
Secretary of the Treasury (2009–)
President, Federal Reserve Bank of New York (2003–2009)

HENRY PAULSON
Secretary of the Treasury (2006–2009)

ALAN GREENSPAN
Chairman, Federal Reserve Board (1987–2006)

LAWRENCE SUMMERS
Director, White House National Economic Council (2009–)

In the Private Sector

JAMES DIMON
Chief Executive, JPMorgan Chase (2005–)

RICHARD FULD
Chief Executive, Lehman Brothers (1994–2008)

KENNETH LEWIS
Chief Executive, Bank of America (2001–)

VIKRAM PANDIT
Chief Executive, Citigroup (2007–)

CHARLES PRINCE
Chief Executive, Citigroup (2003–2007)

ALAN SCHWARTZ
Chief Executive, Bear Stearns (2008)
President or Copresident (2001–2008)

WHATEVER IT TAKES

At the beginning of October 2008, after some of the toughest weeks of the Great Panic, the lines in Ben Bernanke's face and the circles under his eyes offered evidence of more than a year of seven-day weeks and conference calls that stretched past midnight. Sometimes all that seemed to keep Bernanke going was the constantly restocked bowl of trail mix that sat on his secretary's desk and the cans of diet Dr Pepper from the refrigerator in his office. But the balding, bearded chairman of the Federal Reserve managed a smile as he confided that he had a title for the book he would write someday about his watch as helmsman of the world economy: *Before Asia Opens...*

The phrase was a reference to the series of precedent-shattering decisions that Bernanke and others at the Fed and Treasury had been forced to make with insufficient sleep and inadequate preparation on Sundays so they could be announced before financial markets opened Monday morning in Asia, half a day ahead of Washington and New York.

Before Asia Opens... was not a laugh line. The subprime mortgage mess was made in America, and that meant the U.S. government was forced to lead the cleanup. Ben Bernanke had more immediate power to do that than any other individual. The president of the United States can respond instantly to a missile attack with real bullets; he cannot respond instantly to financial panic with real money without the prior approval of Congress. But Bernanke could and did.

Yet the United States had become so dependent on the flow of money from abroad and the business of American financial institutions was so intertwined with those overseas that Bernanke didn't have the luxury of waiting until the sun rose over Washington to make decisions and pronouncements. Hence the subject line Goldman Sachs economists put on one of their weekly e-mails: "Sunday is the new Monday."

There was the Sunday in March 2008 when the Federal Reserve shattered seventy years of tradition and lent $30 billion to induce JPMorgan Chase to buy Bear Stearns, a flailing investment bank the Fed neither regulated nor officially protected.

And the Sunday in August 2008 when Bernanke and Treasury Secretary Henry Paulson, the nation's self-appointed investment banker in chief, decided to seize Fannie Mae and Freddie Mac, the government-sponsored, shareholder-owned mortgage giants that had borrowed heavily from abroad.

And the Sunday in late September 2008 when Bernanke and his Wall Street field marshal, Timothy Geithner, then president of the Federal Reserve Bank of New York, pressured the Federal Deposit Insurance Corporation to invoke an emergency law to subsidize Citigroup's attempt to strengthen itself by acquiring Wachovia.

Yet no Sunday of the Great Panic would prove as consequential and controversial as September 14, 2008, the day Bernanke, Geithner, and Paulson allowed Lehman Brothers to fail after a desperate search for someone to buy it.

The government-sanctioned bankruptcy of a Wall Street firm founded before the Civil War marked a new phase in the Great Panic, a moment when financial markets went from bad to awful. The *Wall Street Journal* dubbed it the "Weekend That Wall Street Died." Lehman's bankruptcy was the largest in U.S. history. The financial market reaction was ugly. At the end of trading on Monday, the Dow had plummeted over 500 points, its biggest one-day drop since September 17, 2001, when trading resumed following the 9/11 attacks. While financial giants led the way down — Goldman Sachs stock lost 19 percent, Citigroup 15 percent — every major sector on the S&P 500 index posted a loss. Other economic indicators were also negative: In anticipation of a global slowdown, oil prices plunged, while spooked investors sent the price of supersafe Treasury bills soaring. In a sign of what was coming, dozens of traders crowded around the specialists who trade American International Group, America's largest insurance company, on the New York Stock Exchange floor as Monday's trading began. AIG shares, which had closed on Friday at $12.14, opened Monday at $7.12 and ended the day at $4.76.

As horrible as the first day after Lehman was, the bigger fear was that nobody knew where the collapse might end. Bernanke, Geithner, and Paulson confronted the biggest threat to American capitalism since the 1930s, and their responses were commensurately big.

Within one week, they:

- married venerable brokerage house Merrill Lynch to Bank of America
- all but nationalized AIG, pumping in $85 billion of Fed money to keep it alive
- risked taxpayer money to halt a run on money market mutual funds no one ever considered guaranteed by the government
- administered last rites for Wall Street's investment-banking business model by converting Goldman Sachs and Morgan Stanley into Fed-protected bank-holding companies
- pleaded with Congress to give the Treasury $700 billion to prevent catastrophe, a request that ultimately led to a Republican administration taking a government ownership stake in the nation's biggest banks

The Fed was the first responder. It acted as quickly and forcefully as its leaders could manage in order to prevent the country — and the global economy — from plunging into the abyss. Bernanke bluntly said as much later: "We came very, very close to a global financial meltdown, a situation in which many of the largest institutions in the world would have failed, where the financial system would have shut down, and…in which the economy would have fallen into a much deeper and much longer and more protracted recession."

In ways that the public and politicians had never before appreciated, that weekend, and the months that followed, would reveal that the Federal Reserve had become a *fourth branch of government,* nearly equal in power to the executive, legislative, and judicial branches, though still subject to their constitutional authority if they chose to assert it.

Ben Bernanke and a small cadre of advisers would vow to do *whatever it takes* to avoid a possibility that, until 2008, was unthinkable: a repeat of the Great Depression.

THE REPUBLIC OF THE CENTRAL BANKER

The Federal Reserve—one chairman, six other Washington-based governors, the twelve presidents of regional Fed banks that dot the map from Boston to San Francisco, 21,199 employees—is given extraordinary latitude. Few checks exist on its actions beyond the oath of the chairman and other governors to obey the Constitution and laws of the United States and the admonitions of its lawyers, a strong unwritten sense of what constitutes sound central banking, and the awareness that Congress has the power to curb the Fed's independence if it strays too far from what the public deems acceptable. As Berkeley economic historian and prolific blogger Brad DeLong put it: "It is either our curse or our blessing that we live in the Republic of the Central Banker."

During the reign of Alan Greenspan—which wasn't much of a republic—the smart people of the Federal Reserve allowed the housing bubble to inflate. They stood by as banks and investors made ever bigger bets on the flawed assumption that housing prices would never fall across the country. They encouraged financial engineering that created securities so complex that neither inventor nor seller nor buyer could fully understand them, instruments that proved toxic to those who bought them and to everyone around them. They shielded financial engineers from attempts at government regulation and restraint. With huge sums at stake, they trusted investors and traders to protect themselves—and the rest of us—better than even the smartest government regulator could hope to. Ultimately, they failed to see that the big banks that the Fed was charged with supervising were gambling with the global economy. It was, among other things, a colossal failure of imagination.

When the bubble burst, Greenspan was gone. Ben Bernanke, the Princeton professor who had devoted an academic career to understanding the Great Depression, had taken his place. The Bernanke Fed initially misdiagnosed the condition. It underestimated the harm that the bursting housing bubble was doing to the U.S. economy and its banking system. It was surprised repeatedly and was forced to apply ever-larger tourniquets to stop the bleeding until the Fed and the Treasury finally talked Congress into a $700 billion blood transfusion — and even that was insufficient.

As the crisis accelerated, the Fed came under fire from all sides — accused of being overly generous to Wall Street by helping JPMorgan Chase buy Bear Stearns, overly punitive in its terms for lending to AIG, and overly complacent for letting Lehman die. The Fed was simultaneously charged with putting so much credit into the economy that it was creating tomorrow's inflation and putting in so little that it was ignoring today's risk of deflation.

Like central banks elsewhere, the Fed is traditionally the "lender of last resort," a phrase borrowed from the French in the eighteenth century by Sir Francis Baring, who described the Bank of England as "the dernier resort." The phrase conveys the Fed's role as the ultimate protector of the financial system on which the entire economy relies. Until the Great Panic, "lender of last resort" usually meant lending to sturdy banks at times when frightened customers wanted to pull out their money. The point was to allow healthy banks to reimburse depositors without forcing the banks to demand early repayment of sound loans or to dump securities in overwhelmed markets — or to sell the furniture — none of which would be good for the overall economy. Banks were regarded as special: taking savings from millions and channeling them into loans for productive investments that individual savers would never have made directly. If banks stopped lending, the economy stopped. The Fed was there to look after the banks. When other companies, even other financial companies, ran into trouble, well, that was someone else's problem — or so the Fed thought.

AUTHORITY AND ABDICATION

In the Great Panic, Bernanke took the Fed beyond the traditional role of lender of last resort to the core of the banking system. When he took office in February 2006, the Fed had $860 billion of loans and securities on its books, nearly all supersafe U.S. Treasury securities. By the end of 2008, the Fed had more than $2.2 trillion of loans and securities on its books, most of them riskier than U.S. Treasury securities. The Fed was lending not only to conventional commercial banks, but also to investment banks, to insurance companies, to auto finance outfits like GMAC, to industrial companies like General Electric, and indirectly to homeowners and consumers. As the law required, the Fed demanded collateral, a security or something else that it could sell if the borrower didn't pay back the loan. But as the Great Panic intensified, the Fed became less picky about collateral. A widely circulated comment on one blog labeled it "the pawnbroker of last resort."

And when it looked like even that wasn't enough and that the political system was paralyzed, Bernanke's Fed in March 2009 said it was prepared to put an additional $1 trillion into the economy — buying up Treasury bonds and mortgages in the markets.

The Great Panic was different from the succession of lesser panics and recessions that occurred in the late twentieth century. As frightening as some of those seemed at the time, the Fed managed them with the standard central banker tools — moving interest rates up and down, lending to healthy banks that needed quick cash, cajoling the chief executives of big banks to do what was needed to prevent crises that threatened the financial system. Jimmy Carter had recruited Paul Volcker to restore global confidence in the U.S. economy and the U.S. dollar and to end an inflationary spiral that, at the time, seemed unstoppable. In Ronald Reagan's years, Volcker helped big American banks cope with massive losses on loans they had made to Latin American governments. His successor, Alan Greenspan, steered the economy through the storms of the 1987 market crash and then helped clean up the mess left by savings and loan associations that were pulled under by a combination of shortsighted regulation and lousy real estate loans.

But the Great Panic was much bigger — in price tag, in geographic scale, and in duration. And so was the Fed's response. What the Bernanke Fed did was necessary. Inaction at a time of such pervasive economic peril would have been devastating. But the Great Panic challenged the ideology of capitalism: economies do best when markets, not governments, decide who gets credit and who does not. What's more, the Fed's actions challenged the essence of democracy: the people's elected representatives levy taxes and spend money.

Barney Frank, the sharp-tongued sharp mind who chaired the House Financial Services Committee, captured the issue clearly. Labeling Bernanke "the loan arranger" with his sidekick, Paulson, Frank said, "I think highly of Mr. Bernanke and Mr. Paulson. I think they are doing well, although I think it's been inappropriate in a democracy to have them in this position where they were sort of doing this stuff unilaterally. They had no choice. And it's not to their discredit, but…this notion that you wait until there's a terrible situation and you just hope that the chairman of the Federal Reserve would pop up with the secretary of the Treasury and rescue you. It's not the way in a democracy…you should be doing this.…

"No one in a democracy, unelected, should have $800 billion to spend as he sees fit," he said.

The Great Panic exposed the alchemy of central banking: the Fed could create money from nothing. Printing money, they called it, although it was actually creating money with electronic keystrokes that showed up in the account of a bank somewhere. In the early stages, the Fed came up with over $115 billion to get Bear Stearns sold to JPMorgan Chase and to prevent insurance company AIG from rushing to bankruptcy court. By early 2009, with some help from the $700 billion financial-rescue fund that Congress eventually agreed to give the Treasury, it was prepared to create more than $3 trillion. *Whatever it takes.*

The Great Panic challenged the competency of those best equipped to calm it. Yet for all that the Fed did, it was often clumsy. Bernanke at times deferred so much to Paulson — always forceful, often impulsive, sometimes politically inept — that he undermined the Fed's credibility as the one economic institution of government that does what is necessary regardless of the politics of the moment. Tim Geithner often said that at times of crisis, the government had to get both the *substance* and the *theater* right. How a line was delivered and how a policy was framed — the setting, tone, and backdrop — could matter as much in a media-saturated environment as the actions themselves. At its best, this approach made wise policy decisions more effective; at its worst, it led Geithner to overestimate his ability to use words — detractors would call it "spin" — to disguise a mistake or to explain away actions that were not always consistent. Bernanke, Geithner, and, even more so, Paulson muffed the theater. Because they didn't tell a convincing story about what was happening or offer a clear explanation of what they were doing, other accounts of varying plausibility filled the vacuum on cable TV, on the Internet, on trading floors, in executive suites, and in the imaginations of frightened investors.

At the outset, the Fed did not do enough soon enough to prevent what has become the most painful recession in more than a generation: Once Bernanke did step up, the Fed became such a whirlwind of activity that it took President George W. Bush, Treasury Secretary Paulson, and the U.S. Congress off the hook, allowing them to avoid timely, but politically uncomfortable, measures that might have prevented some of the worst of the damage.

But with no textbook or contingency plan beyond Ben Bernanke's lifelong obsession with the Great Depression, he and those closest to him responded aggressively and creatively enough to reduce the chances of the Great Panic becoming another Great Depression. Using tools invented by discredited financial engineers, the Fed devised ways to lend money and buy assets that Bernanke's predecessors hadn't dared to contemplate.

Despite resistance from inside the Fed — and a sluggish start — Bernanke ultimately took to heart his own critique of the Japanese central bank, which over a decade earlier had proved unwilling to experiment or try any policy that wasn't absolutely guaranteed to work. "Perhaps it's time for some Rooseveltian resolve in Japan," Bernanke had suggested in 1999. "Many of [FDR's] policies did not work as intended, but in the end FDR deserves great credit for having the courage to abandon failed paradigms and to do what needed to be done."

This is the story of the Bernanke Fed abandoning "failed paradigms" in order "to do what needed to be done." It is the story of what the Fed saw and what it missed, what it did and what it didn't, what it got right and what it got wrong. It is a story about Ben Bernanke deciding to do *whatever it takes*. Above all, it is a story about a handful of people — overwhelmed, exhausted, beseeched, besieged, constantly second-guessed — who found themselves assigned to protect the U.S. economy from the worst economic threat of their lifetimes.

Chapter 1

LET OL' LEHMAN GO

The Fed's embassy on Wall Street is an iron-barred, neo-Florentine fortress built in the 1920s. Even before completion, it was criticized as so "luxurious and lavish" that it "will make Solomon's temple of old seem quite cheap in comparison." The building sits atop $195 billion worth of gold in a vault that rests fifty feet below sea level on the bedrock of Manhattan. Carved into the lobby wall, the Fed's mission statement includes some archaic words ("to furnish an elastic currency") and some still relevant ("to unite the resources of many banks for the protection of all"). A center of power itself, the Federal Reserve Bank of New York also is a key nexus between the worlds of Wall Street finance and Washington politics. Few dramas in its building have played out as momentously as the events of September 13 and 14, 2008, when the building played host to the death of Lehman Brothers, the shotgun marriage of Merrill Lynch to Bank of America, and the preparations to effectively nationalize AIG, the nation's largest insurance company.

Lehman and Merrill Lynch had been on worry lists around the globe since the Fed had brokered the sale of failing investment bank Bear Stearns to JPMorgan Chase seven months earlier. As the financial rot from the housing market spread during the summer of 2008, Lehman's basic problem was not uncommon: a huge pile of bad real estate loans that it couldn't sell. What was unusual was the size: in just six months, it had taken $6.7 billion in losses on its commercial real estate portfolio. Its shares had fallen by 90 percent since the beginning of the year.

Both Paulson, the hyperactive Treasury secretary, and the New York Fed's coolly analytical president, Tim Geithner, had been fielding calls from Lehman's longtime CEO, Dick Fuld, for months — even before the firm announced a couple of days after the Bear Stearns rescue that its first-quarter earnings were down 57 percent from the year before. Both Paulson and Geithner told him to raise capital or find a buyer. Fuld looked — with all of Wall Street watching intently.

At one point, Fuld suggested that Lehman could split into two pieces — putting the rotting real estate assets in a separate entity — if only the government would come up with $4 billion. Lehman had flirted with becoming "a bank-holding company," a way to wrap itself in the Fed's protective blanket and assure investors that it would always have access to Fed loans in a crunch. The Fed listened, but Geithner, among others, was skeptical that an identity change would solve Lehman's underlying problem. "No naked bank-holding companies," he told Lehman. (Translation: a change in legal status without a fundamentally different business strategy wouldn't suffice.)

Paulson, who never thought much of Lehman when he was running Goldman Sachs, found Fuld unrealistically optimistic. But unlike some, even among his own staff, Paulson didn't think the problem was that Fuld was asking too much for his company. "Everyone out there knew that Lehman was sitting there. If they wanted to do a deal with Lehman, they weren't going to be constrained by the price Dick was asking," Paulson said later. A last-minute attempt to raise equity from a Korean bank fell through.

Lehman's time was running out.

COMMANDERS IN CHIEF

Just a few days after orchestrating the government takeover of mortgage giants Fannie Mae and Freddie Mac — a maneuver that would have consumed all their attention for months in ordinary times — Ben Bernanke and

Paulson met for their usual weekly breakfast. This week, they sat in a small antiques-furnished conference room adjacent to Paulson's larger corner office in the Treasury building. In calmer times, the two would have chewed over the surprisingly smooth execution of their plan to seize control of Fannie Mae and Freddie Mac, which were in danger of losing their ability to borrow money because of mounting losses on mortgages they held in their portfolios or had guaranteed. But Lehman pushed itself to the top of the worry list. At midmorning, Bernanke and Paulson convened a conference call to talk Lehman strategy with their top lieutenants and Christopher Cox, the former California congressman who was chairman of the Securities and Exchange Commission and ostensibly Lehman's regulator.

With Lehman clearly struggling for survival, Paulson and Bernanke assured each other — and the others on the call — that all the companies and traders that did business with Lehman had been given time to protect themselves from a possible Lehman bankruptcy. They comforted themselves that, since the Bears Stearns bailout, the Fed had found new ways to lend to other investment houses that might be hurt by a Lehman collapse. They were wrong.

Paulson and Bernanke were directing the entire response of the U.S. government. There had been no high-powered, explore-all-the-options meeting at the White House to contemplate a looming problem as significant as Lehman. Oddly for an administration that had made a habit of interventions and micromanagement throughout the government, Bush and his team had delegated almost unconditional responsibility for managing the Great Panic to the Treasury and the Fed.

Paulson called the plays and kept the White House informed, most commonly through phone calls to Keith Hennessey, the economic-policy coordinator, or Joel Kaplan, the deputy White House chief of staff. Paulson didn't do e-mail. When the Smithsonian's National Museum of American History later asked for his BlackBerry, Paulson said he didn't have one and gave the museum his overused cell phone.

After meeting with Bernanke, Paulson flew to New York on a private plane he paid for himself. He could afford it. He had earned $40 million as Goldman's

CEO in 2005 and had sold nearly $500 million worth of Goldman shares accumulated over his thirty-two years at the firm when he took the Treasury job in 2006. Goldman Sachs had sent so many alumni to positions of power in both Democratic and Republican administrations that it was sometimes called "Government Sachs."

Paulson had played on the offensive line of the Dartmouth College football team, and had a permanently bent little finger on his left hand as a result. After getting an M.B.A. from Harvard, he worked in the Pentagon and later in the Nixon White House as a liaison with the Treasury and Commerce departments. A Christian Scientist with a passion for nature, Paulson initially worked in Goldman's Chicago office, and he and his wife raised their son and daughter on his family farm in Illinois.

Paulson was a physically restless man, even when sitting down, and brought to the Treasury the impatience and drive that had taken him to the top of Goldman Sachs. He issued orders to his secretaries while they were on the phone talking to someone else. He made assignments to staffers and then checked on progress ten minutes later. He convened Sunday-afternoon meetings at his house and focused so intently on the work that he didn't offer drinks or snacks. And he had a tendency to talk more than listen, thinking through a problem by talking about it out loud instead of reflecting quietly or making a list of issues on a legal pad as Bob Rubin, a previous Goldman Sachs executive turned Treasury secretary, did. His closest advisers learned that he often stopped listening to them before they stopped talking, prompting them to tell him explicitly when they were making a crucial point.

With him were Dan Jester, a forty-three-year-old Goldman Sachs investment banker Paulson had drafted out of retirement, and Steve Shafran, another Goldman alum. "Our purpose," Paulson said, "was to either get a deal done for Lehman or have the rest of the industry help one of their competitors make an acquisition."

Paulson wanted a deal for Lehman, and he was prepared for tough negotiations, but he did not want a huge taxpayer-funded bailout: "We said: 'If you're not going to do the acquisition, you're going to need to figure out what you're going to do to help with the wind-down of Lehman because...you have to understand the powers that we have and we don't have.'"

Bernanke stayed in Washington, in nearly constant touch by phone. His immediate interests in New York would be represented by his lieutenant, Kevin Warsh, a role Warsh filled during several pivotal moments of the Great Panic. A young and ambitious former investment banker, Warsh split his time between his Washington office at the Fed — the same office that Bernanke had occupied earlier in the decade when he was a Fed governor — and an office he had commandeered next to Geithner's temporary quarters on the thirteenth floor of the New York Fed. (The Great Panic coincided with the renovation of the cavernous, wood-paneled, tenth-floor executive suite at the New York Fed, its arched hallways modeled on those of the fifteenth-century Palazzo Strozzi, built by a rival of the Medici, the greatest banking family of the Renaissance.)

As Paulson and Jester rode from the Teeterboro, N.J., airport to the New York Fed, a gaggle of Bank of America executives called Jester's cell phone. Bank of America and Britain's Barclays bank were the two potential Lehman buyers — and the best remaining hope for doing for Lehman what had been done earlier for Bear Stearns. For weeks, Paulson had brought all his energy and training as a mergers-and-acquisitions banker to the effort, pressing Bank of America's CEO, Ken Lewis, to buy Lehman without any government help.

But the Bank of America executives now said buying Lehman without help wasn't possible.

Paulson's reply: tell them to show me their best offer.

The executives told Jester that Lehman was carrying assets on its books that were worth about $25 billion less than Lehman said they were. If Bank of America were to do a deal, someone — the government or a consortium of other financial firms — would have to take $25 billion to $30 billion of Lehman's bad real estate assets.

"I'M BEING CALLED MR. BAILOUT. I CAN'T DO IT AGAIN"

Government bank bailouts were hardly unprecedented in the United States or abroad. Between 1986 and 1995, the government shuttered more than a thousand savings and loan associations with assets totaling over $500 billion — for a total cost that ended up at about $150 billion. In that case, as in most others, the decision to spend huge sums of money was made by democratically elected leaders, not unelected central bankers. Now, however, the clock was ticking: if $30 billion was needed this weekend to seal a deal to save Lehman, it was going to have to come from the Fed. For its part, the Fed *could* come up with large sums of money quickly, but neither Bernanke nor Paulson was comfortable with doing so — especially after facing so much criticism for the assertive government role in getting Bear Stearns sold in March 2008.

In a conference call with Bernanke and Geithner, Paulson had stated unequivocally that he would not publicly support spending taxpayers' money — the Fed's included — to save Lehman. "I'm being called Mr. Bailout," he said. "I can't do it again." Though Paulson had no legal ability to stop the Fed, Bernanke and other officials were extremely reluctant to put money into any Lehman deal over the Treasury secretary's objections — unless, as Paulson often did, he changed his stance.

Paulson was a deal maker. He didn't build relationships by socializing. He focused relentlessly on studying his clients, figuring out what motivated them, and reaching the desired outcome. It was a style that helped him in February 2008 negotiate an emergency $152 billion tax cut with a Democratic Congress to try to give the economy a jolt. But like many on Wall Street, he could shout "No! No!" before, citing changed circumstances, abruptly saying "Yes!" The approach provided flexibility in negotiating the best business deal; it didn't build lasting credibility in Washington. He would later argue that each of his exaggerations or unqualified statements was justified by prevailing circumstances or tactics. His "Mr. Bailout" outburst, he insisted months later, was calculated to stop any lower-level government employees on the conference call from weakening the government's bargaining position by leaking that the government might put in money. But his words were so emphatic that listeners later were stunned by his subsequent actions.

As Lehman's problems deepened, the Treasury secretary's style occasionally brought him into conflict with Geithner, his partner in managing the crisis. Geithner's approach — at least when he was at the New York Fed — was more disciplined, calmer, and politically savvy. A veteran of the U.S. Treasury's management of the Asian financial crisis of the 1990s, Geithner had learned at the side of Clinton's agile Treasury secretary, Bob Rubin. Rubin placed a high premium on what his then-deputy Lawrence Summers called "preserving optionality"—deferring final decisions until they had to be made and avoiding any public statement that could limit his political wiggle room. Rubin prized flexibility, and so did Geithner. That made sense in an ever-changing panic, but this approach risked turning crisis management into a series of ad hoc decisions that left everyone from traders in the markets to politicians in Congress guessing at the rules of the game.

Geithner had strenuously cautioned Paulson and Bernanke against publicly displaying any regret about the Bear Stearns bailout. In the calm, methodical manner that earned him respect inside the Fed and Treasury, Geithner counseled that the best approach now would be to ask: Is the system at risk if Lehman defaults? Is there a way to prevent default? If so, can the government help legally?

The Geithner method, however, required a certain team discipline, and that had fallen apart Thursday night when a couple of Paulson's aides—Jim Wilkinson, his chief of staff, and Michele Davis, his spokeswoman and chief of policy planning—jumped the gun, spreading the word of Paulson's no-taxpayer-money-for-Lehman vow to the press. "U.S. Helps Lehman Go Up for Sale; Regulators Are Seeking a Weekend Deal Not Involving Public Money" read the front-page story in the *Washington Post* on Friday, September 12. Reuters news service, citing "a source familiar with Paulson's thinking," said the Treasury secretary was "adamant" that no government money be used. The Associated Press and the *Wall Street Journal* said much the same thing.

Davis and Wilkinson didn't want Paulson to walk into a roomful of Wall Street CEOs who expected him to pull out the Treasury's or the Fed's checkbook to help one of them buy Lehman. Better to save the checkbook until the last minute. It also seemed plausible that Paulson was doing something more than staking out a tough bargaining position. Perhaps, as the press put it, Paulson was "drawing a line in the sand." After all, he had said emphatically a few months before: "For market discipline to constrain risk effectively, financial institutions must be allowed to fail."

Whatever Paulson's reasons—and Wilkinson and Davis's reasons for previewing them—Geithner thought that publicly drawing "a line in the sand" during a financial crisis was lunacy. Paulson's staff seemed to be telling the world that the Treasury and the Fed had decided to cut Lehman loose to punish Wall Street miscreants. Sending a tough message — "Washington to Wall Street: Drop Dead" — at a moment of panic was wrong. Geithner lost his customary cool, telling Paulson emotionally: "The amount of public money you're going to have to spend is going up, more than you would have otherwise! Your statement is way out of line!" Geithner understood, but Paulson and some of his staff didn't appear to, that a tough bargaining stance in a room full of investment bankers made sense, but that the press, the markets, and foreign officials abroad couldn't distinguish a bargaining position from a policy position.

"YOU'RE DOING THIS ONE"

Paulson and Geithner's differences were suppressed as the CEOs of the twenty largest banks and investment houses gathered in a conference room on the first floor of the New York Fed at 6 P.M., Friday, September 12. Paulson sat at one end of the table with Christopher Cox, the chairman of the Securities and Exchange Commission, beside him. Geithner sat at the other end. The goal: to get Wall Street to come up with enough money to make Lehman Brothers attractive to one of its two surviving suitors, Bank of America or Barclays, much as Bear Stearns had been married to JPMorgan Chase.

"We did the last one," Paulson told the men, according to a person who was there. "You're doing this one." There would be no government bailout for Lehman. Either someone would buy the company, sharing the losses with other Wall Street firms, or the government would let it go under. He told the CEOs that if the government did put money in, the political reaction would be overwhelming, and Wall Street firms would feel the pain.

Geithner — in phrasing that would fuel speculation that he would have saved Lehman had it been up to him — told the assembled executives: "There is no political will for a federal bailout."

Then, as Geithner always did in a crisis, he divided the necessary work among task forces. "He is very iterative," one of Geithner's aides said. "What's the best idea? Go back and work on it. Come back in two hours. He's incredibly tenacious. He just keeps going. How many iterations are required to get to where we want to go? Five hundred? OK, I'll go to five hundred."

Morgan Stanley, Merrill Lynch, and Citigroup were assigned to see if the industry could band together to run what Geithner called "a liquidation consortium" to sell off Lehman in pieces. Their mission was to do essentially what had happened back in 1998 when the New York Fed had summoned the heads of Wall Street firms to prevent an untidy collapse of a hedge fund, Long Term Capital Management. That episode demonstrated how one large and leveraged institution, in this case a hedge fund that had recruited Nobel Prize–winning economists to hone its strategy, could threaten the entire financial system. But back then the Fed managed to cajole Wall Street firms into paying the tab; this time the problems were bigger and more widespread.

Goldman and Credit Suisse, which had been working with Lehman for weeks, were assigned to look over Lehman's commercial real estate assets to determine their worth. Everyone in the room believed their value to be far below the value Lehman had been carrying on its books. Their job was to look particularly at the assets no buyer would take, figure out "how big the hole is," and devise some way to share the risk in order to get one of their competitors to buy the rest of Lehman.

A third group was asked, in Geithner's phrase, to "put foam on the runway" — that is, prepare for a Lehman bankruptcy.

"Come back in the morning and be prepared to do something," Geithner told them.

Geithner and Paulson were asking a lot. They wanted the firms present to put in big bucks in the middle of a financial panic to strengthen a competitor, and they knew that Lehman wasn't the end of the line. As the CEOs filed out of the conference room shortly before midnight, everyone was aware that even if Lehman were saved, big brokerage house Merrill Lynch and giant insurer AIG were next in line and perhaps Morgan Stanley, too. Or as Fed governor Kevin Warsh put it later: "We were running out of buyers before we were running out of sellers."

On Saturday morning, Bank of America executives told Paulson and Geithner that Lehman was in deeper trouble than they had realized just twenty-four hours before: someone would need to take between $65 billion and $70 billion of smelly real estate assets if Bank of America were to buy the firm, it said.

That was enough to convince Paulson, Geithner, and Warsh that Bank of America didn't really want to do the deal. Their attention turned to Barclays, the British bank.

All day Saturday, Paulson and Geithner talked in person and by phone with Barclays executives and fielded frequent calls from Lehman's Fuld, who had been told to stay away. Paulson shuttled constantly between Geithner's thirteenth-floor office and the first-floor conference room, where in excruciating detail he briefed executives from other firms on the latest developments.

The group assigned to think through liquidating Lehman quickly concluded that their mission was impossible. So attention shifted toward "filling the hole," somehow coming up with a way for a group of Wall Street firms to take the assets that Barclays didn't want so a deal could be struck.

But, the conversation made clear, no one was confident Lehman would be the last firm to be rescued. "If we're going to do this deal, where does it end?" asked Morgan Stanley's John Mack. Everyone knew AIG and Merrill Lynch were vulnerable. The big question hanging in the air: Would banding together to save Lehman reduce the odds that AIG or Merrill would also need rescuing, or were they in such deep trouble already that they would need rescuing anyway?

To put pressure on the executives, Geithner emphasized the limits to the Fed's and Treasury's ability to shield them from the fallout of a Lehman bankruptcy. "You need to know," Geithner told the CEOs, "that if we are unable to work out some solution, we do not have the capacity to insulate you or the system from the consequences."

The pressure from the government officials was intense. Paulson made it clear to Merrill Lynch's John Thain—in front of his peers—that it was time for him to find a buyer. Paulson pulled Thain aside and said without nuance: find a buyer. Geithner reinforced the point. Merrill's shares had fallen by 36 percent the week before.

Thain took the hint and called Ken Lewis, of Bank of America, Saturday morning, and the two men met that afternoon. Thain tried to sell Lewis a 9.9 percent stake in the company, but before the weekend was over he had agreed to sell the whole company. At the time, Bank of America wasn't asking for any government aid to do the deal.

The rest of Wall Street saw the merits of the Paulson-Geithner argument that their firms would be better off if Lehman didn't go into bankruptcy. By Saturday night, the Wall Street firms had agreed on a way to help "fill the hole," or at least most of it, if a deal to buy Lehman could be struck.

Despite all of Paulson's assertions, Geithner, Bernanke, and Warsh all expected the Treasury to endorse a Bear Stearns–style loan by the Fed if Barclays and the Wall Street firms couldn't come up with enough money. The numbers kept changing, but in the end, other Wall Street firms and the government would have had to come up with roughly $10 billion to close a gap that would remain if Barclays did the deal. The eight firms agreed to pitch in about $4 billion, basically to protect themselves from the consequences of a Lehman bankruptcy.

"If there had been a buyer, the guys on the first floor would have filled the hole, and if they wouldn't have, we would have," Warsh said later.

If there had been a buyer.

Paulson had been warned even before going to New York that the British government was unenthusiastic about Barclays's eagerness to buy Lehman. In a phone conversation, Alistair Darling, the finance minister, told him so. "We are not going to import your cancer," Darling said.

Paulson joked, hopefully, that perhaps the British regulator, the Financial Services Authority (FSA), truly was independent of the British finance ministry and would bless the Barclays deal. He didn't see any alternatives to Barclays, and it *was* interested.

Paulson, Geithner, and Warsh left the New York Fed late Saturday hoping to seal a deal on Sunday.

THE BRITISH AREN'T COMING

On Sunday morning, September 14, U.S. officials were troubled to discover that the British FSA was, in fact, an obstacle. Geithner and SEC chairman Cox had been talking frequently with Hector Sants, the FSA head. They had assumed he was at least neutral, if not an ally. He was proving anything but.

The technical issue was that the Fed and Treasury insisted Barclays guarantee all of Lehman's liabilities so the firm could open for business Monday morning, just as JPMorgan Chase had done with Bear Stearns earlier. Without that, no one would be willing to do business with Lehman the next day. At the last minute, though, Barclays discovered that stock-exchange listing rules would require a shareholder vote on such a guarantee—unless the FSA waived the rule. The FSA refused to grant the waiver. Geithner pressed the New York Fed's lawyers for some way that the Fed might provide the guarantee, but they couldn't find a way. The deal died.

Paulson and Geithner concluded that the British regulator, with good reason, didn't want its bank to swallow a problem as large as Lehman. (Barclays later bought Lehman's core U.S. business from the bankruptcy court, including a $1 billion Manhattan skyscraper, for $1.75 billion.)

Without a buyer, the only alternative to bankruptcy was a Fed-financed takeover of Lehman, one that would have cost two or maybe three times as much as the $30 billion the Fed spent on Bear. Neither Paulson nor Bernanke nor Geithner audibly advocated that step, according to their own recollections and those of others involved.

There would be no show of Roosevelt-like resolve this time. Lehman signed bankruptcy papers on Sunday, September 14, a day that will live in financial infamy because it coincided with, or triggered, a devastating intensification of the Great Panic.

On Sunday afternoon, Paulson recounted in the book he published in 2010, President George Bush telephoned. "Will we be able to explain why Lehman is different from Bear Stearns?" he asked. It was a very good question. "Yes, sir," Paulson said he replied. "There was just no way to save Lehman. We couldn't find a buyer even with the other private firms' help. We will just have to try to manage this."

Paulson, Geithner, and Bernanke came into the weekend with different pressures. Paulson had been singed by previous bailouts and, though given extraordinary leeway by President Bush, was hardly getting encouragement from the White House or Republicans in Congress to bail out another big financial house. He wanted to avoid spending taxpayer dollars, and he had great confidence in his ability to push CEOs to do deals that would serve both their own and the U.S. economy's interests.

Geithner was nearly always the most "forward leaning" of the three, the one most ready to intervene to stop something bad from happening. Though closest to the center of pain on Wall Street, he was also convinced that smart people could find a good-enough solution to almost any crisis and then could deal with the unintended consequences later.

Bernanke usually was as eager to act as Geithner and as worried about the damage that a major financial institution's collapse would cause at a time of panic and distrust. But Bernanke, too, had been facing intense pressure over the Fed's new activist role. He was hectored from all directions by fundamentalists who saw the Fed's role in the Bear Stearns rescue as a dangerous precedent.

"We got a lot of flak on Bear Stearns," Bernanke said in a September 2008 interview. "It's not that long ago that we had the Jackson Hole meetings" — an annual Fed conference in the Grand Tetons — "and a lot of economists there were saying: 'Oh, you know, you should be in favor of the market. Let them fail. The market will deal with it.'"

Bernanke thought that was idiocy. "I was unpersuaded," he said. "I believed that a failure of a major institution in the midst of a financial crisis would not only create contagion through effects on counterparties, but would likely have a tremendous negative effect on broader market confidence."

But worry that the Fed had gone too far was heard deep inside the Fed — and not just with fundamentalists. One Fed official confided later in September that he had acquiesced in the decision to let Lehman go. Why? "Because I thought people had anticipated it. They [Lehman Brothers] were still very big [but] they had shrunk a lot. It was time to find out what would happen if we didn't stand behind all these guys. It had been a long time coming." With hindsight, that tough-guy stance looked, at best, naïve.

All the pressures notwithstanding, Paulson, Geithner, and Bernanke were all willing to put in *some* Fed money to close a deal with Barclays — even Paulson, otherwise he wouldn't have kept talks going with the British when it was clear that some government money might be needed to close a deal.

But once the Barclays deal fell through, neither Bernanke nor Geithner was prepared to nationalize Lehman without Paulson's backing—even if their lawyers found a way to do so. The three had started the weekend hoping that they could sell Lehman and prevent a catastrophic collapse of the firm.

But in what would prove a colossal mistake, they hadn't come prepared with a plan to prevent a bankruptcy if they couldn't sell Lehman as they had managed to sell Bear Stearns. Once a sale proved impossible, they would be forced to scramble to explain why they didn't do more.

"Everything Fell Apart"

Nobody at the Fed expected it to be pretty, but none anticipated the severity of the reaction that came the day after Lehman died. The Dow Jones Industrial Average lost over 4 percent of its value, and losses were just as steep in international markets.

Criticism, though, came not only from stock tickers: the rest of the world was stunned, too. Christine Lagarde, the French finance minister, called the decision "horrendous" in an interview with French radio network RTL. "For the equilibrium of the world financial system, this was a genuine error." The same complaint came from the European Central Bank. "[T]he failure of Lehman Brothers could have and should have been avoided," said Lorenzo Bini Smaghi, a University of Chicago Ph.D. and a member of the European Central Bank's executive board. In private, Jean-Claude Trichet, Bernanke's counterpart at the ECB, said the same thing. Another ECB banker a few weeks later confided: "We don't let banks fail. We don't even let dry cleaners fail. It never occurred to us that the Americans would let Lehman fail."

One of the distinguishing features of the Great Panic was that the United States was the source of the disturbance, not the financial stalwart that would protect more vulnerable or mismanaged economies from harm. Ten years earlier, during the financial crisis that swept through Asia to Russia to Latin America in the late 1990s, small-country central bankers asked their local banks if they had *borrowed* from U.S. banks and thus were vulnerable to being cut off from the flow of money if the small country's finances looked shaky. This time, in a reversal, the same central bankers asked their local banks if they had *lent* to U.S. financial institutions and thus faced potentially huge losses should an American behemoth fail.

Back in Washington, Paulson went to the White House press room Monday morning and made what sounded like an unambiguous declaration that he had been unwilling, not unable, to save Lehman: "I never once considered that it was appropriate to put taxpayer money on the line...in resolving Lehman Brothers." That was not true. Paulson said months later he meant that he never considered using taxpayer money to keep Lehman alive as a stand-alone company.

Nine days later, on September 24, Bernanke and Paulson sat side by side on Capitol Hill. Bernanke, always extremely careful to avoid any sign of disagreement with Paulson in public, also implied that a choice had been made. "In the case of Lehman Brothers," he said, reading from prepared testimony, "the Federal Reserve and the Treasury declined to commit public funds to support the institution. The failure of Lehman posed risks. But the troubles at Lehman had been well known for some time, and investors clearly recognized—as evidenced, for example, by the high cost of insuring Lehman's debt in the market for credit default swaps—that the failure of the firm was a significant possibility. Thus, we judged that investors and counterparties had had time to take precautionary measures."

Paulson and Bernanke's statements were more than after-the-fact window dressing. Although Lehman was already dead, the cause of death wasn't a secondary issue. Lehman's collapse caused—or coincided with—so much financial turmoil in large part because of the lack of a consistent story. Did the government let Lehman fail to teach Wall Street a lesson? Or were they legally powerless to save it? Was Bear Stearns a one-time-only rescue? Would the United States let other major financial firms fail? Every financial firm viewed its trading partners with suspicion.

"Everything fell apart after Lehman," Alan Blinder, a Princeton economist—Bernanke's former colleague—and former Fed vice chairman, later wrote. "People in the market often say they can make money under any set of rules, as long as they know what they are. Coming just six months after Bear's rescue, the Lehman decision tossed the presumed rulebook out the window. If Bear was too big to fail, how could Lehman, at twice its size, not be? If Bear was too entangled to fail, why was Lehman not? After Lehman went over the cliff, no financial institution seemed safe. So lending froze, and the economy sank like a stone. It was a colossal error, and many people said so at the time."

Bernanke and Paulson implied initially that they deliberately let Lehman go. But their later accounts were, well, different. In a January 2009 interview, a few days before leaving Treasury, Paulson said that the truth could not be spoken in September 2008. "We were unable to talk about it in a way in which we wanted to talk about it," he said. "You're unable to say: 'We let it go down because we were powerless to do anything about it.'" After Lehman's collapse, Merrill Lynch had been saved for the moment, but Paulson feared Morgan Stanley would be threatened next and perhaps his own Goldman Sachs would be next. In that climate, publicly admitting that the U.S. government was impotent to stop Lehman's failure would have made everything worse. "You don't want to say 'the emperor has no clothes,'" Paulson explained.

Bernanke never disavowed his testimony, and nothing in it was untrue. But as time passed, he emphasized the legal constraints that had stopped the Fed and Treasury—rather than repeating the sense that the markets were ready for Lehman's collapse. With a commercial bank, one that took deposits that were insured by the federal government, the law established ways to tap the Federal Deposit Insurance Corporation to rescue a systemically important bank, he said. But Lehman wasn't a commercial bank. The law didn't provide a clean way for the government to take over or close an investment bank—no matter how important.

The law said that the Fed could lend to nearly anyone if the Fed board in Washington declared circumstances to be "unusual and exigent," provided that the loan was to be "secured to the satisfaction" of Geithner's New York Fed. That was a problem, both Geithner and Bernanke said days after Lehman's bankruptcy. With Bear Stearns, the Fed had a reasonable chance of selling the assets it bought at close to what the Fed had paid for them, or so they argued. But Lehman was literally worthless. Its debts were overwhelming its assets, and much of its collateral already had been pledged for other loans. There wasn't enough wiggle room in the law to do a deal as big as Lehman, they insisted.

By the end of 2008, Bernanke, Paulson, and Geithner had coalesced around the explanation that—without a buyer—neither the Treasury nor the Fed had the authority to spend what it would have taken to save Lehman. "Neither the Department of the Treasury, the executive branch, nor the Federal Reserve had been given the authority by the Congress that would...have made it possible for the government to put in capital on a scale necessary to avoid default," Geithner told the Senate during his January 2009 confirmation hearings to replace Paulson as Treasury secretary.

Bernanke also made it clear that had Congress given the Fed and the Treasury more authority sooner—for example, had the Troubled Assets Relief Program (TARP) been enacted earlier—he would not have let Lehman fail. "We could have saved it. We would have saved it," he said in an interview in October 2008. "Even then, it would have been politically tough because of the risks to the taxpayer that would have been involved. And, of course, if Lehman hadn't failed, the public would not have seen the resulting damage and the story line would have been that such extraordinary intervention was unnecessary."

WHATEVER IT TAKES

Two harrowing days after Lehman's collapse, with markets bruised and panic spreading, the Fed shelled out $85 billion to prevent AIG, the big insurer, from following Lehman to bankruptcy court. While the federal government took an 80 percent stake in the insurance company and planned to replace senior management, the move undermined the case that the Fed and the Treasury had been unable to save Lehman.

To be sure, there were legal differences: AIG had profitable operating businesses that were pledged as collateral for the Fed loan. But the primary motivation was more practical than legal: Bernanke and Paulson believed that the global financial system *could* absorb Lehman's bankruptcy without catastrophe. A second shock only two days later was a different matter.

"Why not Lehman and why AIG?" Bernanke asked aloud in an interview days after he'd helped keep the insurance giant from bankruptcy. The short answer: AIG was bigger. The markets weren't expecting it to go. And Lehman had just gone under.

"The impact of AIG's failure would have been enormous," Bernanke continued. "AIG was bigger than Lehman and was involved in an enormous range of both retail and wholesale markets. For example, they wrote hundreds of billions of dollars of credit protection to banks, and the company's failure would have led to the immediate write-downs of tens of billions of dollars by banks. It would have been a major shock to the banking system." Even banks that weren't intertwined with AIG would have been hurt, he said. "Since nobody really knew the exposures of specific banks to AIG, confidence in the entire banking system would have plummeted, putting the whole system at risk."

"A disorderly failure of AIG," Bernanke told Congress the same week, "would have severely threatened global financial stability—and, consequently, the performance of the U.S. economy."

It was becoming clear that Bernanke had adopted a new mantra: *whatever it takes*. He would not go down in history as the chairman of the Federal Reserve who dithered and delayed during a financial panic that threatened American prosperity. Sunday, September 14, 2008, would be the last day the Fed would say "No!" to any financial institution of significance. Just two days later, it did the AIG deal. Within weeks, the Fed would successfully press the rest of the U.S. government to guarantee the debts of all the nation's banks, to buy shares in banks to bolster their financial conditions, and to declare that the government would not let another "systemically important" financial institution go under.

Barney Frank, the congressman from Massachusetts, proposed declaring Monday, September 15, to be Free Market Day. On Sunday, the Fed and the Treasury let Lehman fail; on Tuesday, they took over AIG. "The national commitment to the free market lasted one day," Frank said. "It was Monday."

Chapter 2

"PERIODICAL FINANCIAL DEBAUCHES"

I n the fall of 1907, the U.S. economy was hanging by a thin thread over a very deep pit. With stock prices tumbling, a number of prominent brokerage houses already had closed their doors. Faced with runs on their assets, bank managers instructed tellers to count out withdrawals in slow motion. Without fresh loans, New York City was a week or two away from declaring bankruptcy. What became known as the Panic of 1907 was on, and the only man who could save the nation from financial ruin was attending an Episcopal Church convention in Richmond, Virginia.

Telegrams flew back and forth between his offices in lower Manhattan and the convention site. Racing back to work would only stoke the hysteria, it was decided. Instead, he waited until the weekend, then boarded his private railroad car and started for home. Press dispatches followed his progress breathlessly until at last seventy-year-old J. Pierpont Morgan — known by friend and foe as "Jupiter," god of the skies — stepped onto the platform in New York on Sunday, October 20, and the work of rescuing the financial system could begin in earnest.

One hundred one years later, the same scenario would unfold in a Great Panic that remarkably parallels the earlier one, even to the point of Morgan's progeny at the firm of JPMorgan Chase being summoned to rescue Bear

Stearns. This time the starring role of Jupiter would be played by a far more complex mechanism: the Federal Reserve.

The opening years of the twentieth century had been a time of prosperity. The nation rebuilt its economy after the depressions and deflation of the 1890s. Exports doubled between 1897 and 1907. Foreign capital flooded what was the emerging-market economy of its day, the United States, though the term hadn't yet been invented. Banks, insurance companies, brokerage firms boomed. J. P. Morgan bestrode it all like a colossus. Campaigning to end what he called "ruinous competition," Morgan merged companies that had been rivals to create enduring giants such as General Electric and U.S. Steel. Between 1894 and 1904, more than 1,800 companies were merged, acquired, and consolidated into just 93. A joke of the day had a schoolchild telling a teacher: "God made the world in 4004 B.C. and it was reorganized in 1901 by J. P. Morgan."

But the political and financial waters were far from calm. "War was fresh in mind. Immigration was fueling dramatic changes in society. New technologies were changing people's everyday lives. Business consolidations and their Wall Street advisers were creating large, new combinations through mergers and acquisitions, while the government was investigating and prosecuting prominent executives — led by an aggressive prosecutor from New York. The public's attitude towards business leaders, fueled by a muckraking press, was largely negative," University of Virginia business professors Robert F. Bruner and Sean D. Carr wrote in a history published on the hundredth anniversary of the Panic of 1907.

The world economy was tethered to gold, as countries tried to maintain the value of their currencies for a fixed amount of gold, a "gold standard." In 1900, for instance, the U.S. government declared that one dollar would be worth 1.505 grams of gold, setting the price of a troy ounce of gold at $20.67. In years when little new gold was mined, the global economy grew slowly and prices of goods and services tended to fall. After gold was discovered in Alaska and South Africa in the 1890s, the opposite occurred. The mining of gold and its flow from other countries into the United States did essentially what the Federal Reserve does today — expand and contract the supply of money.

A gold standard can restrain inflation and provide certainty for businesses trading internationally. With it, everyone the world around knew exactly what a dollar was worth — one reason nostalgia for the standard still surfaces periodically. But the inherent rigidities of pegging the dollar or any currency to a specific quantity of gold meant that in an unwelcome economic disturbance, governments were limited in their response. The gold standard, for instance, offered no way to expand the money supply temporarily to cope with the seasonal cash flow to farm states to pay for newly harvested crops. And there was no way for the government to flood the economy with money in a crunch, as the Fed did after the stock market crash in 1987 or the 9/11 terrorist attacks in 2001. (The world flirted with a gold standard off and on until Richard Nixon finally killed it in 1971, declaring that the U.S. government would no longer exchange dollar bills for gold at any price.)

By default, the gold standard and the absence of any central U.S. bank often left it to individuals to fill the gap, and that individual was often J. P. Morgan. When the U.S. Treasury's gold reserves fell dangerously low in 1893, Morgan rescued the government by organizing a private syndicate to raise $100 million in gold for the United States and personally guaranteeing that the gold wouldn't flow back to Europe. It was an extraordinary show of financial courage and muscle, far in excess of the power held by modern-day financial guru Warren Buffett and the $5 billion he invested in Goldman Sachs and $3 billion in General Electric during the Great Panic. Yet while Buffett is celebrated and almost universally admired for sagacity, Morgan was often vilified. For populist, and popular, demagogues like three-time presidential candidate William Jennings Bryan, Morgan and his vast private holdings were the problem — not the solution — to the inequities and periodic turmoil in the United States. No one doubted to whom Bryan was referring when he excoriated "the idle holders of idle capital" and vowed to liberate "the struggling masses who produce the wealth and pay the taxes of the country" from "the cross of gold" in his 1896 oration to the Democratic convention.

OFF TO SEE THE WIZARD

Gold and silver, money and banking, the tension between urban lenders and rural borrowers, were at the center of American politics almost from the beginning. The nation's early history is marked by what Bray Hammond, a 1940s Fed staffer turned historian, called the "agrarian antipathy for city, commerce and finance." Thomas Jefferson was famously suspicious of banks as well as of paper currency. "I sincerely believe...that banking establishments are more dangerous than standing armies," he wrote in an 1816 letter. The tensions over the power of money were very close to the surface in the late nineteenth and early twentieth centuries and for good reason: thirteen banking panics careened through the economy between 1814 and 1914 by one scholarly tally, more than one a decade.

Monetary debates were even the stuff of popular culture. Indeed, L. Frank Baum's enduring *The Wonderful Wizard of Oz*, published in 1900, has been read as an elaborate allegory for the monetary politics of the era. Dorothy stands for the American people at their best; Aunt Em and Uncle Henry, the struggling farmers; the cyclone, the financial storms and political unrest of the 1890s. Slippers of silver (not the ruby ones of the movie version) tread the path of gold (the Yellow Brick Road) that leads to the Emerald City of power (Washington). There are the unemployed urban factory worker (the rusting Tin Man), the farmer (Scarecrow), and in some interpretations, pacifist William Jennings Bryan himself (the Cowardly Lion with a frightening roar). The wizard, in allegorical readings, is a political charlatan, in some versions Mark Hanna, the strategist widely seen as manipulating William McKinley. (If only the book had been written later, literary economists could have painted the wizard as chairman of the Federal Reserve. Alan Greenspan, after all, was likened to the Wizard of Oz, the man whose aura of mystery and power exaggerated his wisdom and capacity to control events.)

Populism and the campaign to promote silver as a supplement to gold died when McKinley beat Bryan in the 1896 presidential election, but tension between borrower and lender, farmer and financier, worker and Wall Street, didn't disappear. Hostility to big money ebbed and flowed, but American workers, farmers, and debtors had a recurrent suspicion that "Wall Street" or the "money trust" or "the robber barons" were responsible for economic misery. This recurrent American suspicion went into remission during much of the 1990s and 2000s when Americans enjoyed rising stock prices and climbing home values, but it returned with virulence during the Great Panic with multibillion-dollar bailouts of banks and bonuses paid to executives of failing companies.

In 1901, McKinley was assassinated and succeeded by Teddy Roosevelt, who railed against "malefactors of great wealth." Five years into his presidency, in 1906, the prosperity of the moment was disrupted by a devastating earthquake in San Francisco, then the financial center of the West, and that, in turn, sent shock waves throughout the financial markets. By the spring of 1907, the economy was weakening, stock prices were sinking, gold reserves were low, and interest rates were rising — the makings of a financial perfect storm.

As would be the case a century later, tinder was scattered throughout the financial system. All that was needed to start a calamitous fire was a match, and that was provided by a botched October 1907 attempt by speculators to corner the market for shares of United Copper Company. The idea was to buy up the bulk of the company's shares, drive up the price, and profit by selling them to other investors who had bet that the shares would fall. It didn't work. United Copper shares soared to $62 on October 14, then plunged to $15 two days later. The clumsy speculators couldn't repay the loans they had taken — loans not from conventional banks, but from banklike institutions called trust companies. With that, the panic was on.

Just as lightly regulated mortgage companies and investment banks would prove troublesome in 2008, so the trust companies of a century ago were disasters waiting to happen. Trust companies weren't full-fledged members of the consortiums of banks — called "clearinghouses" — that agreed to stand behind one another at times of stress to stabilize the financial system. Instead, trust companies had to rely on clearinghouse banks to process checks written by their customers.

Knickerbocker Trust Company, the Bear Stearns of its day, had lent heavily to the copper speculators. When word of that circulated, scores of depositors descended on its offices to withdraw money, the sort of bank run that was frighteningly frequent before government deposit insurance arrived. Never mind that just two weeks before, the state banking examiner had found the institution had funds sufficient to pay its depositors. On October 18, the National Bank of Commerce said it would no longer act as the intermediary between Knickerbocker and the clearinghouse, a move as devastating to Knickerbocker as JPMorgan Chase's decision to stop "clearing"—or processing payments—for Lehman Brothers in September 2008, contributing to that venerable firm's bankruptcy.

On Monday, October 21, after paying out $8 million in less than four hours, Knickerbocker ran out of cash. J. P. Morgan sent a young deputy, Benjamin Strong, to inspect Knickerbocker's books. Confirming Morgan's suspicions, Strong concluded the trust company was insolvent. It would never reopen, and indeed, its president later committed suicide. The panic lit next on the Trust Company of New York.

Morgan summoned the secretary of the Treasury, George B. Cortelyou, to come to him in New York. The summons underscored Morgan's influence and what was effectively his quasi-governmental status. A century later, Treasury Secretary Hank Paulson would demand that the chief executives of the nine largest banks come to *his* office in Washington to be told what they had to do, but Paulson had the Federal Reserve beside him and hundreds of billions of dollars at his disposal.

One constant through both panics, though, was a largely absent commander in chief. As Morgan wheeled and dealed, Teddy Roosevelt was hunting bear in the canebrakes of northern Louisiana. When he finally surfaced a few days later, the *New York Times* reported archly that "he had added several deeper shades of tan to the bronze acquired during the summer months." Though a century later George W. Bush would be in the White House for most of the Great Panic, he turned to Paulson and Bernanke rather than leading any defense against the biggest threat to the U.S. economy in more than half a century.

In a late-night October 1907 meeting with the heads of New York's biggest banks, Cortelyou offered to deposit $25 million of government money in New York City banks at Morgan's direction. When the meeting broke at 2 A.M., it was clear to Morgan and the others that rescuing the Trust Company of New York was crucial. Just as he had been with Knickerbocker Trust, Benjamin Strong was dispatched to look over the Trust Company's books and told to report back by noon.

Strong recalled the scene in a twenty-two-page letter written years later:

I remember Mr. Morgan repeatedly saying, "Are they solvent?" He wanted no details, but the general facts and results, and seemed satisfied with the opinions I expressed. There were two or three large loans in the Trust company which I had to ask Mr. Morgan, Mr. [George F.] Baker [president, First National Bank of New York] and Mr. [James] Stillman [president, National City Bank] for their own opinion, and with what I remember telling Mr. Morgan that I was satisfied that the company was solvent . . . that the capital was not greatly impaired, if at all, although were the company to be liquidated there were many assets with which it would take some years to convert into cash.

The meeting lasted forty-five minutes. At the end, Morgan asked Strong if he thought a rescue of the Trust Company was justified. Strong said it was. Morgan then turned to the bankers and said: "This is the place to stop the trouble, then." And he did. As nearly 1,200 depositors thronged the Trust Company's offices to take out their money, Morgan tried to persuade other trust companies and banks to raise the money the Trust Company needed to avoid collapse — much as Paulson and Geithner attempted to do with Lehman Brothers a century later. When that effort failed, Morgan instructed the Trust Company's president to bring his most valuable securities to Morgan's office. Morgan then went over them one at a time until he had enough collateral to reach the $3 million the Trust Company needed to stay afloat for another day. The next day Morgan persuaded other banks to come up with $10 million.

The crisis, though, did not end there. "The closing months of 1907 . . . were marked by an outburst of fright as widespread and unreasoning as that of fifty or seventy years before," Harvard economist A. Piatt Andrew, later a Republican congressman from Massachusetts, wrote in 1908. The United States, he said, had experienced "what was probably the most extensive and prolonged breakdown of the country's credit mechanism which has occurred since the establishment of the national banking system," a reference to the embryonic network of nationally chartered banks established after the Civil War.

The next acts would involve New York City, the New York Stock Exchange, a major brokerage firm, banks outside New York, and, eventually, steel, rail, and coal companies. But the pattern was established. Morgan ruled and pushed others to do what was necessary to avoid the depressions that had followed previous banking panics. In November, the Treasury issued $150 million in bonds and permitted banks to use the securities to create new currency. (In 1907, paper currency printed by banks circulated freely alongside government-printed greenbacks.) Depression was avoided, but the economy suffered a yearlong recession. Commodity prices fell 21 percent, erasing nearly all the increase that had occurred since 1904. The dollar volume of bankruptcies rose 47 percent in one year. Unemployment went from 2.8 percent to 8 percent. Some 240 banks failed.

BIRTH OF THE FED

J. P. Morgan initially was lauded for his role in turning aside the Panic of 1907. "Crowds cheered when he walked down Wall Street, and world political leaders and bankers sent telegrams expressing their awe that one man had been able to do that," one of his biographers, Jean Strouse, told an interviewer. "But the next minute a democratic nation was really quite horrified at the idea that one man had this much power."

Republican senator Nelson Aldrich of Rhode Island, who was among Wall Street's best friends in Washington, put the matter more practically: "Something has got to be done. We may not always have Pierpont Morgan with us to meet a banking crisis."

The idea of a centralized monetary authority was hardly novel. The Bank of England had been around since 1694, and as early as the mid-nineteenth century had developed the practice of printing cash and lending it to smaller banks at times of crisis. This "lender of last resort" role for central banks was codified by British journalist and economist Walter Bagehot in his 1873 book, *Lombard Street*. To an astounding degree, Bagehot's description remains the basic guide for central bankers more than 125 years later. They cite it as an authoritative guide to behavior and refer to it with the same reverence that ministers and rabbis use when quoting from the Bible.

"A panic," Bagehot wrote, "is a species of neuralgia, and according to the rules of science you must not starve it. The holders of the cash reserve [the central bank] must...advance it most freely for the liabilities of others. They must lend to merchants, to minor bankers, to 'this man and that man,' whenever the security is good. In wild periods of alarm, one failure makes many, and the best way to prevent the derivative failures is to arrest the primary failure which causes them."

In a panic, Bagehot advised, a central bank should lend freely on good collateral and charge a high interest rate to discourage overuse. And a central bank, he said, should lend only to those who were ultimately solvent — that is, to banks with loans and other assets greater than their deposits and other borrowing. The last condition was significant: the point was to keep otherwise healthy banks from being wiped out in a panic, not to sustain banks that were broke or, in the jargon of the trade, "insolvent." In other words, the central bank was the solution to a shortage of liquidity, but not the solution to insolvency. Identifying that fine line between liquidity and solvency in the midst of a financial panic would be perhaps the biggest challenge for the Bernanke Fed. Its biggest gambles hinged on getting this diagnosis right: the difference between lending to Bear Stearns (liquidity) and not lending to Lehman (insolvency), the choice between buying smelly loans and securities from the banks (liquidity) or investing taxpayer money in them (solvency.)

Bagehot understood that — provided the authorities had the right diagnosis — central banking was not simply a matter of turning valves to regulate the flow of money, but also was about offering reassurance and bolstering confidence, what Geithner called "theater." "What is wanted and what is necessary to stop a panic is to diffuse the impression that though money may be dear, still money is to be had. If people could be really convinced that they could have money if they wait a day or two, and that utter ruin is not coming, most likely they would cease to run in such a mad way for money," Bagehot wrote. "Either shut the Bank [of England] at once, and say it will not lend more than it commonly lends, or lend freely, boldly, and so that the public may feel you mean to go on lending. To lend a great deal, and yet not give the public confidence that you will lend sufficiently and effectually, is the worst of all policies."

In ordinary times, a central bank's role was mostly to be seen but not heard: to keep an eye on the banking system and to manage the overall supply of credit in the economy to avoid the problems caused by too many dollars chasing too few goods (the recipe for inflation) or those caused by the opposite condition of not enough dollars (the recipe for recession and deflation). All that changed in the case of financial fires. Then a central bank became the first responder — the lender of last resort.

ALEXANDER HAMILTON PREVAILS – ULTIMATELY

The United States had no lender of last resort in 1907, though not for lack of trying. In 1790, Alexander Hamilton, the first secretary of the Treasury, overcame fierce opposition from Jefferson and agrarian interests and persuaded Congress to charter the first Bank of the United States. The bank was largely an economic success, issuing a stable national currency and regulating private state-chartered banks, but its efforts to restrain commercial banks from lending too readily made it persistently unpopular. Congress narrowly refused to renew the bank's charter when it expired in 1811.

Five years later, after the inflation and financial instability that accompanied the War of 1812, Congress tried again. But the Second Bank of the United States proved, at first, incompetent and corrupt and later came to be seen as a threat to American democracy. Andrew Jackson neutered it in 1832, vetoing legislation that would have extended its charter ahead of schedule and declaring it to be "unauthorized by the Constitution, subversive of the rights of the States, and dangerous to the liberties of the people." During the Civil War, Congress created national banks — previously, only states could charter banks — and the federal Office of the Comptroller of the Currency. But from 1832 onward, the nation was left without a central bank, which was why J. P. Morgan was called upon to fill the role.

The year 1907 proved to be a turning point, and not only because the mortal Morgan, then seventy, couldn't go on forever. Earlier panics had struck banks that came under the sheltering umbrella of the clearinghouses. This panic hit the trust companies, which lived outside the clearinghouse safety net. That led New York bankers to realize the financial system had grown too big and complex for them to manage, while at the same time the public and many politicians decided that the time had come to rein in "money trust."

"The Panic of 1907 was an indication of the extent to which the ability to control crises had moved out of the hands of the New York bankers," historian Gabriel Kolko wrote.

But if the need for a central monetary authority was obvious, there was little agreement on who should control it or even what its objectives should be. A Federal Reserve Bank of Boston monograph captured the conflict succinctly: "While most bankers were interested in reforming the financial structure of the nation to make it more efficient and centralized, the progressives were interested in reforming the financial structure by making the banking system less centralized."

To address these issues, Congress created a National Monetary Commission, but the appointment of Wall Street's friend Nelson Aldrich to chair it inflamed suspicions that it was a front for bankers. (Aldrich's grandson and namesake, Nelson Aldrich Rockefeller, the governor of New York and vice president, would never escape the same suspicions.) Conspiracy theories were further fueled when it was later learned that Aldrich arranged a weeklong secret meeting in November 1910 at Jekyll Island, Georgia, a resort owned by John D. Rockefeller and J. P. Morgan himself, to design a new central bank for the United States.

At Jekyll Island, a handful of bankers — among them Benjamin Strong, the Morgan lieutenant — had agreed to back a version of a plan based on one crafted by investment banker Paul Warburg, who was later a member of the Federal Reserve Board. A twenty-four-volume report released in January 1911, the plan called for a National Reserve Association with branches spread throughout the country that would issue currency and make loans to member banks. The association was not to be an arm of the government but would be controlled instead by a board of directors dominated by bankers.

Proponents said the absence of centralized authority was threatening the national well-being. "The whole world is united in agreement that we have about the worst system of banking that there is anywhere in existence," Frank Vanderlip, then president of National City Bank, forerunner of today's Citibank, said in 1911. "It makes of us... an international nuisance." A century later, Hank Paulson would look at the archaic maze of regulatory agencies in his own time and come to a similar conclusion.

Opposition to the new central bank was fervent. William Jennings Bryan charged that the plan would leave bankers "in complete control of everything through control of our national finances." In May 1912, Representative Arsène Pujo, a Louisiana Democrat and dissenting member of the National Monetary Commission, convened high-profile hearings into "the money trust." Among those called to testify was J. Pierpont Morgan, less than a year away from his grave, his great service to the nation of five years earlier largely forgotten. Pujo's final report found "a great and growing concentration of the control of money and credit in the hands of a few men."

In 1912, Wilson — standard-bearer of the Progressive movement, governor of New Jersey, and former president of Princeton University — was elected president, beating both Republican William Howard Taft, the incumbent, and Teddy Roosevelt, who ran as a third-party candidate. Wilson had promised "speedy and sweeping" financial reform and stood on a Democratic Party platform that rejected the Aldrich proposal, but he had been vague about specifics. The day after Christmas 1912, the incoming chairman of the House Committee on Banking and Finance, Carter Glass of Virginia, and his economic adviser, H. Parker Willis, came to Princeton to lay out an alternative to Wilson. They proposed twenty or more privately controlled regional banks that would issue currency and lend to other banks, a plan crafted to dilute New York's dominance and avoid the creation of a central bank in Washington. Wilson insisted that a presidentially appointed board oversee the regional banks to serve as the "capstone" of the system. Glass eventually acquiesced, preferring Wilson's government-controlled board to Aldrich's banker-dominated scheme.

Months of political wrangling ensued. Wilson eventually turned to Louis Brandeis, later a Supreme Court justice, to fashion a compromise, which the president outlined to a joint session of Congress in June 1913. For six more months bankers and agrarian populists battled over every aspect of the proposal, but the bill finally passed. Wilson signed the Federal Reserve Act on December 23, 1913, the most significant achievement of his first year in office. Proponents were irrationally exuberant. Senator Claude Swanson, a Virginia Democrat, said the creation of the Fed made "impossible another panic in this country."

Bronze bas-relief sculptures of Wilson (identified only as "founder of the Federal Reserve System") and Glass ("defender of the Federal Reserve System") occupy niches on either side of the Constitution Avenue entrance to the Fed's headquarters. Under Wilson's bust is a wonderfully pragmatic, though not particularly eloquent, excerpt from his first inaugural: "We shall deal with our economic system as it is and as it may be modified, not as it might be if we had a clean sheet of paper to write upon; and step by step we shall make it what it should be."

Carter Glass's words are taken from an angry book he wrote to dispel suggestions that one of Wilson's White House aides was the true father of the Fed: "In the Federal Reserve Act," the gold letters say, "we instituted a great and vital banking system, not merely to correct and cure periodical financial debauches, not simply indeed to aid the banking community alone, but to give vision and scope and security to commerce and amplify the opportunities as well as to increase the capabilities of our industrial life at home, and among foreign nations."

In the end, Alexander Hamilton prevailed. As Bray Hammond, the Fed staffer turned historian, wrote, "Americans still maintain a pharisaical reverence for Thomas Jefferson, but they have in reality little use for what he said and believed — save when, on occasion and out of context, it appears to be a political expediency. What they really admire is what Alexander Hamilton stood for and his are the hopes they have fulfilled."

Although neither the legislation nor the gilt lettering that adorns the Fed's building makes mention of the fact, Congress had created what would become a fourth branch of government, nearly equal in power in a crisis to the executive, legislative, and judicial branches. It would take the Fed decades to grow into that role, but by the end of the twentieth century, it would have almost unchallenged power over its domain, the U.S. economy.

GROWING PAINS

The host of politically expedient compromises created a flawed institution. The law provided for a weak Federal Reserve Board in Washington, chaired by the secretary of the Treasury and including the comptroller of the currency and five others to be appointed by the president. It also mandated up to twelve regional or "district" (as the Fed refers to them) Fed banks, each to be owned by the private banks in their districts, each to be run by a "governor." It was a classic American balancing between centralization and decentralization, but the legislation provided no clear division of responsibilities between the board in Washington and the regional Fed banks, a feature that would prove troublesome before and during the Great Depression.

Three Wilson appointees — the secretaries of the Treasury and agriculture and the comptroller of the currency — spent months drawing boundaries and designating headquarters of twelve regional Federal Reserve banks, a politically delicate exercise that, among other things, gave Missouri two Fed banks, one in Kansas City and the other in St. Louis. The memory of the regional fights was so lasting that the boundaries have never been adjusted to reflect the westward movement of the population, leaving only two banks, in Dallas and San Francisco, west of Kansas City.

Benjamin Strong, the Morgan lieutenant, had campaigned against the compromise legislation as too decentralized and too fragmented. With some reluctance, he became president of the Federal Reserve Bank of New York and the most powerful player in the system. "He regarded the twelve reserve banks as eleven too many," Carnegie Mellon economist Allan Meltzer wrote in his voluminous history of the Fed, a sentiment that Strong's successors at the New York Fed shared, Geithner especially.

The institution was still in its adolescence when it confronted and failed its biggest test: misstep after misstep on the Fed's part turned a bad late-1920s recession into the Great Depression, an indictment made by Nobel laureate Milton Friedman and collaborator Anna Schwartz, and later expanded by Ben Bernanke in his years as an academic.

In the preface to a collection of his essays on the Depression, Bernanke described those years as "an incredibly dramatic episode — an era of stock market crashes, bread lines, bank runs, and wild currency speculation, with the storm clouds of war gathering ominously in the background all the while. Fascinating, and often tragic, characters abound during this period, from hapless policy makers trying to make sense of events for which their experience had not prepared them to ordinary people coping heroically with the effects of the economic catastrophe." The words might have applied accurately to the early twenty-first century.

"[M]uch of the worldwide monetary contraction of the early 1930s," he wrote, "was...the largely unintended result of an interaction of poorly designed institutions, short-sighted policy-making, and unfavorable political and economic preconditions." The Depression occurred because the government stood by as the financial system imploded. "That went on for three and a half years without any significant action," Bernanke said. "The banks failed. The stock market crashed, other credit markets stopped functioning, foreign exchange markets stopped functioning and that collapse of the financial system, together with the deflation and monetary policy, was the basic reason why the Depression was as severe as it was."

The bottom line — that the Depression was largely the Fed's fault — dominated Bernanke's thinking throughout the Great Panic. He was determined that no future scholar would convict *him* of similar timidity or complacency in the face of a financial crisis. As Bernanke put it in his book of essays, "To understand the Great Depression is the Holy Grail of macroeconomics." That Holy Grail has been the driving force of his entire professional life.

WHO'S IN CHARGE?

Critics of the Fed's ineptitude in the late 1920s and early 1930s point to an absence of enlightened, strong leadership at the top. Friedman and Schwartz argued that the Depression would have been avoided had Benjamin Strong, who had chronic tuberculosis, not died in October 1928, a year before the crash. Shortly before his death, Strong had written a prescription for the Fed: "Not only have we the power to deal with...an emergency instantly by flooding the street with money, but I think the country is well aware of this and probably places reliance upon the common sense and power of the System."

The Fed didn't take his advice. Its mistakes were many. The original sin was to tighten credit and lift interest rates in 1928 and 1929, in what now appears to have been a misguided attack on speculation in the stock market when the deeper problem was a weakening of the overall economy and an absence of inflation.

As Bernanke retold the story, the post-Strong Fed "passed into the control of a coterie of aggressive bubble-poppers," the most determined of whom was Adolph Miller, an economist who was among the first members of the Fed board and served for twenty-two years into FDR's presidency. Herbert Hoover—a neighbor and friend of Miller—was a fervent foe of "speculation" and encouraged him. Under Miller's influence, the debate inside the Fed shifted from whether to try to stop stock market speculation to how to stop it. The Washington faction threatened to cut off loans to New York City banks as a way to stop them from lending to stockbrokers. It also favored rhetoric, the sort of jawboning that Alan Greenspan tried with his warnings about "irrational exuberance" in 1996.

Strong's successor at the New York Fed, George Harrison, a Harvard-trained lawyer who had been the Washington board's general counsel, argued that the brokers would get money elsewhere and that rhetoric would do nothing. His solution was to raise interest rates in an economy that had hardly recovered from a recession that began in November 1927, and was experiencing no inflation. He prevailed, and the Fed's discount rate on loans it made to banks went from 3.5 percent in January 1928 to 6 percent by August 1929, higher than at any time since 1921.

The Fed tightened credit again in 1931 at just the wrong moment, responding with then-conventional tactics when gold flowed out of the United States. By 1932, with Congress shouting for relief, the Fed reluctantly opened its spigot for a few months, and the economy responded. But when Congress went home in July, the Fed reversed course with Harrison's support, and the economy collapsed. "The monetary policy of the '30s led to a deflation of about 10 percent a year, so it was extraordinarily tight monetary policy, which created, among other things, the greatly increased value of debts, which therefore led to more defaults and bankruptcies," Bernanke said.

Friedman and Schwartz argued the key to the Depression was that the Fed had been too stingy with credit. Bank failures were "important not primarily in their own right" but because they were the vehicle for the "drastic declines in the stock of money," they wrote. Bernanke contended that that wasn't the whole story. In seminal research done while he was still in his twenties, Bernanke emphasized the devastating impact that the collapse of the banking system had even beyond its depressing effect on the money supply. Bank failures and the weakness of surviving banks, he wrote, meant households, farms, and small firms found credit "expensive and difficult to obtain." In turn, the "credit squeeze...helped convert the severe but not unprecedented downturn of 1929–30 into a protracted depression."

As happened in 2008, confidence in financial institutions evaporated. A toxic combination of depression and deflation made borrowers insolvent. Nearly half the banks that existed in 1929 had collapsed or been merged into other banks by the end of 1933. Those that survived suffered massive losses and often could not or would not lend. When they did, they often charged outrageous rates.

As with lesser panics, worries about the safety of banks prompted runs in which depositors pulled out their money. Runs, or even the anticipation of them, forced banks to sell securities or call in loans to raise cash. Dumping assets at the same time other banks were doing so pushed down the market price of virtually all assets, generating losses that actually caused banks to fail. "Thus, expectation of failure, by the mechanism of the run, tends to become self-confirming," Bernanke wrote. The words could have been used to describe Bear Stearns or Lehman Brothers.

"THE FINANCIAL ACCELERATOR"

In seeking to understand why the economy had a disturbing tendency toward growth spurts followed by recessions, panics, and depressions, many economists discounted the financial markets as a sideshow. They believed that financial markets reflected and predicted what was going on in the underlying economy but weren't an independent driver of the business cycle. It was a reflection of much of the profession's amazing proclivity for assuming away reality at times and understating the importance of institutions. Ben Bernanke didn't see the world as they did. The health of banks and other financial institutions and their attitude toward lending was a major driver of the business cycle — and could amplify the impact of Fed policies on the economy, he said. He called it "the financial accelerator," and the Great Depression became his leading case study. His research on this subject provided the lens through which he would later view the Great Panic.

Beginning with an article published in 1983 in the prestigious *American Economic Review* and in subsequent research, Bernanke emphasized banks' role in the economy, employing concepts that later brought Nobel Prizes to Joseph Stiglitz and George Akerlof for their insights into the functioning of markets when one side has more information than the others.

Bernanke, among others, contended that banks and other financial intermediaries were "special" because they did more than funnel money from savers to borrowers; they developed expertise in gathering information about industries and borrowers and maintained ongoing relationships with customers. "The widespread banking panics of the 1930s caused many banks to shut their doors," Bernanke told a 2007 audience. "Facing the risk of runs by depositors, even those that remained open were forced to constrain lending to keep their balance sheets as liquid as possible." The economy, thus, was denied the benefits of banks' unique knowledge and ability to discern the creditworthy borrower from the less desirable. Stingier banks inhibited consumer spending and capital investment and made the Depression worse. His determination to avoid repeating that mistake drove Bernanke during the Great Panic to do *whatever it takes* to resuscitate the financial system.

The other way that financial disturbances exacerbated the rest of the economy in the 1930s, Bernanke said, was through the creditworthiness of borrowers — and, particularly, through the value of the collateral that they could offer as a way to assure lenders that a loan would be repaid. Bernanke viewed the collapse of home prices during the Great Panic primarily through this lens: a decline in the value of American families' best collateral would inevitably make it harder for them to borrow. This reading of economic history also led him to press earlier and harder than Paulson did for the government to take steps to avoid "preventable foreclosures" and reduce the size of mortgages that exceeded the value of the homes on which they were written.

In his dissection of the Fed's mistakes in the 1930s, Bernanke also cited the Fed's misreading of interest rates as a gauge to the availability of credit.

At times of panic and uncertainty, bankers and others rush to the security of the safest securities, especially the debt of the U.S. Treasury. This pushes down the interest rate that the Treasury has to pay to borrow money, a measure that ordinarily is a useful gauge for the Fed. More important, though, are the rates that consumers and businesses have to pay to borrow, if they can borrow at all. If the gap — known as the "spread" — between the rates the Treasury pays on supersafe borrowing and the rates that ordinary borrowers pay widens (if they can borrow at all), then that becomes a much more important gauge of financial distress.

Bernanke found that the gap between medium-grade Baa corporate bonds and supersafe U.S. Treasury bonds widened from 2.5 percentage points in 1929 to 1930 to nearly 8 percentage points in mid-1932. That was more than double the spread recorded during the deep recession of 1920 to 1922. "Money was easy for a few safe borrowers, but difficult for everyone else," he concluded. Exactly the same was true during the Great Panic, and many of Bernanke's innovations at the Fed were aimed at reducing that same spread, which widened sharply from about 1.6 percentage points in December 2006 to over 6 percentage points in December 2008.

INTERVENTIONISTS VS. LIQUIDATIONISTS

In the wake of the Depression, Congress made the only substantial changes to the Federal Reserve Act it has ever made. In 1935, it removed the Treasury secretary and comptroller of the currency from the board in Washington, renamed it the Board of Governors of the Federal Reserve System to emphasize its primacy over the district banks, and changed the title of the heads of the regional banks from "governor" to "president." Even more significant, Congress diluted the power of the regional Fed banks to set interest rates by creating a Washington-dominated committee, the Federal Open Market Committee. All seven governors in Washington have a vote at all times, but only five of the twelve regional bank presidents vote in any one year, serving in a rotation dictated by statute. (The New York Fed president is always one of the five voting presidents.)

That institutional change would prove important during the Great Panic, giving Bernanke the power to act despite the resistance of the presidents of some regional Fed banks. But the broader consequence of the Depression was the nature of received wisdom. Today, the notion that the government should or would stand by as the stock market crashed, credit markets stalled, and the economy tumbled over the abyss seems implausibly bizarre. The public, politicians, professors, and the press have been shaped by searing memories or photographs from the Great Depression, the years in which the unemployment rate rose to 25 percent and the country's output of goods and services declined by 29 percent over four years. The lasting lesson — taught by economists with views as different as John Maynard Keynes and Milton Friedman, the leading economic minds of the twentieth century — is embraced almost universally by politicians and economic policy makers: government can and should act to prevent such a dangerous downward financial and economic spiral. Indeed, during the Great Panic, the Fed took interest rates to zero, and President Barack Obama signed into law a package of tax cuts and spending increases that amounted to $787 billion in fiscal stimulus over ten years, $185 billion of which was to hit the economy in the first year and another $399 billion in the second year.

This notion of the government's role was not universal in the 1930s. In his memoirs, Herbert Hoover described tension within his own administration, putting words in Treasury Secretary Andrew Mellon's mouth that are routinely reported as something Mellon actually said.

In one camp were the "leave it alone liquidationists" headed by Secretary of the Treasury Mellon, who felt that government must keep its hands off and let the slump liquidate itself. Mr. Mellon had only one formula: "Liquidate labor, liquidate stocks, liquidate the farmers, liquidate real estate." He insisted that, when the people get an inflation brainstorm, the only way to get it out of their blood is to let it collapse. He held that even a panic was not altogether a bad thing. He said: "It will purge the rottenness out of the system. High costs of living and high living will come down. People will work harder, live a more moral life. Values will be adjusted, and enterprising people will pick up the wrecks from less competent people."

Several Fed officials saw the financial debacle unfolding around them much as Mellon did: as an avenging angel sent to purge a slack system and fallen people. George Norris—a lawyer and early overseer of a federal farm-mortgage agency who was president of the Federal Reserve Bank of Philadelphia from 1920 to 1936—attacked the Fed for interfering "with the operation of the natural law of supply and demand in the money market," an argument not far from that made by some dissenting Federal bank presidents during the Great Panic.

History has cast Hoover as the do-nothing president who stood firm on conservative principles as the economy crashed and burned, as opposed to his hyperactive successor, Franklin Roosevelt. Hoover wasn't as callous or delusional as his modern caricature suggests, and he believed in the power of government to do good. Some of the seeds of the New Deal were planted in his presidency as he realized that "volunteerism" wouldn't suffice, just as some parts of Obama's recession-fighting policies of 2009 had their beginnings in the Bush years. Hoover created the Federal Home Loan Bank System to rescue savings banks and savings and loans, and to offer sustenance to the beleaguered mortgage market, but Congress watered down his proposals to his bitter regret. He created the Reconstruction Finance Corporation to provide emergency loans to banks, railroads, and other companies. But he was hung up on balancing the budget. He disagreed with, but didn't fire, Mellon as Treasury secretary. And he did not—despite some of the claims in his 1952 autobiography—see how big a government response it would take to conquer the Great Depression.

But in contrast to the Great Panic, Hoover did not have anyone with Bernanke's stature at the Fed pushing him to be bolder. Only a minority of Fed officials, Hoover wrote, "believed with me that we should use the powers of government to cushion the situation."

Bernanke knew this history well. He faulted Hoover for overoptimism and for listening too much to Mellon, among other things, but thought Hoover—a smart, well-intentioned man who was hardly opposed to using the power of government—had been given a "bum rap." The bigger culprit, he said, was Woodrow Wilson, the father of the Fed, because he had so badly botched the Treaty of Versailles after World War I, which produced the global economic and political conditions that led to the Great Depression.

"After Strong's death...," Bernanke said, "the Federal Reserve no longer had an effective leader or even a well-established chain of command. Members of the Board in Washington, jealous of the traditional powers of the Federal Reserve Bank of New York, strove for greater influence; and Strong's successor, George Harrison, did not have the experience or personality to stop them. Regional banks also began to assert themselves more. Thus, power became diffused; worse, what power there was accrued to men who did not understand central banking from a national and international point of view, as Strong had. The leadership vacuum and the generally low level of central banking expertise in the Federal Reserve System was a major problem that led to excessive passivity and many poor decisions by the Fed in the years after Strong's death."

Or as Herbert Hoover put it, the Fed became "a weak reed for a nation to lean on in a time of trouble." Ben Bernanke was determined that *his* Fed would not be a weak reed. "I optimistically think that, while we could still have financial crises and bad outcomes in the world economy, policy makers know enough now to short circuit the impact before it becomes anything like the severity of the 1930s. Certainly that's the hope anyway," he said.

In November 2002, the University of Chicago honored Milton Friedman as he turned ninety years old. Bernanke, then in his fourth month as Fed governor, turned to Friedman and Schwartz and said: "Regarding the Great Depression. You're right, we did it. We're very sorry. But thanks to you, we won't do it again."

A half decade later, faced with the Great Panic of 2008, Bernanke would struggle to keep that promise.

BEYOND "ONE-MAN LEADERSHIP" — OR NOT

As for J. Pierpont Morgan, the man who saved the nation in the Panic of 1907, the glory of his triumph would be subsumed in the shifting sentiments of the times. When he died at the end of March 1913, the nation was more relieved than sad.

"We may look upon Mr. Morgan's like again — there were great men before and after Agamemnon, but we shall not look upon another career like his," the *New York Times* editorialized on April 1. "The time for that has gone by. Conditions have changed, and Mr. Morgan, the mighty and dominant figure of finance, did more than any other man to change them....

"The growth in his time was prodigious, and now Wall Street is beyond the need or the possibility of one-man leadership. There will be co-ordination of effort, the union of resources, but Mr. Morgan will have no successor; there will be no one man to whom all will look for direction."

The *New York Times* editorialist, of course, could not have known about Alan Greenspan.

Chapter 3

AGE OF DELUSION

In the morning cold of February 6, 2006, President George W. Bush made his way by armored limo to the Federal Reserve's Beaux Arts building, only the third time on record that any U.S. president had visited the Fed's headquarters. The official occasion was the public swearing-in of Ben Bernanke as the chairman of the Federal Reserve, but everyone knew Bernanke's ascension wasn't the main event. What really was being celebrated was Alan Greenspan's departure after nearly nineteen years as Fed chairman, the Maestro. To laughter and applause from the invitation-only crowd, Bush said, with substantial accuracy, "Alan Greenspan is perhaps the only central banker ever to achieve...rock-star status."

Indeed, Bush gladly would have done what he had four years earlier, and what his father and Bill Clinton had done before him: extend Greenspan's term as chairman and avoid the search for a successor who would satisfy both financial markets and the president. Bush had plenty of other problems — notably the war in Iraq — and in the years following the September 11 attacks, Greenspan had steered the economy to a place where Bush hardly had to worry about it. But Greenspan was seventy-nine years old, ready to retire and cash in on his celebrity. He rebuffed a quiet White House plea to stay for a while beyond the January 31, 2006, expiration of his term.

BERNANKE'S DASHBOARD
February 6, 2006

Dow Jones Industrial Average:	10,798
Market Cap of Citigroup:	$224.6 billion
Price of Oil (per barrel):	$65.13
Unemployment Rate:	4.7%
Fed Funds Interest Rate:	4.5%
Financial Stress Indicator:	0.09 pp

NOTE: The financial stress indicator, given in percentage points (pp), is the gap between the rate banks charge one another for three-month loans and the expected Fed rate. The bigger the gap, the more stress.

So, in front of a crowd that included Greenspan and his predecessor, Paul Volcker, Bush celebrated Greenspan's successes. The final report card looked impressive. Unemployment was below 5 percent. Inflation was low. The United States had been in recession for only 16 months in Greenspan's 211-month tenure. The housing bubble had yet to burst. The very worst of the subprime mortgages were yet to be written. The Great Panic was unimagined except by a few Cassandras who were routinely dismissed as cranks.

Bush was not alone in his belief that Greenspan's time at the Fed had been barely short of magic. During the 2000 presidential campaign, Senator John McCain had quipped that if Greenspan were to die, the smart response would be to put sunglasses on him, prop him up, and keep him in office. Greenspan's last Federal Open Market Committee (FOMC) meeting had turned into a roast. Richard Fisher, president of the Federal Reserve Bank of Dallas, borrowed from Shakespeare. "I…am but a sprout in the crop of otherwise experienced men and women here…but I'm sure they will agree with me that Henry V's remarks at Agincourt are appropriate: economists and bankers now asleep shall think themselves accursed they were not here."

Greenspan responded with a smile, and then said, "I went to school with Henry V. And the last time I spoke to him he gave me a good notion of strategy." Everyone laughed.

In the 1980s, Greenspan had turned his interest in and facility for understanding the inner workings of the American economy into a successful consulting business when Ronald Reagan's Treasury secretary, James Baker, and chief of staff, Howard Baker, recruited him to succeed Paul Volcker. Volcker had put the U.S. economy through a wrenching recession and accomplished what most people — economists and ordinary folk — thought impossible: bring inflation from the double digits to below 5 percent. But he was not in favor in the Reagan White House. He was a Democrat, for one thing. "Jim Baker didn't necessarily want a puppet. He just wanted a Republican," the *Washington Post*'s Bob Woodward wrote in his 2000 celebration of Greenspan, *Maestro*. "It was not a matter of trust, it was a matter of good politics. He also wanted a Fed chairman with a more agreeable temperament. Volcker's crankiness and his I'm-above-politics air were hard to take."

Greenspan, in contrast, was both reliably conservative — an acolyte of philosopher Ayn Rand — and politically agile. He had come to Washington in the last dark days of the Nixon White House. (His confirmation hearing to be chairman of Nixon's Council of Economic Advisers came the same day Nixon went on national TV to resign.) He stayed on to advise Ford and later candidate Ronald Reagan. He was comfortable with politicians and, having dated TV news stars Barbara Walters and Andrea Mitchell, with the press. He was skillful at courting and manipulating both sets of people to protect the Fed's credibility and independence and to burnish his own reputation.

Volcker was physically intimidating at six feet seven inches and famously opaque in his utterances. Greenspan was not physically imposing. "How did my Jewish uncle get to be the most powerful man in the world?" Clinton's labor secretary, Robert Reich, quipped. But he could be intellectually intimidating, just as opaque as Volcker if not more so, and far better at disarming or disabling his opponents inside and outside the Fed. Best of all, he came through his first early test with flying colors.

Only two months after Greenspan took over from Volcker, in October

1987, the stock market crashed. Thanks in part to the Fed's quick reaction, and some good luck, the crash didn't produce even a mild recession. Thus was born Greenspan's reputation as a wise man. Bernanke, who was still fighting off a financial crisis a year and a half after it began, would later complain good-naturedly that Greenspan had it easy.

Greenspan cemented his status as a guru with unique foresight in the mid-1990s with an intellectually courageous call that the Internet-based New Economy was so fundamentally changing the U.S. economy that the Fed could permit the economy to grow faster than most inflation-fearing economists thought prudent. The result was lower unemployment without higher inflation — and a technology stock market bubble for which Greenspan got substantial blame. But even after that bubble burst, and a recession ensued, the Greenspan Fed managed to get the economy going again by aggressively cutting interest rates — and the United States avoided the misery that followed the bursting of a real estate and stock market bubble in Japan.

Bush was right. Greenspan *was* a rock star — at least at that moment. He had steered the U.S. economy around the Asian financial crisis in 1998, two wars with Iraq, and the September 11 attacks. To economists, bond traders, and businessmen, he was a hero. "No one has yet credited Alan Greenspan with the fall of the Soviet Union or the rise of the Boston Red Sox, although both may come in time as the legend grows," Princeton's Alan Blinder, a former Fed vice chairman, and Ricardo Reis wrote in a 2005 evaluation of Greenspan that pronounced him "amazingly successful." Volcker had been far from anonymous, but the proliferation of business cable TV channels and the arrival of the Internet turned Greenspan into a celebrity of far larger dimensions than the chief justice of the Supreme Court and the leaders of Congress — and with a far longer tenure and more credibility than the president himself.

After he retired as chairman of the Fed, Greenspan kept laughing — all the way to the bank. With the help of Washington's superagent (and lawyer) Robert Barnett, Greenspan landed a reported $8.5 million advance for his memoirs. The book, *The Age of Turbulence,* hit the bookstores in the fall of 2007, a year and a half after he retired, just as the Great Panic was getting under way. The title was apt for a book that looked back to the 1987 crash, the 1989 fall of the Berlin Wall, two U.S. wars with Iraq, the September 11 attacks, and the emergence of China and India as economic powers.

But Greenspan had no idea how much more turbulence lurked just over the horizon, nor how his then sterling reputation would suffer — fairly and unfairly — in the aftermath.

WHAT DID HE KNOW? AND WHEN DID HE KNOW IT?

The causes of the Great Panic are many, the list of culprits long. Ultimately, every check on the system failed to restrain the excess and greed or to correct for the myopia and delusional optimism. Blame the well-paid executives and directors of the nation's financial institutions who gambled with their own companies and the U.S. economy. Blame the bankers' much-ballyhooed approach to "risk management" that disguised rather than illuminated their risks. Blame the credit rating agencies that stamped "AAA" on securities that didn't warrant that excellent status. Blame the chain of subprime mortgage makers — from unregulated mortgage brokers on the front lines to securitizers on Wall Street — who were driven by fat fees to make loans that were unwise for borrower and lender alike. Blame the supposedly sophisticated investors who bought risky, complex mortgage-linked securities they didn't understand. Blame the home buyers with house lust that exceeded their paychecks. Blame the politicians who spent crucial years on the sidelines, swayed either by moneyed interests or excessive trust in markets. Blame the regulators who couldn't or wouldn't keep pace with the evolution of finance. Blame the reporters who failed to press questions or take cranky Cassandras seriously. Blame the Federal Reserve, which was, after all, created to head off financial panics. And, yes, blame Alan Greenspan, who during his nineteen years at the helm had created the Fed in his image.

What did Greenspan and his Fed know, and when did they know it? What did they do — or fail to do — about it? What did the Fed miss? What could the Fed have done differently to prevent the Great Panic or, at least, to minimize the damage the panic did to the global economy? The answers fall into four categories.

THE GREENSPAN FED KEPT INTEREST RATES
TOO LOW FOR TOO LONG

In the wake of the bursting tech-stock bubble and a weakening economy, the Fed began cutting interest rates aggressively in January 2001. The Fed's target for the federal funds rate — its key interest rate, the one at which banks borrow from one another overnight — plunged from 6.5 percent at the beginning of 2001 to 3.5 percent at the time of the September 11 attacks. After the attacks, the Fed kept cutting the rate, ending 2001 at 1.75 percent. As the economy sagged and fears of Japanese-style deflation grew, the Fed later dropped the rate to a forty-five-year low of 1 percent and kept it there until June 2004.

When the Greenspan Fed finally turned to raising interest rates, it did so at what it described as a "measured pace" — very slowly. Taking its foot off the monetary gas pedal ever so cautiously, the Fed raised the fed funds rate by only one-quarter of a percentage point every six weeks or so. The rate didn't cross 3 percent until May 2005. Greenspan took it to 4.5 percent on his last day on the job.

When interest rates are so low, credit is usually cheap and plentiful, and the prices of stocks, houses, and other assets tend to rise. It's cheaper to borrow to buy assets, and the alternative — putting money in the bank or in bonds — is less attractive because returns are so low. The *Wall Street Journal* tracked this phenomenon in a 2005 front-page series called "Awash in Cash" that illustrated how in a world of cheap and plentiful credit people will pay just about anything for anything — and this was before the worst of the subprime mortgage loan craze.

Among the examples:

- A week after Hurricane Katrina, a defaulted loan backed by aging tugboats and barges in coastal Alabama came up for sale. A firm called Mooring Financial Corporation, a firm that buys troubled loans at a discount, was interested but couldn't determine how well the boats had survived the hurricane, or even whether their cash-starved owner had kept up the insurance. So Mooring

bid fifty to fifty-five cents on the dollar, and it considered that
generous. The winning bidder offered about ten cents more on
the dollar.

- Australia's biggest homegrown investment bank, Macquarie
Bank, leased Chicago's Skyway toll road for ninety-nine years
for $1.8 billion, hundreds of millions of dollars more than some
Chicago officials thought it would fetch.

- An investment partnership run by Grantham, Mayo, Van
Otterloo & Co., a Boston money manager with a taste for timber,
bought more than 5 percent of the land in the state of Maine.

To be sure, Fed policy during this first part of the decade kept the economy chugging along, but there is a potential downside to sustained very
low interest rates—a downside that goes far beyond overpaying for assets.
As economic historian Charles Calomiris of Columbia University observed,
"The most severe financial crises typically arise when rapid growth in untested
financial innovations"—such as complicated securities invented to invest in
mortgages—"coincided with . . . an abundance of the supply of credit."

This is exactly what happened during the last years of the Greenspan
Fed. With interest rates low, investors took greater and greater risks to get
higher returns. This risky investing is called "reaching for yield"—and in
the mid-2000s, there was a lot of reaching. The difference between the interest rates that investors demanded on risky securities and those on the safest
U.S. Treasury securities—the "spreads" or "risk premiums"—narrowed.
After years of sunny economic weather, investors acted as if it would never
rain again.

Greenspan himself saw some danger. In an August 2005 speech, he cautioned, "History has not dealt kindly with the aftermath of protracted periods of low-risk premiums." (Translation: You're paying too much for those
stocks, risky bonds, and mortgage-backed securities.) He warned, in his
opaque style, that the likely scenario was that an "onset of increased investor caution elevates risk premiums and, as a consequence, lowers asset values
and promotes the liquidation of the debt that supported higher asset prices."
(Translation: a crash.) But the words weren't chosen to enter the popular

culture the way his December 1996 warning about "irrational exuberance" in the stock market did, nor did he draw any link between these "low-risk premiums" and the abundance of credit. Rather, with some justification, he described the investor optimism as "the apparent consequence of a long period of economic stability." (Translation: The Fed was doing such a good job that people thought the good times would last forever.)

The Greenspan Fed's policy of sustained low interest rates reflected an almost exclusive focus on keeping the economy growing and avoiding falling prices for goods and services, not on restraining the prices of houses or stocks. That was what Greenspan believed central banks should do. Throughout 2003, Bernanke was a strong ally of Greenspan's in making the case that the Fed should keep interest rates low and should say so publicly. In June 2003, transcripts released in 2009 reveal, he suggested to colleagues that it might "make sense tactically to say publicly that we are willing to lower the federal funds rate to zero if necessary," and argued for using the end-of-meeting statement "to signal our willingness to keep policy easy so long as there is a risk of further disinflation and continuing economic weakness." It wasn't clear at the time that the strategy was wrong, a point easily overlooked by those who criticize it now. The fact is, the U.S. economy did keep growing, and deflation didn't arrive. Indeed, one reason investors were willing to pay so much for risky securities was that they believed — or acted as if they believed — that the Fed and other central banks had found a way to keep economies growing with little inflation and with recessions that were mild and infrequent.

But Nassim Nicholas Taleb, an options trader who made his reputation by describing unanticipated but unusually important events that he called "black swans," criticizes Greenspan — and Bernanke — for failing to see that the calm was masking a building of hidden risks. "It was like someone sitting on dynamite and saying, 'It's okay, we're safe because nothing has happened.'"

Despite its apparent successes, the Greenspan Fed had some well-respected contemporary critics. One of the most prominent was Bill White, a veteran of the British and Canadian central banks, who between 1994 and 2008 was a top economist at the Bank for International Settlements, an international organization in Switzerland for central bankers. From that perch, White cautioned the Fed and like-minded central bankers against looking only at conventional measures of inflation. In a 2006 paper, for instance, he warned that easy money might not lead to "overt inflation" of the sort measured by the Consumer Price Index, but rather to an investment boom that would be followed by a painful bust, "an eventual crisis whose magnitude would reflect the size of the real imbalances that preceded it," he wrote. "Mistakes…take a long time to work off."

At that time and since, Greenspan countered that the Fed was impotent: global flows of money were so great they overwhelmed the Fed's ability to make credit scarce or costlier by moving up short-term rates. Even when the Fed raised short-term rates, he said, the longer-term rates on which mortgages depend didn't rise as much. "We tried in 2004 to move long-term rates higher in order to get mortgage interest rates up and take some of the fizz out of the housing market, but we failed," Greenspan said just as the Great Panic was beginning. He publicly labeled this "the conundrum," the fact that the Fed was—albeit slowly—raising short-term interest rates, and long-term rates were not following. Bernanke provided intellectual cover on this front by talking about "a global savings glut," a torrent of savings from China and the rest of Asia that flooded global markets and especially the United States and was overwhelming the Fed's ability to tighten credit. Greenspan concurred. The arrival of billions of Chinese, Indian, and Eastern European workers into the global economy created such an antiinflationary force that long-term interest rates simply wouldn't rise no matter what the Fed did, he asserted.

Not all the members of Greenspan's FOMC were enthusiastic about pledging to keep rates low for, as the Fed put it at the time, "a considerable period." The debate over including the phrase in the end-of-meeting statement at the August 12, 2003, meeting was so vigorous that Greenspan had to ask for a show of hands to see whether the advocates—including Bernanke and Kohn—were outnumbered. "I will stipulate that, unless we get a significant vote in favor of putting it in, I would recommend that we drop it and bring it up for discussion…next time," he said, according to transcripts released in May 2009. Seven of the eighteen members of the FOMC present objected, an extraordinary protest by FOMC standards. "Right on the margin," Greenspan said, ruling that the unusual vow would be included in the statement. But many of those at the Fed who embraced the low interest rates of the early

2000s—or favored even lower rates, such as Bob Parry, former president of the San Francisco Fed—would later contend that the Fed should not have kept rates so low for so long. And, in retrospect, they were correct. Among outsiders, that view became conventional wisdom: the *Wall Street Journal* asked fifty-five economists in March 2008 if they agreed with this statement: "With the benefit of hindsight, the Fed was too slow to raise the federal funds rate after taking the target to 1 percent in 2003?" Some 84 percent said yes. "Bernanke is paying for Greenspan's sins," said one. "I suppose, with hindsight, we are gods," another quipped. Indeed, what was clear later was not obvious at the time.

THE GREENSPAN FED SAW AT LEAST SOME SIGNS THAT THE HOUSING MARKET WAS BECOMING A BUBBLE BUT TOOK NO ACTION

Greenspan long prided himself on understanding housing prices and their role in the economy better than almost anyone; it was a subject he had studied for decades. He saw early that Americans treated their homes as ATM machines, refinancing or taking home-equity loans to turn a home's value into spending money, and he worked with a Fed staff economist to measure this effect. Researchers inside and outside the Fed cautioned that house prices were rising unsustainably. A 2004 Fed working paper by staff economist Joshua Gallin, for instance, said that housing prices had risen 70 percent over the previous ten years while rents had risen only half as much. The strong suggestion: house prices couldn't keep rising. Greenspan himself liked to point to a closed-door November 2002 Fed meeting in which he said the "extraordinary housing boom" and "very large increases in mortgage debt cannot continue indefinitely into the future." (Of course, no one outside the room knew he had said that until transcripts were released five years later.)

But Greenspan thought and said publicly that a nationwide bubble in housing prices was nearly impossible because housing markets—unlike, say, the market for copper—were local markets. "I would tell audiences that we were facing not a bubble but a froth—lots of small, local bubbles that never grew to a scale that could threaten the health of the economy," he recalled, accurately, in his book. After all, he reasoned, housing prices had soared in Britain, Australia, and other countries but then stopped rising without falling across the board. In the United States, housing prices hadn't actually declined across the country since the Depression. A national decline in house prices was extremely unlikely, Greenspan thought—and so did many others. Indeed, this was an assumption on which an entire financial house of cards rested. And it was wrong.

Greenspan's unwillingness to attack the housing bubble wasn't only about misreading signs. It also reflected a philosophical view about central banks targeting rising asset prices. In an approach Bernanke backed at the time, Greenspan argued that central banks shouldn't increase interest rates to attack possible market bubbles because they can't always distinguish a transitory bubble from a sustainable rise in prices. Simply put, the Fed was as likely to aim at a false bubble and kill economic growth as it was to prevent one from inflating.

Greenspan also argued that the central bankers' other tool—talking investors out of their euphoria—was extremely limited. His famous "irrational exuberance" warning came in December 1996 when the Dow Jones Industrial Average was at 6,500. After that headline-making comment, stocks rose for more than three years, by a cumulative 75 percent, before they finally collapsed, as Greenspan frequently reminded those who chastised him for not using his bully pulpit more aggressively.

Greenspan thought the Fed should preach prudence, pounce only if the rising asset prices were pushing up prices of goods and services, and prepare to protect the economy from harm if a bubble burst. Bernanke and his frequent collaborator, Mark Gertler, put intellectual heft behind this doctrine at a Fed conference in Jackson Hole, Wyoming, in 1999. The two argued vociferously that the Fed cannot reliably identify bubbles in assets such as stocks or housing and, therefore, shouldn't use interest rates to try to burst them. Raising rates in response to rapidly rising stock or house prices, Bernanke once said, is like "doing brain surgery with a sledgehammer." He instead argued that the Fed should focus on inflation and helping the broad economy with rate cuts after any bubbles do burst.

"We cannot practice 'safe popping' at least not with the blunt tool of monetary policy," said Bernanke, who cited his Princeton colleague Alan Blinder's quip that doing so is like "sticking a needle in a balloon; one cannot count on letting out the air slowly or in a finely calibrated way."

After the speech, Greenspan quietly showed his support. "He didn't say anything during the session," Gertler recalled. "But after it was over he walked by and said, as quietly as he could, 'You know, I agree with you.' That had us in seventh heaven."

Waiting for a bubble to burst before the Fed responded was called the "mop up after" strategy and was largely deemed a success after the tech-stock bubble burst. "The biggest bubble in history imploded, vaporizing some $8 trillion in wealth in the process," observed Blinder and Ricardo Reis in their laudatory 2005 report card on Greenspan's tenure. "It is noteworthy…that the ensuing recession was tiny and that not a single sizable bank failed…and even more amazingly, not a single sizable stock brokerage or investment bank failed either."

The severity of the Great Panic put this doctrine on the defensive. The global consequences of the current housing market bust have already been so great that Bernanke, among others, is rethinking his previous convictions, and he has company. Blinder has amended his views. When bubbles aren't the result of bank lending, the mop-up strategy still looks good, but the Fed should use its regulatory powers, though not higher interest rates, to respond to bubbles fueled by bank loans, he says. Volcker told Congress that policy makers needed to be "alert" to "persistent and ultimately destabilizing economic imbalances" — a condition that includes bubbles.

And John Gieve, the Bank of England's deputy governor for financial stability, said flatly in a valedictory speech in 2009: "Mopping up after the bust is not a good strategy.…

"It's not at all clear that the post-2000 mopping up strategy worked that well in retrospect — it just stored up more trouble for the future." In light of the economic devastation of the Great Panic, Gieve concluded, "it is evidently not safe to rely on being able to mop up after the crash."

THE GREENSPAN FED MISSED WARNINGS THAT SUBPRIME WAS A MOUNTING PROBLEM, AND WAS RELUCTANT TO USE THE POWERS IT HAD TO RESTRAIN SUBPRIME LENDING

The Fed does more than set interest rates and lend to banks short of cash. It regulates banks, oversees truth-in-lending laws, and, under the 1994 Home Ownership and Equity Protection Act (HOEPA), has the power to prohibit abusive mortgage practices. The Greenspan Fed did not use these powers to restrain subprime lending, nor did its platoons of bank examiners spot the enormous risks that the big banks were taking in packaging or holding securities composed of subprime mortgages.

Greenspan argued he and others at the Fed didn't realize how quickly subprime lending exploded. In fact, he said that when he first saw estimates from a mortgage-industry trade publication in 2005, he doubted them. He didn't believe markets could move that fast. They did.

But there were earlier warning signs that went largely ignored at the Fed. By 2002, members of the Fed's Consumer Advisory Committee — created in 1976 to help the Fed keep tabs on consumer credit issues — saw signs of trouble. Jeremy Nowak, president of a Philadelphia community-revitalization organization, reported that foreclosures in inner-city Philadelphia were escalating significantly. It was time, he said, "to ask some questions about why that is so, and under what context is pushing home ownership too low in terms of income a problem, and under what context is it not a problem?"

At the same 2002 meeting, Agnes Bundy Scanlan, an executive at Fleet Boston Financial, warned of an alarming spread of "predatory lending," costly loans unsuitably targeted at low-income and poor people. "There are days when I feel that the seven, eight, nine, ten years of CRA [Community Reinvestment Act] work that I've been doing has probably all been undone, and that's what I'm going to be spending the next three years trying to fix," she said, bemoaning the many cases of homeowners who had lost all their house equity because they had refinanced on onerous terms. "We have lost everything that we've gained. I think that is absolutely something that the Fed can play a role in, all the regulators can play a role in, and take a very hard look at what some of these financial institutions are doing."

One issue, a big one, was that many subprime mortgages were not made directly by banks that the Fed regulated, but by financial institutions supposedly overseen by other regulators or by less tightly regulated consumer-finance affiliates of Fed-sponsored banks. Edward "Ned" Gramlich, a Fed governor, saw this loophole as a major problem. "In the subprime market, where we badly need supervision, a majority of loans are made with very little supervision," said Gramlich, well after the subprime mortgage market imploded. "It is like a city with a murder law, but no cops on the beat."

An earlier, failed attempt by Gramlich to prompt Fed action on the matter is instructive. A tall, soft-spoken liberal Democratic economist who had been in and out of Washington his whole career, Gramlich was named to the Fed board by President Clinton in 1997 and served as chairman of the committee that handles consumer issues for most of his eight-year tenure. Three months before he died in 2007, Gramlich told *Wall Street Journal* reporter Greg Ip that he had gone to Greenspan in 2000 and suggested the Fed send its examiners to check that the affiliates of the banks weren't pushing abusive loans. Greenspan thought that unwise, and Gramlich didn't press the issue. "He was opposed to it, so I didn't really pursue it," Mr. Gramlich said.

Greenspan said later that while he acknowledged Gramlich's concern, he was reluctant to expand the Fed's regulatory reach. "I told him I was worried that if we extended our reach and pretended to be able to do something about it, we were likely to make the problem worse rather than better," Greenspan said. "I could very readily envisage that, unless we had a huge police force, if we publicly announced that we were regulating these institutions, they would have placed a sign in their window proclaiming 'We are regulated by the Federal Reserve system,' and egregious lenders would have then fleeced subprime borrowers at a much higher rate."

The *Wall Street Journal* story made Gramlich a hero, celebrated by Greenspan critics for having more clairvoyance than the Maestro. In truth, Gramlich hadn't seen the enormity of the subprime problem or the degree to which the entire financial system had bet on housing prices. But he had seen signs of abuse that warranted Fed pursuit, and believed that's what regulators were supposed to do.

Greenspan couldn't escape the Gramlich story. Asked about it by a congressional committee in 2008, he said that Gramlich, like any Fed governor or the Fed's staff, could have pressed the matter — and didn't. But that wasn't the way the Greenspan Fed worked. Greenspan didn't spend much time thinking about regulatory matters, and even less time encouraging new rules. He left that to others. But as Gramlich knew, it was nearly impossible to push a regulatory initiative through the Fed without Greenspan's blessing — and Alan Greenspan gave such blessings sparingly.

GREENSPAN PUT TOO MUCH FAITH IN MARKETS AND THE CAPACITY OF BIG-MONEY PLAYERS TO POLICE THE MARKETS IN THEIR OWN SELF-INTEREST

Greenspan's libertarian leanings were well known, and his skepticism about the capacity of government regulators openly expressed. He often referred to the ten years he spent as a director of J. P. Morgan before going to Washington in 1987, making a point of how much more knowledgeable the bank's loan officers were about borrowers than Fed regulators. Greenspan generally celebrated the benefits of financial innovation and downplayed the risks. In his memoirs, he says he took the Fed job committed to enforcing the laws of the United States—even those with which he didn't agree—but "planned to be largely passive" in matters of regulation. The surprise, he wrote, was that the Fed staff wasn't nearly as eager to regulate as he had feared—a fact that other bank regulators in Washington often attributed to the dominance of market-loving economists at the Fed.

Greenspan did not provoke controversy or attention by attacking regulations frontally; he was too shrewd for that. He emphasized the limits of regulation. He resisted any attempt to broaden the Fed's purview beyond the core of the banking system despite the enormous growth of financial institutions beyond banks. He insisted on the virtues of having multiple bank regulatory agencies, figuring that would prevent any one regulator from being unwisely tough. He scoffed at the counterargument that this would create unhealthy competition among regulators because financial institutions would shop for the softest one. His staff and colleagues knew where he stood.

When Democrats in Congress pressed the Fed in 2002 to use its power to write rules to define "unfair or deceptive acts and practices" in banking, Greenspan resisted. "It is effective for banking agencies to approach compliance issues on a case-by-case basis," Greenspan said in a letter to the then-senior Democrat on the House Committee on Financial Services, John LaFalce of New York, that summed up his attitude toward regulation. "In the absence of specifics generated through case-by-case complaints and enforcement, however, it is difficult to craft a generalized rule sufficiently narrow to target specific acts or practices determined to be unfair or deceptive, but not to allow for easy circumvention or have the unintended consequence of stopping acceptable behavior," he wrote.

In short, the Greenspan view on regulation in general was: either it doesn't work to prevent the abuses at which it is aimed or it will have the unwelcome consequence of stopping activities that benefit the economy. (The one place where government should be more aggressive, he said often, was in fighting fraud. But, of course, that wasn't the Fed's job.)

It was not obvious in the early 2000s that the Fed should have been raising the interest rates it controlled more rapidly to curb the excesses that provoked the Great Panic. But it was clear then — and is more abundantly clear today — that if the Fed wasn't using its interest rate weapon, it could and should have used its regulatory clout and rhetoric to restrain the shortsighted, excessively ebullient players in financial markets and to at least try to resist the worst of the abuses in the subprime lending market.

The enormity of the Great Panic eventually brought many of these points home to Greenspan and challenged his most fundamental assumptions about regulation and the capacity of players with big money in the game to police the poker table themselves. On October 23, 2008, Greenspan faced Representative Henry Waxman, the aggressive chairman of the House Oversight and Government Reform Committee. Knowing he would be grilled, Greenspan hired a PR consultant, David Dreyer, formerly with the Clinton White House, for advice.

In a crowded hearing room with television cameras focused on his face, Greenspan read his prepared testimony, and then Waxman launched his attack. His questions were narrowly focused on the regulation of newfangled securities called derivatives. But Greenspan's answers were broad, a self-indictment.

"I made a mistake in presuming that the self-interest of organizations, specifically banks and others, were such that they were best capable of protecting their own shareholders and their equity in the firms," he said. "And it's been my experience, having worked both as a regulator for eighteen years and similar quantities in the private sector, especially ten years at a major international bank [J. P. Morgan, where he served on the board of directors], that the loan officers of those institutions knew far more about the risks involved in the people to whom they lent money than I saw even our best regulators at the Fed capable of doing.

"So the problem here is something which looked to be a very solid edifice, and indeed a critical pillar to market competition and free markets, did break down. And I think that, as I said, shocked me....I still do not fully understand why it happened."

Waxman knew he was onto something. He pressed Greenspan: "In other words, you found that your view of the world, your ideology was not right. It was not working."

"Precisely," Greenspan replied. "That's precisely the reason I was shocked because I had been going for forty years or more with very considerable evidence that it was working exceptionally well."

Perhaps a better title for Greenspan's book would have been the one that Bernanke chose for the book manuscript he set aside when he came to Washington: *Age of Delusion: How Politicians and Central Bankers Created the Great Depression.*

Chapter 4

THERE ARE JEWS IN BOSTON, TOO

Ben Shalom Bernanke didn't seem to mind that his February 2006 installation as the fourteenth chairman of the Federal Reserve was upstaged by his predecessor's departure. After the paeans of praise heaped on Alan Greenspan, Bernanke added his own heavy measure. He hoped his record would look as impressive as Greenspan's tenure, he told the ceremony. "My first priority will be to maintain continuity with the policies and policy strategies established during the Greenspan years."

When your middle name translates as "peace," as Bernanke's does, you are perhaps inclined by nature to seek harmony. But as much as he did genuinely respect the man he was succeeding, Bernanke was determined to be the un-Greenspan — in style, if not in substance.

Bernanke didn't think a Fed chairman should be a rock star. He wanted to avoid the cult that had attached to Greenspan, the perception that the chairman *is* the Fed. An economy shouldn't rely so much on the instincts of a single man, Bernanke thought, even one as wise as Greenspan. Bernanke wanted to elevate the stature of the institution instead. He wanted to make the fourth branch of government more like the Supreme Court and less like a royal court where the king was surrounded by retainers.

To that end, Bernanke thought the Fed should be more explicit and open about its objectives and thinking than it had been in Greenspan's time. "The Fed needs an approach that consolidates the gains of the Greenspan years and ensures that those successful policies will continue — even if future Fed chairmen are less skillful or less committed to price stability than Mr. Greenspan has been," Bernanke wrote long before coming to Washington. He imagined a day when the Fed was so easy to understand and so open about its objectives and current views of the economy that a few words from the chairman at a congressional hearing or after-dinner speech wouldn't move markets because they wouldn't provide any new information. This would prove a naïve hope, a misreading of the chairman's role that would create confusion in the early stages of the Great Panic.

Ben Bernanke and Alan Greenspan were both brainy and Jewish, life-long baseball fans, and, oddly, proficient saxophone players. The similarities between the two stopped there, though. Bernanke grew up in a small southern town, Greenspan in New York City. Bernanke was a star of academia but unfamiliar with the corporate and Wall Street universe with which Greenspan was a part. Bernanke's wife, Anna, was a Spanish teacher whose passion was launching a new school for minority students. The couple didn't seek to be fixtures at the A-list Washington dinner parties frequented by Greenspan and Andrea Mitchell.

For Ben and Anna Bernanke, excitement was jointly doing the *New York Times* crossword puzzle nearly every day — although they skipped the easier beginning-of-the-week puzzles. "That's the one thing we do together," Bernanke joked. "It shows our sexy social life. We're pretty good. We can do the Sunday puzzle in about forty minutes."

The trouble for Bernanke, though, was that he couldn't just wish away celebrity status. During Greenspan's long reign, the job had become too big for that. After becoming Fed chairman, Bernanke was a clue in at least a dozen published crosswords — including one Wednesday *New York Times* puzzle. (Clue: Federal Reserve chief Bernanke. Answer: Ben.) An August 2007 puzzle in the *New York Sun* offered this clue: "Cause of difficulty in understanding Ben Bernanke?" The answer: FEDOPAQUENESS.

So much for being the un-Greenspan.

THE BANKS OF THE LITTLE PEE DEE

Ben Bernanke's story is an affirmation of the ideal of America as meritocracy. The grandson of European immigrants, he was the clever small-town boy whose ambitious, hardworking parents put him on the education escalator that carried him to the pinnacle of power.

Bernanke's parents met while attending different campuses of the University of North Carolina, his father at the then all-male Chapel Hill and his mother at the then all-women's campus at Greensboro. After marrying, they moved to tiny, segregated Dillon, South Carolina, a once-prosperous tobacco town of 6,400 that sits on both the railroad line and the Little Pee Dee River. In Dillon, Bernanke's father and uncle joined his grandfather Jonas Bernanke in running Jay Bee Drugs, a family business that wove the family into the town's fabric. "In Dillon, a town that was always very short of the more regular kind of doctor, my father and uncle were popularly known as Dr. Phil and Dr. Mort," Bernanke once told an audience, "and the prescriptions they dispensed were often accompanied by their free advice on maintaining good health."

In the middle of this small southern town, Bernanke grew up in a tight-knit Jewish family. Bernanke's mother, Edna, gave up a job teaching elementary school when Ben, the eldest of three, was born December 13, 1953. She often worked in the store, where Ben was supposed to help out as well, although he usually ended up in the comic book section. On May 23, 1958, the *Charlotte Observer* ran the headline "Ben Will Enjoy Grandma's Blintzes" over a photo of Bernanke's grandmother and a recipe (secret ingredient: one tablespoon pineapple jam), plus this quote from four-year-old Ben: "Grandma, why don't you teach my mommy to make blintzes?"

Young Ben's maternal grandfather taught him to play chess when he was five or six. Said Bernanke, "He let me win at first, but after a few years I was no longer a pushover." Bernanke, who skipped first grade, was South Carolina's spelling bee champion at the age of eleven but was eliminated in the national championship at the Mayflower Hotel in Washington, D.C., when he misspelled *edelweiss*. His excuse: There was no movie theater in Dillon, so he hadn't seen *The Sound of Music*, the film that popularized the name of the flower.

At Dillon High School, Bernanke played saxophone in the marching band, taught himself calculus, and scored 1590 out of a possible 1600 on the SATs, an achievement that drew publicity in South Carolina. Edna Bernanke recalled, "One of his teachers said you could put him in a dark closet and he'd still learn. One time, a teacher was sick so he got up and taught the class." The local schools were integrated while he was in high school, and the event made such an impression on him that he wrote a novel, never published, about the best black and white football players of a newly integrated high school forming a team. He sent the first several chapters to a publisher who rejected it but with an encouraging note suggesting that he keep writing. The manuscript disappeared long ago, and Bernanke is hoping no one ever finds it.

Bernanke obviously was destined for college, most likely the University of South Carolina or, following his father, to UNC-Chapel Hill. Bernanke recalls a customer asking his father what colleges his son was considering. "UNC-Chapel Hill," replied Philip Bernanke. "That's a real tough school to get into," said the customer.

But Kenneth Manning, a Dillon native six years older than Bernanke, had different aspirations for Ben. Like other local African Americans, Manning's family had been regular customers of Jay Bee Drugs because it was willing to extend them credit when other stores wouldn't. Manning had gone from Dillon's segregated schools to Harvard with the assistance of a United Presbyterian Church program — and he was aware of Ben's precociousness. "It was a small town," Manning said with understatement. He thought sending Ben to the University of South Carolina would be a waste and approached him about applying to Harvard.

The young Bernanke embraced the idea almost immediately, but his parents worried that their son would be led astray. Manning, now a professor of the history of science at MIT, spent hours assuring them that Ben would not end up on SDS picket lines or lured by drugs or, of most concern to them, lose his Jewish identity. "I assured them there were Jews up in Boston," Manning recalled. Manning, who was close to a Jewish family in Brookline, took

Bernanke to Rosh Hashanah services his first year at Harvard. To the dismay of Bernanke's parents, Manning found Jewish services more meaningful than their son did.

"THE SUPERSTAR OF ALL TIME"

Manning's faith turned out to be well placed. Bernanke "was the superstar of all time as an undergraduate," said Dale Jorgenson, a Harvard professor with whom Bernanke worked. Bernanke won a prize for the best undergraduate economics thesis — for a paper demonstrating how deregulating natural gas prices could be good for the economy — and, in his senior year, was designated the outstanding Harvard economics major. (Pictured nearby in Harvard's alphabetical 1975 yearbook was Lloyd Blankfein, the son of a New York City postal clerk and later chief executive of Goldman Sachs.)

While successfully competing with the children of some of America's wealthiest and most powerful families, Bernanke returned to Dillon after his freshman and sophomore years to wait tables six days a week at Pedro's South of the Border, a tacky tourist stop just below the North Carolina border on I-95, famous for its campy billboards featuring groan-inducing slogans like PEDRO'S WEATHER FORECAST: CHILI TODAY, HOT TAMALE. More than thirty years later, the South Carolina legislature would name another I-95 exit, the one in Dillon, the "Ben Bernanke Interchange" and attribute Bernanke's success to the knowledge, integrity, and values he acquired in small-town South Carolina.

In the mid-1990s Bernanke's parents sold the four-bedroom house in which he had grown up to a couple from Texas and moved to North Carolina. Eventually, the house would become emblematic of the problems Bernanke himself would be called upon to fix. In September 2006 it was sold to Dwayne Thompson, a soldier in the South Carolina Army National Guard, and Sharon Rogers, his former wife with whom he had reconciled but not remarried. When the deal closed early in 2007, they took a $123,000, thirty-year mortgage with a 10.1 percent interest rate, well above the rates that more creditworthy borrowers paid. The couple fell behind on their payments and, under financial strain, broke up again. Twenty-one months after they bought the house, the bank that served as trustee for the mortgage-backed security that held their loan began foreclosure proceedings. Thompson ended up in bankruptcy. The house was sold to a local banker, Travis Jackson, in December 2008. "It's just a great sense of pride to know that one of the greatest leaders we have in our time period walked the same floors I walk," Jackson said.

From Harvard, Bernanke went on to graduate school at MIT, arriving with what his adviser, prominent macroeconomist Stanley Fischer, called "a terrific reputation." But Fischer, now Israel's central banker, said, "He wasn't a prima donna or arrogant. He had the same personality that he has now."

"At that time," he added, "there was a tendency to think that to prove you were a star, you had to write a thesis that was difficult and mathematical." Bernanke didn't. "I used to say that the more work I had to do on a thesis, the worse the thesis. I didn't have to do much work on Ben's thesis."

At MIT — then widely regarded as having the strongest economics department in the world — Bernanke occasionally crossed paths with another wunderkind, the child of two economists and the nephew of two Nobel Prize winners, Lawrence Summers, who earned his undergraduate degree at MIT in 1975 and an economics Ph.D. at Harvard. While at MIT, Bernanke also met Anna, then a Wellesley senior; the two were married the week after she graduated.

In 1979, the couple moved to Palo Alto, California, where Ben took up teaching at Stanford's Business School while Anna pursued a master's degree in Spanish. MIT classmate Jeremy Bulow invited them and another young economist, Mark Gertler, to share a house he had rented from Stanford economist Robert Hall. "My first reaction was how shy and unassuming he was," Gertler said. "If I hadn't heard he was a superstar, I would have thought he was just a good guy. Once you start talking about economics, though, he got animated — or about baseball." It wasn't just the game; it was the stats, the sort of sports minutiae made popular at the time by Bill James and his *Baseball Abstract*.

CLOGGED CREDIT CHANNELS

The late 1970s and early 1980s were a time of ferment in academic economics and in economic policy in Washington. In academia, a school of thought known as rational expectations was arguing that Fed moves to raise or lower interest rates didn't have much impact on the economy if they were anticipated by the public and the markets, as they often were. At the Fed, Volcker wasn't worrying about models. He was exercising the Fed's monetary muscle, raising interest rates to double-digit levels to bring down inflation at the cost of a severe recession.

At Stanford, seminar rooms and coffee rooms were thick with talk about the ways markets work or don't work when one side has much better ("asymmetric") information than the others and about the divergence of the interest of principals (such as shareholders) and those of their agents (corporate executives), especially when the agent has more information than the other. Bernanke applied that theory to the way banks and borrowers work, making his initial mark with the *American Economic Review* article on the causes of the Depression that was published in 1983, a couple of years after Bernanke finished it.

The conventional textbook explanation of the Fed's influence on the economy is simple: the Fed raises interest rates, which makes borrowing more costly for businesses — so they borrow and invest less — and more costly for consumers, too, so they borrow and spend less, particularly on houses, cars, and appliances. Lowering interest rates has the opposite effect: more borrowing, more investing, more spending. The uncomfortable secret among economists, though, was that they had a hard time documenting this story. Something was missing.

Working with Gertler, Bernanke built on his initial 1983 paper on the Depression and claimed to have found the missing link: the functioning of banks and financial markets. It was a subject that macroeconomists for a couple of generations had treated as intriguing, but not crucial to understanding booms and busts. Bernanke and Gertler emphasized the expertise, information, and relationships on which banks relied to decide to whom to lend. When this "credit channel" got clogged — because banks were closing (the Depression) or because they were trying to rebuild their capital cushions (the Great Panic) — the economy suffered.

Eventually, Bernanke and Gertler broadened their thinking and came up with the notion of a "financial accelerator" to describe the way shocks were transmitted — through the credit channel, among other ways — from the economy to the financial system and then back to the economy. A quarter century later, the Great Panic became a frightening illustration of the phenomenon Bernanke and Gertler had described. As the housing bubble burst, falling real estate prices reduced the value of houses (the collateral families had used to get mortgage loans) as well as the value of the mortgage-linked securities that banks held. The first phenomenon made borrowers much less appealing to lenders. The second ate into banks' capital cushion; with less capital and the prospect of even more losses in the future, banks grew reluctant to lend. That further weakened the economy. Inevitably, looking at this unraveling through the lens of his early work shaped Bernanke's response.

THE CHAIRMAN . . . OF THE ECONOMICS DEPARTMENT

After six years at Stanford, Bernanke, then thirty-one, took a tenured position at Princeton, and he and his wife moved to New Jersey, where they raised two children, Joel, now at Weill Cornell Medical College in New York, and Alyssa, who graduated from college in the spring of 2009. Bernanke seemed destined to live out his career in the world of academia, looking at the Fed from the outside. In 1996, Bernanke became chairman of Princeton's economics department, a post that often offers more hassle than honor. When Bernanke returned to Princeton for a speech early in his Fed tenure, Alan Blinder noted that he had spent six years as chairman. "Six *and a half*," Bernanke said, wanting credit for every month. In Bernanke's own speeches, the term stretched to seven years.

By all accounts, Bernanke was good at the administrative job. He helped strengthen the economics department by courting prominent names in the field — including Paul Krugman, who later won the Nobel Prize in economics. (Bernanke might have had reason to regret the Krugman coup; he proved generally unpopular with students and colleagues and occasionally used his popular *New York Times* column to snipe at his former colleague for, among other sins, propping up "zombie" financial institutions.) Bernanke was an aggressive fund-raiser and found a way to establish a successful and lucrative center on finance, overcoming resistance from some economics professors who feared it was a stealth business school. Despite his successes, though, Bernanke was passed over for provost, the top academic management post at Princeton, in favor of political scientist Amy Gutmann, who later became president of the University of Pennsylvania.

WASHINGTON CALLING

In early 2002, the Bush administration had two vacancies to fill on the seven-member Fed board, now one of the very few politically safe ways a president can try to influence the Fed. Lyndon Johnson and Richard Nixon openly pressed their Fed chairmen to keep interest rates down, while President George H. W. Bush made no secret of his displeasure with what he considered Greenspan's stinginess prior to the 1992 election. Although nothing in the law demands it, recent presidents have taken a hands-off, mouth-shut approach to the Fed. Both Bill Clinton and Bush the younger made a fetish of respecting the Fed's independence on interest rates; Barack Obama shows signs of doing the same. This approach reflects the international consensus that a politically insulated central bank is the best way to counter inflation.

By 2002, confidence in the U.S. government's management of its economy rested almost exclusively on the reputation and health of the aging Greenspan, then seventy-six years old. Greenspan's allies at the Clinton Treasury, Robert Rubin and Lawrence Summers, were gone. Greenspan was the only remaining member of what a *Time* magazine cover famously called "The Committee to Save the World" for a story that described how the trio had "prevented a global meltdown — so far" during the financial crisis that enveloped Asia in 1999. Bush's other economic advisers saw an urgent need to put some economic heavyweights on Greenspan's board in case the old man slipped in the shower.

Glenn Hubbard, then on leave from Columbia University's Graduate School of Business to chair Bush's Council of Economic Advisers, had his eye on Bernanke, a longtime acquaintance. Fearing that Greenspan might be uncomfortable with a Princeton professor — the last one, Clinton appointee Alan Blinder, chafed at Greenspan's dominance of the institution — Hubbard assured the chairman that Bernanke would be less confrontational. To sweeten the deal, Hubbard proposed packaging Bernanke with the promotion of Greenspan loyalist Donald Kohn. That part, the chairman liked.

Bernanke had thought a lot about the Fed, particularly about the post-Greenspan era. He coauthored a *Wall Street Journal* op-ed in 2000 with the provocative headline: "What Happens When Greenspan Is Gone?" His answer: "Fix the roof when skies are sunny" and declare an explicit, public, numerical target for inflation "to ensure that monetary policy stays on track after Mr. Greenspan." Given his interests, Bernanke had thought about — but never pursued — a Fed job; thus, when Hubbard called a few months after September 11, he was intrigued and made several trips to Washington for interviews.

"All I had in mind," he said, "was taking a couple of years off from the university and doing some public service. It was still in the penumbra of 9/11.... I had never been in the military, and so I felt I needed to do something. The best thing I had to offer was my knowledge of monetary economics and monetary history."

Indeed Bernanke, who once described himself as an "academic lifer," had seen precious little of life outside of the university. To academics, he was among the best and brightest: degrees from Harvard and MIT, teaching posts at Princeton and Stanford, editorships of prestigious journals, and a catalog of academic writings that put him among the twenty economists most often cited by peers, according to the Research Papers in Economics database. But Bernanke had barely tasted politics and never the high-stakes Washington flavor.

A few colleagues at Princeton knew he was a Republican, but he hadn't flaunted it or publicly advised any candidate. His only political experience was on a local school board. "On the administrative side," he once joked, "I served seven years as the chair of the Princeton economics department, where I had responsibility for major policy decisions such as whether to serve bagels or doughnuts at the department coffee hours." Bernanke had never worked on Wall Street, in government, or in business. But the White House wasn't looking for a Renaissance man; they wanted to strengthen the brainpower at the Fed.

As is the custom for significant presidential appointments, Bernanke's ultimate interview was in the Oval Office with Bush. "He talked a bit about his own economic goals — Social Security privatization at the time — but the thing I remember the most was, he asked, 'Do you have any political experience?'" Bernanke recalled later.

"I said, 'Mr. President, it won't count for much in this office, but I've served for two terms as the elected representative on Montgomery Township's school board.'

"And he said, 'No, no, I think that counts for a lot in this office, and I think that's really terrific.'"

HELICOPTER BEN

Bernanke was a solid citizen on the Greenspan Fed, but few governors had much impact on Greenspan's decisions. Colleagues confided privately that Bernanke's interventions at the Fed's policy meetings were undistinguished — though several incidents illustrated his dry, if sometimes nerdy, sense of humor.

In August 2002, Bernanke noted that revised government data showed the 2001 recession to be worse than initially reported. "We were always pessimistic about *forecasting*, and now *backcasting* seems to be a problem as well!" he said. "I have a modest proposal…if the BEA [Commerce Department's Bureau of Economic Affairs] can restate GDP figures and firms can restate their earnings, the Fed should have the option to go back and restate interest rates from last time." The wonks around the table laughed, according to the transcript of the meeting.

Four months later, at a December 2002 meeting, Greenspan skipped his usual lengthy soliloquy preceding the discussion of interest rates and recommended that the Fed leave interest rates unchanged. Bernanke told him: "I support your recommendation, Mr. Chairman. But if your brevity is going to be a habit, though, I would like to get my tuition back."

An advocate of relaxed academic dress codes, Bernanke joked that one of the biggest changes in his life that came with working at the Fed was wearing a suit to work every day. Wearing uncomfortable work clothes, he once said, is a way that people signal that they take official responsibilities seriously. He lamented that his proposal that Fed governors wear Hawaiian shirts and Bermuda shorts had gone unheeded.

His speeches, however, were tightly reasoned, influential, and closely read, both inside and outside the Fed. Among Bernanke's most visible roles was promoting, explaining, and defending Greenspan's strategy of keeping interest rates very low. This was, in part, a deliberate campaign to reduce the risk of deflation—a generalized decline in prices, which can lead to a debilitating disease that makes it ever harder for borrowers to pay back debts. Deflation was a major feature of the Great Depression, and most economists thought it had been eradicated until it reappeared in Japan in the 1990s. As U.S. inflation rates fell in early 2002, the Fed saw deflation as a possibility for which it had to prepare.

So in November 2002, to a group of economists in Washington, Bernanke delivered a talk titled "Deflation: Making Sure 'It' Doesn't Happen Here." The speech described all the ways the Fed could fight deflation, a mix of standard textbook talk and speculation about innovative maneuvers the Fed might undertake if interest rates fell so low they couldn't go any lower. (When a similar threat emerged in late 2008, the earlier speech was revived and scrutinzed because it was such a useful guide to the options he was putting before the Fed.)

Bernanke clearly meant for his November 2002 speech to be reassuring. But the reaction to it underscored the differences between a professorial lecture and words spoken by a Fed governor. Bernanke argued that even if the Fed cut interest rates all the way to zero—then an almost unimaginable event—it wasn't out of ammunition. Obviously, it couldn't cut the price of borrowing below zero, but it could increase the supply of credit by simply pumping money into the economy. The government might, he suggested, cut taxes, increase the federal deficit, and issue bonds that the Fed would buy by printing money. This, he said, was "essentially equivalent to Milton Friedman's famous 'helicopter drop' of money." (Friedman used the line in 1969 to argue that depression and deflation were avoidable. If nothing else worked, the Fed could send a helicopter to drop dollar bills to get people spending.)

The reference wouldn't have raised an eyebrow in one of his old seminar rooms, but Bernanke wasn't at Princeton any longer. Bond traders quickly derided him as Helicopter Ben, prompting political cartoons and blog ridicule. One faux ad circulated on the Internet showed a bald, bearded Ben Bernanke action figure in camouflage, getting into a yellow plastic helicopter with a satchel of currency. "Now YOU can drop money out of a helicopter," it said. But the helicopter line had a more serious effect, prompting bond traders to suspect that Bernanke might be soft on inflation. And that led others to worry that, to erase that perception, he might be tempted to be stingier with credit than he otherwise thought necessary in order to establish his credentials as an inflation fighter.

The metaphor would reappear — appropriately — when the Fed confronted the circumstances that Milton Friedman had envisioned and responded aggressively to the Great Panic. "Big Ben Fires Up the Choppers," read a *Forbes* December 2008 headline.

WHERE DID YOU GET THOSE SOCKS, BEN?

Bernanke's initial appointment to the Fed was for a term that extended to January 31, 2004. In late 2003 he was nominated and confirmed for a full fourteen-year term. About then, Bernanke decided he would stay in Washington more than the couple of years initially planned. Princeton extended his leave of absence. He and Anna sold their house ten minutes from the Princeton campus and bought a town house on Capitol Hill. If he needed any personal evidence of the housing boom, he had only to track his former residence: the Bernankes sold the New Jersey house in June 2004 for $630,000; sixteen months later, it sold again — for $781,000.

In May 2005, in his third year as a Fed governor, Bernanke was still ruminating like an academic economist, not like a man ready to take the controls from Greenspan. His academic training had not included contemplating the month-to-month movements in the economy, a shortcoming he acknowledged publicly. "A part of monetary policymaking for which my background left me imperfectly prepared is what central bankers call 'current analysis' . . .

getting an accurate assessment of the current economic situation," the synthesis of data, anecdotes, and judgments "to construct a 'story' about how the economy is evolving," he said, contrasting himself to Greenspan, with a public humility that the elder man rarely displayed. "Current analysis is not taught in graduate school, probably for good reason; it seems more amenable to on-the-job training.... It is, nevertheless, an intellectually challenging activity—analogous, it seems to me, to the efforts of a detective to reconstruct a sequence of events from a range of diverse and subtle clues—and I have enjoyed the opportunity to become more proficient at it."

The candor was disarming, perhaps admirably so. But it was the kind of comment that sowed doubts among Fed watchers that Bernanke had the Greenspan touch for knowing just when to tap the monetary brakes and when to wait. Nonetheless, the doors kept opening for him.

When Greg Mankiw decided to leave the chairmanship of the Council of Economic Advisers (CEA) to return to Harvard, Bernanke was high on the list of potential successors. Perhaps because the CEA post has more cachet among academic economists than among the power-hungry in Washington or the Fed-fixated on Wall Street, perhaps because being a Fed governor in the Greenspan years was like being in a gilded cage, Bernanke was interested in the change. Just as important, the job offered Bernanke an important step toward succeeding Greenspan: an opportunity to get close to Bush.

Greenspan himself had served as chairman of Ford's CEA, the three-member panel created by Congress in 1946 to provide economic advice to the president. Janet Yellen, now president of the Federal Reserve Bank of San Francisco, had left the Fed board to serve as Clinton's chairman. The introverted Bernanke nearly missed out on his opportunity, flunking his first few interviews for the job. Al Hubbard, the president's buddy and economic coordinator, initially thought Bernanke too low key, too bashful, too hard to relate to. That impression was eventually dashed when Hubbard began working closely with Bernanke and as he watched Bush take to him.

During his short, seven-month tenure at the White House, Bernanke's primary accomplishment was establishing a rapport with the president, but on that point, he scored a major success. Bush tended to be uncomfortable with professorial advisers. However, in briefings, Bernanke was clear and understandable. He never raised his voice but wasn't reticent. One aide recalled Bush echoing a view then widespread among politicians and the public, and complaining that "speculators" were driving up the price of oil and making markets more volatile. Bernanke quietly but firmly disagreed, telling the president that every study he knew suggested that speculators dampen, not amplify, the volatility of oil prices.

"I came to trust his judgment, his calm demeanor, and his sly sense of humor," the president would say as Bernanke was leaving his White House post.

Bernanke also disarmed the president with probably his most famous prank. One day, Bernanke showed up for a monthly Oval Office economic meeting wearing a dark blue suit and light tan socks.

Bush noticed. "Ben," the president said, according to one participant, "where did you get those socks?"

"Gap," replied Bernanke. "Three pair for seven dollars."

The president wouldn't let it go, mentioning Bernanke's light tan socks repeatedly during the forty-five-minute meeting.

When the time came for the next meeting of the same group, Bernanke and White House economic staffer Keith Hennessey agreed they would both wear tan socks and recruit others to do the same. Hennessey asked his boss, Al Hubbard, what he thought about the whole team's wearing tan socks. Hubbard was game but said he didn't own any. Hennessey volunteered that he had some.

Hennessey then asked, "Do you think the VP would wear them?" Hubbard, who had been on the job only six months, called Dick Cheney and asked, with considerable trepidation, if he would join the prank. Cheney agreed but said he didn't have any tan socks either. "Well, I've got some," Hubbard replied. When Bush arrived for the meeting, nearly everyone was wearing tan socks. The president roared with laughter.

HOUSING: IT'S THE FUNDAMENTALS

Bernanke was chairman of Bush's CEA for less than seven months and had little apparent impact on the president's economic policies during that time.

After he was anointed as Greenspan's successor in October 2005, he almost disappeared from public view as he prepared for Senate confirmation hearings. Bernanke did breed loyalty among those beneath him by resisting the rigidities of the White House hierarchy. In general, "principals" — like Bernanke — go to "principals" meetings. Their "deputies" — the other two members of the council — go to "deputies" meetings. CEA chairmen tend to jealously guard their time with the president in the Oval Office.

Bernanke was different. In late 2005, the CEA got a request from Bush's chief of staff for an economic briefing before the president traveled to Asia. Matthew Slaughter, an international economist on leave from Dartmouth's Tuck School of Business, was sitting in his office when Bernanke walked in and asked Slaughter to take the lead on the briefing. Slaughter agreed, saying he assumed Bernanke meant taking the lead on preparing the briefing. "No," Bernanke said. He wanted Slaughter to join him in the Oval Office — in itself unusual — and to do the talking. "I will go to his funeral because of that," Slaughter said.

If Bernanke was worrying about house prices at the time, he wasn't saying so very loudly. "While speculative behavior appears to be surfacing in some local markets, strong economic fundamentals are contributing importantly to the housing boom," he said in March 2005. "These fundamentals include low mortgage rates, rising employment and incomes, a growing population, and limited supply of homes or land in some areas.... However, our best defenses against potential problems in housing markets are vigilant lenders and banking regulators, together with perspective and good sense on the part of borrowers."

As would later become painfully clear, neither lenders nor regulators were being "vigilant," and "good sense" was in very short supply.

FIVE FINALISTS, ONE WINNER

The search for Alan Greenspan's successor began in the spring of 2005 and was conducted by Vice President Dick Cheney; Scooter Libby, Cheney's chief of staff; Andy Card, the White House chief of staff; Josh Bolten, Card's deputy; Liza Wright, the White House personnel director; and Al Hubbard. After consultations with Greenspan among many others, the group came up with a long list that was winnowed to five finalists. Bernanke's proximity to Bush inevitably had heightened the public speculation that he would be among the finalists, and he was.

The other finalists included Mankiw, the Harvard economist who had preceded Bernanke at the CEA; John Taylor, the monetary policy scholar who had received mixed reviews as the Treasury's top international official earlier in the administration; Marty Feldstein, the prominent and outspoken Harvard Republican professor, who had long been mentioned as a potential Fed chairman; and a dark horse whose name never surfaced in the press, Stephen Friedman, the former Goldman Sachs chief executive, who had preceded Al Hubbard as Bush's White House economic-policy coordinator.

Each was interviewed by the entire search committee in Cheney's office for about ninety minutes. Bernanke talked about housing, a growing concern by then. He and the others were asked how they would handle hypothetical situations—like a call from the CEO of Citigroup saying his bank was in trouble.

In the end, Bernanke wasn't the unanimous first choice of the committee. He had the intellect and the credentials as well as the respect of his peers, but he seemed, as he often did, nervous in the interview and had never been tested in a crisis. Friedman had a great interview but would have been a surprise, out-of-the-box choice, and the White House had just seen an out-of-the-box choice for the Supreme Court — White House counsel Harriet Miers — turn into an embarrassment. The committee eventually coalesced around Bernanke and recommended him to Bush.

But so much time had passed between his interview and the decision that Bernanke figured someone else had been chosen. One Thursday afternoon, he got a message to stop by Andy Card's office in the White House West Wing before the next day's 7:30 A.M. White House senior staff meeting. He told his wife he expected Card to make the bad news official; she was relieved. Bernanke showed up as requested, sat down facing Card, and heard him say: "How would you like to be Fed chairman?" When he telephoned his wife with what he considered to be good news, she burst into tears. She realized, more than he did, that the job would be all-consuming and change their lives.

If Bernanke was daunted by filling Greenspan's shoes, he didn't admit it. He figured he was as well equipped as anyone available, better at some things than Greenspan was, not as good at others.

"I felt that I had my own set of distinct skills," he said, "and I had a lot of confidence in the support I would get from the staff and my FOMC colleagues."

The nomination was announced the following Monday, October 24, well in advance of Greenspan's planned retirement. To offset Bernanke's inexperience on Wall Street, the Bush White House pursued Hank Paulson at Goldman Sachs for Treasury secretary.

After only a few years in Washington, the brainy kid from South Carolina had stepped into a post sometimes described as the second most powerful in the country.

"GREENSPAN NEVER WOULD HAVE DONE THAT"

Bernanke's first year as Fed chairman was uneventful, especially given what was to follow. The handoff from Greenspan to Bernanke went surprisingly smoothly. Greenspan had been steadily raising the Fed's key interest rate for years; Bernanke continued to do so and indeed left many of his predecessor's monetary policies untouched. But true to his determination to dampen the cult of personality that had grown up around Greenspan, Bernanke set out to give other Fed policy makers more say and to be more open with the public.

Vincent Reinhart, a senior Fed staffer until September 2007, said Bernanke "embarked on a fundamentally selfless act by attempting to make the Federal Open Market Committee more central to policy making." Under Greenspan, the Fed's policy-setting Federal Open Market Committee extended its one-day meetings to two days only twice a year; under Bernanke, by 2009, all eight scheduled meetings were two days long.

Greenspan had relied on the staff to satisfy his insatiable appetite for obscure data or for intense one-on-one discussions of economic data. Bernanke shot hoops with them in the Fed gym. Greenspan rarely confided in the other Fed governors. Bernanke conducted a running seminar with several of them. Greenspan was famously cryptic, even boasted of his ability to put fewer thoughts into more words than almost anyone. Bernanke vowed and tried to be more "transparent."

Despite the respect Bernanke won from his staff for these changes, financial markets weren't fully prepared for another of Bernanke's innovations, his new brand of "clarity." In April 2006, when markets were preoccupied with how much further the Fed would lift interest rates, Bernanke told a congressional committee that the Fed might not raise rates at every scheduled meeting. "Future policy actions will be increasingly dependent on the evaluation of the economic outlook," he said, adding that "at some point in the future the committee may decide to take no action at one or more meetings in the interest of allowing more time to receive information relevant to the outlook."

When Greenspan said something "might" happen to interest rates, he meant it was almost a sure thing. Financial markets, conditioned to listening to Greenspan, read Bernanke as sending a clear signal that the Fed was going to take a break in its interest-rate lifting campaign at the next meeting. That wasn't Bernanke's intent, and he said as much a few days later in what he assumed was an off-the-record conversation with CNBC's Maria "The Money Honey" Bartiromo at a *Wall Street Journal* cocktail party before the annual black-tie Saturday-night dinner of the White House Correspondents Association. The following Monday afternoon, Bartiromo broadcast the news, jarring markets and unleashing a firestorm of criticism of Bernanke. The Fed raised rates at each of the next two meetings and then paused. Bernanke later told Congress that his conversation with Bartiromo was "a lapse in judgment" and promised "in the future, my communications with the public and with the markets will be entirely through regular and formal channels."

Bernanke's communication problems were hardly uncommon. No matter how often they are cautioned, new Fed chairmen (and Treasury secretaries) rarely appreciate how large and loud the megaphone they've been handed is until an offhand comment or private whisper moves financial markets around the world. Bernanke's mistake was humiliating—and in retrospect inconsequential—but it bred uneasiness about his command of the job. Grumbles of "Greenspan never would have done that" became commonplace. The markets didn't want to know what he was thinking; they wanted to know what he was going to do next. Clarity and transparency, it turned out, were noble goals, but what the markets wanted was a clear guide to the Fed's intentions, and Bernanke hadn't mastered that art yet.

TARGET PRACTICE

With few hints of the meltdown that was to come, Bernanke devoted himself to a pet project: setting a target for inflation and trying to meet it. Inflation targeting is an effort both to avoid a repeat of the inflationary 1970s and to employ the insights of scholars concerning the importance of public expectations about inflation. Some foreign central banks—including the European Central Bank, the Bank of England, and the Bank of Japan—are given one and only one explicit goal: price stability. The Fed, in contrast to most other central bankers, was instructed by Congress in 1977 to aim at both "maximum employment" and "stable prices." Democrats in Congress warned Bernanke against any unilateral move to alter the Fed's priorities, an admonition that Bernanke, like Greenspan before him, countered by maintaining that price stability *was* the road to maximizing employment and economic growth.

Bernanke was not the first Fed chairman to consider inflation targets. In 1996, the Greenspan Fed had come close to a consensus on setting 2 percent as an internal inflation target. But while Bernanke advocated an explicit public inflation target, Greenspan had admonished Fed officials to keep the consensus quiet. "I will tell you that if the 2 percent inflation figure gets out of this room," Greenspan told his colleagues, "it is going to create more problems for us than I think any of you might anticipate." Greenspan prized flexibility and resisted rules that limited his discretion; Kohn and, later, Geithner sided with him.

The Greenspan Fed's semiannual reports to Congress avoided anything approaching specificity about the Fed's goals. At one FOMC meeting, Fed governor Frederic Mishkin, a proponent of explicit inflation targeting, derided the reports as "sex made boring."

Bernanke reopened the inflation targeting question soon after becoming chairman, but the process dragged on for so long that even fans of the approach and his usual allies grew impatient and began pressing for a resolution. The compromise called for the Fed to publish an economic forecast from each governor and regional bank president four times a year, instead of twice as had been the practice since 1979. More detailed than in the past, the forecast looked out three—and later more—years, instead of the two years that had been the custom. The reports amount to unofficial inflation targeting; most Fed officials in early 2009 predicted inflation would fall between 1.9 percent and 2.0 percent several years into the future. Everyone in the Fed and in the markets understood that was tantamount to a target.

Bernanke is proud of the expanded forecasts; he hopes that someday they may be seen as a significant innovation. However, his change initially was overshadowed by the beginning of the Great Panic, which, among other things, exposed the shortcomings of inflation targeting über alles. The targets provided no guidance for how the Fed should respond to the collapsing housing market or the financial calamity it triggered. As Blinder put it, the Fed essentially said: "Mr. Inflation, you're going to have to wait, which is the opposite of inflation targeting." But as the recession deepened and the inflation rate fell lower than the Fed thought desirable, the inflation target issue resurfaced — as a way for the Fed to assure everyone that it wouldn't let inflation fall *too low* or let the economy lapse into a devastating deflation, where prices and wages fall and borrowers find it harder to repay their debts.

"CONTAINED"

Ben Bernanke was just getting the hang of being Fed chairman when the housing market deteriorated and, contrary to expectations (including his own), refused to bottom out. Both inside and outside the Fed, a sense spread that this might be the end of an era in which the economy and markets had been too good to be true. One of the most prominent warnings came from Lawrence Summers, who had been Clinton's last Treasury secretary and later president of Harvard (until he crashed and burned). As the housing situation spun out of control, Summers was teaching, writing, and—successfully—positioning himself for a perch in a future Democratic administration and a run at succeeding Bernanke.

In a December 27, 2006, op-ed piece in the *Financial Times*, Summers wrote: "Changes in the structure of financial markets have enhanced their ability to handle risks in normal times." Translation: Lenders were more willing to lend because they share with the investors the risk that borrowers wouldn't repay. Derivatives allowed investors to hedge their bets, making them comfortable with positions they might once have shunned. Hedge funds and other huge pools of capital reduced volatility by pouncing when markets push an asset price even slightly out of line.

That was all to the good, but recalling the 1987 stock market crash and the 1998 Asian financial crisis, Summers observed presciently: "Some of the same innovations that contribute to risk spreading in normal times can become sources of instability following shocks to the system as large-scale liquidations take place." (Translation: Everyone was counting on always being able to quickly sell any newfangled financial instrument.) Normally, that made sense. But if something bad happened, and everyone tried to sell at once—look out! Looking back over the preceding twenty years, Summers suggested that financial crises seem to occur in about one out of every three years. The beginning of the Great Panic was less than one year off.

Soon, cracks in the subprime market began to surface. In January and February 2007, several subprime mortgage originators filed for bankruptcy court protection. In March, New Century Financial—one of the largest subprime lenders—stopped making loans and said it needed emergency financing; a month later, it, too, was in bankruptcy.

Nonetheless, the concern about potential problems found no official voice in Washington. After Bernanke and Paulson met their counterparts from the Group of Seven major economies in February 2007 in Essen,

Germany—where the Germans were obsessed with the risks posed not by house prices but by hedge funds—Paulson confidently predicted that "housing activity appears to have stabilized" and observed that the strength of consumer spending and exports was offsetting the "cooling" housing market.

The Fed was similarly optimistic. At the March meeting of the Federal Open Market Committe, officials agreed that "the economy was likely to expand at a moderate pace" and cited data that suggested "demand for homes was leveling out." They did acknowledge that the "downside risks" were growing—Fedspeak for a sense that any surprises are more likely to be bad ones than good ones. As for the subprime market, it was in trouble but wasn't big enough to overturn the entire U.S. economy. Bernanke told the Joint Economic Committee of Congress at the end of March, "At this juncture... the impact on the broader economy and financial markets of the problems in the subprime market seems likely to be contained," he said.

Soon, the word *contained* would become a mantra for both Bernanke and Paulson, an attempt to reassure everyone that housing might be bad but the rest of the financial system and the overall economy would muddle through. It was neither accurate as a description nor successful at reassurance.

READY FOR THE AVIAN FLU

Bernanke, Geithner, and Paulson all had a gut sense that the U.S. economy was overdue for a financial crisis of some sort and thought they were doing what was necessary to prepare for one. Geithner organized teams at the New York Fed to attempt to get a more comprehensive view of the financial system than was provided by looking at individual banks or markets. In Washington, Bernanke also asked existing Fed task forces to prepare "financial stability reports" twice a year. The Fed created an online crisis manual so officials could instantly check Wall Street prices and find contact information on their foreign counterparts. But, in fact, the Fed spent more time preparing for physical disruption to the banking system, such as a terrorist attack, and for the avian flu than it did for anything resembling the scope and magnitude of the Great Panic.

Bernanke and Geithner simply never imagined that things could get so bad, that the crises they would confront would be so much larger than the worst of those that Greenspan had managed. It was, as much as anything, a failure of the imagination, similar to the failure to anticipate terrorists hijacking big airlines and steering them into the World Trade Center. Yes, there was a sense that something bad might happen someday. And, yes, someone somewhere probably did predict exactly what happened. But to the officials overseeing the economy and many others, a crisis as big and broad as the Great Panic simply wasn't considered a plausible scenario — and they weren't preparing for anything this large.

Geithner did muse, occasionally, that the evolution of financial markets might produce fewer crises, but bigger ones. (The "bigger" so far has proven dead-on. "Fewer" remains an open question.) And he did help clean up one mess: an alarming backlog of paperwork in a rapidly growing corner of the markets, the securities called credit default swaps, which allow banks and other lenders to buy insurance against borrowers going bust. The buyers and sellers used sophisticated twenty-first-century finance; but the back office was more circa the late nineteenth century. One firm confessed in June 2006 that it had 18,000 undocumented trades, several thousand of which had been languishing in the back office for more than ninety days. The risk was that in a crisis, no one would be sure who owed what to whom — and everyone would stop doing business. With the help of his predecessor, Gerald Corrigan, then at Goldman Sachs, Geithner summoned representatives of fourteen big Wall Street firms — "the Fourteen Families," they called themselves — and prodded them to automate the process before a crisis hit. It worked. On September 30, 2006, the firms counted 97,000 unconfirmed trades outstanding for more than thirty days. By October 2008, the backlog had been reduced by 75 percent. And in all the turmoil of the Great Panic, the failure to process credit default swaps was one problem that *didn't* occur. Big players on Wall Street knew who their counterparties were — even if they didn't completely trust them.

No one at the Fed, however, rang the gong and warned investors, lenders, business executives, and consumers that years of easy credit even for risky borrowers, placid markets, and shared optimism were unsustainable. There was no analog to Alan Greenspan's famous — and unheeded — admonition about "irrational exuberance" in the stock market in 1996. Nor would any Fed official be able to point to a warning as dramatic as ECB president Jean-Claude Trichet's headline-making caution in January 2007 that "elements in global financial markets...are not necessarily stable" and prediction of a "repricing" — also known as a crash — in asset prices.

Occasional bursts of public prescience by Fed officials were so circumspect they were hardly noticed, let alone heeded. Geithner's expressions of concern were enveloped in so much jargon that only sophisticated listeners sensed any anxiety on his part. For instance, there was this 2005 passage in one of his speeches: "We are in the midst of an unusual dynamic in financial markets, in which low realized volatility in macroeconomic outcomes [Translation: everyone thinks we've licked the boom-bust cycle], low realized credit losses [Translation: even deadbeats are paying their loans], greater confidence in the near term path of monetary policy [Translation: everyone assumes the Fed will never surprise them], low uncertainty about future inflation and interest rate [Translation: everyone *really* believes the Fed will never surprise them], rapid changes in the nature of financial intermediation [Translation: the rise of finance outside the core banking system in the securities markets], and a large increase in the share of global savings that is willing to move across borders [Translation: the huge sums of money sloshing around the world economy], have worked together to bring risk premia down across many asset prices [Translation: all of which have led prices of stocks and other assets to rise awfully high]."

His bottom line, but only if you could understand him: don't invest as if these unusually good times will last forever.

Mixed Messages

Outside the Fed, warnings were starting to pile up. Larry Summers was increasingly pessimistic. Housing, he warned in March 2007, was becoming a brake on the U.S. economy and would eventually make lenders reluctant to make home equity, auto, and credit card loans. It was "premature" to predict recession, he said, but "the U.S. economy will slow down very significantly in 2007."

Summers suggested that, with hindsight, policy makers should have better restrained imprudent subprime lending, and the Greenspan Fed should have raised interest rates sooner. These, however, were solutions to yesterday's problems. "Economic policy makers who seek to correct past errors by doing today what they wished they had done yesterday actually compound their errors. They are in their way as dangerous as generals fighting the last war," Summers wrote, adding that "if recent developments mark a genuine change, let us hope that policy makers look forward rather than backwards."

How bad were things really? In an early warning of what was to come, a couple of Bear Stearns–sponsored investment funds that had borrowed heavily to invest in subprime mortgages ran into trouble and were initially bailed out by the parent company. One of them, the deliciously named High-Grade Structured Credit Strategies Enhanced Leverage Fund, had taken $600 million from investors and borrowed $6 billion to make huge, and ultimately losing, bets. The global consequences of a collapsing U.S. housing market became equally evident when big Swiss bank UBS fired its chief executive after discovering how exposed the company was to the U.S. subprime market. Yet the Fed could take comfort from the impressive resilience of the overall U.S. economy despite the spreading subprime stain. On July 20, 2007, the Dow Jones Industrial Average crossed 14,000 for the first time; the stock market kept rising until October — as did the price of oil, widely seen as a sign of the strength of economies around the world.

With all these mixed messages, Bernanke tried to strike a balance in his semiannual report to Congress in July 2007. Distinctly more cautious than he had been, Bernanke still conveyed a generally optimistic tone. He mentioned deteriorating conditions in the subprime mortgage market, mounting mortgage delinquencies, and increased worry among investors about the risks of various financial instruments. The spread between rates on loans to shakier businesses and rates on U.S. Treasurys had widened, he said, but were still "near the low end of their historical ranges."

To be sure, there was concern in Bernanke's words, but his conclusions were far from grim. "Overall," he said, "the U.S. economy appears likely to expand at a moderate pace over the second half of 2007, with growth then strengthening a bit in 2008 to a rate close to the economy's underlying trend." The "downside risk," he told Congress, was "that the ongoing housing correction might prove larger than anticipated, with possible spillovers onto consumer spending." (Bad dreams *can* come true.) Still, he told Congress, the Fed saw "upside risks to inflation"—not recession or the ill effects of the bursting housing bubble—as its "predominant policy concern."

Housing, however, was very much on the mind of the senators and congressmen who questioned him. At a July 2007 hearing, responding to a question from Republican senator Richard Shelby of Alabama, Bernanke acknowledged that there would be big losses from subprime mortgage loans that weren't likely to be repaid and from securities linked to those mortgages. He cited estimates of between $50 billion and $100 billion, which he called "fairly significant." That understated the problem enormously. In April 2009, the International Monetary Fund (IMF) estimated that global losses on subprime and other loans made in the United States would eventually reach $2.7 trillion—with another $1.4 trillion coming from loans made overseas.

"He Has No Idea!"

Over the summer of 2007, the housing market continued its collapse. In June, Standard and Poor's downgraded over a hundred bonds backed by subprime mortgages; the ratings company later placed 612 securities backed by subprime mortgages on the list of securities likely to be downgraded. Countrywide Financial Corporation, a huge California-based mortgage company, warned of "difficult conditions" as its problems with subprime mortgages spread to conventional loans. On the last day of July, the two Bear Stearns hedge funds that had been teetering for several months finally filed for bankruptcy and were liquidated.

Then, on August 3, 2007, the growing anxiety on Wall Street found a voice in CNBC commentator Jim Cramer, the lawyer turned journalist turned hedge fund manager turned cable TV star who, according to his official biography, "believes that there is always a bull market somewhere, and he wants to help you find it."

Responding to a question from business news anchor Erin Burnett, Cramer launched into an explosion that became a YouTube favorite. "This is about Bernanke! Bernanke needs to open the discount window! Bernanke needs to focus on this! Bernanke is being an academic. It's not a time to be an academic. . . . Open the darn Fed window."

BERNANKE'S DASHBOARD
August 7, 2007

Dow Jones Industrial Average:	13,504
Market Cap of Citigroup:	$241.6 billion
Price of Oil (per barrel):	$72.43
Unemployment Rate:	4.7%
Fed Funds Interest Rate:	5.25%
Financial Stress Indicator:	0.12 pp

In characteristic fashion, Cramer then began shouting and slamming his hand down. "He has *no idea* how bad it is out there! He has *no idea*! . . . My people have been in the game for twenty-five years, and they are losing their jobs, and these firms are going to go out of business. . . . The Fed is asleep. . . . Cut the rate! Open the window! Relieve the pressure! . . . We have Armageddon in the fixed-income markets. . . . We'll spend billions in Iraq to build homes . . . we have thousands of people losing their homes now."

The Fed's discount window, the way in which it lends directly to banks, *was* open, though few banks were coming to it. But that was a technicality. Cramer's red-faced tirade was a plea to Bernanke to cut interest rates, to pump money aggressively into financial markets as Bagehot had recommended, and to shout reassuringly that the Fed understood that Wall Street players were terrified. As loud as it was, though, Cramer's indictment didn't seem to make much of an impression on the man who bore the brunt of it.

Neither the Fed's actions nor its words suggested Bernanke appreciated how bad things were, and how much worse they would become. From his study of the Depression, Bernanke knew that a severe financial crisis could disable an economy. He could explain how it happened and how it could be cured. He simply didn't — yet — see the subprime mortgage mess as the beginning of a crisis that had any resemblance to the one that confronted the earlier generation of central bankers whom he had criticized with such vehemence.

Chapter 5

PAS DE DEUX

The European Central Bank is a monument to the faith that modern capitalist democracies put in central banks, the high point so far in the post–World War II effort by European nations to bind themselves together not only to avoid another intra-European war but also to build an economy big enough to rival that of the United States. Eighty-five years younger than the Federal Reserve, the ECB occupies a gleaming thirty-seven-story skyscraper in Frankfurt's financial district. Outside the building stands a triumphant blue statue of the symbol of the euro, the multinational currency that has replaced the French franc, Italian lira, German mark — sixteen currencies in all.

Both the Fed and ECB were structured as political compromises. The Germans, surrendering the continent's sturdiest currency, got the headquarters. The French — after tolerating an undistinguished Dutchman for a couple of years — got the presidency: Jean-Claude Trichet, a veteran bureaucrat with thick, graying hair and the demeanor of a duke. The Fed has a couple of advantages: It has only one set of elected politicians to cope with; the ECB has sixteen. All Fed officials speak English as a first language; the ECB does business in English, which is a second language for most of its leadership, and then has to translate its decisions into twenty-one other languages. The ECB has the advantage of clarity of mission: its legal mandate is to resist inflation and ensure stable prices. Period. The Fed's legal mandate is broader and during a crisis more flexible: maximum employment and price stability.

Both central banks are designed to be independent. The ECB's independence is enshrined in a treaty, but it gets frequent, often hostile, public advice from European heads of state and finance ministers about what it should be doing with interest rates and whether it should be trying to talk the euro down to help European exports. The Fed's independence is more by tradition than law, but — at least now — the president and his Treasury secretary rarely offer it advice in public.

But as central banks, both the ECB and the Fed concentrate on the same things: credit and liquidity. If the economy is a car, then credit is the gasoline that powers it, and liquidity is the oil that lubricates the engine. Although liquidity doesn't fuel the economy, it is every bit as essential. The central bankers *knew* lubrication was essential but spent most of their time on the gas pedal, tinkering with just how much fuel to give the engine: less when they wanted to slow the economy, more to speed it up.

On Tuesday, August 7, 2007, the ECB's monetary mechanics in Frankfurt saw a warning light flashing on their computer-screen dashboard: European commercial banks were flush with cash, yet the rates they were charging to lend to one another were rising sharply. It was a clear warning that liquidity was drying up. The mechanics sent word up the chain of command to Trichet and other officials, who shared their staff's concern but didn't want to overreact. Just days before, on August 2, Trichet had dismissed the market's gyrations as a "normalization of the assessment and pricing of risks." (Translation: Investors were coming to their senses.) The ECB officials decided to wait until Wednesday to see if markets were more normal.

What Transparency?

Despite the situation developing in Europe, no sense of urgency was in the air as Fed officials gathered on August 7 in Washington for a previously scheduled meeting of the Federal Open Market Committee (FOMC), known as the "EFF-oh-em-SEE" to insiders. Sitting around a twenty-seven-foot-long oval table of Honduran mahogany and black granite, beneath the twenty-three-foot ceiling of the Fed boardroom, were the six sitting governors based in the nation's capital (one seat was vacant), plus the presidents of the twelve regional Fed banks. A never-used marble fireplace sits at one end of the stately boardroom beneath a huge bas-relief of the coat of arms of the United States, sometimes (though not during FOMC meetings) obscured by a large screen used for projecting charts. On the wall opposite is a map of the United States painted in 1937, showing the location of the district Fed banks and their branch offices.

FOMC meetings followed a nearly religious ritual. Bernanke sat at the middle of the table, as Greenspan had, with each president in the same seat at each meeting. The Fed's influential staff, all sworn to secrecy, reported first on the markets, then on the economy. After each of the governors and Fed bank presidents added their comments on the economy, Greenspan usually would sum up, and then, after a break, the staff would outline options for moving or not moving interest rates. In this round, Greenspan almost always spoke first — and then went around the table. He always prevailed. Bernanke, in pointed contrast, let other committee members go first, then gave his views on rates last, as if to express a consensus rather than dictate an outcome.

Despite Bernanke's attempts to stir debate, many participants stuck to prepared statements, aware that a transcript would be released five years later. At one meeting, Frederic Mishkin, the Columbia economics professor who joined the Fed board in the fall of 2006, turned to Kohn and said, "Don, this is worse than a faculty meeting." Kohn replied, "Yeah, but it's important."

At these meetings the most important decision was whether to change the Fed's most important interest rate. Like the ECB, the Fed manipulated rates up or down, based on its best guess at the future direction of the economy. Its primary tool was still the "federal funds rate," the interest rate at which banks lend to one another. No consumer ever borrows at the overnight federal funds rate, but any change in that rate normally ripples through the economy by moving other interest rates.

To lower rates, the Fed (or any other central bank) creates money from nothing, a process called "printing money," even though it is electronic, and uses that money to buy U.S. Treasury securities from the portfolios of the banks. The banks then have fewer securities but more money to lend. This increased supply of money lowers the federal funds rate, the price of money. When the Fed wants to push up rates, it siphons money out of the market by selling government securities from its vast portfolio; this reduces the credit supply and raises the price of money. The Fed's balance sheet — its portfolio of government securities and loans on one side (its assets) and the reserves of the banks and currency in circulation on the other (its liabilities) — is part of the magic of central banking. Because the Fed can create money, it can buy as many bonds and make as many loans as it wants. In August 2007, the Fed had a $900 billion portfolio, of which $850 billion was in U.S. Treasury securities of one kind or another.

At their August 2007 meeting, Fed officials discussed what was going on in Europe. They noted that housing was apt to remain a drag on growth and acknowledged the "volatility" in financial markets and the deepening problems in subprime housing. Just one day before the meeting, American Home Mortgage had joined fifty or so other mortgage lenders in collapsing into bankruptcy. Bernanke was uneasy that deteriorating financial markets might hurt the economy, and so were Geithner and Mishkin. But no one used the word *crisis*. Those who were worried didn't have enough evidence, conviction, or time to sway the consensus behind a rate cut.

"There was an appreciation this was unusual," remembered Eric Rosengren, the president of the Federal Reserve Bank of Boston. "It wasn't clear how bad it was going to get. The hope was that it would be temporary and that we wouldn't have a lot of spillover effects. And given the knowledge that we had at the time, given what had happened at times of previous liquidity problems, I'm not sure that was a bad guess at that time."

The meeting concluded at 1:25 P.M., but following well-established ritual, the world had to wait another fifty minutes for a statement summarizing the meeting's key decisions. Predictability is the mantra of modern central bankers. Thus, a few minutes before or after 2:15 P.M., a small band of wire-service reporters stationed a few blocks away at the U.S. Treasury flashed the news around the world: the Fed had left its target for the federal funds rate at 5.25 percent, where it had been since June 2006. Despite all that was going wrong, the words of the Fed's statement were almost identical to the ones used in June. Altered wording would have been seen as a signal that a rate cut was imminent, and Bernanke hadn't maneuvered the committee to that point yet.

"Although the downside risks to growth have increased somewhat, the Committee's predominant policy concern remains the risk that inflation will fail to moderate as expected," the Fed said. (Translation: The odds of recession are growing, but we're more worried that inflation will take off.) The statement implied that the Fed was shrugging off the unfolding credit crunch. There was no hint of Bernanke's concern about the risks to the economy posed by disintegrating credit markets. So much for transparency.

"Sometimes the role of the release is more to placate nineteen people sitting around the Board table in Washington and less to educate the public," said ex-Fed staffer Vincent Reinhart, who helped write the statements for six years.

The statement would quickly be overtaken by events — a reminder that behind the curtain at the Fed are a bunch of men and women, some smarter than others, trying to predict the course of an economy that stubbornly refuses to be predictable.

The day after the FOMC meeting found Bernanke occupied with ceremonial duties: a 10 A.M. reception for graduate students in economics interning at the Fed, a 10:45 A.M. taping for a video tribute to ailing Fed governor Ned Gramlich, an 11:30 A.M. meeting with the Turkish ambassador and his wife, a 2 P.M. session with consumer advocate John Taylor of the National Community Reinvestment Coalition.

At day's end, Robert Rubin, the then-much-respected former Treasury secretary and top Citigroup executive, telephoned Bernanke. His message: you did the right thing in not cutting rates. It was classic Rubin, a reassuring call at a key moment, a genuine gesture that helped build a relationship that could be useful later.

FINE-TUNING?

At 8:30 A.M. on the following day, August 9, the huge French bank BNP Paribas made a startling announcement: it was suspending withdrawals from three funds that had invested in U.S. subprime mortgages. The bank said it couldn't put a value on the funds assets because of "the complete evaporation of liquidity in certain market segments of the U.S. securitization market."

This news was as unsettling to investors in 2007 as it had been to depositors in 1907 when a bank shut its doors and said the cash vault was empty. Rumors circulated that other banks were similarly exposed. Banks with cash husbanded it, reluctant to lend even to other banks because they were no longer sure they would get paid back.

Investors scurried to the safety of short-term German government bonds. Liquidity lock was overwhelming the ECB's attempts to maintain control over lending rates. Normally no more than a few hundredths of a percentage point separate the overnight rate and the ECB target rate. Suddenly, skittish European banks had pushed overnight lending rates to 4.7 percent, a huge distance from the 4 percent target. Clearly, the engine was in danger of seizing up.

The ECB had been derided for years for moving too slowly. This time, it reacted with unusual speed. At 10:26 A.M. Thursday — 4:26 in the morning Washington time — it issued a statement to markets that it stood "ready to act." Two hours later, at 12:32 P.M., it said it would lend an unlimited quantity of funds at the 4 percent rate, a sharp break from its usual practice of limiting how much it would lend at any one time. To listeners, this was a loud signal that the ECB was on high alert; it was also a way for the ECB, which has surprisingly little detailed information about European banks, to gauge banks' appetite for liquidity.

The ECB gave banks until 1:05 P.M. to ask for money. At 2 P.M., the ECB announced it was pumping 94.8 billion euros into the banking system, the equivalent of $131 billion — a stunning sum, more than the ECB had put into the markets after the shock of September 11.

The ECB told reporters in Europe and Fed officials who called to inquire that this was just "fine-tuning," a term central bankers generally use to describe minor, inconsequential maneuvers. The Fed, though, knew better. In Washington and New York, it looked as if the ECB had panicked.

Thus began a series of extraordinary responses by central banks to extreme circumstances, the beginning of a cycle of crisis and ever-larger responses that would stretch on for more than a year. "We were the first central bank to react immediately when the international financial turbulence first appeared," Trichet would boast repeatedly in the months that followed, especially when the ECB was criticized for moving more slowly than Bernanke's Fed to cut interest rates or for its reluctance to follow the Fed and the Bank of England in buying long-term government bonds to put more credit into its economy.

THE SPARE TIRE THEORY

The ECB announced its massive cash infusion just as Bernanke was having breakfast — which happened to be his weekly breakfast with Hank Paulson, the Treasury secretary. Bernanke knew the emerging liquidity crisis in Europe was not just a European phenomenon. He saw similar strains in the American banking system. The yelps from Wall Street were growing louder. Jim Cramer's CNBC rant looked more rational than it had the week before. Bernanke moved nearly as swiftly as his ECB counterparts, but with far less force. That morning, the Fed pumped $24 billion into the U.S. markets in overnight loans; an additional $38 billion would follow the next day.

To those who watched the Fed closely, the message was that the managers of the nation's economy were now on alert. The old diagnosis had been that home construction and consumers would suffer a bit from the housing bust, but the overall economy would be able to move forward. That now looked questionable. Officials had also expected the strength of exports and the banking system, which they regularly pronounced "well capitalized," to keep the economy moving forward. The early days of August had dampened that optimism as well.

"In August, *it* crossed into the banking system. That's when things got really complicated," said Donald Kohn, the Fed's vice chairman, who had long taken comfort from what Greenspan once dubbed — in another automotive metaphor — the "spare tire" theory of finance.

The spare tire theory holds that when the banks run into trouble, companies and consumers can borrow directly or indirectly in credit markets where money market funds, insurance companies, pension funds, and others lend cash. Likewise, when credit markets are tight, companies and consumers can borrow from banks. Problems in one sector are offset by the other, in short, and the economy keeps right on rolling.

This theory had held up pretty well over the past two decades. In the 1980s, the banks were stingy and credit markets generous; in the late 1990s, the markets were clogged and banks generous. One advantage that the United States had over other big economies was that it relied on both banks and credit markets; economies in Europe and Asia relied much more on banks to move money from savers to borrowers and thus had nowhere to go when banks got in trouble. "The lack of a spare tire is of no concern if you do not get a flat. East Asia had no spare tires," Greenspan had said in 1999.

Until August, spare-tire theorists thought this episode was largely limited to the markets, save for a few hapless banks. Now both appeared to be going flat—and the Fed amounted to the only available spare. The housing bust was contaminating both credit markets and banks—only the first of what would become a long list of surprises during the Great Panic.

When the Music Stops

Behind this surprise was a misunderstanding of what had been happening in the banks. The Fed and nearly everyone else had taken false comfort in labeling the behavior of twenty-first-century banks as "originate and distribute." The notion was that by packaging loans into securities that were sold to investors all over the world, the banks wouldn't get stuck if loans went bad.

Don Kohn, among others, had celebrated all this as a major advance that was promoting economic growth. The new financial instruments, he said in a reprise of the Greenspan years at a 2005 Fed conference at Jackson Hole, Wyoming, "enable risk and return to be divided and priced to better meet the needs of borrowers and lenders...permit previously illiquid obligations to be securitized and traded, and...make obsolete previous divisions among types of financial intermediaries and across the geographical regions in which they operate." Financial innovation made banks and other financial institutions "more robust" and made the financial system "more resilient and flexible" and "better able to absorb shocks without increasing the effects of such shocks on the real economy."

A more apt description might have been "originate and hide." Banks hadn't distributed nearly as much risk as even sophisticated observers thought. The bad loans—and massive losses—would end up with the banks, eroding their capital cushions to the point where, eventually, their only option for survival was a government bailout.

"All of a sudden," Kohn said months later, "it became very clear the risk had not been distributed. So all I had said at Jackson Hole about risks being distributed and people being safer and people knowing what they had and people could choose and diversify and all that—it turned out to be not entirely true."

Citigroup had pioneered entities called "structured investment vehicles," or SIVs. In essence, mortgage loans were sliced into pieces, with some sold and others kept in these stand-alone units. The SIVs borrowed money by selling short-term IOUs on the market, making them vulnerable to a change in investor appetite for short-term lending. And SIV loans frequently were not shown on the banks' books. A bank has to set aside capital—a cushion to absorb losses—for every loan it makes and every bond it buys. By parking the loans and securities in SIVs off the banks' balance sheets, Citibank and other banks that used SIVs didn't have to set aside capital to absorb any losses. That made the potential profits far greater than if the loans had been on the banks' books. But it also meant there was no capital cushion to absorb losses if the banks ended up taking back the losses, either because they had legal promises to the SIVs or felt maintaining reputations required them to bail out the SIVs. "We didn't recognize how much the stuff would flow back onto the bank balance sheets," Kohn said.

In 2006, Citibank's off–balance sheet assets amounted to $2.1 trillion; its on–balance sheet assets were $1.8 trillion. Not only were these enormous loans hidden, but several top Fed staffers confessed later that they hadn't even heard the term "SIV" until the end of July. Neither had some senior Fed officials—even though they were charged with being guardians of the financial system. In fact, that was typical. An astounding array of derivative products had exploded across the marketplace over the past few years. Even market sophisticates faced a steep learning curve to keep up with what was happening, and that included Citigroup's own chief executive, Chuck Prince.

Dubbed "Prince of the Citi" by the financial press when his bank was flying high, Prince was a lawyer who had taken over the big bank in 2003 when Sandy Weill, the financial entrepreneur, retired. Prince famously dismissed worries that his bank and others were counting unwisely on cheap and plentiful credit to make ever bigger and riskier loans. "When the music stops, in terms of liquidity, things will be complicated. But as long as the music is playing, you've got to get up and dance. We're still dancing," he told the *Financial Times* in early July 2007. It was, actually, a profound observation: a banker who didn't dance, who didn't make ever more risky loans, would find his bank's market share falling and near-term profits less impressive than his competitors'. Prince was one of several Wall Street chief executives who, it turned out, didn't understand the risks their own institutions were taking or who were powerless to stop them. Citi, it would become clear, was not only too big to fail, it was too big to manage. (By November 2007, Prince would be gone.)

Ben Bernanke soon would discover what happens when the music stops, but he had good reason to believe that his team had the experience, smarts, and tools to manage the situation.

Chapter 6

THE FOUR MUSKETEERS:
BERNANKE'S BRAIN TRUST

By the summer of 2007, the Fed was stocked with veterans of market crises: the stock market crash of 1987, the savings and loan scandal of the late 1980s and early 1990s, the commercial banking and real estate woes of the early 1990s, the Asian financial crisis of the late 1990s, the bursting of the tech-stock bubble in 2000, and the September 11 terrorist attacks. The conventional wisdom was that crises were unavoidable despite all the best efforts at prevention. The countervailing comfort was that cleverly conceived and targeted responses by the Fed and Treasury — even if flawed in detail — could limit the economic damage from even the most frightening shocks.

The thinking wasn't as excessively self-confident as it had been back in July 1990 when Frederic Mishkin, then a Columbia University professor, later a Fed governor, declared that: "Since 1945 . . . in no instance has there been a financial crisis that has had serious adverse consequences for the aggregate economy." But within the Fed, self-confidence still ran high. No crisis was unmanageable if you had the brainpower on hand to deal with it, and the Fed had plenty of brains.

Assembled with Bernanke to deal with the emerging grim economic reality were vice chairman Don Kohn, sixty-six, the levelheaded economist who had joined the Fed staff when Richard Nixon was president; Kevin Warsh, thirty-eight, the well-connected Gen-X investment banker who had come to the Fed from the White House shortly after Bernanke had; and Tim Geithner, forty-seven, who was president of the Federal Reserve Bank of New York and the baby-boomer protégé of Treasury secretaries Bob Rubin and Larry Summers.

The composition of this core group was born from background, personality, and legislative strictures. Under the Government in the Sunshine Act, no more than three Fed governors can meet to consider action without formal notice. Bernanke, Kohn, and Warsh made three; Geithner, even though he was president of the most powerful regional Fed bank, didn't count because he wasn't a member of the Fed board of governors. As events unfolded rapidly, the Fed needed maximum operational flexibility for the daily barrage of meetings and conference calls. This meant that other governors, including Bernanke's friend and like-minded academic Mishkin, were frequently left on the sidelines.

Bernanke, Kohn, Warsh, and Geithner became known to some inside the Fed as "the Four Musketeers" — the group that would call every significant play during the Great Panic at the Fed until Geithner left to serve as Obama's Treasury secretary.

KOHN: GREENSPAN'S CONSIGLIERE

Don Kohn began working at the Federal Reserve Bank of Kansas City even before finishing his Ph.D. at the University of Michigan and had never worked outside the Fed. Kohn moved to the Fed's Washington headquarters in 1975, climbing the staff ladder under Chairman Paul Volcker and becoming one of Alan Greenspan's closest advisers. Eventually he inherited one of the three princedoms in the Fed staff hierarchy — director of monetary affairs. In that job, he prepared a series of options on interest rates before each FOMC meeting and discussed them there. Laurence Meyer, a former Fed governor, said Kohn was "always calm and thoughtful, and perhaps the staff member the FOMC members relied upon most frequently for guidance at meetings."

Greenspan relied on him, too, particularly in fashioning the market-moving words he used to describe the Fed's thinking and intentions. During the 1998

Asian financial crisis, Kohn was at Greenspan's side as the chairman wrote a sentence into a speech to signal that the Fed would cut interest rates even if the U.S. economy didn't appear to be in imminent danger: "It is just not credible that the United States can remain an oasis of prosperity unaffected by a world that is experiencing greatly increased stress." The wording was meant and received as a signal that the Fed would cut its interest rates even though the U.S. economy wasn't then feeling much pain from the Asian crisis. The power of the Fed — and its chairman — is such that a sentence like that can lead traders and investors with multibillion-dollar hands to change their bets.

Kohn kept a loose-leaf binder by his desk that held every statement the FOMC had made since it began making public pronouncements in 1994, nearly all of which he helped write. After fourteen years in the grueling monetary-affairs post, Kohn took a step away from the center ring in 2001 to serve as an "adviser," a job created for him, to the Federal Reserve Board. That's what he was doing in 2002 when the White House personnel office called to inquire about his interest in serving as a Fed governor. His first reaction was to walk down the quiet hallway to Greenspan's office. Greenspan had been tipped off by the White House but acted surprised — and pleased. Kohn aced his interview with White House personnel chief Clay Johnson and began preparing for a grilling by the president. He rehearsed with his wife at home and then tried out his pitch on Greenspan. The chairman stopped him. "You don't have to prove anything. Just don't say anything stupid or bad, and it's yours," Greenspan told him.

A few days later in the Oval Office, the president asked Kohn if he thought there were limits to economic growth. "I thought, 'Oh man, if I tell him that there are limits to how fast the economy grows, then he probably doesn't like to hear that.' So I danced around his question," Kohn recalled. Bush noticed and pressed for an answer. So, Kohn said, "I gave him the honest answer: 'Yeah, I think there's a limit to how fast the economy grows...and if you push past that, you're going to get inflation.'" If the president didn't like the answer, he didn't let on. "You'll do fine," he told Kohn.

For decades, Kohn's most prominent moments were showing up on CNBC, sitting behind Greenspan while the chairman testified before Congress. After becoming a governor, his public profile rose significantly.

As Greenspan's retirement neared, *The Economist* endorsed Kohn to be the Great Man's successor. Instead, Bush appointed Kohn to be Bernanke's vice chairman in the spring of 2006, passing over Mishkin, who was named a plain old governor.

Kohn was the institutional memory in the Bernanke brain trust, the one man in the room who could plausibly say: "This is what Greenspan would have done in this situation." He was often the one to find the flaws in Bernanke's latest bit of creative financial engineering.

Kohn had been among Bernanke's intellectual adversaries when both were mere governors. Bernanke thought Greenspan's approach to monetary policy relied too much on the chairman's discretion and not nearly enough on well-explained rules. Along with Geithner, Kohn long had been on the other side, defending Greenspan's approach. Before Bernanke ascended to the throne, Kohn took the lead in making the public case against his inflation-targeting proposal, squaring off against Bernanke face-to-face at a St. Louis Federal Reserve Bank forum on the topic in 2004. Aware of skepticism about inflation targeting both inside the Fed and on Capitol Hill, Bernanke knew he couldn't make progress without Kohn's support. So Bernanke appointed Kohn to head a subcommittee to examine "communications"—a euphemism for "inflation targeting." Bernanke knew that Kohn commanded enormous respect and affection among the Fed staff and policy makers, and he knew that Kohn was unfailingly loyal to the chairman, whoever it happened to be.

By August 2007, Kohn had sold his house in northern Virginia and was planning to spend more time at his weekend place in Annapolis, Maryland. Meanwhile, he and his wife were spending weeknights in a basement apartment of their son's Takoma Park, Maryland, house. Before the work hours demanded by the credit crisis became overwhelming, Kohn often rode his bicycle to work, parking it in the space in the Fed garage reserved for governors' cars. He also had a thing for running up and down the stairs at the Fed instead of taking the elevator.

His low-key personality, experience, and credibility made Kohn a trusted mediator—sometimes among members of the Fed board who felt excluded from the inner circle; sometimes between Geithner and Sheila Bair, the chairman of the Federal Deposit Insurance Corporation, whom Fed and Treasury officials viewed as reluctant to expose the $45 billion deposit-insurance fund to potential losses even when the entire economy was at risk.

WARSH: THE NETWORKER

Kevin Warsh was in many ways Ben Bernanke's opposite.

Bernanke was cerebral, introverted, an alpha in academic networks such as the National Bureau of Economic Research, but an outsider on Wall Street and in Washington. Warsh was outgoing and practical, maintained a rich network of Wall Street contacts, and moved easily among conservative Republicans in the Bush White House and Congress.

Warsh, whose father made his living manufacturing school uniforms, had been a high school tennis star in upstate New York. While he was still a Stanford undergraduate, Warsh finagled his way into the inner circle of West Coast Republican economists at Stanford's Hoover Institution. A math geek, he got a job helping Hoover economists build computer models. One of them, John Cogan, a veteran of the Reagan White House, recalled Warsh asking for help in bringing conservative icon William F. Buckley to campus.

Buckley came, spoke to the student body, and predictably drew pickets. At a dinner for about thirty people before the speech, Cogan asked Warsh to make a few remarks. When he finished, Buckley leaned over to Cogan and said, "This is the most impressive college senior I've come across in years." It was typical Warsh, the agile networker successfully impressing those senior to him in years and experience.

Warsh majored in public policy, graduated with his class in 1992, and contemplated staying on at Stanford to pursue a Ph.D. in economics, but his father deemed that a waste of time and encouraged Warsh to do something else: Harvard Law School. From there, Warsh worked seven years as a mergers and acquisitions investment banker at Morgan Stanley.

In 2002, Warsh married his Stanford classmate Jane Lauder, an heir to the Estée Lauder cosmetics fortune and the daughter of reliable Republican campaign contributor Ronald Lauder. The marriage made Warsh wealthier than all his fellow Fed governors combined. The couple has a penthouse duplex in the trendy NoLita neighborhood of lower Manhattan for which she paid $12.6 million in 2005 as well as a town house in Georgetown for which they paid $2.3 million after Warsh was appointed to the Fed. (Ethics lawyers advised him to take a mortgage from the White House Federal Credit Union to avoid any hint of favoritism from a lender overseen by the Fed. He did promise to avoid anything involving JPMorgan Chase because his wife had money there. Ethics lawyers later waived that restriction so he could deal with JPMorgan Chase during the Great Panic.)

Warsh's connections to the Hoover mafia led to a job on the White House staff in 2002 just as Bush was junking his initial economic team. Warsh ended up working for Stephen Friedman, the former Goldman Sachs chief executive, on corporate finance and capital markets issues and on the administration's efforts to rein in Fannie Mae and Freddie Mac, the government-sponsored mortgage giants.

When Bernanke arrived at the White House in 2005, he and Warsh were often at the same meetings — Bernanke talking about the economy, Warsh about the markets. Warsh also helped prepare Bernanke for his confirmation hearings, and in a sign of his unusual agility at the Washington game, he maneuvered to get himself nominated as a Fed governor, then won confirmation despite being the youngest appointee in Fed history.

Arriving at the Fed less than a month after Bernanke became chairman, Warsh established himself as the chairman's protector in Republican circles and Bernanke's bridge to Wall Street chief executives. When CEOs didn't feel comfortable calling Bernanke directly, they would call Warsh and know their message had been delivered. Bernanke's reliance on Warsh for advice on Republican and Wall Street politics became enshrined in the chairman's frequent query to his staff: "Have you run it by Warsh?"

GEITHNER: DIPLOMAT WITH AN ATTITUDE

The fourth Musketeer, Tim Geithner, was about a decade older than Warsh but was a lithe marathoner and tennis player who looked younger than his forty-seven years. His good looks later earned him a spot on *People* magazine's

100 Most Beautiful People list. His youthful appearance not only made him less threatening to big-ego superiors but, before he'd achieved his current prominence, led some interlocutors to underestimate him. However, it proved to be a major liability when he became Treasury secretary.

As a result of his father's work with the Ford Foundation, Geithner spent most of his childhood overseas. He returned to the United States to attend Dartmouth College and graduate school at Johns Hopkins University. Then Geithner had a stint at Henry Kissinger's consulting firm before joining the Treasury in 1988 as a career bureaucrat. For a time, he was the Treasury's attaché in Tokyo, but after he came back to Washington, Rubin and Summers promoted him rapidly. Geithner entered the Clinton administration as undersecretary for international affairs, the position Summers had started in 1993 (and one that comes with one of the best offices at the Treasury, a room restored to look as it did in 1865, when Andrew Johnson used it while waiting for Abraham Lincoln's widow to vacate the White House). Geithner was at the epicenter of the U.S. government's response to the Mexican and Asian financial crises of the 1990s. The experience had taught him a lot about crisis management and an enduring lesson: smart people solve crises one at a time and worry about dealing with unintended consequences tomorrow. It seemed to work in the past but, with much higher stakes, didn't prove as successful a strategy in the Great Panic.

Geithner wasn't on anyone's short list in 2003 when the New York Fed was looking for a successor to retiring William McDonough. The New York Fed's search committee first considered more likely candidates: Peter Fisher, a former top New York Fed staffer who had coordinated the rescue of the Long Term Capital Management hedge fund, and then done a stint at the U.S. Treasury in the early George W. Bush years; Stanley Fischer, the former MIT professor who had been Bernanke's adviser and had gone to the World Bank and the number two job at the International Monetary Fund; and John Taylor, a Stanford economist whose expertise in monetary policy earned him an international reputation. But Peter Fisher had rubbed some Fed insiders the wrong way. Taylor's time as the Bush Treasury's top international hand suggested he was a better professor than manager. And Stan Fischer had just taken a well-paid post at Citigroup.

Bob Rubin had tried to lure Geithner to join Stan Fischer and other veterans of the Rubin Treasury at Citigroup, but without success. Geithner had taken a job at the IMF instead — where, to his later embarrassment, he failed to pay all the U.S. taxes he owed. Still, Rubin remained an admirer, and as others fell off the short list, he offered Geithner's name to Pete Peterson, the cofounder of the Blackstone private equity group and chairman of the New York Fed Board. In response, Paul Volcker, who was on an advisory committee for the search, asked, not completely seriously: "Who's Geithner?"

When Peterson reached Geithner in London, Geithner's first reaction was, "It isn't plausible." The job, he said, was usually for someone at a later stage of life. But he discovered that Peterson had done his homework and that Greenspan had endorsed the idea. He respected Geithner but also knew Geithner wouldn't challenge him. Not wanting to appear excessively eager, Geithner refused the search committee's suggestion that he write an application and went directly to the interview phase.

Peterson would later say that he had found Geithner disturbingly young-looking and wondered if he was tough enough to say "No!" to Wall Street bankers when necessary. Peterson called Summers. "I wanted to be sure the soft-spokenness, the diffidence, didn't translate into a lack of courage," he explained. In an often-repeated anecdote, usually printed without the profanity that peppered Geithner's conversation, Peterson said, "I told Larry what my concerns were, and Larry burst out laughing. He said, 'Don't worry about that, Pete. He's the only person who ever worked with me who'd walk into my office and say to me, 'Larry, on this one, you're full of shit.'"

By tradition, the president of the Federal Reserve Bank of New York serves as vice chairman of the FOMC. Geithner's immediate predecessor, Bill McDonough, a former banker, usually was the first to speak after Greenspan, almost always responding with fawning enthusiasm. By contrast, Geithner generally waited until everyone else on the committee had spoken and then weighed in, loyal to Bernanke but not a sycophant. His capacity to size up a situation and lay out options coherently and calmly won him admirers among the other Musketeers and made him among the most influential advisers not only to Bernanke but also to Treasury's Paulson, who had a habit of bolting from a telephone call with Geithner and giving his aides orders with the introductory phrase: "Geithner says..."

Paulson, a forceful personality, liked Bernanke and relied on him but sometimes was surprised by his unwillingness or inability to act like the five-star general that he was. He greatly admired and respected Geithner. Treasury staff would chafe and complain to counterparts at the Fed in Washington about Geithner's outsized influence. Longtime Fed hands would fret that Geithner was so close to Paulson and so sympathetic to the Treasury, where he had worked for years, that he was undermining the Fed's cherished reputation of being independent of elected politicians.

Despite a well-cultivated image as a diplomat, Geithner grew testy at the persistent second-guessing from those who were far from the chaos of the battlefield. After sparring with the Richmond Fed's hard-line Jeffrey Lacker at one meeting, Geithner warned him and other Fed bank presidents that their dissents and public hectoring might provoke Congress into stripping them of their vote on interest rates—a possibility that Barney Frank, the chairman of the House Financial Services Committee, had mentioned more than once. Both inside and outside the Fed, Geithner often was seen as too close to the banks, too ready to rush to their rescue. Some of this came with the job, and some of it reflected his long-standing ties to Bob Rubin at Citigroup, the largest of the banks under the New York Fed's supervision.

This, then, was the core group that was going to face down the worst economic and financial threat since the Great Depression: a brainiac from South Carolina who had once worked summers at the tackiest roadside attraction on I-95; a sober sixty-something bicyclist and technocrat who had the confidence of both the Fed's Old Guard and new leadership; an ambitious thirty-something Republican investment banker; and a diplomat whose cool demeanor masked an iron will.

Chapter 7

RE: RE: RE: RE: RE: RE: BLUE SKY

On the afternoon of August 9, 2007, only hours after the Fed had joined the European Central Bank in throwing money on the table, Ben Bernanke assembled the Musketeers. He wanted to brainstorm or, as he put, to "blue sky." One of Bernanke's e-mails on the subject circulated so furiously around the Fed that by day's end the subject heading read: "RE: RE: RE: RE: RE: RE: Blue Sky." (Unlike Paulson, Bernanke was a BlackBerry addict.) The iterations tell the tale: the moment was growing urgent.

At that afternoon huddle, Bernanke and Warsh sat close to the coffee table in Bernanke's office so they could be heard on the Polycom speakerphone. Kohn was in his car on the way to a wedding in New England, talking on a cell phone while handing quarters for tolls to his wife, who was doing the driving. Geithner phoned in from his vacation on Cape Cod. Although they were scattered from Washington through the Northeast, the Four Musketeers were of one mind: they had misjudged the severity of the problem.

That same day, unseen by the public and well beneath the shadows cast by the ECB and Fed actions, the St. Louis Federal Reserve Bank sent up a flare. It was an unlikely source. Bill Poole, the seventy-year-old economist trained at the University of Chicago in Milton Friedman's heyday and now the St. Louis Fed's president, was more determined to resist inflation than many others at the

Fed and was prone to dissent in favor of higher interest rates. But at a meeting of the St. Louis Fed's board of directors, Poole sought a request to cut the discount rate—the rate that the Fed charges on loans it makes directly to individual banks. (The phrase "discount window" refers to the Fed's original practice of "discounting"—or buying at a discount from the face value—IOUs that businesses had given banks. The size of the discount these days is known as "a haircut." The riskier the security offered as collateral for a discount-window loan, the bigger the haircut.) Such requests, though technically from the private-sector directors of a district Fed bank, are a way for a Fed bank president to signal his or her druthers on interest rates. They are closely guarded secrets; no one outside the Fed knew. Poole said later he had been stunned by the severe strains in the market for commercial paper: short-term corporate IOUs.

The next day, Bernanke started early, convening a 7 A.M. conference call with the Fed governors in Washington and the presidents of the twelve regional banks. They agreed to do the first thing that the Fed always does in a crisis: try the calming effect of words. There would be neither action nor a stated change in policy, only a promise to provide enough money to keep the federal funds rate close to its 5.25 percent target and to lend through the discount window.

Their job was to keep the banking system functioning by serving as the lender of last resort at a time of stress, and the banks, at least at this point, weren't facing a run from depositors. In the infinitely more complicated financial system of the twenty-first century, though, ancient nostrums were running up against intractable modern realities.

While they weren't facing runs, banks were increasingly reluctant to lend to one another, and other parts of the money markets were showing signs of malfunction. This was threatening to freeze the pistons of the economy. One vulnerable market was the one where financial houses borrowed money overnight from money market funds and other institutional investors with spare cash, the "tri-party repo market." The word *repo* is short for "repurchase." In the standard deal, the borrower sells a security to a lender and agrees to *repurchase* it at a fixed price later. In effect, a repo is an overnight mortgage. In the same way that a homeowner pledges a house to the bank in exchange for a loan, a financial institution pledges a bond in exchange for funds. If the borrower doesn't pay back the loan, the lender gets the bond, often a U.S. Treasury note or mortgage-backed security of some sort. The "tri-party" term refers to a three-cornered arrangement that was devised in the mid-1980s after the collapse of a couple of dealers in government securities. Two banks dominate the middleman part of the business, Bank of New York Mellon and the ubiquitous JPMorgan Chase.

The tri-party repo market was just one manifestation of the ways finance had moved away from traditional banking, the business that the Fed was accustomed to supervising. "The structure of the financial system changed fundamentally during the boom, with dramatic growth in the share of assets outside the traditional banking system," Geithner said. The overall repo market had boomed over the past couple of decades. In 1990, the market amounted to $372 billion, or roughly 13 percent of the size of the $2.8 trillion in federally insured bank deposits. By 2007, the market had grown to $2.6 trillion, equal to 60 percent of the $4.3 trillion in bank deposits. A market practice that had evolved in response to a 1980s vulnerability was creating a new one in the 2000s.

One of the first to get crushed was California's Countrywide Financial. One of the nation's largest and most aggressive mortgage lenders, Countrywide was cofounded in the 1970s by Angelo Mozilo, the entrepreneurial son of a Bronx butcher who rode the subprime roller coaster up and then down. Countrywide used the "originate and distribute" model of spreading risk around: it bought mortgages, then quickly sold them to Fannie Mae and Freddie Mac and others. In June 2009, Mozilo was formally accused by the Securities and Exchange Commission of securities fraud for misleading investors of the risks the company was taking to maintain its market share from 2005 through 2007. In an April 2006 e-mail released by the SEC, Mozilo referred to one Countrywide mortgage product and told a top lieutenant: "In all my years in the business I have never seen a more toxic prduct [sic]."

Unlike traditional banks, Countrywide relied heavily on borrowing overnight in money markets to finance loans that hadn't yet been sold, often using the tri-party repo market. That proved to be a major vulnerability as the Great Panic tightened up lending. Countrywide was now increasingly being viewed as risky, and the downward slide in its stock price accelerated. Countrywide shares, which had been trading at $42 at the beginning of 2007, fell below $30 at the end of July and below $20 in mid-August. (They would end 2007 at $8.94.)

By mid-August, growing anxiety around mortgages, however, was putting the value of Countrywide's collateral in doubt. On the evening of the fifteenth, Bank of New York Mellon, the middleman with whom Countrywide dealt, told the New York Fed that unless Countrywide came up with more collateral, it wouldn't give investors their cash the next morning, and would instead pay them with Countrywide's securities. Tim Geithner knew what was at stake: money market funds wouldn't want the securities and would try to sell them immediately, creating a fire sale of billions of dollars in securities dumped onto an already jittery market.

Geithner mediated talks that stretched past midnight, at which point he left, telling his staff to call if discussions fell apart. Eventually, the two sides agreed on additional collateral. "We worked it out beautifully," Countrywide CEO Mozilo told the *Wall Street Journal*. Bullet dodged, or so it appeared.

BERNANKE'S DASHBOARD
August 16, 2007

		Change from August 7, 2007
Dow Jones Industrial Average:	12,846	down 4.9%
Market Cap of Citigroup:	$236.4 billion	down 2.2%
Price of Oil (per barrel):	$71.01	down 2.0%
Unemployment Rate:	4.7%	—
Fed Funds Interest Rate:	5.25%	—
Financial Stress Indicator:	0.61 pp	up 0.49 pp

The next morning, August 16, Countrywide made public that it was drawing down its $11.5 billion credit lines, unnerving the markets. (Within a week, it had sold a $2 billion stake to Bank of America, which later acquired the whole company.) Countrywide was an early warning of the susceptibility of the tri-party repo market to sudden bouts of distrust among big players in financial markets, the same virulent distrust that would sink Bear Stearns seven months later.

At 6 P.M. on the sixteenth, Bernanke convened a videoconference of the entire FOMC. The Fed's cavernous boardroom — so well fortified that it was used for meetings between U.S. and British military chiefs during World War II — isn't equipped with video. So Bernanke and the other governors used a small conference room nearby, known as "the special library," and faced a TV screen that was wheeled in on a cart. Each regional Fed bank president appeared on the screen in his or her own box, the outline of which was highlighted when the person spoke. A couple of Fed presidents dubbed it *Hollywood Squares*, after the TV game show. They joked about leaning over and punching the president in the next box if there was a disagreement.

Bernanke had devised a two-pronged response with the other Musketeers. The first was to reduce the rate at which the Fed lent directly to banks by one-half percentage point and let banks borrow for thirty days, instead of the usual overnight. The point was to lubricate the economy, not add more fuel. The Fed long had charged a penalty — one percentage point above the federal funds rate — on loans from its discount window so that banks would have good reason to keep themselves healthy enough to borrow more cheaply from other banks in the federal funds market.

Rick Mishkin, the Fed governor, applauded the Bernanke innovation as an attempt to put more liquidity into the markets without increasing the total amount of credit, targeting the remedy at what appeared to be the most serious symptom at the moment. A student of the history of financial crises, Mishkin was convinced that this was the opening act of what could be a much more serious crisis and argued that the Fed needed to be very aggressive very quickly. In a fifteen-minute conversation before the FOMC meeting, he had told Bernanke that he wanted an even bigger cut in the discount rate and said so at the meeting itself. On the other side, Jeff Lacker of the Richmond Fed didn't want to cut the discount rate at all, and told Bernanke as much.

The second prong of Bernanke's action plan was more conventional: crafting words to undo the impression left at the end of the FOMC meeting ten days prior that the Fed was fixated on inflation. Don Kohn, as a veteran of Greenspan's artful market communication, considered this more important and worked on the wording of the sentences with Brian Madigan, a tall, red-bearded career Fed economist who now was in the pivotal monetary-affairs staff job that Kohn had once held.

"DOWNSIDE RISKS"

To those fluent in Fedspeak, the Friday-morning message of August 17 was clear: a cut in interest rates was now on the table for the first time in Bernanke's tenure. "Downside risks to growth have increased appreciably" (Translation: It's going to be worse than we anticipated), and the Fed "is prepared to act as needed to mitigate the adverse effects on the economy arising from the disruptions in financial markets." (Translation: We will cut rates unless markets turn around soon.)

Theater and substance wound around each other. At moments of panic, the financial system acts less like the automobile engine of the favorite metaphor and more like a collection of worried people, with emotions and trust that wax and wane. When people are concerned about money, they make choices — such as delaying purchases, hoarding cash, distrusting each other — that are completely rational acts of self-preservation but that worsen an already bad situation.

A successful central bank attacks on both fronts, and that's what Bernanke had hoped to do. The substance: the Fed belatedly acknowledged that a weakening economy meant that it would cut the interest rate that mattered most, the federal funds rate. The theater: the Fed was shouting that it was eager to lend to cash-short banks through the discount window. But banks were reluctant to borrow from the discount window because doing so, if word leaked, could be seen as a sign of their own financial weakness. If a bank suddenly stopped bidding for short-term funds in the open market, others would guess that it had gone to the Fed. The Fed hoped to dispel that stigma.

Geithner and Kohn convened an unusual conference call with bankers and urged the strong and weak alike to borrow from the discount window. The first to do so — the American arm of Germany's biggest bank, Deutsche Bank — quietly let the press know, figuring other banks would be doing the same. But none of the others did initially, embarrassing Deutsche. So the Fed cajoled four big banks into borrowing $500 million each and saying so loudly.

The effort was a flop. "The thing about 'lending freely and at a penalty rate' only works when people want to borrow," Kohn said, referring to Bagehot's prescription. Banks, it turned out, didn't want to borrow sufficiently at the discount window to lubricate the system.

Bernanke, though, didn't have time to ponder what Greenspan might have done, or even to mull over if there was something he and his lieutenants might have done differently. Events were moving too fast for that. He canceled plans to join his family on vacation in Charlotte, North Carolina, and Myrtle Beach, South Carolina. He no longer even had time to shoot baskets with the staff in the Fed gym, although he did occasionally don T-shirt and shorts to shoot baskets alone.

Until August 2007, the Fed was something like a firehouse in a town of brick houses: long stretches of boredom punctuated by the occasional one-alarm blaze. The pace was slow, the routine almost unvarying. That changed in August. Now the houses were frame, the weather bone dry, and the alarms were ringing incessantly. In response, the Four Musketeers began a series of daily early-morning and late-afternoon conference calls with key staffers to monitor markets and reassess strategy.

RETHINKING GREENSPAN

As they did every year, the biggest names in global central banking — Fed officials, their overseas counterparts, Wall Street's Fed watchers, and a handful of journalists — gathered from August 25 to 27 at Grand Teton National Park in Jackson Hole, Wyoming, for golf, hiking, socializing, and sometimes ponderous, sometimes provocative, academic presentations sponsored by the Federal Reserve Bank of Kansas City, in whose turf the spectacular park is located.

Jim Wolfensohn, the former president of the World Bank, hosts a dinner Friday night at his house nearby. Friedman, the former Goldman CEO, hosts one Saturday night. Invitations to Jackson Hole are coveted by academics and Wall Street analysts, who prize the schmoozing with the Fed's elite.

Bernanke and four other Fed governors were at Jackson Hole that late August 2007, as were all but one of the twelve Fed bank presidents. Greenspan hadn't been since 2005, a session that had turned into an almost unrestrained celebration of his tenure. Now, two years later, the hangover from the

Greenspan years was giving his successors a massive and growing headache. The formal topic was timely and reinforced the pain: housing and housing finance.

This year, a revisionist account of the Greenspan years began to take hold inside the fraternity. John Taylor, the noted Stanford monetary expert, indicted Greenspan for having created the current housing crisis by keeping interest rates too low too long earlier in the decade. Taylor believed that government economic policy worked best when the people who made policies publicly described the rules that governed their decision making. He was famous among central bankers around the world for "the Taylor rule," a simple formula for setting interest rates that depended on where inflation was versus the Fed's goal for it, how far from full employment the economy was, and what the short-term interest rate should be when the economy was perking along. Taylor had been among George H. W. Bush's economic advisers, and nearly made it to the Fed board then until internal political squabbles thwarted him. In 2005, he had been among the unsuccessful contenders to succeed Greenspan, for whom he had once worked when Greenspan was a private consultant. Taylor's critique particularly stung Greenspan because of Taylor's stature and because it gave legitimacy to other critics with lesser pedigrees.

He wasn't Greenspan's only critic at Jackson Hole. At lunch one day, in a speech that had to be read by a designated hitter because severe illness kept him from attending, former Fed governor Ned Gramlich underscored warnings he had made to Greenspan about the risks of refraining from regulation of the subprime mortgage market. Coming from a revered figure — and a dying one — and after the subprime debacle had been exposed, Gramlich's implicit criticism of Greenspan also stung.

NONCURES FOR NON-BANKS

Fed officials had little time to reevaluate the past. They were preoccupied by the present and near future. From the podium at Jackson Hole, Rick Mishkin, the Fed governor, choosing his words with great care to avoid triggering an unwelcome market reaction, explained what the Fed officials were worried about: "I generally do not place the housing and mortgage markets close to the epicenter of previous cases of financial stability," he said. But "periods of rapid financial change...often lead to lending booms...[and] lending booms can sometimes outstrip the available information resources in the financial system, raising the odds of costly, unstable conditions in financial markets in the short run." (Translation: Housing and mortgage booms don't usually burst in ways that disrupt an entire economy, but they can.) It would prove a prescient warning.

In a small conference room on the second floor of Jackson Lake Lodge, the Four Musketeers met to figure out what to do next. Their initial response: the discount rate maneuver and the hint of lower interest rates to come hadn't been sufficient. Banks were reluctant to lend to one another, but they were reluctant to borrow from the Fed, too. The new solution: auction Fed loans to banks, a more anonymous way of getting funds than applying at the discount window. They asked the staff to work on the technicalities. Although most of the officials didn't realize it at the time, the notion was similar to one the Fed had considered during a deflation scare in 2002.

From the sidelines, Larry Summers sounded an even louder alarm. Writing in his regular column for the *Financial Times*, Summers suggested that the real threat to the economy might lie in financial institutions either beyond the Fed's purview or resistant to its carrot-and-stick remedies. "The problem this time," Summers wrote, "is not that banks lack capital or cannot fund themselves. It is that the solvency of a range of *non-banks* is in question, both because of concerns about their economic fundamentals and because of cascading liquidations as investors who lose confidence in them seek to redeem their money and move into safer, more liquid investments." (Emphasis added.)

The commercial banks, it would turn out, weren't nearly as well capitalized as Summers asserted. But the "non-banks" — Freddie Mac and Fannie Mae, big investment banks and brokerage firms, insurance companies — would prove major threats to financial stability in the months ahead and highly resistant to the Fed's traditional cure of cutting interest rates.

Chapter 8

RUNNING FROM BEHIND

The Federal Open Market Committee had a passing resemblance to high school. There were the cool guys, the jocks, and the geeks. Bernanke, Don Kohn, Tim Geithner, and Kevin Warsh fell into the first category, the cool ones. The jocks were regional Fed bank presidents determined to show their manhood by talking tough about inflation and economic rectitude: economists Jeffrey Lacker in Richmond and Charles Plosser in Philadelphia, investor-turned-policy-maker Richard Fisher in Dallas. The geeks included monetary policy scholars who shared Bernanke's view of the world: Rick Mishkin in Washington, Janet Yellen in San Francisco, Eric Rosengren in Boston. And then there were the wannabes: among them Randy Kroszner, the book-smart University of Chicago professor who managed to rub much of the Fed staff the wrong way, and newcomers James Bullard of St. Louis and Dennis Lockhart of Atlanta.

The FOMC can be a fractious group, as even Alan Greenspan discovered. In 1988, the cacophony of competing views was so pronounced that the *Wall Street Journal* labeled the FOMC the "Open Mouth Committee." As Greenspan accumulated clout, he fixed that. With occasional exceptions, renegade governors in Washington and district bank presidents were replaced by appointees with views closer to the mainstream and personalities more inclined toward following the leader. By the late 1990s, Greenspan's papal-size reputation for infallibility made insiders wary of challenging him. And then there was his masterful ability to silence internal critics when he grew weary of them. "You challenge Greenspan, and he tolerates it — at first," one Fed bank president said. "If you keep going, it's like a cartoon: a sixteen-ton weight drops on you from the ceiling, and it's clear the conversation is over."

BERNANKE'S DASHBOARD
September 18, 2007

		Change from August 7, 2007
Dow Jones Industrial Average:	13,739	up 1.7%
Market Cap of Citigroup:	$240.5 billion	down 0.5%
Price of Oil (per barrel):	$81.52	up 12.6%
Unemployment Rate:	4.7%	—
Fed Funds Interest Rate:	4.75%	down 0.5 pp
Financial Stress Indicator:	0.96 pp	up 0.84 pp

Bernanke had neither Greenspan's skill at cowing critics nor his desire to dominate the committee. He was "influenced by his own experience on the Board as a governor, by academic research that tended to show groups perform better than individuals, and by the foreign precedent of argumentative yet still successful monetary policy committees," according to Vincent Reinhart, who was the top Fed monetary staffer until the summer of 2007. Bernanke admired the Bank of England, which consists of five insiders and four outsiders, some of whom sharply disagree in public with Bernanke's counterpart and former MIT office mate Mervyn King, to no apparent harm.

All that won Bernanke high points for collegiality, but as the Great Panic unfolded through 2007, several things became clear: in a fast-breaking crisis that demands a prompt, decisive response, waiting for a committee to reach consensus can be a mistake. In such a crisis, the markets and the public prize clarity, and clarity will always be elusive when a Fed chairman allows everyone else to outshout him. Just as bad, waiting for a consensus to form didn't guarantee a positive outcome. No matter how much smarts they command or how expansive their powers, central bankers can and do badly misread their economies. Finding central bankers who can avoid making such mistakes is preferable, but finding central bankers who recognize their mistakes and then change course may be the best any country can expect.

TAKING OUT INSURANCE

By the time the FOMC convened in Washington on September 18, a couple of weeks after Jackson Hole, the government had reported that employers had cut their payrolls for the first time in seven years. Britain had witnessed its first bank run in a century, humiliating Mervyn King at the Bank of England. King had chided the Fed and ECB for rushing to pump money into credit markets. Doing so "encourages herd behavior and increases the intensity of future crises," he charged. Then in response to a run on a bank misleadingly named Northern Rock—which employed a Countrywide-like strategy of borrowing in short-term markets to finance mortgages that it planned to sell to securities markets—King had been forced to do in the markets what other central banks had. In Washington, the ghost of Greenspan loomed as he released his memoir with an appearance on *60 Minutes*, an excerpt in *Newsweek*, and headlines nearly everywhere days before the FOMC meeting.

Bernanke didn't need a cudgel to persuade the FOMC to cut interest rates. Reducing short-term interest rates was traditionally the Fed's best weapon against the prospect of an unwelcome weakening of the economy, and there was no reason — yet — to doubt they'd be ineffective. The only issue was how much to cut.

Financial markets and the Fed play a constant mutual guessing game. Traders, analysts, and investors scrutinize the Fed's words, the whispers they hear from people who seem to talk to folks at the Fed, and accounts in the press. Out of that stew of speculation and innuendo, the markets gauge the likely reaction of Fed officials to incoming data on the economy, and move market interest rates in anticipation of the next Fed maneuver. The Fed, in turn, looks to markets for the collective judgment of huge numbers of people with money about the likely direction of the economy—even though Fed officials know that looking at the markets is sometimes like looking in a mirror and seeing what the market thinks the Fed is planning to do. Finally, after both sides have studied each other, bets are placed on which way the Fed is going to move, often in the federal funds futures market. In September, the betting was that the Fed would cut its target, then at 5.25 percent, by a quarter percentage point.

Despite the misgivings of some regional bank presidents, the Fed delivered a rate cut twice that size. The stock market cheered the news loudly. The Dow Jones Industrial Average had its best day since 2003, rising 2.5 percent. In Fedspeak, the aggressive half-point move amounted to "taking out insurance," preemptively cutting interest rates to reduce the risk of a nightmare scenario becoming reality. Especially in the wake of the run on Northern Rock, the Fed needed—as Geithner often put it—to get the ratio of drama to impact right. Too much drama, and the Fed conveyed unsettling panic. Too little action, and the Fed looked wimpy. The September rate cut was one instance in the Great Panic where the Fed appeared to hit the ratio exactly right. The first rate cut of Bernanke's tenure was a clear success.

Yet despite the deft touch, surprising numbers of ordinary Americans were angry, and getting more so. They saw the Fed helping Wall Street and irresponsible home buyers. "The Federal Reserve needs to stand its ground and not bail out hedge funds—they should have known better to begin with!" Suzanne Mitchell, an administrative assistant at a Houston real estate company, told the *Wall Street Journal*. "I'm very sorry that people took out $450,000 mortgages with no money down…people ought to be responsible for the loans they take out."

"THE BANKING SYSTEM IS HEALTHY"

An angry public aside, the Fed had reason for optimism in September and October 2007. In the weeks that followed the rate cut, the economy and markets did better than Fed officials had expected. So the Fed put aside plans, discussed in the back room in Jackson Hole in August, to experiment with new ways to lend money to banks. Cutting interest rates and the few modest other steps the Fed had taken to provide liquidity seemed sufficient. Banks had taken a blow, for sure, but Bernanke and Geithner believed banks had begun the Great Panic with enough capital to absorb the anticipated losses.

At a closed-door workshop on financial stability in Washington in October, Geithner said that though it was too early to tell how well the system was functioning in this crisis, one thing was encouraging: "The capital cushions at the largest banks proved strong enough to withstand the shock.... This was absolutely critical." (He was wrong.)

Bernanke was just as reassuring when he appeared before the New York Economic Club, a group of Wall Street economists, executives, and traders. "Fortunately, the financial system entered the episode of the past few months with strong capital positions and a robust infrastructure. The banking system is healthy," he said. It was not one of his more prescient observations, but where the Great Panic was concerned, almost no one got a gold star for guessing the future right.

Bernanke wasn't in a Pollyanna mode. He had plenty of worries, but they were more question marks than alarm bells. Prompted by a question from Henry Kaufman — nicknamed Dr. Doom for his gloomy predictions while at Salomon Brothers years earlier — Bernanke told the Economic Club that one issue was the difficulty Wall Street was having in valuing securities, particularly those linked to mortgages. With so little trading, market prices were nonexistent or possibly misleading. What information did Bernanke most wish he had that he lacked? Kaufman asked. "I'd like to know what those damn things are worth," the chairman replied.

The response drew a laugh, but it turned out to be far more profound than it sounded at the time. The difficulty in putting a value on loans, securities, and exotic financial instruments banks were carrying on their books became one of the most debilitating features of the Great Panic. With the usual market mechanisms dysfunctional, no one could be sure the assets were properly valued — and that all the losses had been disclosed — so everyone assumed the worst, a problem that would persist into 2009. But in the fall of 2007, the Fed didn't yet appreciate just how big an issue that was or would become.

"The mistake I made was to think about the damage being primarily limited to subprime lending," Bernanke would admit later. "After all, the subprime losses involved an amount of money equal to one day's movement in the stock market, and that isn't enough to make a big difference in the economy," he said, with the perspective that comes only with time. "But we know now this was much bigger than subprime lending. It was a credit bubble much more broadly construed. The subprime crisis triggered a much broader retreat from credit and risk taking. It became a much bigger deal than I anticipated. And on top of that, we didn't — nobody really did — understand the interconnections to off–balance sheet vehicles and complex credit derivatives and all those other things that followed."

All that, though, was by way of retrospection. By the end of October, the economy seemed to be gaining traction. Fed officials saw "scant evidence of negative spillovers from the ongoing housing correction to other sectors of the economy." Instead, they predicted the economy would rebound to normal growth in 2009. Mishkin's histories of financial crises found that they often turned around after three or four months. Why shouldn't that happen this time, too? At the October 31 FOMC meeting, Bernanke led the majority to a one-quarter percentage point cut and an end-of-meeting statement that indicated the Fed thought it was done with rate cuts for a while. That, too, would prove a widely overoptimistic assessment.

HAWKS, DOVES, AND JEWISH MOTHERS

While economists on the outside worried that the Fed was doing too little, some regional Fed bank presidents thought Bernanke was doing too much. Among those arguing for holding interest rates steady was a band of central bankers from the middle of the country derided by their internal foes as "presidents from the flyover states." One of them, Thomas Hoenig, longtime president of the Kansas City Fed, said that the U.S. economy was growing at "a reasonable pace" on its own and didn't need the Fed's ministrations. By lowering rates to cure what didn't need curing, the Fed instead had "elevated" the risk of inflation, he said. By law, only five of the twelve district bank presidents vote on rates at any meeting; Hoenig was one of the five and thus allowed to formally object to the rate cut.

Fed officials are the Jewish mothers of the global economy. They always have to worry about something, and that something is often inflation — not today's inflation, but the possibility of inflation tomorrow. It's no idle concern: when the Fed took its eye off that ball in the late 1970s, the United States ended up with debilitating double-digit inflation. In late 2007, Hoenig and others were worrying that the Fed had taken its eye off the inflation ball again. Oil prices were rising, and he and the like-minded feared that would lead companies and consumers to anticipate price increases throughout the economy, an anticipation that often becomes self-fulfilling. The U.S. economy wasn't so weak that it would prevent wage and price increases, the inflation-wary feared, and the world economy wasn't weak at all.

In Fedspeak, Hoenig was a hawk, while Boston's Rosengren and San Francisco's Yellen were doves. The labels were used loosely to distinguish between Fed officials who tend to favor higher interest rates to ward off any risk of inflation and those who tend to favor lower rates to head off higher unemployment. Economic forecaster Laurence Meyer, a keen observer of the Fed who spent five years on Greenspan's Fed board, noticed that traditionally hawkish FOMC members minimized the risks to the economy from financial turmoil, while dovish members tended to emphasize the risks — even though issues of financial stability had little in common with the usual inflationary dynamics.

"The hawks are very passionate in their views about the appropriate course of monetary policy and tend to speak with loud voices, both in their speeches and inside the FOMC," he wrote to clients in a memo that circulated widely within the Fed. "The doves...tend to be stunned by the belief of the hawks that the credit shock does not have to be offset by easier monetary policy."

"Call it a genetic predisposition," he said.

That internal divide would plague Bernanke throughout the Great Panic, particularly when the Fed began to devise new ways to lend money.

MISHKIN, SMISHKIN

October proved a false dawn. As financial stresses resurfaced in November, Rick Mishkin — who wasn't by nature patient — grew antsy about the inadequacy of the Fed's response. A scholar of financial crises of the past, Mishkin finished his Ph.D. at MIT a few years ahead of Bernanke and, in 1983, landed a teaching job at Columbia. Except for a brief stint at the New York Fed in the mid-1990s, where he was recruited to strengthen a lackluster research department, Mishkin had become a fixture at Columbia in the years since, authoring a college textbook on money and banking that dominated the market and sweetened his personal finances. (Mishkin disclosed $434,000 in royalties in 2007, more than double his Fed salary of $172,200. He left the Fed in August 2008, largely because government ethics rules wouldn't permit him to revise his textbook while remaining in office. By the end of 2008, he already had revised the chapter on financial crises to refer to this latest one.)

Mishkin thought of himself as entertaining — and sometimes was. Despite uneasiness among the Fed's public relations staff, he titled one speech "Comfort Zones, Shmumfort Zones," an uncomplimentary reference to an alternative to inflation targeting that called for the Fed to set a vague "comfort zone" for the acceptable level of inflation. "Putting the 'shm' before a word is a way to cast a bit of skepticism on it," he explained to a Lexington, Virginia, audience unaccustomed to Yiddish-spouting New Yorkers. "Thus, if your friend tells you that you are 'fancy, shmancy,' then you might be overdressed for the occasion.... Of course, there's also a significant distinction between the expressions 'shlemiel' and 'shlimazel,' but that's more advanced material that I will defer until another speech."

Mishkin had been close to Bernanke professionally and personally before arriving in Washington seven months after Bernanke assumed the chairmanship — three of the twelve references in Bernanke's first published paper cited Mishkin. And Mishkin remained unswervingly loyal to his friend. Excluded from the Four Musketeers, he resorted to one-on-one meetings with Bernanke to try to influence him directly. Frustrated at the FOMC's inertia and the caliber of some of the discussions, Mishkin eventually decided that public speeches might have a bigger influence inside the Fed than arguments he made at the Fed's closed-door meetings. Speeches, after all, could be cited by outsiders, giving them credibility with insiders, and they could be contemplated outside the meeting room.

Better still, well-conceived phrases in speeches could frame debates at the

Fed. In the 1990s, Greenspan repeatedly described banks' reluctance to lend as "50 mph headwinds" holding back the economy, and those headwinds became the justification for cutting interest rates. Mishkin's contribution a decade-plus later was a wonky phrase: "adverse feedback loop." The notion was that financial disruptions hurt consumer spending and business investment. That, in turn, made lenders and investors more cautious, which led to an even worse economy.

The notion wasn't original; Bernanke's "financial accelerator" concept was much the same thing. But neither the phrase nor the policy it implied — sharply lower interest rates — caught on when Mishkin began using it in internal debates in the fall of 2007. He didn't give up, though. After he dropped "adverse feedback loop" into a November 5, 2007, speech, it got more attention — though not immediate endorsement. Two days later, for example, the Atlanta Fed's Dennis Lockhart cited it in a speech before dismissing the idea as being "quite unlikely." A few months later, though, in February 2008, Lockhart would use Mishkin's argument to defend the Fed's dramatic cuts in interest rates, and Janet Yellen, the San Francisco Fed president, would declare that mitigating the possibility of an adverse feedback loop was a major Fed objective. And in June 2008, the whole FOMC cited the loop as "a worrisome possibility" in its economic forecast.

Long before then, though, the term's rising acceptance had given Mishkin a platform for arguing that the usual, gradual, one-step-at-a-time monetary policy was precisely the wrong approach to use in a situation like the Great Panic. The Fed, he argued, needed to be "preemptive" to disrupt the adverse feedback loop that would otherwise engage. With hindsight, his was the right diagnosis.

While Mishkin was laying the foundation for the Fed to do more, he was careful to hedge his public predictions about precisely what the Fed would actually do. Fellow Fed governor Randy Kroszner was less careful. In a speech in New York on November 17, he took the usually safe course of reciting the Fed's last public statement, but he couldn't resist a little update: "I would add that the limited data and information received since the October FOMC meeting have not changed my thinking in this regard." Unfortunately for him, it soon became clear that Bernanke and Kohn had changed *their* thinking in this regard. Less than two weeks later, Kohn and then Bernanke sent unmistakable flares: the worsening markets were casting a shadow over the benign economic forecast on which the Fed had been relying. More rate cuts were likely.

A QUARTER-POINT BABY STEP

Bernanke realized that his quest to be the un-Greenspan was having unintended consequences: the people who mattered in the markets had grown accustomed to Greenspan's peculiar prose and counted on him to point them in the direction he was headed. Bernanke was more candid, confessing uncertainty and almost thinking aloud at times. That is, when he could be heard above the divergent perspectives offered by other Fed officials.

"The public should understand that the FOMC members' . . . views are likely to be especially diverse when, as in the current situation, circumstances are changing quickly and are subject to many different analyses," Kohn said plaintively, in the Fed's defense. Still, there was a reason why the Fed had a chairman, and Bernanke had to begin talking like one. He resolved to give more regular — and authoritative — updates on their outlook for the economy.

It worked. Bernanke's speeches in 2007 and 2008 had five times the market-moving impact of the next most influential speaker — and number two was Don Kohn, the chairman's public reinforcer. In contrast, in 2006, Bernanke's impact was only double that of the next most influential speaker — and number two was attention-grabbing dissenter Bill Poole from St. Louis.

Mishkin, meanwhile, was putting on his own version of a full-court press. He knew that his advocacy of aggressive rate cuts alarmed hawkish bank presidents like Hoenig, but he had allies heading into the December FOMC meeting: Geithner was nearly always more worried than anyone else about the credit crunch. San Francisco's Yellen and Boston's Rosengren were also both inclined to cut rates another half-percentage point. The federal funds futures market was betting on a half-point cut as well. Most regional Fed bank presidents, though, used their discount-rate requests as a signal that they were leaning toward a one-quarter point cut. A couple of the hawks — Richard Fisher in Dallas and Tom Hoenig in Kansas City — didn't want any rate cut at all.

Several Fed officials believed the economy would recover gradually and be back to normal by late 2008 as weakness in the housing sector abated and financial conditions improved. Their faith in the tendencies of market capitalist economies to right themselves hadn't yet been shaken. "Underpinning this story is the view that our modern market economy has a keen ability to self-correct as opportunistic capital moves into depressed markets. Markets correct. And market solutions are preferable," Lockhart said in a speech that could have been delivered by one of several others. "This transition already is happening in the market for subprime mortgages. In this story, financial markets may endure some more weeks or months of volatility, but I believe they will find a restructured state of 'normality,'" Lockhart said, putting a slightly optimistic sheen on the Fed's thinking at the time.

While some presidents used speeches to be provocative and get attention, Lockhart tried to avoid making waves. "When I'm out there speaking," Lockhart confided, "I always run my remarks through a filter of, gee, is this going to contribute to something we don't want to have happen. I want to be frank and candid. I don't want to be a Pollyanna. But I don't want to be a Jeremiah unnecessarily."

Mishkin, though, wasn't as sanguine as Lockhart and the like-minded. Drawing from his work on past financial crises, he argued — as he put it later — that "monetary policy that is appropriate during an episode of financial market disruption is likely to be quite different than in times of normal market functioning." At a time of a significant disruption of financial markets, the Fed needed to display "less inertia than would otherwise be typical."

Unhappy that the FOMC was heading to a one-quarter point rate cut, Mishkin arranged to have lunch with Bernanke on Monday, December 10, the day before the meeting. The Fed would be making a huge mistake if it didn't try to get ahead of the Great Panic and cut rates by a half-percentage point, he told his friend. He felt so strongly that he was contemplating casting a dissenting vote. Bernanke talked him out of it: a dissent from a Washington governor intellectually and personally close to Bernanke would be seen by outsiders as a sign that Bernanke was losing control of the committee. Mishkin reluctantly voted with the majority.

Bernanke, in fact, had sympathy with those who wanted the more aggressive rate cut, but he didn't think he could sway the FOMC—and didn't force the issue, to his later regret. It was another lesson in the limits of prizing consensus in the committee. "Democracy is a good thing, but in times of 'war' quicker and more decisive decision making is needed," Ethan Harris, then a Lehman Brothers economist, wrote in an account of Bernanke's first year.

The Boston Fed president, Eric Rosengren, in his fifth month as a Fed president, did dissent and argued for a bigger rate cut. Although not nearly as quotable and thus not as prominent as some other presidents, Rosengren emerged as a thoughtful, low-profile Bernanke ally during the Great Panic. He and the Richmond Fed's Jeff Lacker had gone to the same New Jersey high school, although they didn't know each other then, and were graduate students in economics at the same time at the University of Wisconsin. Rosengren began his Fed career in the Boston Fed's research department, focusing for a time on the credit crunch and banking woes of New England in the 1990s as well as Japan's banking crisis. In 2000, he moved into the nitty-gritty of bank supervision and regulation, an unusual move for a Ph.D. economist but one that gave him highly relevant expertise during the Great Panic and a clear view that some fellow bank presidents lacked. Where others saw signs of hope, Rosengren saw "a deteriorating housing sector, slowing consumer and business spending, high energy prices, and ill-functioning financial markets."

"It was a tough decision," Rosengren said later of his dissent. "You should really feel strongly before you dissent. I hadn't been on the FOMC for very long. We were moving in the right direction, just not at the same magnitude that I thought was appropriate." The attention his dissent drew surprised him, he said. "I probably underappreciated that." For their part, markets were disappointed with the miserly rate cut and the absence of any innovative attacks on the nascent credit crunch. The Dow Jones Industrial Average responded by plunging nearly 300 points. "From talking to clients and traders, there is in their view no question the Fed has fallen way behind the curve," David Greenlaw, economist at Morgan Stanley told the *Wall Street Journal.* "There's a growing sense the Fed doesn't get it."

THE GREAT EXPERIMENTER

Bernanke might have been wary of overreaching, but he had not been idle. The Friday before Tuesday's FOMC meeting, he convened a conference call — unannounced at the time — to approve two innovations tailored to the peculiarities of the Great Panic. One was a new way to lend money directly to U.S. banks that were reluctant to come to the Fed's discount window. The other was a long-discussed deal to help European central banks satisfy their banks' craving for U.S. dollars. To fight the Great Panic, Bernanke was becoming the Great Experimenter.

BERNANKE'S DASHBOARD
January 22, 2008

		Change from August 7, 2007
Dow Jones Industrial Average:	11,971	down 11.4%
Market Cap of Citigroup:	$121.3 billion	down 49.8%
Price of Oil (per barrel):	$89.86	up 24.1%
Unemployment Rate:	4.8%	up 0.10 pp
Fed Funds Interest Rate:	3.5%	down 1.75 pp
Financial Stress Indicator:	0.81 pp	up 0.69 pp

The Fed's Tuesday afternoon statement gave no indication that anything more was coming, though there were a few Fed-supplied hints in the next day's *Wall Street Journal* and *Financial Times* that something was up. The big announcement came at 9 A.M. Wednesday, timed so word of international cooperation would come during daylight hours in Europe. That annoyed Fed watchers on Wall Street, who were embarrassed Tuesday when the Fed did less than they had predicted, and it hurt investors who lost money when the stock market dropped on the small rate cut. Neither was a big deal, but this was another instance where the Bernanke Fed seemed to be stepping on its own story and contributing to the confusion about what it was doing. After the Fed initiatives were announced, the stock market recovered all that it had lost the day before and then some. And in any event, the significance of the moves outlived the kvetching about the timing of the announcement.

The Fed in the fall of 2007 had two basic pipelines to the credit market. One was open market operations. The New York Fed bought and sold government securities through twenty or so big banks and government-securities trading firms, known as primary dealers, to influence the federal funds interest rate — that is, the rate at which banks lent to one another overnight. When the Fed bought securities and put cash into the markets, the fed funds rates went down; when it sold them and sucked cash out, rates went up. The resulting changes in the federal funds interest rate would provoke changes in other interest rates throughout the economy. (By June 2009, the number of primary dealers was down to seventeen because of mergers and bankruptcies.)

The other pipeline was to lend directly to individual banks through the discount window. But banks were reluctant to go to the discount window, for fear that they would be deemed unstable if word leaked out that they had borrowed from the Fed. Indeed, this stigma had become so feared as the economy spiraled downward that for 30 percent of the days since August, banks had been paying more to borrow from one another than they would have had to pay to borrow from the Fed. This was definitely *not* the way things were supposed to work.

As economist Stephen Cecchetti explained it, "Central banks have great tools for getting funds into the banking system, but they have no mechanism for distributing it to the places where it needs to go. The Fed can get liquidity to the primary dealers, but it has no way to ensure that those reserves are then lent out to the banks that need them."

To unclog the financial circulatory system — and to get the blood flowing to where it was needed — the Fed decided to try a bypass operation that it called the Term Auction Facility, or TAF as it was named by one of its architects, Bill Dudley, who then served as the New York Fed's markets chief and later succeeded Geithner as its president.

Through TAF, the Fed would begin auctioning off funds to any of the seven thousand or so banks in the country, not just twenty primary dealers. The acceptable collateral would be anything that a bank might have pledged as security for an overnight loan at the discount window, a much broader set of securities than the Fed usually bought and sold in open market operations. For banks, it was a way to get money—initially for twenty-eight days, later extended to eighty-four days—that was hard to secure in ordinary markets without the potential embarrassment of being seen waiting in line at the Fed's discount window.

For the Fed, TAF was a small but significant step toward selling the sterling U.S. government securities that it owned and using the proceeds to take riskier securities that were out of favor. In peacetime, the Fed occasionally used its Treasury securities to solve a peculiar shortage in the markets. It once had even contemplated seriously buying securities other than Treasury debt in the long-ago days when the U.S. government surplus was so large that speculation focused on whether the supply of Treasury debt might just dry up. But this was the financial equivalent of war. In one market, the Fed was taking riskier-than-Treasury securities onto its balance sheet, and in another, it was offsetting those purchases with sales of U.S. Treasury securities.

The purpose—unlike nearly everything the Fed had done for decades—was not to lower the overall level of interest rates in the economy. That's what changes in the federal funds rate were supposed to do. The purpose was instead to reduce an important gap once of concern only to bond geeks: the spread between Fed-influenced rates and the rates banks were charging one another for loans, the London Interbank Offered Rate (LIBOR). This spread usually was a few hundredths of a percentage point. By early December, though, it had widened to around a full percentage point—a huge move, though not nearly as wide as it would get later. Basically, the gap revealed that banks were so wary of one another and so worried about their own balance sheets that they were hoarding cash instead of lending it out. And the interest rates their customers paid on many of the loans they had made in the past were tied to the now-rising LIBOR rate.

Although modest in light of what was waiting down the road, the TAF was still controversial inside the Fed. The notion had been cooked up in August when Fed officials brainstormed at Jackson Hole, and it was raised with FOMC in September, where it came under hostile fire from Bill Poole of St. Louis and Jeff Lacker of Richmond. Before Bernanke convened the FOMC conference call to consider the TAF on December 6, Lacker circulated a memo to the entire committee arguing against it. He didn't buy the underlying diagnosis. The market *was* working: banks were paying more to borrow because they were, for good reason, seeing greater risk of losing money in deals with other banks, he argued. Fed lending was unlikely to change that in the short term; in the long run, the TAF would lead markets to expect the Fed to jump in every time some new crisis loomed.

The concerns were noted and duly disregarded. Geithner — in the *only* public speech he made between August 2007 and March 2008 — described the TAF on December 13 to a conference of academics as a way to provide banks with "a more effective form of access to liquidity" that he hoped would reduce their appetite for hoarding cash or lending it to each other "in ways that might lead to a further deterioration on market conditions." The Fed auctioned off the first $40 billion in December. A year later, it would be lending $450 billion through the auctions versus $90 billion through the traditional discount window. The TAF was widely seen as a success — despite a skeptical reading of the markets by Stanford economist John Taylor. Most Fed officials saw it as implementing Walter Bagehot's nineteenth-century basics of central banking in a panic.

Geithner, in the same speech, hinted that providing liquidity might not be enough because that didn't "directly address the balance sheet or capital constraints facing financial institutions" — in other words, the possibility that they might have much deeper problems than a temporary inability to borrow. But other than lauding those financial firms that had raised capital privately, he offered little guide to the Fed's thinking about how to cope with the looming possibility that some banks might be insolvent, or have losses so great that their capital cushions had vanished.

You Need Dollars? We Have Dollars!

Bernanke quickly discovered that the Fed couldn't think only about lubricating American banks. European banks had a problem, too, and one that their central banks couldn't solve. In what Bernanke delicately described as "a novel aspect of the current situation," European banks craved U.S. dollars — and couldn't easily find them in malfunctioning markets.

For years, there had been hand-wringing and naysaying about the U.S. dollar losing its status in the global economy to other currencies. But the value of securities issued outside the United States denominated in U.S. dollars — as opposed to home currencies of the countries in which the borrowers were located — rose from $322.5 billion in 2005 to $753.3 billion in 2006. That 134 percent increase far surpassed the 25 percent increase in euro-denominated issues. During the credit boom that preceded the Great Panic, the U.S. dollar was gaining market share in global finance, not losing it. With one hand, British and continental European banks were lending dollars to corporate customers and buying U.S. mortgage-linked securities. With the other, they were borrowing dollars in money markets to balance their positions. U.S. banks do the same thing but have one huge advantage: they have billions in ordinary deposits in dollars, so they don't have to borrow as much. European banks, especially those not large enough to have branches in New York or Chicago or Los Angeles, didn't have that option. So they had to rely almost exclusively on borrowing in the very wholesale markets for dollars that were suddenly seizing up.

The European banks' desperate scramble for dollars all over the world was obvious to men and women who constantly watch markets on the trading floor of the New York Fed, the one place where the Fed actually lays its hands on the market. It has the Bloomberg screens that are now ubiquitous and digital clocks that give the time in Tokyo, Frankfurt, London, and New York, but little of the unrelenting frenzy and buzz of moneymaking trading rooms. Its primary job is straightforward: to drip just enough money into the markets or drain just enough to keep the federal funds rate — the one that banks charge one another for overnight loans — close to the target set by the FOMC.

The European banks' lust for dollars was making that job difficult. Global finance is nearly a round-the-clock operation these days, but time zones still matter. The traders of the New York Fed could see rising demand for dollars in the bank-to-bank market during daylight in Europe, pushing up the federal funds rate in the market. The demand then would abate when the sun set in Europe—early afternoon in New York—and the federal funds rate would come down.

All this amounted to a classic liquidity shortage in Europe, the kind that "the lender of last resort" can usually solve, but this time the problem had a twist. The ECB could print euros, the Swiss National Bank could print Swiss francs, but their banks didn't need those. They needed U.S. dollars. In ordinary times, the ECB would hand out euros and let the banks exchange them for dollars on global markets, but those markets weren't working normally. It was an early manifestation of the global nature of the Great Panic: many of the loans and securities that proved to be poisonous were grown in the United States, but they were consumed by banks and investors all over the world whose appetites appeared to be insatiable.

The solution was for the Fed to give dollars to the ECB and take euros in exchange. Then the ECB could lend dollars to its own banks. That was easily done mechanically, but egos and national pride interfered. Key players at the Fed and at the ECB, for different reasons, were reluctant to make what seemed the obvious move.

Some at the Fed had objections in principle, others thought there were ways for the ECB to get dollars other than borrowing from the Fed. At the ECB, the plan ran up against a strong effort to pin the Great Panic on the United States. The Fed, as early as August, offered dollars in exchange for euros. But in an Alphonse-Gaston routine, the ECB replied, "It's a dollar problem. It's *your* problem." The Fed's position was that you have to ask for dollars if you need them.

By December, the dollar shortage was so acute that reluctance melted away. The swaps began, with the FOMC approving up to $20 billion for the ECB—with only half that immediately available—and $4 billion to the Swiss National Bank in December. The Fed got euros (and Swiss francs) in return, about as solid collateral as any available. The ECB and the SNB took the risk that banks might not be able to pay back the dollar loans. Over the next year, the Fed expanded both the list of countries to which it was offering to swap dollars and the size of the swaps. In October 2008, it decided to lift altogether the cap on swaps with the European, British, Swiss, and Japanese central banks and provide as many dollars as their banks wanted.

With this, the Fed became the lender of last resort—of dollars—to the entire world, and the world responded the way parched desert travelers do to an oasis. In the first week after the cap disappeared, the total sum of dollars the Fed had offered the foreign central banks doubled to $135 billion and grew by another $100 billion the week after that. By the end of December 2008, the Fed's swaps amounted to $545 billion, about a quarter of all the credit it had put into the economy. One in every four dollars that the Fed was lending was going not to Bear Stearns or Bank of America but, through the ECB, to France's BNP Paribas or Germany's Commerzbank.

This didn't get as much attention as the Fed's aggressive lending in the United States. But it was a major—and innovative—way to fight the Great Panic. "Central banks have been in constant communication, which of course they also were in the 1930s," observed Barry Eichengreen, a Berkeley economic historian. "But in contrast to the '30s, this time there has been a readiness to back words with deeds."

BERNANKE WAKES UP

By the end of December 2007 and the beginning of January 2008, Bernanke realized he had misread the economy. It was worse than he anticipated, and he began thinking he should deliver a speech that said so as a way to signal that the Fed would be cutting interest rates soon. He didn't yet know that the U.S. economy had slid into recession in December. (That verdict would not be delivered until much later by the official arbiters of such things, a committee of academics at the nonprofit National Bureau of Economic Research on which Bernanke had served before going to the Fed.) But whatever was happening to the economy looked and smelled alarmingly like a recession.

Thinking about the speech and other matters, Bernanke talked to Greenspan and Paulson. Then on Thursday evening, January 3, he got the customary heads-up from the White House Council of Economic Advisers that the next morning's Bureau of Labor Statistics monthly employment report would be bad: the unemployment rate had leaped from 4.7 percent to 5 percent, the

BLS said. The stock market responded to Friday's announcement by giving up six months of gains in three days. Inside the Bush White House, discussions intensified among the president's economic advisers about proposing a tax cut to provide emergency first aid to the economy before it got worse — and Bernanke encouraged them.

Around 5 P.M. on Wednesday, January 9, Bernanke and the other Fed governors gathered in the Fed's "special library." They sat around three sides of a small table that had been used by the original Fed board back in 1914 and faced the camera so the Fed's regional bank presidents could see them and they, in turn, could see the presidents' faces. The next stage of Rick Mishkin's "adverse feedback loop" had arrived: the weakening of the job market in an economy starved for credit. A further constriction of credit and a decline in house prices were all but certain to follow, which would make financial markets even worse.

BERNANKE'S DASHBOARD
March 14, 2008

		Change from August 7, 2007
Dow Jones Industrial Average:	11,951	down 11.5%
Market Cap of Citigroup:	$107.7 billion	down 55.4%
Price of Oil (per barrel):	$110.21	up 52.2%
Unemployment Rate:	4.8%	up 0.10 pp
Fed Funds Interest Rate:	3.0%	down 2.25 pp
Financial Stress Indicator:	0.83 pp	up 0.71 pp

Clearly, the Fed was going to cut interest rates — a lot. The issue was when. Although some presidents anticipated Bernanke would press for an immediate rate cut, he didn't. In part, he hoped to avoid any hint of panic by waiting until the FOMC meeting scheduled for the end of the month. Waiting two or three weeks to cut usually didn't make much difference — at least in normal times. So Bernanke told his colleagues he was planning a speech the next day — evidence of the new, more alpha-male chairman. He planned to send a clear signal, and indeed he did. Speaking before a lunchtime gathering in Washington, Bernanke came about as close to announcing an imminent rate cut as any Fed chairman ever has. The Fed, he said, already had cut rates from 5.25 percent to 4.25 percent because credit was scarce and housing was weak. But its forecast for the economy was growing grimmer, so "additional policy easing may well be necessary," he said.

Down, Down, Down

Bernanke wouldn't need long to regret not pushing the FOMC to cut rates on January 9. His speech wasn't the boost to confidence he had hoped it would be. Very soon afterward, the economy—and, particularly, the markets—got very much worse.

U.S. markets were closed on Monday, January 21, for Martin Luther King Jr. Day and so were Fed offices. But Bernanke was in his office—as he was nearly every day, weekends included—watching Asian and European stock markets plummet. Futures markets Monday were predicting a 4 percent plunge Tuesday in U.S. stocks. Facing what seemed to be yet another meltdown of the economy, Bernanke convened a videoconference call of the FOMC with little advance notice. He and Kohn could no longer deny that the Fed was seriously "behind the curve," as they put it at the time, and they were determined to remedy that.

Basically, they told the videoconferees, the target for the federal funds rate was more than a percentage point too high for the Fed's then-current forecast. Cutting interest rates that much in one move would have been seen as panic and desperation, but Bernanke and Kohn thought that a demonstration of the Fed's "commitment to act decisively" to support the economy might make markets more sanguine and avoid another twist in the "adverse feedback loop." Flexing his muscles as he had rarely done before, Bernanke won the FOMC's backing for what—for the Fed—was a king-size rate cut: three-quarters of a percentage point, with a strong hint of more to come at the FOMC meeting scheduled for the following week. It was the first time the Fed had cut rates in between regularly scheduled meetings since the after-math of September 11, 2001. *Whatever it takes.*

One president dissented—St. Louis's Bill Poole. It was his last hurrah as an official naysayer. Poole surrendered his vote at the next scheduled FOMC meeting and retired before St. Louis's turn to vote came around again. Poole said he wanted to wait till the scheduled meeting to make the move, but he wasn't the only reluctant member of the committee. A few warned that the Fed's newfound aggressiveness at cutting rates would need to be matched by similar aggressiveness once the economy rebounded. The concern was rea-sonable, especially given the widespread regret that the Fed had held rates too low too long earlier in the decade, but it was also evidence that, if they wor-ried about anything, Fed officials thought they might be doing too much.

The move was what Rick Mishkin had been pushing a month earlier. But he wasn't on the conference call to savor the victory. He was cross-country skiing at Lake Tahoe in California when he was alerted by cell phone that Bernanke had called an emergency FOMC meeting, and he couldn't get to a secure phone line in time to take part—the standard requirement for Fed offi-cials who dial into a call that could move the markets if it were intercepted.

RIGHT WAR, WRONG BATTLE?

After the Fed's morning announcement the next day, January 22, financial markets showed their approval after a bearish start. Down as much as 464 points Tuesday morning, the Dow Jones Industrial Average reversed course and gained back over 300 points to end the day down "only" 128 points. European stock markets, which had also been falling sharply, did their own about-face when word of the Fed rate cut arrived. They closed up for the day.

Despite the temporary good news, Bernanke knew he was going to be accused of cutting rates to rescue the stock market, rather than to manage the economy. The same accusation had been made about Greenspan. Bernanke had already discounted the complaints. In his mind, plunging stock markets—along with all the troubling indicators—threatened to undermine confidence in an economy that was already showing signs of weakness. The Fed was "behind the curve," he concluded. He wanted to get ahead of it.

The timing, though, was terrible. Stock markets, it turned out, weren't plunging on intensifying worries about the health of the global economy. Prices were falling because a big French bank, Société Générale, was secretly rushing to sell off a huge book of bets that one of its traders had made. (The bank lost about €4.9 billion, or more than $7 billion, undoing unauthorized trades done surreptitiously by a thirty-one-year-old trader, Jérôme Kerviel.) The head of the French central bank, Christian Noyer, knew what was going on but, having no reason to suspect the Fed was preparing an emergency rate cut, didn't alert Fed officials until Wednesday.

Bad enough that the Fed was accused of rushing to rescue the stock market, rather than the overall economy; now it looked like the stock market hadn't really needed a rescue. "It does look like they were snookered into cutting rates," Lou Crandall, a veteran Fed watcher at Wrightson ICAP, said at the time.

If successful central banking is equal parts substance and theater — what the Fed does with interest rates and whether it looks to be calm and in control — then Bernanke had botched the theater this time. He shrugged it off, though, and the Fed cut interest rates by another one-half percentage point the following week, at its regularly scheduled meeting. The cumulative 1.25-point rate cut was the swiftest in the Fed's recent history. Not everyone was happy: Dallas's Richard Fisher dissented this time, fretting about inflation. But the Four Musketeers thought, finally, they had been aggressive enough to get ahead of the curve. They were wrong.

Chapter 9

"UNUSUAL AND EXIGENT"

I n the Great Panic, there will always be Before Bear Stearns and After Bear Stearns.

Before Bear Stearns, no major financial institution had failed.

Before Bear Stearns, the Fed was doing what central banks have done for generations: lending money for a few days, sometimes a few weeks, to solid commercial banks that couldn't raise cash quickly on their own. The Fed lent readily, but only to banks, after the 1987 stock market crash and the September 11, 2001, terrorist attacks. It lent nothing in 1998 when it rallied Wall Street to rescue hedge fund giant Long Term Capital Management.

That nearly sacrosanct principle was violated in March 2008 when the Fed lent billions not to a bank that it supervised but to Bear Stearns, a broker-age house that had never been required to play by the Fed's rules about how much it borrowed or how it managed its business. And Bear Stearns wasn't a one-shot deal: the Fed said other Wall Street securities firms and investment banks could drink from the Fed's trough, too.

For the Fed, this was, as one longtime staffer put it, "crossing the Rubicon or at least a very large tributary." Just ten days before the Bear Stearns loan, Don Kohn, the Fed's vice chairman, was asked at a Senate hearing about lending to institutions other than ordinary banks. Kohn's answer: legally permissible, but prudent only in "an emergency, very, very unusual situation."

"I would be very cautious about opening that window more generally," he told Christopher Dodd, chairman of the Senate Banking Committee.

All that was before, though.

After Bear Stearns, potential buyers of any failing financial institution — Lehman Brothers, Wachovia — would ask the Fed not whether it would lend, but how much it was willing to kick in.

After Bear Stearns, the debate would not be *whether* the Great Panic would require government bailouts but would instead be *who* would be bailed out and on what terms.

After Bear Stearns, the line between Fed-protected, deposit-taking Main Street banks and less tightly regulated, more leveraged Wall Street investment banks was obliterated.

After Bear Stearns, the Fed's elastic interpretation of its power to lend to almost anyone in "unusual and exigent circumstances" would lead the Bush administration to see the Fed as the lender of *first* resort, rather than in its traditional role as the lender of *last* resort.

After Bear Stearns, although not immediately, many members of Congress would realize for the very first time just how much power Ben Bernanke wielded and how much money was at his disposal.

Seeing imminent danger to the financial system, Bernanke and the New York Fed's Tim Geithner had no choice but to improvise, but this was improv with stakes greater than those at any time since the 1930s. In pushing the loan for Bear Stearns, the two were discarding decades of practice intended to discourage investors and institutions from taking reckless risks on the expectation that they would profit if they were lucky and the Fed would rescue them if they weren't.

"Central banks typically have rules. When the rules cannot easily be broken...there is frequently trouble," the late economic historian Charles Kindleberger wrote in his classic, *Manias, Panics and Crashes*. "There is also trouble when rules are too readily broken."

Or as Berkeley economist and blogger Brad DeLong paraphrased him during the Great Panic: in normal times, the central bank's appearance should always be in doubt. But it should always show up when really needed.

The Fed, it was clear, was "really needed."

"WHEN CONFIDENCE GOES, IT GOES"

By late winter 2007, all of Wall Street was confronting losses on bad mortgage investments and displaying extraordinary reluctance to lend even to one another. The shadow banking system — investment banks, hedge funds, private-equity funds, producers of and investors in securitized loans — had grown larger than the core of the banking system that the Fed was created to protect. The lesson drawn from the Panic of 1907 that led to the creation of the Fed was that banks play a unique and vital role in the economy: they take deposits and borrowed short term (the savings of the society), and they lend money for the long term to finance the investments of the society. This mismatch between taking money that can be withdrawn at any time and lending it in ways that will be paid back only over time makes them vulnerable. So they are required to set aside some money for emergencies, maintain substantial capital cushions to absorb losses, submit to government regulation to restrain them from taking imprudent risks, and are offered the privilege of borrowing from the Fed in a crisis.

After the Depression, the government tried to give savers confidence that their money was safe by offering them government-backed insurance on their deposits. It created the Securities and Exchange Commission to assure stock market investors that the game wasn't rigged. And, with the Glass-Steagall Act of 1933 (pushed by the same Carter Glass who had played such a big role in creating the Fed), it built a wall between traditional banking (lending money) and what was seen as the riskier business of investment banking (helping companies raise money by selling securities and trading those securities).

These rules could be a nuisance to the banks and could limit their profits. So institutions outside the core banks — sometimes owned by the same parent companies — grew and evolved to dominate the financial system. Encouraged by Greenspan, Congress repealed the Glass-Steagall Act in 1999. Big financial firms grew into banking-insurance-brokerage-trading behemoths like Citigroup. Investment banks, supposedly just outside the Fed's safety net, became a bigger, more vital part of the system. As loans were made by one outfit, packaged into securities by another and sold to investors, and then other outfits bought and sold insurance (called "credit default swaps") on those loans, the "shadow banking system" outside the brand-name, Fed-protected commercial banks exploded with a bewildering array of securities, each with its own acronym.

The U.S. financial regulatory system had not kept up with this change. In a division of labor that dated to the 1930s, the Fed and other bank regulators kept a close eye, sometimes not close enough, to be sure, on the banks. The Securities and Exchange Commission worried about the big securities firms (Bear Stearns, Lehman Brothers, Goldman Sachs, and the like), but more to protect their customers' money and to enforce laws about disclosure and fraud than to make sure that the firms didn't put the entire financial system in harm's way. The walls dividing those businesses had eroded over time, and Congress had undone much of the New Deal legislation without finishing the job of reconstructing the financial regulatory apparatus, which was shared by a bewildering number of federal and state agencies of varying competence.

It was fine in good times. "The bottom line is simple: shadow banks use funding instruments that are *not* just as good as old-fashioned [government]-protected deposits," said Paul McCulley, who periodically offered acerbic comments from his post as a portfolio manager at Pimco, a big West Coast bond manager. "But it was a great gig so long as the public bought the notion that such funding instruments were 'just as good' as bank deposits—more leverage, less regulation and more asset freedom were a path to (much) higher returns on equity in shadow banks than conventional banks."

Suddenly, the times weren't so good. The "public"—or at least big-money investors—didn't view the shadow banks as quite so safe, and grew reluctant to provide the short-term money on which the shadow banks depended. In proliferating numbers, Wall Street executives were beseeching the Fed for the same loans available to ordinary commercial banks at times of duress.

Of all the firms on the Street, Bear Stearns was widely regarded as the weakest link. Funds it managed had been among the early high-profile victims of the subprime mess. Just as bad, the firm was thought to suffer from a severe leadership vacuum. The *Wall Street Journal*, in a devastating front-page November 1, 2007, story described the CEO, Jimmy Cayne, as a detached, marijuana-smoking executive who spent more time playing bridge than tending his company. Cayne, who had almost died the previous September from a severe prostate infection, stepped down in January.

On Monday, March 10, 2008, Moody's Investors Service downgraded mortgage-backed debt issued by a Bear Stearns fund, and with that, rumors began to circulate in the market that there were liquidity problems at Bear Stearns itself. Bear Stearns denied the rumors, but the market ignored the denials. When new CEO Alan Schwartz went on CNBC Wednesday to try to shore up confidence in the firm's finances, his appearance got upstaged by news that New York's governor Eliot Spitzer was resigning after law-enforcement authorities discovered his dalliance with prostitutes. The run on Bear Stearns continued.

Bob Steel, the former Goldman executive who had come to Treasury to serve as Paulson's undersecretary for domestic finance, told his boss: "They've got a month or so."

"I don't buy that," Paulson said. "When confidence goes, it goes." He was right.

UNCLOGGING THE CREDIT CHANNEL

For weeks, the Fed had been looking for a way to aid Wall Street by lubricating markets that weren't functioning well. The week of March 10, as Bear Stearns edged toward the precipice, the Fed finally offered securities houses a deal: give us your troubled assets yearning to be sold, the wretched refuse of your lending. Specifically, the Fed created the Term Securities Lending Facility (or TSLF) to take up to $200 billion worth of Wall Street's hard-to-sell mortgage-backed securities and exchange them for supersafe U.S. Treasury securities from the Fed's vast portfolio for up to twenty-eight days.

Like several of the subsequent Fed interventions in the money markets, this one was devised largely by Bill Dudley. An economist with a Ph.D. from the University of California at Berkeley, Dudley had spent twenty years at Goldman Sachs, ending up as its chief U.S. economist. Geithner hired him to run the New York Fed's markets desk—the place where the Federal Reserve actually buys and sells in the markets. Dudley arrived at the beginning of 2007 in the opening acts of the Great Panic, which turned his new post into a 24/7 job. He even did a press briefing on the TSLF from a hospital room where his wife was recovering from surgery. (When Geithner became Obama's Treasury secretary, Dudley edged out Fed governor Kevin Warsh to become president of the New York Fed.)

The thinking behind the move was simple: Bernanke was trying to unclog what he dubbed the "credit channel." Since the investment houses' collateral was increasingly suspect, he reasoned, giving them a chance to replace bad paper with something nearly as good as cash would get credit flowing again. Confidence would rise. Players would know that even in the event of default, securities with already depressed prices wouldn't be dumped on the market, avoiding the acceleration of a downward spiral. The TSLF didn't increase the size of the Fed's portfolio or the total amount of credit it was providing to the economy. The Fed wasn't yet printing extra money. But the Fed had taken a big step toward using its portfolio to arrest the Great Panic. By temporarily trading a chunk of its own holdings of the safest securities in the world, U.S. Treasury debt, for the far riskier ones the investment houses would be off-loading from their books, the Fed was expanding its "lender of last resort" protection beyond commercial banks. It was a maneuver designed to offer liquidity to the system but was not a long-term solution, because the investment banks were still on the hook if those securities turned out to be worthless because the ultimate borrowers defaulted. The money wasn't flowing out yet, but Bernanke and the others had just left the vault door ajar.

BEAR AT THE DOOR

A few hours after the Fed announced the TSLF, Geithner hosted a closed-door lunch for Bernanke in the New York Fed's Washington Dining Room, one of several get-togethers he had convened so the Fed chairman could meet Wall Street's brass. Paul Volcker and Alan Greenspan were familiar faces long before they became Fed chairmen. Each had a mystique that conveyed competence and wisdom. But Wall Street was not Bernanke's milieu, and it showed. "Greenspan was at home at the markets," one executive at the lunch said. "I don't think Bernanke has a feel for this stuff."

That was a problem. The notion that the Fed did banks (Citigroup, Bank of America, JPMorgan Chase) and the SEC did investment houses (Bear Stearns, Lehman Brothers, Goldman Sachs) went up in smoke on Wednesday, March 12.

That evening, Bear CEO Alan Schwartz called Rodgin Cohen, the dean of the banking bar, for strategic advice. Cohen's firm, Sullivan & Cromwell, wasn't representing Bear Stearns, although it had handled a few projects for the firm. But Cohen was the go-to banking lawyer in a crisis — so much so that he had ended up with a client in nearly every significant financial controversy in modern memory.

Cohen heard Schwartz out, then said: "We've got to call the Fed." Moments later, the lawyer had Tim Geithner on the phone. "I think I've been around long enough to sense a very serious problem, and this seems like one," he said. That message alone was more dire than anything Bear Stearns had delivered directly to the Fed.

"If Alan is worried, he needs to call me," Geithner replied.

Schwartz did so the next morning. He explained that, while Bear Stearns was continuing to look for a partner to provide long-term financing, its problems weren't only long term. Two days earlier, he told Geithner, Bear Stearns had opened for business with $18 billion in cash or securities that were so easily sold that they were as good as cash. By day's end, $6.5 billion of that was gone. The firm was down to its last $11.5 billion. This was the bad news that builds on itself once word gets out, so the next few days would be deeply challenging.

The problems were the ones that would recur throughout the Great Panic: credit and collateral. Commercial banks use deposits, insured by the government, so they aren't wholly reliant on short-term borrowing. Investment banks like Bear Stearns hadn't any deposits, so they were reliant on borrowing in the markets, often overnight. Bear had pledged collateral in the repo market, the market that had caused a scare for Geithner in the Countrywide episode months earlier. The repo market, in its collective wisdom, had now decided that Bear Stearns collateral wasn't good enough to secure loans, even when that collateral was U.S. Treasury securities.

Bear couldn't borrow, and without borrowing, it couldn't do business. It was the twenty-first-century equivalent of a bank run in a world organized for twentieth-century finance. "I just never, frankly, understood or dreamed it could happen as rapidly as it did," Bear Stearns's Schwartz said.

Neither did Geithner nor Bernanke. In fact, though, the problem — the reliance on borrowing in the wholesale markets to keep the business going without realizing how ephemeral credit was — had been building for a long time.

Months later, Fed governor Kevin Warsh tried to put it in perspective. "You know that line in *Fletch* when Chevy Chase tells a doctor that it was a shame that 'Ed' died so suddenly. 'He was in intensive care for eight weeks,' the doctor says. To which Chevy Chase replies: 'But in the very end, when he actually died...that was extremely sudden.'"

"Same thing here," Warsh said about Bear Stearns. "Very sudden, but..."

THE LAST $2 BILLION

By Thursday night, Bear Stearns was down to $2 billion in cash. The company asked Gary Parr, a Lazard Frères investment banker who had been helping the firm to try to raise money, to contact the most likely savior: Jamie Dimon of JPMorgan Chase. Parr interrupted Dimon's birthday dinner with his family at Avra, a Greek restaurant, and told him Bear needed $30 billion. Dimon balked. Well, Parr replied, how about buying the whole company overnight? Schwartz followed up with a call to Dimon.

Dimon, in turn, called Geithner. JPMorgan didn't have enough information to make an overnight decision to buy Bear Stearns. "Tim, look," he said, "we need more time. Just do something to get them to the weekend."

Geithner took Dimon seriously. Once a contender for the top job at Citicorp before he was tossed out by his mentor, Sandy Weill, in 1998, Dimon was one of a handful of top financial executives to escape the worst of the subprime fiasco. He went from Citi to run Bank One, a big bank based in Ohio that was acquired by JPMorgan in 2004. By 2007, Dimon was at the top of one half of the original J. P. Morgan empire—the other half was at Morgan Stanley. Citi was struggling. Dimon, a Democrat, would have been on the list of potential Obama appointees to the Treasury—the job Geithner eventually got—had a banking résumé not become a disqualification for the post.

Bear Stearns's fate was in the hands of a very tight fraternity. Dimon was a member of the Federal Reserve Bank of New York's nine-person board of directors. That board hired Geithner and set his salary, an extraordinary historical anomaly that gives the regulated the power to pick the regulator.

From the beginning, the regional Fed banks were organized not as government agencies, but as private companies in which local banks own shares, a remnant of a time when central banks raised capital privately as well as publicly. Under the 1913 law, each bank has nine directors, the majority chosen by the banks in the district. Three are bankers. Three are nonbankers picked by the local banks. Three are chosen by the Fed board in Washington to represent the public. On the New York Fed's board, Dimon fell into the first category, a banker picked by bankers. Richard Fuld, CEO of Lehman Brothers, was in the second; since Lehman wasn't a bank in the legal sense, he was a nonbanker picked by bankers. Stephen Friedman—the former CEO of Goldman Sachs and then a member of Goldman's board of directors—was in the third, legally a nonbanker picked to represent the public. He chaired the New York Fed board and stayed in close touch with Geithner.

Later in the Great Panic, Goldman would change its legal status and become a Fed-regulated bank-holding company. Under Fed rules, holding shares and sitting on Goldman's board made Friedman ineligible to represent the public on the New York Fed board. The Fed, with the approval of the Fed governors in Washington, quietly gave Friedman a waiver to serve through the end of 2009, but was embarrassed when the *Wall Street Journal* reported that he had been adding to his Goldman stake during the tumult of late 2008 as the Fed was making moves that benefited Goldman. Friedman quit the New York Fed board in May 2009. He said his continued presence there was an unwelcome distraction for the Fed, and insisted unapologetically that his actions had been "mischaracterized" and above reproach.

Directors of regional Fed banks didn't vote to approve Fed loans like the one Bear Stearns was seeking; the loans went to the Fed board in Washington, where all the power was with government employees like Bernanke. And directors weren't supposed to participate in formal conversations about their own institutions. But the incestuousness was obvious, the kind of crony capitalism that the U.S. government criticized in Indonesia and other developing countries. Geithner was hired by bankers he was supposed to supervise and, now, was being asked to bail out. The arrangement underscored the New York Fed's peculiar relationship with Wall Street. It was supposed to be a regulator and guardian of the public interest, but sometimes was seen — by banks, by other factions inside the Fed, and by the public — as Wall Street's advocate, rather than its overseer. And on some days, it was more advocate than overseer.

Geithner's most prominent predecessors, Paul Volcker and Gerry Corrigan, were career Fed (and, in Volcker's case, Fed and Treasury) employees who balanced the perception of excessive chumminess with gruff schoolmaster personalities and physiques. Volcker towered over everyone in the room unless he happened to show up at a Knicks game, while Corrigan played the beefy Irish rugby player. Volcker made his mark as the Fed chairman Jimmy Carter appointed to restore global confidence in the American economy, the man who brought inflation down from the double digits. While at the Fed, Corrigan was known as the chief worrywart, frequently warning of the fragility of the financial system or imminent crisis.

Geithner's public persona as a technocrat and his slight build didn't offer him the advantages that Volcker and Corrigan had. The circumstances didn't help either. He believed firmly that protecting the American economy at a time like this meant rescuing the banks, even if they had caused their own misery. But that didn't stop the critics from suggesting that he was looking out for the banks' interests first.

"So what can taxpayers expect from an increase in the Fed's discretionary authority over investment banks?" asked Carnegie Mellon economist Allan

Meltzer. "The likely answer is rescues, delays, and lax supervision — followed by taxpayer-financed bailouts. Throughout its postwar history, the Fed has responded to the interests of large banks and Congress, not the public."

SHOWTIME

While Bear Stearns and its investment bankers desperately sought a partner with very deep pockets, the guardians of the U.S. financial system convened an almost nonstop series of conference calls. On Thursday afternoon, "the DK committee" — named for Don Kohn — chewed over the situation: Kevin Warsh, Bob Steel at Treasury, John Dugan at the Office of the Comptroller of the Currency, and Geithner. The climactic call came around 7:30 P.M. when Bernanke and Paulson came on the line and the SEC staff told them all that Bear Stearns was going to have to file for bankruptcy the next morning.

It was showtime.

Geithner, as he usually did, divided the work among small task forces. He stayed at the office until midnight, then left for a couple of hours' sleep at a nearby hotel. Before he left, he asked his staff to e-mail Kohn, Warsh, Steel, and a few others to dial into a 6 A.M. conference call. A couple of staffers at the Securities and Exchange Commission were on the e-mail; the chairman, Christopher Cox, a former Republican congressman from California, was not.

But that plan was discarded. Geithner came to the office to get financial firefighters on the phone around 4:45 A.M. Bernanke, Kohn, and Warsh dialed in from home. So did Treasury's Paulson and Steel, and several top staffers, including the Fed's lawyer, Scott Alvarez, and Bernanke's spokeswoman, Michelle Smith.

The SEC was legally Bear Stearns's chief regulator, but Cox, its chairman, wasn't on the call. Apparently, he wasn't missed. Top officials at both the Fed and the Treasury had decided the SEC and its chairman weren't up to the job of coping with the collapse of an investment bank. Cox was largely a bystander. Around 7:40 A.M., an SEC staffer, Robert Colby, deputy director of the trading and markets division, e-mailed the Fed's Don Kohn and the Treasury's Bob Steel and begged someone to call Cox and fill him in.

The big question: save Bear Stearns so it could continue to seek a buyer, or let it go under and try to protect the financial system and the economy from the damage. The call stretched on for more than two hours. "There were one or two points where someone said, 'Well, suppose we don't? What happens then?'" recalled Don Kohn, the Fed vice chairman. In 1990, the Fed had stood by when Drexel Burnham Lambert went under after it was accused of illegal shenanigans in the market for junk bonds pioneered by Michael Milken, the creative financier who ended up in jail.

But this was a very different time.

"It was the whole market environment," Kohn said. "People were running from all kinds of financial counterparties," he said. "Bear happened to be the weakest, so it was kind of the leading edge of the run. But it was clear that spreads were spiking out" — meaning that investors were demanding unusually high yields to buy anything besides the safest securities — "that banks and other financial firms were having increasing trouble raising money, that hedge funds were cutting back their exposure to all kinds of counterparties. It just felt like the system was kind of imploding. And everybody was running for the safest asset: Treasury bills." Neither the overseers of the nation's financial plumbing nor anyone else understood the workings of the system until the pipes were seriously clogged.

Around 7 A.M., Geithner tried to bring the conversation to a conclusion. "We've got to make a call here before markets open. What's it going to be?"

The consensus was clear: make the loan. "Let's do it," Bernanke said.

The fact that such a significant decision was made on the fly before daybreak speaks volumes. The financial regulatory system had become overwhelmed by the evolution of the markets it was supposed to supervise. "Things happened very quickly and left very little time window," Bernanke said. "In most cases when firms, banks, have problems, they have a considerable amount of time to take preemptive actions in terms of raising capital, finding a partner, and taking other measures to avoid these problems."

In the end, the Fed agreed to lend Bear Stearns enough to get to the weekend. Technically, the money went from the Fed's discount window to JPMorgan Chase to Bear Stearns. But the Fed, not JPMorgan, was on the hook if Bear didn't pay it back. For its part, Bear had to place $14 billion worth of collateral Friday to borrow $12.9 billion. When the Fed lends, it takes a "haircut" from the collateral's market value to be sure that it will avoid losses if the loan isn't paid back. In this case, the Fed was fully paid back — and got $4 million in interest — on Monday.

Lending to a financial firm outside the Fed's regulatory net would eventually force long-overdue changes in the U.S. financial regulatory regime: the Fed could no longer pretend that it supervised banks and someone else supervised the shadow banking system. The Fed would now have to begin examining the books of *all* investment banks because the Bear Stearns loan was certain to be seen as a precedent. "Everybody on the phone knew that this was hugely consequential, an irreversible decision that would have consequences that were very hard to say at the time," Don Kohn said. "My stomach hurt for sure."

Others would later say that Bear wasn't too *big* to fail; it was too *interconnected* to fail, a new standard. Bear Stearns had open trades with 5,000 other firms and was a party to 750,000 derivatives contracts. It would not have gone into bankruptcy quietly.

"In my mind, what was foremost was that lots of other folks would be brought down with it with consequences I couldn't imagine," Kohn said. "So it just felt like the beginning of the Great Depression or something. If you didn't do [the loan], you would be destroying lots of financial intermediaries." What Bernanke had dubbed the "credit channel" in his examination of the Depression was obstructed, and the Fed had to clear it out or bypass it.

"Unusual and Exigent"

The Fed's ability to come up with billions of dollars overnight to prevent a Bear Stearns bankruptcy and for subsequent loans to borrowers, from insurance companies to car buyers, rested on an undefined phrase — "unusual and exigent circumstances" — in a 1932 federal law that had atrophied from lack of use. "Unusual and exigent" was basically the legal license to do *whatever it takes.*

At its birth in 1913, the Fed lent to businesses only indirectly. Businesses would take IOUs from other businesses, and use those IOUs as security to borrow from commercial banks. The banks, in turn, would use the IOUs as collateral to borrow from the Fed. By 1932, businesses were finding bank credit scarce. Despite Hoover's reservations about "a gigantic centralization of banking and finance to which the American people have been properly opposed for the past 100 years," Congress tucked a provision into a public works bill that gave the Fed the power to bypass banks and lend to any individual, partnership, or corporation.

That authority is still found in Section 13(3) of the Federal Reserve Act: the Fed may lend "to any individual, partnership or corporation" if five members of the Federal Reserve Board in Washington declare the circumstances to be "unusual and exigent." After the 1932 law passed, the Fed declared the times to be "unusual and exigent" but didn't do much actual lending: over the five unusual and exigent years from 1932 to 1936, 123 businesses borrowed a grand total of $1.5 million, the equivalent of about $25 million in today's dollars, adjusted for inflation, a pittance compared with the Bear Stearns loan.

In 1934, Congress further expanded the Fed's purview, authorizing it to make up to $280 million in *unsecured* loans of up to five years to businesses, particularly small ones, that couldn't find working capital elsewhere. That brought a brisker trade, but demand fell off sharply in 1935 because terms offered by the government's Reconstruction Finance Corporation, created by Hoover and expanded by Roosevelt, were more attractive.

By the 1950s, the Fed had changed its mind about the whole idea. Fed chairman William McChesney Martin told Congress that the central bank wanted to stick to "guiding monetary policy and credit policy so as to exert its influence toward maintaining the value of the dollar and fostering orderly economic growth," and to avoid lending to individuals or companies, a view that prevailed inside the Fed until the Great Panic. In 1958, Congress terminated the Fed's authority to make the working-capital loans, turning that task over to the Small Business Administration.

Congress left the 1932 "unusual and exigent" escape clause on the books, and the Fed invoked the power in 1966 and 1969 to offer loans to savings banks and savings and loan associations struggling with interest-rate ceilings, though none actually took the money. After that, it pretty much shut down the operation, refusing even to consider making loans to airlines after 9/11 (although the Fed did help oversee an airline-loan operation created by Congress).

Some of the most savvy on Wall Street, though, realized that the Fed's capacity to lend instantly in an emergency might be needed in a financial crisis — and wanted to be sure it had the powers it needed. Immediately following the 1987 stock market crash, the then-president of the New York Fed, Gerry Corrigan, leaned heavily on reluctant commercial banks to lend to securities firms. Among those most troubled by the vulnerability of securities firms to the whims of commercial banks were Bob Rubin and Steve Friedman, then cochief executives of Goldman Sachs, the politically well-connected investment bank where Corrigan would end up after retiring from the Fed in 1993.

The problem was that the law delineating the Fed's powers had vestiges of the old doctrine that limited the Fed to financing agricultural, industrial, and commercial transactions, not speculation — which was just another word for the business of Wall Street. Specifically, the act barred the Fed from lending to anyone who would use the money for "merely investments" or "for the purpose of carrying or trading in stocks, bonds, or other investment securities" other than U.S. government bonds and notes.

At the urging of Goldman Sachs lobbyists, Congress dropped the prohibition in a little-noticed section of broader banking legislation enacted in 1991. Don Kohn, then a Fed staffer, told the Senate Banking Committee at the time that the changed wording of the statute would remove any "ambiguity" about the Fed's powers to lend to securities firms. The committee agreed. "In... an emergency, the Federal Reserve must be able to ensure the liquidity of the financial system, including if necessary by the use of advances [loans] to securities firms," the committee report said. Sixteen years later, that tiny legislative maneuver, remembered only by the handful of lawyers and lobbyists involved in it, would prove vital to the Fed's ability to do whatever it takes.

Bernanke and Geithner knew Section 13(3) of the Federal Reserve Act existed but never thought they would use it. Indeed, within the Fed, there long had been anxiety that any public declaration of circumstances to be "unusual and exigent" would be so alarming it could make matters worse. When the Fed initiated the Term Securities Lending Facility a few days before

Bear Stearns, its general counsel advised that the action went beyond the Fed's usual money market operations and recommended that it invoke the "unusual and exigent" clause. The Fed board did so but didn't announce that.

Everyone in on the decision knew that the Fed was going where it hadn't gone since the 1930s. "We recognized, of course, that the use of this legal authority was, in itself, an extraordinary step," Geithner told a Senate committee a couple of weeks later. "At the same time, we were mindful that Congress included this lending power in the Federal Reserve Act for a reason, and it seemed irresponsible for us not to use that authority in this unique situation."

"IT SEEMS I SHOWED UP AT AN INTERESTING MOMENT"

After the Bear Stearns conference call finally ended around 8 A.M. on Friday, March 14, Bernanke, Kohn, and Warsh — joined by the only other Fed governor in town, Randy Kroszner — immediately went to the Fed's boardroom to formally approve the Bear Stearns loan. Rick Mishkin, the other sitting board member, was flying home from Finland; two other board seats were vacant. (Recalling that Mishkin had been skiing when the Fed abruptly cut interest rates in January, one Fed colleague suggested he avoid further travel to cold climates.)

The empty seats posed a slight problem: the Federal Reserve Act required five votes to lend to anyone other than an ordinary bank. But a post–September 11 change in the law provided an escape hatch: a unanimous vote of the available governors could approve a loan if it was urgently needed "to prevent, correct or mitigate serious harm to the economy or the stability of the financial system of the United States." The Fed's formal approval cited "the fragile condition of the financial markets at the time, the prominent position of Bear Stearns in those markets, and the expected contagion that would result from the immediate failure of Bear Stearns." Although the Fed didn't say so publicly on Friday, the vote gave Bernanke and Geithner the authority to lend to any other investment bank.

The subsequent Fed press release was terse even by the usual standards, saying only that the Fed board had voted to approve the arrangement announced by JPMorgan Chase and Bear Stearns. It offered no details beyond those that JPMorgan had offered: the Fed was making a loan of unspecified size, a "no-recourse, back-to-back loan," meaning JPMorgan wouldn't have to pay back the money if Bear didn't. In a phrase that hadn't received much attention inside the Fed, both JPMorgan and the Fed said the loan was made for *up to* twenty-eight days. Bear Stearns executives later said they took that to mean that they had four weeks to find an ultimate solution. But Paulson and Geithner both had told Bear Stearns executives that they had lost control of their fate when they accepted the Fed's money.

The fact that the Fed itself was on the hook was such a departure from tradition that some insiders on Wall Street didn't grasp instantly what happened when Paulson and Geithner briefed them Friday morning. At Morgan Stanley, for instance, executives who participated in the call didn't realize that the Fed was putting money at risk until a JPMorgan investor-relations person explained it.

President Bush — inconveniently — was scheduled to speak that Friday at noon at the New York Economic Club, a group of economists and Wall Street executives, all of whom were certain to be focused on Bear Stearns and its implications. Bob Steel, Paulson's undersecretary for domestic finance, had flown to New York Thursday night to surprise his daughter, who was celebrating her twenty-first birthday at a restaurant in Greenwich, Connecticut. He showed up for dessert but then hurried into New York to join the Bear deathwatch. Friday morning, Steel was dispatched to meet the presidential helicopter and bring Bush up-to-date.

"It seems like I showed up in an interesting moment," Bush told the crowd at the New York Hilton. They laughed. Then he turned to his role as cheerleader in chief. "In a free market, there's going to be good times and bad times. And after fifty-two consecutive months of job growth, which is a record, our economy obviously is going through a tough time.... [B]ut I want to remind you, this is not the first time since I've been the president that we have faced economic challenges. We inherited a recession. And then there was the attack of September the 11th, 2001, which many of you saw firsthand, and you know full well how that affected our economy. And then we had corporate scandals. And I made the difficult decisions to confront the terrorists and extremists in two major fronts, Afghanistan and Iraq. And then we had devastating natural disasters. And the interesting thing, every time, this economy has bounced back better and stronger than before."

Bush alluded to the morning's announcements and then praised Bernanke. "I respect Ben Bernanke. I think he's doing a good job under tough circumstances. The Fed has cut interest rates several times."

As much as the president wanted to take credit for Bernanke's actions, he was also careful to genuflect at the altar of Fed independence. "We also hold dear this notion of the Fed being independent from White House policy. They act independently from the politicians, and they should. It's good for our country to have that kind of independence."

Such words undoubtedly would have been comforting to the Fed's New York contingent, but none of them had joined the Economic Club lunch. They were too busy working.

"How's Your Finger?"

The Friday-morning loan solved very little. The run on Bear Stearns continued, just as Paulson had predicted days earlier. "It's over for Bear Stearns," he told an aide. "It's over for the shareholders. We've got to find a way out of it that doesn't tank the [whole] market."

By day's end, Bear's already depressed stock had lost nearly half its remaining value. That night, Paulson and Geithner decided the problem had to be solved before markets opened Monday. Around 7:30 P.M., they reached Schwartz in his car on his way from Manhattan to nearby Greenwich, Connecticut. He didn't have twenty-eight days to find a buyer, they told him. He had the weekend. Either he would sell the company by Sunday night, or he would be forced into bankruptcy.

"It was just clear that this franchise was going to unravel if the deal wasn't done by the end of the weekend," Paulson said a few days later.

No one at the Fed had ever anticipated a weekend like this one. Although the New York Fed has three dorm-style rooms for emergencies, Bill Dudley, the markets' chief, slept on the floor of his small office off the trading floor instead of trying to make it home to New Jersey. Tom Baxter, the Fed's general counsel, who lives in Staten Island, bought an air mattress and pillow and slept on his office floor, too — and stored the mattress and pillow in a file drawer in case there was a next time. Bernanke himself spent a night or two on the couch in his office.

On Saturday morning, after checking in with Bernanke and Paulson, Geithner went to see Paul Volcker at his Manhattan apartment. It was classic Geithner, acknowledging the older man's experience and stature, and seeking his advice and his blessing. Geithner had an almost Asian reverence for his elders, making time to play tennis with Greenspan even after he retired. By now, Greenspan's star was waning. Volcker — who had been vilified by the public for causing a deep recession in the 1980s, though celebrated by the bond market and economists for vanquishing inflation — was on the rise. Indeed, events had turned him into something of a seer. In recent years, he had been a notable and vocal skeptic about financial engineering and had further let it be known that he thought Greenspan hadn't worried enough about the banks.

Volcker, about a foot taller than Geithner, greeted Geithner with a reference to the little Dutch boy and the dike: "How's your finger?"

Volcker's advice: find a buyer for Bear Stearns — quickly.

That was the plan. But it proved difficult.

Running Out of Options

Hank Paulson figured that every potential buyer knew that Bear Stearns was desperate and available. He was skeptical of rumors that Germany's big Deutsche Bank might be interested, but called its CEO, Josef Ackermann, anyhow. Deutsche wasn't interested. Private equity investor J. C. Flowers was interested but couldn't raise the $20 billion or so he needed. As one option after another disappeared, a solitary potential buyer was left: JPMorgan Chase. No one else was strong enough to say with credibility on Monday morning that it stood behind every trade on Bear Stearns's books.

On Saturday night, after talking with Jamie Dimon, Geithner and Paulson were relieved. "I've talked to Jamie," Geithner told his team. "We've got a deal. They're going to buy them." The price was between $8 and $12 a share—somewhere between $945 million and $1.4 billion. And the Fed wouldn't need to put in a dime.

To monitor the talks, Paulson dispatched Neel Kashkari. He was thirty-five years old, a junior Goldman Sachs investment banker on the West Coast who had failed at his first attempt at a Washington foothold with an unsuccessful application to be a White House fellow, a prestigious internship for thirty-somethings. When Paulson was named Treasury secretary, Kashkari volunteered, and Paulson hired him. Around 10:15 P.M., Kashkari e-mailed Bob Steel, the undersecretary for domestic finance, and David Nason, a securities lawyer who had worked at the SEC before becoming an assistant Treasury secretary, that he had heard from Paulson and Geithner that "the deal is basically agreed to."

"Tim confirmed that to the group," Steel e-mailed back, referring to government officials Geithner had been informing. Nason typed back: "Awesome. TG [Tim Geithner] seemed pretty relaxed."

It sounded too good to be true, and it was. The next morning, Dimon called Geithner to say JPMorgan had changed its mind. After a night of scouring Bear Stearns's books, the deal looked too risky. In particular, Morgan didn't want to take Bear Stearns's mortgage-linked securities. Bear had sold the best of its book already, Dimon told the Fed and the Treasury, and Morgan didn't want to add to the mass of mortgage securities it already had.

Paulson didn't get the word right away. He was doing the Sunday talk show circuit, and Kashkari couldn't immediately reach him. Geithner labored to keep JPMorgan interested while pressing Fed staff to figure out if there was some way the Fed could close the gap. Bernanke stayed in touch by phone but left the on-the-ground negotiating to Geithner. As for Jamie Dimon, he held the best cards, and he knew it. The government wanted to sell Bear Stearns before the markets in Asia opened, and Morgan was the only potential buyer left. Ergo, the government was going to have to subsidize this deal. The only question was who and how much. (One question would linger for months: How much would JPMorgan have lost, given that it had sold insurance to others against a Bear Stearns default in the credit default swaps market?)

Geithner and Bernanke had few doubts that the U.S. government, broadly defined, should pony up, but they knew this was a step beyond the Fed's traditional role of pumping liquidity into the markets. The lawyers would devise language to get around the requirement that the Fed could make loans, not buy assets. But that would be legal semantics. The fact was, the Fed was about to purchase assets that it would likely hold for up to ten years, assets that had more than a little stink on them. But the spirit of the law was clear: the Fed should not make a deal if it anticipated a loss. Its job was to keep healthy banks functioning and provide liquidity; if a bank was broke, if losses had depleted its capital, that was supposed to be a problem for the keepers of taxpayer money in the executive branch and in Congress.

The Fed's first choice was to get Treasury to put up the money. Had Bear Stearns been a conventional bank, funding might have come from the Federal Deposit Insurance Corporation, a government agency financed by insurance premiums paid by banks and backed by the full faith and credit of the U.S. government. But Treasury lawyers said they couldn't spend money without an act of Congress, and there was no time to seek that. The Fed pushed for the Treasury to promise to "indemnify" the Fed if the mortgage-linked securities ultimately weren't worth the $30 billion. Paulson was willing to go along. Treasury lawyers rejected that, too, and with that, the Fed's options came down to a precious few — three, to be exact.

One was to let Bear go under and try to contain the damage. Geithner and Bernanke weren't willing to take that risk. "It became clear that Bear's involvement in the complex and intricate web of relationships that characterize our financial system, at a point in time when markets were especially vulnerable, was such that a sudden failure would likely lead to a chaotic unwinding of positions in already damaged markets," Geithner said. It would have "cast a cloud of doubt" on Lehman Brothers, Merrill Lynch, and others "whose business models bore some superficial similarity to Bear's, without due regard for the fundamental soundness of those firms." The consequences, Geithner concluded, would have been "unpredictable but severe" and almost surely would have meant lower stock prices, lower house prices, and less credit for companies and households.

A second option was to buy time to see if the Fed could find an offer to compete with JPMorgan's. "My question then was whether we could get through another several days to run a more robust auction," Warsh said. "And the answer I think was that we probably could not."

Geithner saw it the same way: "The only feasible option for buying time would have required open-ended financing by the Fed to Bear into an accelerating withdrawal by Bear's customers and counterparties," he said.

That left the third choice: subsidizing JPMorgan's acquisition of Bear Stearns. Geithner told Paulson that Dimon was talking about offering $4 or $5 a share for Bear Stearns. Paulson thought that was too much. In large part, he figured that every nickel JPMorgan Chase's Dimon paid Bear shareholders was another nickel he would be asking the government to provide. But he also believed that shareholders in all financial firms needed to be reminded of the rules of capitalism: shareholders take risks and get the rewards of success and the pain of failure. Paulson called Dimon, and the secretary told the banker that $4 or $5 "sounded high." JPMorgan offered $2, or about $236 million in all.

An e-mail circulating inside Treasury captured the apparent bargain price Jamie Dimon had struck: "Did you know the LA Glaxy [sic] paid more for Beckham than JP [Morgan] did for Bear??" (The LA Galaxy soccer team signed the British soccer superstar to a five-year $250 million contract in 2007.)

C.Y.A.

To satisfy Fed lawyers, the Fed subsidy was cast in the rhetoric of a loan. But the Fed was effectively spending $30 billion of its money to buy mortgage-linked securities that JPMorgan didn't want. JPMorgan, to the Fed's discomfort, described them unattractively as "illiquid assets, largely mortgage related" on a Sunday-night conference call with securities analysts, a reference that implied it was sticking the Fed with the worst of Bear's holdings. The structure of the deal stretched Section 13(3) of the Federal Reserve Act. Because the Fed wasn't supposed to buy the securities outright, it borrowed a tool from financial engineers whose handiwork had led to the Great

Panic. It created a "special purpose vehicle" to hold the assets. Then it made a loan to that entity and argued that the loan had been secured by those Bear Stearns securities. And if they proved to be worth a lot less than the price the Fed had paid, the Fed — not JPMorgan Chase — would eat the loss.

"It took some time before the political class realized that the Fed had not just lent money to JPMorgan to buy Bear Stearns, but in effect now owned the downside of a portfolio...of possibly dodgy assets," wrote Phillip Swagel, who had been the Treasury's top economist at the time, in a 2009 reprise of the Treasury's actions during the Great Panic.

Beneath such technicalities, though, lurked some big unresolved issues. The Treasury and the Fed were united on the necessity of the Bear Stearns deal, but neither side wanted to take all the blame when the inevitable bailout backlash erupted. To the Fed, the Treasury seemed to be maneuvering to put as much of the responsibility as it could on the Fed. At the Treasury, the often-repeated view was that "all money is green"—that it didn't matter which branch of the government was putting the money on the table, it was all the taxpayers' money ultimately. The Fed was uneasy that it was stepping over lines it had traditionally drawn. It wanted a veneer of political cover for using its money for what Fed officials thought was properly the responsibility of the Treasury—if only Congress had given it the power to act.

At the very least, Bernanke and Geithner wanted Treasury to endorse putting taxpayers on the hook for an action that went well beyond lending to keep markets lubricated. They settled for a terse thank-you note signed by Paulson, offering his "support" for the Fed's extraordinary action "as appropriate and in the government's interest," and even that took hours of negotiations. Paulson didn't explicitly say taxpayers were behind the loan — his lawyers said he couldn't — but he did acknowledge that if the Fed lost money, it would have fewer profits to turn over to the Treasury, so the tab eventually would fall on the taxpayers. The Treasury didn't release the letter, though. To the surprise of Paulson's staff, neither did the Fed. It became public only when a congressional committee asked for it later.

The pattern was established. Paulson was a stubborn, forceful, and experienced negotiator. He didn't care if the folks on the other side of the table detested him. Bernanke was different. He was, by nature, more conciliatory.

And he was prepared to do *whatever it takes* to save the economy—even if that meant taking flak inside the Fed for allowing Paulson to push him around or stretching the Fed's mandate and intervention in the economy beyond what was customary.

KNOCK, KNOCK

On Sunday afternoon, the Fed board met to ratify the $30 billion deal and invoke the "unusual and exigent" clause for the third time in less than a week. Mishkin was back from Finland and in on this vote—by phone from New York. He believed the Fed had no choice. "The issue is not recession," he said. "The issue is can we get something that we just can't control."

Mishkin and his wife had plans to see *Sunday in the Park with George* in New York on Sunday afternoon, and he went, anticipating that he would have to leave for a Fed board meeting. When the call came during the second act, Mishkin left the theater and took the call in his car, which he had parked nearby for this purpose.

This being New York, the driver of a passing car noticed him in the car and thought he'd spotted a choice parking place about to open up.

He knocked on Mishkin's window.

"Go away!" Mishkin told him, gesticulating with one hand while holding his cell phone with the other. Eventually, the guy got the message. "We are bailing out Bear Stearns, and this guy is knocking on my damn window," he recalled. "It was like a *Seinfeld* episode."

Mishkin and his colleagues did more than sign off on the Bear deal that Geithner had negotiated. Declaring circumstances to be unusual and exigent, they formally and publicly expanded the ranks of firms to which the Fed would lend directly to include all remaining securities firms of consequence through what they called Primary Dealer Credit Facility, or PDCF. The objective was to shore up confidence in the remaining investment banks by making clear that they could borrow directly from the Fed, reducing the risk of a Bear Stearns–like run on any other investment bank. As the New York Fed's Dudley put it, "The Primary Dealer Credit Facility essentially puts the Federal Reserve in the position of tri-party repo investor of last resort." (Translation: The shadow banking system was collapsing, and the Fed was taking its place, one market at a time.)

It was a good idea; it wouldn't prove sufficient.

DEAL? NO DEAL?

Except for Geithner, the regional Fed bank presidents hadn't been part of the conversations about Bear Stearns. Bernanke and Kohn tried to reach them all Sunday. San Francisco's Yellen was on a plane on her way to Washington for Tuesday's FOMC meeting and missed the call from Kohn. Alerted by a San Francisco Fed staffer, she dialed into a conference call that the Fed had with reporters to fill them in on the details. The twelve bank presidents had planned to have dinner together Monday night at the Fairmont Hotel in Washington, where they always stay during FOMC meetings. An e-mail alerted them that Bernanke was going to show up to field questions about Bear Stearns along with Geithner, who came late.

Overt criticism was almost nonexistent. It was all too sudden, and everyone knew Geithner had just walked off the battlefield. Even those suspicious of his proclivity for intervention and rescues were restrained. There were lots of questions—about the Treasury's role, about the assets the Fed was taking, and about other details. Geithner criticized the SEC, saying that when he asked for Bear Stearns's balance sheet, he got an old one because the SEC didn't have daily data.

Near the end of the dinner, Bernanke offered up a prediction. "This has completely changed the political debate," he said, according to a person in the room. "Congress is going to have to do something about the mortgage market."

He was right. Before Bear Stearns, the argument in Washington about whether the government should help homeowners with mortgages they could no longer afford had focused on practicality, fairness, and the difficulty of distinguishing deserving homeowners from undeserving. After Bear Stearns, the argument was about bailing out Wall Street versus bailing out ordinary American homeowners, a debate that would persist for another year.

In fact, though, the deal that occasioned all this reflection and soul-searching wasn't quite yet done. Public statements made it seem as if the Fed had walked down the aisles of Bear Stearns and taken $30 billion worth of mortgage-backed securities off the shelves. It hadn't. The terms of that deal hadn't been settled when the Fed board voted its approval and delegated details to Geithner.

A week later, the details were still pending, and the deal was in danger of collapse. Sloppy legal work by JPMorgan's lawyers meant the bank had agreed to stand behind Bear Stearns trades until its shareholders voted — even if it took a year to get their approval. Many Bear shareholders weren't happy with the $2-a-share price, and it wasn't clear they would approve the merger — which meant JPMorgan might have to guarantee Bear's trades for a long time without owning the company. With the prospect of a Bear Stearns bankruptcy once again darkening the horizon, JPMorgan eventually agreed to pay $10 a share instead of $2.

Geithner said that if the shareholders were getting a better deal, the Fed wanted one, too. So JPMorgan agreed to eat the first $1 billion of losses in the $30 billion pool of assets that the Fed was taking. When it was finally signed on March 28, the renegotiated deal between the Fed and JPMorgan set criteria for what sort of securities were in and which were out. They had to be investment-grade securities, and the property owners on all the underlying mortgages had to be making their monthly payments. The two sides agreed to value the securities at what Bear Stearns had been carrying them on March 14. But Bear had hedged some of its exposure, and figuring out which hedge went with which security was complicated. Three more months would pass before JPMorgan Chase and the Fed — working with the money manager it had hired, BlackRock, and the auditing firm of Ernst & Young — agreed on what was in and what wasn't. Even then, it was all so complicated that the parties couldn't quite agree on securities that added up to $30 billion, ultimately falling about $30 *million* short.

Each side privately accused the other of nickel-and-diming, but the economy was doing its own value-cutting as well. By the time the New York Fed and JPMorgan had agreed on exactly what was in the Bear Stearns portfolio at the end of June 2008, the best guess at the market value of the portfolio was $1 billion less than it had been valued in mid-March. By the end of 2008, the Fed said the portfolio had lost another $3.2 billion in value.

"This cost...must be weighed against the effects on the American economy and American financial system of allowing this firm to collapse," Bernanke told a Senate committee a few weeks after doing the Bear Stearns deal. By then, anyone listening closely would have recognized the chairman's mantra implicit in his testimony: *whatever it takes.*

What Next?

The day after the Fed sold Bear Stearns to JPMorgan Chase, Larry Summers stood up for the Fed on PBS's *Charlie Rose* show. "Did the Federal Reserve need to act in an extraordinary way to preserve the system?" he asked himself. His answer: "History will judge that acting to preserve the system was wise." While cautioning that the worst might still be ahead for the U.S. economy, Summers said his protégé Geithner and future rival Bernanke had made "an important contribution to the restoration of confidence."

But others — including some usually sympathetic — weren't so complimentary.

Paul Volcker told the New York Economic Club that the Fed had gone to "the very edge of its lawful and implied powers, transcending certain long embedded central banking principles and practices." That could have been an endorsement — going to the edge is *not* going over — but Volcker's comments were taken as criticism of Geithner and Bernanke.

Volcker's admirers at the New York Fed were stung by what appeared to be the suggestion that Geithner and Bernanke had gone too far. A former New York Fed staffer tried to use a sports metaphor to defend the move: "If you think about basketball, you can have your toes on the line and you don't commit a foul unless you go over the line." Volcker later insisted to reporters — and to Geithner and Bernanke — that his point was that the law needed to be changed so someone other than the Fed was doing the rescuing. But there was a very fine line between saying (a) that the Treasury or Congress should have found some alternative way to cope with the imminent collapse of a big financial firm so the Fed wouldn't have to be the first responder, and (b) that Bernanke and Geithner had gone too far.

Anna Schwartz, who had been Milton Friedman's collaborator, was unambiguous. She picked (b). She denounced the Fed–Bear Stearns loans as "a rogue operation" in a May 2008 interview: "To me, it is an open-and-shut case. The Fed had no business intervening here."

And Vince Reinhart, who had been one of the Fed's senior staffers before leaving in 2006, stunned his former colleagues by condemning their action as "the worst policy mistake in a generation." It meant that the Fed would always be expected to bring money to the table when trying to arrange the rescue of a big financial firm, he said.

Three months after Bear Stearns, the Richmond Fed president, Jeffrey Lacker, made headlines with a denunciation of the Bernanke-Geithner rescue in a speech in London. The Fed should always move to stop irrational runs on the banks, the self-perpetuating kind where panic by some bank depositors leads to panic by many, Lacker said. But by preventing Bear Stearns from failing, the Fed was sowing the seeds of future crises. It was creating "moral hazard," a term borrowed from the insurance business to describe the temptation to take bigger risks because someone else will pay the cost if things go wrong.

Like Lacker, Philadelphia's Charles Plosser and a few other Fed officials saw the Bear Stearns rescue as the original sin that led to the risk taking that worsened the turmoil that would follow later: the Fed, they argued, had led markets, executives, and creditors of big financial institutions to take unwise risks with the understanding that they expected the Fed to step in if anything bad happened. From Stanford, John Taylor, who had criticized Greenspan, emerged as a counterweight to Larry Summers. Well before the Lehman debacle, Taylor — who was big on making rules that guided policy — attacked Bernanke, Geithner, and Paulson for failing to explain to the markets and the public the criteria for rescuing Bear Stearns so everyone would know how the same trio planned to respond the next time a big financial house got into trouble.

Most inside the Fed, though, swallowed hard and concluded Bernanke and Geithner had made the best battlefield decision possible. "There is no question we created moral hazard by doing this. But there are moral hazard extremists who think moral hazard is such a big problem that we should never do anything that creates it," Mishkin said after returning to Columbia University's business school. "It is unfortunate that we didn't have more time to think about this, but the risk is that you may go into a depression if you screw it up."

In early April, Bernanke, Geithner, the SEC's Cox, and Treasury's Steel were called before the Senate Banking Committee. Senator Jim Bunning — a Kentucky Republican, former major league pitcher, and perennial critic of the Fed — ended a run of hostile questions with a particularly pertinent one: "What's going to happen if a Merrill or a Lehman or someone like that is next?"

Congressional committees limit the time any one senator can hog the microphone, and Bunning's time was up. The committee chairman, Chris Dodd of Connecticut, asked Bunning if he wanted a response. Bunning declined, and Bernanke and Geithner were let off the hook. Five months later, though, there would be no place to hide.

Chapter 10

FANNIE, FREDDIE, AND "FEDDIE"

On Tuesday, April 15 — almost a month to the day after orchestrating the Bear Stearns sale — Paulson, Bernanke, and a handful of aides met for an hour in the Fed's "anteroom," a small conference space adjacent to the boardroom decorated with portraits of Fed chairmen past. Paulson carried with him a ten-page memo titled "'Break the Glass' Bank Recapitalization Plan." The "glass" reference had come from a late-2007 discussion among Bush aides about a potential economic stimulus during which White House economic-policy coordinator Keith Hennessey had asked, "How big is the ax behind the glass?"

The plan — really more of a bare-bones outline — was the closest thing the Treasury had to a contingency scheme. It had been drafted by Phillip Swagel, the Treasury's economist, and Neel Kashkari, the young former Goldman Sachs banker. Kashkari was a low-profile player back in April 2008. Still, he had been prescient in realizing that housing would require more aggressive action than the Bush administration was acknowledging publicly. In fact, as early as January 2008, he had joked to colleagues that the *next president* would be forced to use taxpayer money to buy mortgage-backed securities. Over and over he would repeat, "The next president is going to bring the hostages home"—a reference to Iran's 1980 release of U.S. hostages just a few minutes after Ronald Reagan succeeded Jimmy Carter. Kashkari, it turned out, was right on the inevitability, wrong on the timing. Like others in the Paulson Treasury, Kashkari and Swagel were suspicious of housing-rescue schemes being discussed by the staff of Barney Frank's House Financial Services Committee and the Fed staff, particularly housing specialist Wayne Passmore. The April 15 meeting, which Passmore attended, was the Treasury's attempt to offer alternatives.

The centerpiece of Kashkari and Swagel's "Break the Glass" plan was a proposal to ask Congress for $500 billion to buy mortgage-backed securities from banks and securities firms—not the safe sort guaranteed by government-sponsored mortgage companies Fannie Mae or Freddie Mac, but the riskier sort, including subprime loans. The goal was to remove toxic assets weighing on bank balance sheets and replace them with easily traded Treasury bills so banks would look and feel healthier, and thus would be more willing to lend and more attractive to investors. With excessive optimism, Kashkari and Swagel predicted the first auction could be held just one month after the legislation was signed.

The two Treasury officials also offered four less detailed alternatives to buying assets. The government could guarantee mortgage-backed securities to make them more attractive to investors. The Federal Housing Administration could refinance mortgages one by one. The Fed could buy mortgage-backed securities, as it had from Bear Stearns. And then there was the fourth option, labeled "Alternative D." It filled half of the last page of the relatively brief memo. It detailed a plan whereby the Treasury would ask Congress for permission "to purchase equity stakes in financial institutions" to help them "rebuild capital and resume lending without purchasing their toxic assets"—precisely where Paulson ended up six months later.

Although Bernanke knew from earlier banking crises in the United States and elsewhere that the government ultimately spent a lot of taxpayer money fixing banks, the Treasury contingency plan went nowhere, essentially because the situation didn't look bad enough yet. Bernanke and Paulson agreed that there was no point in offering Congress a plan so far-reaching unless the crisis was so severe that Congress would see no other option. They hoped that day wouldn't come. In fact, it came sooner than they ever imagined.

At the New York Fed, at about the same time, Geithner asked a top lieutenant, Terry Checki, a veteran of financial crises in emerging markets, to think about what the government might do about this ever-emerging crisis. Checki devised what came to be called the Consolidated Asset Management Trust, or CAM-T. The notion was to create a freestanding entity that would draw money from private investors and borrow more on the private markets — with government backing in some form — to buy residential and commercial mortgage-linked securities from banks at then-current market prices. The banks would get most of the proceeds in cash, but a portion would be paid in an IOU good only if the ultimate borrowers paid their loans. CAM-T was meant to help the banks, restore liquidity to the moribund mortgage market, and lure investors from the sidelines. The idea went nowhere, bogged down, among other things, in arguments over which part of the government would put up the money. Whether it might have worked — and avoided some of the pain that came later — is impossible to know. It never surfaced in public.

NOT IN AN ELECTION YEAR

In July, as Congress reprised Bear Stearns and all that followed, Bernanke and Paulson testified before Barney Frank's House Financial Services Committee. They told Frank and his colleagues that federal law needed to be changed so the government could better cope with the failure of big financial institutions other than conventional banks. Although there was no argument on the necessity of this legislation, neither Bernanke nor Paulson gave any hint that they thought large sums of taxpayer money might be needed soon. Nor did either man suggest that they wanted Congress to move during 2008 on anything except legislation tightening regulation of Fannie Mae and Freddie Mac, the big mortgage companies.

Paulson and Frank — who had fashioned a good working relationship before the Great Panic — talked privately ahead of the hearing. Frank told Paulson and Bernanke in person what he had told the secretary on the phone: take an expansive view of your powers, and I won't criticize you for that. If you need more power, don't ask us to give it to you until you're sure we can do it. The last thing we need now is for you to ask us for something and we say no. Paulson and Bernanke replied that they didn't have all the power that they'd like, as both had pointed out before, but they had enough to cope with what they currently confronted. Paulson softened his testimony to suit Frank's request. "The chance of our getting this in an election year was zero," Paulson said in an interview a few months later.

In the public hearing, Paulson and Bernanke said bluntly that they didn't think Congress could tackle major changes to financial regulation in an election year. "The more complex issues like resolution [of failing financial institutions] or even financial regulatory restructuring are simply not likely to happen in the short term, and we need to take the time to make sure it's done right and thoroughly worked through," Bernanke said, his words reflecting Barney Frank's advice. "So we will continue to think about what steps might be taken on a shorter-term basis and be in close touch with Congress. But…I just want to be clear that it's not that we don't have any tools. We have plenty of tools, and we are working together very well, I think, to address a difficult situation."

Paulson—who was less inclined than Bernanke to accommodate Frank's request—was less reassuring and did just a little finger-pointing. "[R]egulators are working together seamlessly to address some of the issues that have arisen, and I think progress has been made," he said, but there were problems. "Work should begin immediately and urgently on…these steps we've suggested. We're just telling you that realistically, because we've heard from you and we know it to be the case, realistically it's going to be difficult to get things done this year. But this is going to take some time, so begin work urgently on that."

Frank, Paulson, and Bernanke came away from their private conversation and the hearing with different interpretations. Frank concluded that Paulson and Bernanke couldn't make a strong case that they needed more power to deal with the "next Bear Stearns," so Congress didn't need to do anything urgently. Paulson and Bernanke concluded that there wasn't any point in asking Congress—unless the crisis intensified to the point where there were no other options. Either way, it boiled down to the same result: waiting until it was too late. There was no serious attempt to get Congress to swiftly grant the Treasury or the Fed the power to deal with the imminent collapse of another financial institution that wasn't a bank.

A BAZOOKA IN PAULSON'S POCKET

Fannie and Freddie wouldn't wait. Their capital issues were quickly turning into another financial emergency—an unsurprising situation given that the two highly leveraged mortgage giants were wholly invested in housing and the housing bubble was bursting. Warnings about the two companies stretched back to well before their current troubles. Larry Summers, when he was at Treasury in the Clinton years, and Alan Greenspan, when he was at the Fed, had warned that the two companies had grown so large that they posed risks to the whole financial system. In the Bush White House, encouraged by chief of staff Andy Card, Kevin Warsh pressed a campaign to rein in the companies—and he had plenty of allies at the Fed when he moved there.

More than a year earlier, in March 2007, Bernanke himself had warned, "Financial crises are extremely difficult to anticipate, and each episode of financial instability seems to have unique aspects. But two conditions are common to most such events. First, major crises usually involve financial institutions or markets that are either very large or play some critical role in the financial system. Second, the origins of most financial crises (excluding, perhaps, those attributable to natural disasters, war, and other nonfinancial events) can be traced to failures of due diligence or 'market discipline' by an important group of market participants. Both of these conditions apply to the current situation of Fannie Mae and Freddie Mac." At the time he spoke, the companies had $5.2 trillion in debt and other obligations outstanding, even more than the federal government's $4.9 trillion in publicly held debt.

Fannie and Freddie were unusual companies. Since 1972, they had been owned by shareholders and run for profit, but they borrowed all over the world at low interest rates because investors, including the Chinese government, assumed—correctly—that the U.S. government stood behind their debt, even though it didn't have any legal obligation to do so. The companies used the money not only to guarantee repayment of mortgages that they had turned into securities but also to build massive portfolios of mortgages. They made their money by exploiting the difference between the low rates they paid to borrow (thanks to the perceived U.S. government backing) and the higher rates on the mortgages they held. For years, the fear had been that Fannie or Freddie would mismanage the risks they were taking by borrowing big and lending big and counting on sophisticated hedging techniques to be sure that an unanticipated swing in interest rates didn't sink their portfolios and bring down the companies. But that wasn't the big problem now: Fannie and Freddie hadn't anticipated that housing prices would fall so far so long and that so many homeowners would stop paying their mortgages. No one had. These losses — which hit their portfolios of mortgages as well as the guarantees they had made on mortgages turned into securities sold to others — were eroding their capital. But markets and the Chinese traditionally hadn't worried about the skimpiness of their capital because they figured the U.S. government would never let them fail.

The companies long had been targeted by the banks that competed with them and Republican champions of free markets, but they cultivated strong political backing in Congress, particularly (although not exclusively) among Democrats and the housing industry. The national goal, Bush himself had proclaimed, was homeownership for all. Fannie and Freddie styled themselves as the means to that end, and they used their political clout to stymie Bush administration attempts to restrain them. Much like Goldman Sachs, Fannie and Freddie seemed to be the employer of last resort for people moving out of government or preparing to go into government, and not only for Democrats. Stephen Friedman, the former Goldman executive who was for a time Bush's economic-policy coordinator, had been on Fannie's board, for instance, and, as result, was recused from dealing with the issues. A top Freddie Mac executive, Hollis McLaughlin, had been Treasury Secretary Nick Brady's chief of staff. Bob Zoellick, who was Bush's first trade representative and then president of the World Bank, had been an executive vice president at Fannie Mae. (The Obama administration continued the tradition: Thomas Donilon, the deputy national security adviser, had overseen Fannie Mae's lobbying. But in a telling sign that the companies had lost their mojo, candidate Obama bowed to criticism after he designated former Fannie Mae CEO Jim Johnson to oversee his vice presidential search and then quickly replaced him.)

Both companies had been weakened—both politically and otherwise—by accusations of improper accounting, which claimed the jobs of their chief executives. But their size, unique ability to borrow huge sums, and vulnerability to falling house prices placed them high on the worry list at both the Fed and the Bush White House—though not on Paulson's own worry list when he arrived at Treasury in 2006.

Over the summer of 2008, however, housing prices sank and Fannie's and Freddie's losses mounted. Foreign governments began peppering the Treasury and the Fed with questions about the safety of the loans they had made to the companies and the mortgage-backed securities they had purchased because Fannie and Freddie guaranteed them. By early July, the shares of the two companies had fallen more than 60 percent since the beginning of the year, and they had to pay more to borrow.

Alarmed at the prospect that one or both of the companies might falter at a moment when the housing market needed them more than ever, Paulson and Bernanke and their staffs scurried to devise an emergency rescue. By Thursday, July 10, Paulson had concluded that Fannie Mae and Freddie Mac would need help the following week. By the weekend, he was saying that the companies needed support before—when else?—Asian markets opened Sunday night, Washington time.

That Sunday night, on the steps of the Treasury building, Paulson unveiled the rescue plan as TV cameras filmed. He asked Congress to give him the power to lend unlimited sums to the companies or to invest taxpayer money in their shares if they needed capital. Because Congress couldn't act before the markets opened, the Fed declared the circumstances to be "unusual and exigent"—again—and said on Sunday that it would lend Fannie and Freddie the money if they needed any before Congress acted. Once again, the Fed ended up the first responder; no alternative existed. The government hadn't gone all the way toward explicitly guaranteeing Fannie's and Freddie's debt, but it had—as the officials put it—"hardened the implicit guarantee."

To the consternation of some at the Fed, the Treasury had managed to make it appear to many outsiders that Bear Stearns was a Fed-run operation. This time, even though the Fed and its staff were all over Fannie and Freddie, the rescue was seen as Treasury-led. While this relative anonymity was a relief, the Fed wasn't off the hook. The Paulson legislation assigned the Fed—for the first time—a formal "consultative" role in overseeing the mortgage giants, another broadening of its purview that made some insiders uncomfortable. The more the Fed got involved in these politically charged bailouts, the more it risked its prized independence in setting interest rates in the future to guide the economy without fear of political interference.

Paulson still had to sell Congress on giving him nearly unlimited authority to pump money into the mortgage giants. It was a hard sell. "If you're not used to thinking about these issues, it seems counterintuitive," Paulson told a Senate committee. "But if you're used to thinking about the issues, it is very intuitive.... [I]f you've got a squirt gun in your pocket, you may have to take it out. If you've got a bazooka, and people know you've got it, you may not have to take it out.... By increasing confidence, it will greatly reduce the likelihood it will ever be used."

BERNANKE'S DASHBOARD
August 22, 2008

		Change from August 7, 2007
Dow Jones Industrial Average:	11,628	down 13.9%
Market Cap of Citigroup:	$99.8 billion	down 58.7%
Price of Oil (per barrel):	$119.38	up 64.8%
Unemployment Rate:	5.8%	up 1.10 pp
Fed Funds Interest Rate:	2.0%	down 3.25 pp
Financial Stress Indicator:	0.79 pp	up 0.67 pp

As graphic as it was, the ad-lib was a mistake. The strategy made sense; talking about it didn't. It was as if the Treasury secretary were waving a gun and threatening to shoot, but at the same time promising he didn't expect to use it. When he fired the bazooka a few weeks later, he hurt his credibility with members of Congress who felt misled. *Fortune* magazine labeled the remark one of 2008's 21 Dumbest Moments in Business. Paulson had, again, messed up the theater, the managing of expectations and the appearance of calm, reasoned policies that are essential ingredients at a moment of widespread anxiety and panic.

By the end of July, after intensive lobbying by Paulson, Bernanke, and — this time — the White House, Congress granted the Treasury's request, an extraordinary grant of power to the Treasury secretary that some of Paulson's aides thought he would never be able to convince Congress to give him. Paulson considered passage of the legislation one of his biggest successes, and cited it as evidence that he had built strong relationships with key members of Congress of both parties. But handing Paulson his bazooka didn't solve Fannie's and Freddie's problems immediately. For one, the whole operation seemed to call attention to the fact that Fannie's and Freddie's debt hadn't actually been legally guaranteed by the U.S. government — causing consternation among top political leaders in China and other nations whose underlings had invested money.

From retirement, where he showed no interest in fading into obscurity, Greenspan blasted the operation: "They should have wiped out the shareholders, nationalized the institutions with legislation that they are to be reconstituted — with necessary taxpayer support to make them financially viable — as five or ten individual privately held units," which the government would eventually auction off to private investors, he said.

When Fed officials traipsed off to their annual conference at Jackson Lake Lodge in the Grand Tetons over the weekend of August 23 and 24, the formal presentations were about housing, subprime mortgages, and the dynamics of financial crises. In the second-floor hideaway that had become the Fed's summer war room, Fed officials chewed over options for Fannie Mae and Freddie Mac.

One mystery in August 2008 was why the U.S. economy was doing as well as it was, a fact that gave Bernanke and the rest of the Fed some comfort. "Although it is widely described as the worst financial crisis since World War II, the real economy in the United States is still growing, albeit at a slower rate," Stanley Fischer, the Israeli central banker and Bernanke's thesis adviser, told the conference. He offered three alternative scenarios: Fiscal and monetary policy actions had worked. The obvious financial mistakes of the recent past weren't damaging to the economy. The worst was yet to come.

Bernanke, Kohn, and Warsh returned to Washington from Jackson Hole determined to keep Fischer's pessimistic scenario from coming true. They spent Labor Day weekend at the Treasury building, plotting the government takeover of Fannie and Freddie. Fortunately, this takeover wouldn't have to be executed in a single sleepless night.

On Labor Day afternoon, Bernanke and Paulson finally left the Treasury — Bernanke to see Washington's baseball team, the Nationals, play the Philadelphia Phillies, while Paulson and his wife biked through Washington's forested Rock Creek Park. Paulson, though, couldn't get his mind off Fannie and Freddie. While his wife rode on ahead, Paulson pulled out his omnipresent cell phone and called Bernanke. The two conferred about the unresolved details of the takeover while the home crowd cheered a Nationals' victory. Aware that Lehman and Merrill Lynch were teetering, Paulson wanted to get Fannie Mae and Freddie Mac settled soon. Fannie had raised capital on its own and was in better shape than Freddie, but the Treasury decided it was impossible to treat them differently.

FIRING THE BAZOOKA

In the days that followed, a firm plan emerged. Bernanke and Paulson pressured Fannie and Freddie's regulator, James Lockhart, head of the Federal Housing Finance Agency, to use the powers Congress had just provided. The government would put the companies into "conservatorship" — essentially taking control of them and replacing their chief executives. And Paulson would fire the bazooka: Treasury would promise up to $100 billion in taxpayer money to companies if they needed it. By promising the markets that the government would keep the companies solvent — known on Wall Street as a "keep well" commitment — Paulson and Bernanke hoped investors would keep lending the companies money.

The Treasury and the investment bankers from Morgan Stanley it had hired for advice thought $25 billion was the most Fannie and Freddie could possibly need. But they asked aloud: "What is the investor in China going to say?" The U.S. officials wanted to leave no doubt that the two companies would be strong enough to pay their debts: $50 billion would be impressive, but $100 billion was an overwhelming sum, so that's the number they settled on. (Five months later, the Geithner Treasury would double the offer to $200 billion to shore up confidence in the two companies as their losses mounted.)

The chief executives of Fannie Mae and Freddie Mac—Dan Mudd, a Marine veteran and former General Electric executive, and Dick Syron, an economist and business executive who had been president of the Boston Fed in the 1990s—knew something was up, but they had no idea that the government was plotting a takeover. On Thursday night, September 4, Mudd and Syron were asked to show up separately at the Federal Housing Finance Agency offices the next day. The hope was to keep the meetings secret, but *Wall Street Journal* reporter Damian Paletta had been tipped off and was waiting outside when Mudd and his squad arrived. Paletta then spotted Bernanke arriving. Soon headlines were flashed around the world.

The presentations had been rehearsed. Lockhart and Paulson did most of the talking. Bernanke was there to show that the Fed was behind them. "This is important to the economy," Paulson first told Mudd and then, in a meeting later that afternoon, Syron. "The quality of your capital is not what we would have hoped for," Paulson explained. "Nobody did anything wrong. There's a flawed business model." He gave them a choice: accept the government's conservatorship, or we will use our power to force it down your throats.

The Freddie and Fannie boards of directors met on Saturday, first with the government officials and then without them. Freddie caved first; then—with some hesitation and talk of fighting the government in court—Fannie did the same. This time, Paulson got the all-important theater right. Faced with a determined secretary of the Treasury and chairman of the Federal Reserve, their powers newly bolstered by Congress, the two companies decided there was little point in resisting.

By Monday, the two chief executives had been replaced, and the government was in control. The companies — to the relief of both Bernanke and Paulson — opened for business Monday with only a few hiccups. Freddie's and Fannie's preferred shareholders were wiped out, but the government had protected debt holders. Paulson saw the whole episode as one of his successes and pronounced it to be "nearly perfect."

Bernanke marveled at Paulson's ability to organize the military-style operation. New chief executives were at work on Monday, and human resources consultants were on hand to keep key staff from defecting. "The Fannie/ Freddie thing was a brilliant operation, absolutely necessary," Bernanke said later. "It stabilized an important part of the financial system at a critical time." Yet despite the explicit federal government support for the companies, investors continued to demand higher rates on their debt than on U.S. Treasury debt or government-guaranteed bank debt — pushing up the rates that most American home buyers had to pay on new mortgages.

It soon became clear, too, that the Treasury, the Fed, and the regulator didn't have a well-defined strategy for running the companies. They found new chief executives and a way that they hoped would keep the markets, and the Chinese, lending to the companies. But they hadn't a way to resolve the long-standing tension between operating the companies prudently to make profits and using them as an arm of the government to support the beleaguered housing market. The result was that neither Fannie nor Freddie collapsed and caused a financial catastrophe, but the two huge now government-run companies weren't as effective in rescuing the mortgage and housing markets as had been hoped. Fannie's ex-CEO, and Marine veteran, Dan Mudd later likened the takeover to the U.S. invasion of Iraq. "The troops got to Falluja in a couple of weeks and seized the radio towers, but there was no plan to run the country once the shooting stopped," he said.

Bernanke and Paulson, though, had other things to worry about. Lehman Brothers' Dick Fuld was calling. In less than a week, the Fed chairman and the Treasury secretary, along with the president of the New York Fed, would be unable — or unwilling — to prevent the largest bankruptcy in U.S. history. Fannie and Freddie had been painstaking and exhausting. Now things were about to get really serious.

Chapter 11

BREAKING THE GLASS

Bernanke, Geithner, and Paulson expected collateral damage from the enormous Lehman Brothers bankruptcy, but their preparations didn't come close to anticipating how badly global financial markets would react. They hadn't put nearly enough foam on the runway.

This wasn't for lack of trying. On Sunday, September 14, after it became clear that Lehman would not be salvaged, the other big Wall Street firms were told to open their books to one another at the New York Fed. Firms that had bet one way with Lehman could settle up with firms that had bet the other way, reducing the eventual burden on the bankruptcy court. Some did, but not many.

From Washington, Bernanke called his counterparts in Frankfurt, London, and Tokyo to alert them to Lehman's bankruptcy. That didn't do much to limit the damage, though.

At noon, the Fed board in Washington convened to expand recently created emergency-lending programs to shield other securities firms by expanding the collateral eligible for Fed loans in an effort to keep the tri-party repo market going. The Fed told Wall Street: if you lend to someone and get stuck with the collateral because they can't pay you back, we'll take the paper off your hands. The dealers jumped at the offer: the week before Lehman, none of them were borrowing from the Fed, not even Lehman; a few days after Lehman's demise, both the remains of that firm and others were borrowing nearly $60 billion.

Geithner used the runway-foaming metaphor to explain the strategy for containing the damage from Lehman's now inevitable bankruptcy. Kevin Warsh, the Fed governor, just as aptly explained it: "We hoped a lot of the underbrush was cleared away so that when the fire started there wouldn't be an inferno." Foam or underbrush, it didn't work as well as they had hoped.

Largely unanticipated problems overwhelmed the preparations. The Fed was lending Lehman's U.S. brokerage unit more than $50 billion a day to keep it functioning, but the firm's bankruptcy was messier than anyone had contemplated—and the mess was global. Finance houses all over the world had lent Lehman money and couldn't get it back, or even get clarity if they would ever get repaid.

The havoc in the financial markets didn't leave Bernanke, Geithner, or Paulson much time for contemplation. All three men could see another big plane—AIG—about to crash. Worse, the engines on the two remaining independent investment banks, Morgan Stanley and Paulson's former employer, Goldman Sachs, were now sputtering.

It became apparent to Bernanke that the government was now in the business of forcing instant mergers to save and restructure the American financial system. Bernanke wondered: What is going to solve this? What is going to stop this? As the deal to save Lehman Brothers fell apart, he had an epiphany: "That weekend really hit home to me that this was a fiscal issue."

Paulson came to the same realization. In an early Monday morning telephone call, he told the president that the time to ask Congress for money was approaching. For months, Congress had been on the sidelines saying, in effect: Let the Fed do it. Wink, wink. And we'll just yell at the Fed in public. That day was past.

Next Up: AIG

AIG's chief executive, Robert Willumstad, first alerted Geithner on Thursday, September 11, that the giant insurance company was having trouble borrowing short term. Geithner was stunned. AIG had been on the worry list but wasn't thought to be in imminent danger. With Geithner and Paulson watching closely, the company and its bankers spent the weekend trying to raise money from private equity sources, sovereign wealth firms, and others. Late Sunday, Geithner briefed key members of the New York Fed's board of directors, telling them that—at that point—he couldn't imagine that an insurance company posed such a big risk to the financial system that the Fed should bail it out. Big banks, investment banks, hedge funds, sure, Geithner knew they had placed and taken so many big bets with so many other players in the game that the collapse of any one of them could overturn the table. But an insurance company?

Over the next twenty-four hours or so, Geithner got a crash course in New York State rules for managing the insolvency of an insurance company; in the size and reach of the hedge fund that AIG had built without any regulator realizing what it was doing; in the number of banks, particularly in Europe, to whom AIG had sold insurance against borrowers' defaulting; and in the consumer businesses that would likely suffer runs if the parent company failed. At each turn, options for the giant insurer looked worse.

At the end of the weekend, Paulson returned to Washington, leaving behind ex–Goldman banker Dan Jester to monitor the situation. The markets were having a horrendous day. "I left expecting the markets to be bad, but I didn't really totally understand—none of us did—what 'bad' was," Paulson recalled later. The Dow Jones Industrial Average lost 500 points, or 4.4 percent.

Amid a plunging stock market, AIG gave up trying to raise capital and turned, instead, to trying to borrow $75 billion from a syndicate of banks to keep itself alive long enough to sell off some of its most attractive businesses. The effort was hurt by Monday afternoon's downgrading of AIG's debt by the major rating agencies, which forced the company to post more collateral under the terms of its lending agreement.

On Tuesday morning, AIG and its bankers told Geithner and Paulson's man Jester that there would be no private rescue for AIG. The sums were just too big for Wall Street to manage at a time of such anxiety. JPMorgan Chase and Goldman couldn't raise $50 billion—and even if they could have, that wasn't enough.

AIG's difficulties grew more intense by the hour. With its debt downgraded and its stock price plummeting, the insurance giant's trading partners were refusing to do business with it. Over the weekend, AIG executives had told the Fed and the Treasury it had enough money to make it until Thursday. By Tuesday morning, AIG said they could make it till the next day. By Tuesday afternoon, they were saying they might need $4 billion by the end of the day—and even that proved optimistic.

"I JUST CHANGED MY MIND"

Just as with Bear Stearns, the intense deathwatch on Wall Street inconveniently preceded a scheduled FOMC meeting in Washington. Bernanke and Kohn tried to call the regional bank presidents in advance so they wouldn't arrive in Washington angry that they knew no more than had been in the newspapers. Geithner stayed in New York to tend to AIG, missing the meeting entirely. Around 8 A.M. he dialed into a conference call and told Bernanke, Paulson, and Kevin Warsh that Wall Street wasn't going to rescue AIG. The update made Bernanke uncharacteristically late for the 8:30 A.M. start to the FOMC meeting, akin to a priest showing up late for morning mass.

The FOMC discussion of the economy and interest rates was straightforward and dull. The Fed hadn't cut rates since April and agreed to keep rates unchanged in September, as markets had anticipated. Bernanke briefed his colleagues on the ugliness of the Lehman weekend and explained vaguely about the condition of the next patient in the emergency room: AIG. Warsh chimed in with a few details from the weekend, but they didn't tell the full committee that the Fed was on the verge of swallowing AIG.

The meeting broke up around 12:30 P.M. The plan was for the governors and presidents to grab food from the buffet in the adjacent room, as was the routine, and then bring the food back to the boardroom to hear from Laricke Blanchard, the Fed's congressional lobbyist.

But before lunch began, Geithner telephoned with an urgent plea to Bernanke: convene a meeting of the governors. It was time for the Federal Reserve Board to consider another "unusual and exigent" loan, a move Geithner had considered unimaginable just two days earlier. "I just changed my mind, and I wasn't alone in changing my mind," Geithner later explained.

So Bernanke, Kohn, Warsh, Kroszner, and Betsy Duke — a banker whom Bush had appointed to the Fed board in August — huddled around the coffee table in Bernanke's office so they could hear Geithner on the Polycom speakerphone. Lunch with the rest of the FOMC never happened. Eventually, the bank presidents realized they had been abandoned, and wandered off to cars and airports with little idea of what was going on in Bernanke's office just a few steps away.

The other Fed officials didn't know much about AIG. Geithner described what had caused him to change his mind: the realization that AIG had become more than a big insurance company; it was now a company that had made financial promises on which hundreds of financial firms around the world depended. AIG, he told them, was a sprawling set of profitable insurance businesses trapped beneath a parent company that had become a giant hedge fund that had massive losses. Options for saving the company were limited: recapitalizing AIG in the midst of a financial panic was impossible. Yet in the wake of the messy Lehman bankruptcy, Geithner added, the system couldn't withstand another disorderly disintegration of a major financial institution. Only later did the public learn the specifics of what Geithner already knew: nearly every major financial institution in the world had bought financial insurance of some sort or placed huge bets with AIG. (AIG disclosed in early 2009, for instance, that Société Générale, the big French bank, had $4.1 billion at stake, and Goldman Sachs had nearly $6 billion.)

And unlike Lehman's and Bear Stearns's largely wholesale businesses — trading with other financial institutions — AIG's businesses also touched hundreds of millions of American companies and households. In addition to its foundering hedge fund, AIG sold insurance to more than 100,000 big and small companies, pension plans, and municipalities, and sold insurance or managed retirement plans for thirty million Americans.

In his relentless, disciplined manner, Geithner posed these questions: Was there an alternative to the Fed lending money? Was there some way for the Fed to rally Wall Street to avoid an AIG default? Was the Fed confident it could contain the damage if AIG went under? Was there some way the Fed could buy AIG a few weeks with a short-term loan? To each, Geithner answered: "No."

Warsh pushed back, asking if there was any way to lend AIG money for thirty days, send in SWAT teams of regulators, and find some way out. Geithner accused him of "temporizing," by which he meant avoiding a tough decision to do the uncomfortable but inevitable. Warsh backed off. Bernanke mostly listened, looking more grave than usual.

"LET'S DO THIS ONE"

After Geithner's stark briefing, the Fed began looking for someone else's money. Geithner and Treasury's Dan Jester had kept Paulson in the loop; now the Fed started pressing the Treasury to kick in, especially since putting money into AIG would go far beyond conventional Fed lending to banks. There was talk of tapping the $50 billion in the Treasury's Exchange Stabilization Fund, a war chest created by Congress in 1934 so the Treasury could intervene in foreign exchange markets. The statute gives the secretary and the president the power to use it to "deal in gold, foreign exchange, and other instruments of credit and securities," broad enough for almost anything. But Treasury lawyers said the link between AIG and the dollar was too tenuous. Paulson knew that when Bernanke saw the system at risk, he would find a way to make a loan. Tapping the FDIC insurance fund was floated, even though AIG wasn't a bank that the FDIC had insured. That didn't work either.

BERNANKE'S DASHBOARD
September 15, 2008

		Change from August 7, 2007
Dow Jones Industrial Average:	10,918	down 19.1%
Market Cap of Citigroup:	$83.0 billion	down 65.6%
Price of Oil (per barrel):	$95.71	up 32.1%
Unemployment Rate:	6.2%	up 1.50 pp
Fed Funds Interest Rate:	2.0%	down 3.25 pp
Financial Stress Indicator:	1.06 pp	up 0.84 pp

Soon the question became the same as in the earlier crescendos of the Great Panic: Was there some way the Fed could come up with the money? The answer, eventually, was yes. The Fed general counsel in Washington, Scott Alvarez, and the New York Fed general counsel, Tom Baxter, found a justification for doing with AIG what the Fed hadn't done for Lehman: lend enough to keep it out of bankruptcy. Lehman's only collateral, they reasoned, was the franchise of an investment bank that no one wanted to buy, and that wasn't worth much. AIG had businesses that the Fed believed had substantial value and could be sold; they would be collateral for the Fed loan.

Bernanke and Geithner got Paulson on the phone. All of the alternatives were ugly, but Paulson was no longer shouting about "no taxpayer money."

Bernanke called the question: "Let's do this one."

"We did this very unhappily," Bernanke later remembered. "AIG came to us on the brink of a default. They had not found a private-sector solution, and we were the last, the only chance. The company shouldn't have been saved in terms of its own quality and management, etcetera. But we thought that on top of Lehman, this would be just a complete disaster for the markets and the banking system."

"If there's a single episode in this entire eighteen months that has made me more angry, I can't think of one, than AIG," Bernanke told a congressional committee in March 2009, echoing what he had said inside the Fed each time the price tag of the AIG operation grew — and grow it did. By March 2009, the Fed and the Treasury, which chipped in after it got money from Congress, had $183 billion sunk into the company.

"AIG exploited a huge gap in the regulatory system," Bernanke complained. "There was no oversight of the financial products division. This was a hedge fund, basically, that was attached to a large and stable insurance company, made huge numbers of irresponsible bets, took huge losses. There was no regulatory oversight because there was a gap in the system," he said.

He said the Fed "really had no choice" but to sink billions into the company to try to stabilize it because the failure of what had become such a major financial operation in the midst of a crisis could be "disastrous for the economy." With millions of policyholders and thousands of derivatives and credit-insurance counterparties, Bernanke said AIG's downfall would have been "devastating to the stability of the world financial system." In an obvious reference to those who had criticized the Fed's emergency rescue of Bear Stearns, he added, "If there's been any doubt about the power of financial stress to affect the real economy, I hope that it's been removed at this point."

The unanswered, and perhaps unanswerable, question was whether AIG would have survived without a Fed rescue if Lehman hadn't gone into bankruptcy. The shock waves from Lehman clearly made AIG's problems worse. The bankruptcy gave all its creditors and counterparties good reason to protect themselves in ways that threatened the stability of the financial system. But AIG was in trouble before Lehman's collapse — and the weight of its debts and bad bets was so heavy that it might have gone under even had Lehman been sold to Barclays or rescued by the government.

In part so they wouldn't be seen as soft touches, the Fed and the Treasury decided to offer AIG the same, tough interest rate that AIG's investment bankers had been discussing with Wall Street. There was talk about whether it would be too onerous, and there was a debate: Should the government make a loan to AIG on terms more generous than the commercial market had been discussing? The answer, at least in retrospect, was that the government was not just another investor: it was trying to save the system, not make a profit. The terms of the deal would be relaxed later, when it became clear that the company couldn't survive them.

To move quickly, the government arranged for a law firm that had been working on the deal for AIG's bankers, Davis Polk & Wardwell, to switch teams and represent the Treasury and the Fed. In the end, the Fed offered AIG up to $85 billion at 8.5 percentage points above the rates banks were charging one another, and said the government would take a 79.9 percent interest in the company in exchange. This wasn't a loan; this was a takeover. And it was a take-it-or-leave-it offer.

Geithner was told to give AIG until 8 P.M. to accept or decline the terms. The terms were tough — too tough, AIG and some others argued later. But Bernanke and Paulson had a signal to send: if you have to crawl to the government to recapitalize yourself, it's not going to be on easy terms.

Around 3:15 P.M., Bernanke, Paulson, and Warsh cut off the conference call and rushed to the White House for a previously scheduled meeting of the President's Working Group on Financial Markets—a coordinating committee that the Treasury secretary chaired that was created after the 1987 stock market crash. The markets were so fragile that the White House canceled plans to let reporters and photographers record the beginning of the meeting; it feared a stray comment from the president or someone else would make a bad day worse.

Bernanke and Paulson focused on AIG and the reasons they were trying so hard to keep it from following Lehman into bankruptcy court. They didn't tell the president that they probably were going to need a lot of money from Congress. But White House aides at the meeting noticed a change in tone. The one-company-at-a-time rescue wasn't working. Bush did as he did at almost every stage of the Great Panic: he delegated. "If you are comfortable with this, then I am comfortable with it," he told Bernanke and Paulson.

More than a year into a financial panic that had become the biggest threat to American prosperity in a generation, the president of the United States remained largely a spectator as the Treasury secretary and Fed chairman he had appointed made and executed the plays. One presidential adviser explained that Bush, aware how unpopular he had become, figured he would make Paulson's job tougher if he appeared to be calling the shots. Others said the White House, stumbling through its last few months, was simply exhausted and understaffed.

"THE ONLY PROPOSAL YOU'RE GOING TO GET"

Around 4 P.M. on September 16, the government's three-page offer was delivered to AIG in New York. Robert Willumstad, the former Citigroup executive who had been chairman of the AIG board for a couple of years and became its CEO in June 2008, called a board meeting for 5 P.M.

At 4:50 P.M., Paulson and Geithner called. "This is the only proposal you're going to get," said Geithner, making it clear that there wasn't going to be any bargaining.

"And there's one condition," Geithner added. "We'll replace you as CEO."

At least one AIG director objected. Marty Feldstein, the Harvard economist who had been among Bernanke's rivals for the Fed job, said it wasn't the government's role to forcibly buy private companies. "We are faced with two bad choices," Willumstad told the board. "File for bankruptcy tomorrow morning or take the Fed's deal tonight."

At 7:50 P.M., Willumstad told the Fed that AIG accepted the terms. Fedwire, the Fed-maintained network for moving large sums among banks, was kept open past its usual 6 P.M. closing so AIG could get its cash transfusion. AIG had said that afternoon that it anticipated needing $4 billion; Fed officials were stunned when AIG drew $14 billion that night and another $23 billion over the next few days.

"We're All in This Mess Together"

While the AIG board was meeting in New York, Paulson called Senate majority leader Harry Reid of Nevada and said he and Bernanke wanted to come to the Capitol around 6:30 P.M. The crisis had overwhelmed the call-one-congressman-at-a-time approach.

Bernanke and Paulson entered Reid's office on the second floor of the Capitol, looking like two exhausted surgeons about to deliver grim news to relatives. Most of the senior congressional leadership from both parties had rushed to be there. Senator Judd Gregg, the New Hampshire Republican, showed up in a tuxedo but no tie.

Bernanke and Paulson explained the outlines of the AIG deal and why they had decided that allowing AIG to follow Lehman into bankruptcy was unwise. They emphasized how interconnected everything was. They didn't seek the blessing of the congressional leaders, and none was offered. Instead, Harry Reid told them: We've listened, but don't go out and tell people that we've approved this. This is your responsibility. Both Bernanke and Paulson acknowledged as much.

At one point, Barney Frank recalled, he asked Bernanke: "Do you have

$80 billion?" And Bernanke replied: "Well, we have $800 billion," a reference to the value—then—of the Fed's assets. "And that's when many of us, for the first time, understood the full scope of this ["unusual and exigent circumstances"] statute."

For many members of Congress, the Fed's ability to come up with $85 billion overnight led to the realization that the Fed increasingly was acting like a fourth branch of government. Most politicians, indeed, most American citizens, had a vague idea that the Fed could move some interest rates up or down. But they had no idea that the Fed could—with the push of a button on a computer keyboard—create that much money from nothing and without seeking the approval of Congress or the president.

The meeting lasted nearly an hour. The members of Congress left one at a time, most ducking reporters waiting outside. Representative Spencer Bachus of Alabama, senior Republican on the House Financial Services Committee, offered a promise of unity: "We're all in this mess together."

Frank, the committee's chairman, came out later and growled, with substantial accuracy: "We've had a series of ad hoc interventions. This is one more ad hoc intervention."

Bernanke and Paulson rebuffed reporters. Bernanke went back to his office and called Geithner to settle last-minute details on the AIG deal. Around 10 P.M., after AIG had agreed to the terms, Bernanke convened a conference call to brief the Fed bank presidents, several of whom were disgruntled because they had been told so little even though they were in Washington while the AIG drama unfolded.

Paulson allowed himself a little hope—"not an expectation," he emphasized, just hope—that perhaps the markets would stabilize. "Fannie and Freddie were off the table. Lehman was off the table. Merrill Lynch was off the table," he said. One big West Coast bank was teetering, Washington Mutual, or WaMu. But he already was talking to JPMorgan Chase's chief executive, Jamie Dimon, about that one. "WaMu was about to be off the table. Maybe the situation would get better," he said. He was wrong.

ANAPHYLACTIC SHOCK

As the markets opened Wednesday morning, September 17, Bernanke — with Kohn and Warsh sitting beside him — called his counterparts in Europe, the U.K., and Japan to explain the AIG deal. Jean-Claude Trichet, who had been privately critical of letting Lehman sink, was relieved that the United States had come to its senses and dismissed any suggestion that this had been a tough call for Bernanke.

An hour later, the Four Musketeers assembled by phone to hear the New York Fed's Bill Dudley give his daily report on the markets. It was ugly. The Dow Jones Industrial Average fell 449.36 points, or 4.1 percent, to 10609.66, its lowest close in nearly three years. Trading was so heavy it nearly matched the record — which had been set just two days earlier. European and Asian stocks were down. General Electric, usually considered so creditable that it borrowed close to the Fed funds rate target — then 2 percent — was forced to pay 3.5 percent for overnight money. And yields on the safest securities of all, short-term U.S. Treasury bills, fell nearly to 0 percent because so many investors wanted to park their money there.

"It was becoming clear that the markets were going into anaphylactic shock, and that we needed to do something," Bernanke said. The Fed could no longer cope with the Great Panic by itself.

Based on his years of studying previous financial collapses and telephone conversations with his Swedish and Japanese counterparts who had coped with recent banking crises, Bernanke had suspected for months that he and Paulson would eventually end up asking Congress to spend substantial sums of taxpayer money to rescue the banks. In every major banking crisis he had studied, the government had had to put capital into the banks, take bad loans off the banks' books, and guarantee the banks' debts. So far, Bernanke had deferred to Paulson on the timing of going to Congress, while Paulson had been reluctant to propose anything that Congress might, in an election year, reject.

Bernanke and Geithner saw this as the inevitable and costly politics of responding to banking crises in a democracy. The most effective solution always called for lots of taxpayer money upfront — "overwhelming force," as Geithner called it. Politicians, ever sensitive to public opinion, never responded early enough. The usual political solution was to wait until the crisis was bad enough to dominate the headlines, driving up the ultimate cost. Now, that moment had arrived.

At 7:30 P.M., after a day of nearly constant conference calls, the financial firefighters convened for the last session of the day. Warsh and Kohn sat beside Bernanke in his office, all facing the omnipresent speakerphone. Geithner was on the phone from New York. Paulson was at his desk. More than a dozen Treasury aides stood around him to listen, or huddled in corners in separate conversations.

Bernanke was usually soft-spoken and mild-mannered. He was not this time. "We can't do this anymore, Hank. We have to go to Congress," Bernanke told Paulson, according to one of the participants in the call. The Fed was at its limit.

Paulson was uncharacteristically silent. He didn't argue with Bernanke. He didn't signal agreement. He didn't tell Bernanke that he already had scrambled his staff to prepare to go to Congress. They worked all night.

When asked by CBS's *60 Minutes*, in an interview taped September 26, 2008, to name the worst moment of the Great Panic thus far, Paulson would reply: "I've had a lot of knots in my stomach, but I would say...Wednesday night [September 17], when the capital markets froze, when there started to be a run on money markets, banks stopped lending to each other. And, I know people in America won't understand what that means, but if money doesn't flow freely between financial institutions, then it impacts everyone in the country."

"The economy had a heart attack in that moment," the reporter suggested.

"I would say this: whether it had a heart attack or not, the arteries were clogged," Paulson responded.

Around 9:30 A.M. the following day, September 18, Bernanke, Paulson, and their lieutenants reconvened by telephone. Bernanke launched into his pitch for going to Congress. Paulson cut him off: "We have to go to Congress — today."

It was time to break the glass.

BUSH'S UH-OH MOMENT

When Bush, with an assist from chief of staff (and Goldman alumnus) Josh Bolten, wooed Paulson from the top of Goldman Sachs to the Treasury secretary's office overlooking the White House, Paulson let it be known that he had a deal his two predecessors didn't. The first two Bush Treasury secretaries — Paul O'Neill, a veteran of the Ford White House and a former aluminum company CEO, and John Snow, a former railroad executive — were overshadowed and overruled by the Bush White House staff and the powerful vice president. Paulson, it was said, had the president's assurances that he, not the White House staff and not Dick Cheney, would be in charge.

Though there was much skepticism in Washington about that arrangement at the time, it turned out to be true. When Paulson arrived, the pendulum of power swung all the way from the White House to the Treasury next door. During the Great Panic, he, Bernanke, and Geithner called the shots, keeping the president's White House economic team "informed," as one senior Treasury staffer put it.

Keith Hennessey, a congressional staffer who came to the White House in 2002 and rose to be the coordinator of economic policy there, often fielded Paulson's telephone calls. He typed them into e-mailed memos — "I just got a Hank call," he would write — for the rest of the White House staff. Paulson didn't do e-mail; he did phone calls, frequent ones.

But going to Congress for hundreds of billions of dollars would require more political firepower than either Paulson or Bernanke had. At the same time, Bush aides were growing uneasy with the public perception that the president was a bystander in the biggest economic crisis in a generation. There was no way to keep the White House on the sidelines any longer.

Paulson summoned Joel Kaplan, the deputy White House chief of staff and another of his frequent telephone partners, to Treasury early in the afternoon to listen to the Fed-Treasury-SEC conference call. There wasn't enough time for bringing him up to speed after the meeting.

Around 2:30 P.M., Edward Lazear, chairman of the president's Council of Economic Advisers — a lanky, bald Ph.D. economist from Stanford, nicknamed "Stork" by Bush — left the White House compound to go to the Fed's headquarters to find out what was going on.

The conference call ran until 3:30 P.M., ending abruptly so Paulson and Bernanke — accompanied by Kevin Warsh, on whom the Fed chairman had come to rely for political advice — could go and give the president the bad news: his final months in office were going to look uncomfortably like those of Herbert Hoover.

They made an impression. "I remember sitting in the Roosevelt Room with Hank Paulson and Ben Bernanke and others," Bush would later recall to ABC News's Charles Gibson, "and they said to me that if we don't act boldly, Mr. President, we could be in a depression greater than the Great Depression."

"But," asked Gibson, "was there an 'uh-oh' moment — and I could probably use stronger language than that [laughter] when you thought this really could be bad."

"When you have the secretary of the Treasury and the chairman of the Fed say, if we don't act boldly, we could be in a depression greater than the Great Depression, that's an 'uh-oh' moment," Bush replied. "But you got to understand, leading up to that we had been bailing water in this way: AIG was failing; other big houses on Wall Street needed to be merged; one failed."

In the Roosevelt Room meeting, Paulson reminded Bush that the Treasury secretary's authority to spend or lend money that Congress hadn't appropriated was extremely limited. The Treasury secretary was agitated, talking a lot about the treacherous politics in Congress. At times the president's face suggested he wasn't following Paulson's line of reasoning, one participant recalled. Bernanke, calling on his years of classroom teaching, calmly made the case so the president could better grasp its dimensions.

At one point, according to participants, Paulson made an oblique reference to the possibility that the Fed could continue to finance the rescue of Wall Street if Congress balked. Someone — several participants recalled it was Bush, but others insisted it was Vice President Cheney or Chief of Staff Josh Bolten — pressed Bernanke. Could the Fed keep doing it if Congress was a problem? No, Bernanke said. He recited the limits of the Fed's legal authority even in "unusual and exigent circumstances." He told the president that the sums involved were now so great that the legitimacy of the enterprise required the approval of the entire political system.

With that, Bush gave his assent. The plan was to ask Congress for $500 billion. At the time, that seemed like more than enough.

HUNG OUT TO DRY

On his way back to the Treasury from the White House, Paulson fielded a call from Nancy Pelosi on his cell phone. She proposed a meeting between congressional leaders and Paulson and Bernanke for Friday morning. Paulson said it couldn't wait. So Bernanke, Paulson, and the SEC's Cox went to Capitol Hill that Thursday night. No one from the White House accompanied them. The White House was simply irrelevant.

Before the meeting, according to a person who overheard him, Paulson confided to Bernanke: "They'll kill me up there. I'll be hung out to dry." He knew that many members of Congress, influenced by constituents who saw everything he and Bernanke were doing as a bailout of moneyed interests in Wall Street, would resist his plea to give him the power to spend hundreds of billions of taxpayer money.

Bernanke reassured him: "I'll be with you. I'll go to any meeting. You can count on me." They agreed that Bernanke would talk first.

By taking the lead, Bernanke was attempting to leverage congressional trust in not only the Fed but also his personal credibility in a moment of economic terror. The move would inextricably link Bernanke to Paulson, but there was good reason for Bernanke to permit that: at a time of economic crisis, any hint of daylight between the Treasury secretary and the Fed chairman would undermine whatever confidence was left. Nonetheless, Bernanke was risking both his and the Fed's reputation by sticking so close to the sometimes impolitic Paulson. "Managing Paulson was like riding a bull," one Fed staffer said.

The meeting of the dozen or so top congressional leaders convened in the conference room off Speaker Pelosi's offices. She opened the session, then turned it over to Bernanke. "I spent a lot of time as an academic studying the Depression," he said, according to notes taken by a Hill staffer. "If we don't act in a very huge way, you can expect another Great Depression, and this is going to be worse." The financial system was "only a matter of days" away from "a meltdown," he said. "Our tools are not sufficient."

Fed chairmen, aware that even their private comments can trigger market turmoil, usually speak delicately, especially when predicting bad things for the economy. Bernanke was not delicate. "No economy has ever faced the financial meltdown we're facing without undergoing a major recession," he said. Without congressional action, it would be deep and prolonged.

"I kind of scared them," Bernanke later said. "I kind of scared myself."

Paulson then explained what they wanted from Congress. He outlined a plan to get bad real estate loans off the banks' books — the "break the glass" plan that had been on the shelf at Treasury for months. He talked about auctions where many sellers (the banks) would vie to offer mortgage-linked securities to one buyer (the Treasury), which would turn to private money managers to manage and eventually sell the portfolios. He told the representatives and senators that the Treasury's purchases of such securities could drive up their price and thus help the banks, a notion that would prove a sticking point later on.

A couple of members of Congress asked about using taxpayer money to invest directly in banks instead of buying what came to be called "toxic assets." It was an idea popular with academic experts in finance. And it was one that Bernanke quietly favored. Advocates saw rebuilding banks' capital cushions as a necessary step toward a return to normal lending. The Democrats liked the idea, but for different reasons: they wanted to be sure the taxpayers got some of the upside if they were going to bail out the banks, and they saw ownership as a lever on what banks did. Paulson was discouraging. Bernanke was silent on the point, reluctant to display any disagreement with Paulson.

How much money do you need? Paulson was asked.

"Several hundred billion dollars, for starting off," he said, refusing to be more precise. No one needed to be told that he was talking a lot of money.

Republican leaders Senator Mitch McConnell and Representative John Boehner as well as Pelosi, all stunned by the bad news, were quick to assure Bernanke and Paulson that Congress would give them what they needed.

Nevada's Harry Reid, the Senate majority leader, wasn't so sure. "This is not an easy thing to do. You are coming here to ask taxpayers to spend hundreds of billions of dollars....We're elected. You're not. This needs hearings....I know the Senate. It takes two weeks to pass a bill to flush the toilet."

His Senate colleagues, both Republican and Democrat, abruptly contradicted him. McConnell said, "If what's at stake is saving the country, then we can get it done in record time."

But there were hints of the political difficulties that lay ahead. Senator Richard Shelby of Alabama, senior Republican on the Banking Committee, said, "It sounds like a blank check. When's this going to end?"

Barney Frank and Chris Dodd pushed to include something for beleaguered homeowners whose mortgages exceeded the value of their houses. "You aren't selling this plan to a boardroom. You are selling it to the American people," Frank said, warning Paulson and Bernanke that Congress would impose conditions.

Asked what would happen if it didn't pass, Paulson replied, "If it doesn't pass, then heaven help us all."

The congressional leaders asked Paulson to submit a written plan over the weekend and then — joined by Paulson and Bernanke — faced the television cameras and stoically promised to do *whatever it takes*.

As he drove to the office along Washington's Rock Creek Parkway a few days later, Don Kohn, the Fed vice chairman, thought to himself with relief: as the Treasury stands up, the Fed stands down — a play on a Bush line about Iraq: "As the Iraqis stand up, we will stand down." With financial wars as with real ones, though, timing can be everything.

In hindsight, the U.S. economy would have been much better off had Bernanke and Paulson gone to the president and Congress sooner and won the power and money that they later won. After Bear Stearns, both men had talked publicly about the need for new laws to cope with the imminent collapse of brokerage houses or other financial firms that weren't a conventional bank. But they didn't describe it as an emergency. And from their conversations with Barney Frank and others, they concluded that the odds of Congress acting on any request were very slim.

"Our political calculation was that we had to wait until we got to the point where the case would be palpable and clear — that it would be early enough to do some good, but not so early that it wouldn't be given serious consideration," Bernanke said a few months later in an interview. "Our sense and our intelligence was, there was no hope of getting something like this, given the very short legislative schedule, given the complexity of such a thing, given the lack of appetite for such a thing. So we didn't make a serious attempt to get Congress to pass anything," he explained.

But then, second-guessing himself, he added, "If we had, we wouldn't have gotten it . . . but at least we would have been able to say we tried."

Breaking the Buck

The turmoil in the financial markets during the week of September 15 didn't revolve only around newfangled financial instruments, cross-border sophisticated bets, or the collapse of major financial institutions. In fact, the biggest surprise of Lehman's collapse came from money market funds, the $1-a-share mutual funds that Americans had come to consider as safe as bank accounts. Money market funds had been on the Fed list of things to worry about for months, dating back to the fragility of the tri-party repo market and the Bear Stearns episode. But with so much advance speculation about Lehman's frailties, it didn't occur to Bernanke, Geithner, or Paulson — or any of their staff — that a major money market fund would hold a significant chunk of Lehman's short-term debt. But the Reserve Primary Fund, the oldest of all the money market mutual funds, had 1.2 percent of its $63 billion in Lehman — holdings that would prove devastating and which couldn't wait for Congress to act.

In a classic run, Reserve Primary Fund shareholders tried to withdraw $24.6 billion in the first twenty-four hours after Lehman's bankruptcy, less than half of which the fund actually paid. Shortly after noon on Tuesday, the fund's directors, desperate to avoid having to cut its share price below $1, decided to ask the Fed for help. Bruce Bent II, president of the fund's management company, called Geithner's office and ended up explaining the situation to a secretary who promised to relay the information.

A couple of Fed staffers called back an hour or so later, listened, and said they would pass the request along. "The Fed officials cautioned the participants on the call not to be overly optimistic," the minutes of the Reserve Fund's board record drily. Around 3:45, the Fed said, "No."

At 4:15 P.M., the fund issued a press release. The Lehman paper in its portfolio was worthless and the Fund's shares were worth not $1, but only 97 cents: breaking the buck. The news triggered a run that spread through the $3.4 trillion industry. (Bruce Bent II and his father, Bruce Bent Sr., were later accused of fraud by the SEC, which said they had misled investors, credit rating agencies, and the money market fund's trustees in failing to disclose "key material facts" about the fund's vulnerability when Lehman collapsed, among other transgressions. The elder Bent said in a statement that he remained "confident that we acted in the best interest of our shareholders.")

The run was another manifestation of the U.S. economy's dependence on the shadow banking system — major financial intermediaries other than the banks, regulated by the government and covered by deposit insurance. Money market funds were formed in the 1970s to *avoid* regulation, to allow investors to earn a higher yield than regulations permitted banks to pay. Neither the funds nor federal officials considered them in any way insured by the government. But suddenly the economy was as vulnerable to a run on money market funds as it was to runs on banks.

And it wasn't only ordinary savers who stood to get trampled. Scores of brand-name industrial companies — General Electric, Caterpillar, Dow Chemical — relied on the money market funds for their short-term borrowing, often issuing the funds IOUs called commercial paper that were backed only by the companies' promise to pay. The Fed and the Treasury decided that to avoid a stampede out of money market funds, they had to find a way to assure consumers that the Reserve Primary Fund wouldn't be followed by scores of other money market funds breaking the buck.

At the Fed, Don Kohn took charge of the response while Bernanke went to Capitol Hill and Warsh to New York. At the Treasury, the job fell to David Nason, the assistant secretary for financial institutions. Nason recently had recused himself to look for a job. After AIG imploded, he dropped the job hunt and returned to work.

In the frantic search for a solution, talk bubbled up about the Fed lending directly to the money market funds. It turned out SEC rules forbid the funds from borrowing. There was talk about asking the Federal Deposit Insurance Corporation to insure the money market fund deposits; that went nowhere. There was talk about allowing industrial companies to come directly to the Fed for loans, an idea that resurfaced a few weeks later. The money market fund industry itself was split on the question of government aid. The biggest funds thought they could protect themselves and the $1-a-share value and didn't want to pay for government insurance or invite politicians into their business. The smaller funds were desperate.

Kohn, his office crowded with Fed staffers, worked into the night Thursday to come up with another Fed lending initiative that would get around the inability of the money market funds themselves to borrow. Otherwise, the funds would end up having to dump securities in a falling market. Patrick Parkinson, a veteran economist in the Fed's research unit, came up with the solution. Invoking the "unusual and exigent circumstances" power again, the Fed said it would lend money to banks which, in turn, would use the money to buy commercial paper from money market funds — provided the commercial paper was backed by assets of some sort (often loans or leases) so there was collateral if the issuer of the IOU didn't pay. The Fed, not the bank, would get the collateral and take the hit if the company that issued the IOU didn't pay. Within a week, the Fed had financed $73 billion worth of commercial paper; within two weeks, the demand was so great it was up to $150 billion. Step by step, the Fed was becoming the lender of last resort not only to the banks but also to the entire U.S. economy.

The Treasury, moving for the first time to put its money on the table, said it would stand behind any money market mutual fund that agreed to pay an insurance premium so it could insure customers that it wouldn't break the buck, an extraordinary move by the government. To pay any claims, Paulson turned to the Exchange Stabilization Fund, the kitty Congress had created in 1934. After some back-and-forth between the Treasury and the White House over the legalities, Bush signed an order late Thursday night, September 18, allowing the Treasury to announce the agreement Friday morning and attempt to stem the outflows. In the end, Treasury didn't pay any claims, but Congress later forbid future Treasury secretaries from using the Exchange Stabilization Fund for this purpose.

PAULSON'S PITCH: BLOWING HIS LINES

Despite the April 2008 "break the glass" memo, the Treasury hadn't done much detailed work on exactly what it would ask of Congress if the time came. Work intensified after the AIG loan, once it became clear that a trip to Congress was imminent. The original plan was to ask for $500 billion. But Treasury staff recalled that when Congress had given the Treasury up to $100 billion for Fannie Mae and Freddie Mac, the Treasury thought it was a figure close to infinity, and the markets shrugged and said it wasn't enough. So Paulson and company agreed to up their request to $700 billion. No one thought that could possibly be insufficient. Once again, they were wrong. Every time officials at the Treasury or the Fed thought they finally had gotten ahead of the Great Panic, they turned out to be insufficiently pessimistic. This would be a distinguishing characteristic of this chapter in American economic history: even when officials thought they were planning for the worst-case scenario, they weren't.

When it came to dealing with the White House and Capitol Hill, Bernanke largely left the politics to Paulson—and occasionally to Kevin Warsh. Unlike Greenspan, Bernanke didn't have long-standing relationships with senators like Utah's Bob Bennett or Chris Dodd of Connecticut, ties that were useful at times like these. Bernanke wanted just two things: the Treasury to have some money in its pockets so the Fed could stop being Paulson's piggy bank, and a law to give the government the flexibility to buy shares in the banks—to invest taxpayer money in them. The calculus was simple, though very hard to explain to politicians and the public. Banks set aside a certain amount of capital for every loan—the riskier the loan, the more capital. When banks take big anticipated losses, the capital cushion absorbs the pain. With less capital to support lending or purchases of securities, a bank has only two choices: shrink by lending less and selling securities, or raise more capital so it can lend more and buy securities. The first option can be profitable for a bank and its shareholders, but the economy as a whole greatly prefers the second one.

For his part, Paulson didn't want to speculate about injecting capital into the banks, even though some inside the Treasury did. His reasoning was both political and practical. Politically, a Bush administration proposal to buy bank shares would be seen as socialism by Republicans and a lever to pursue a social agenda by Democrats. Practically, Paulson figured any hint that the government would buy bank shares would scare off any *private* investors — especially after the terms on which the government had forced capital on AIG and Fannie Mae and Freddie Mac.

"I'd watched Fannie and Freddie, and watched us get authority to inject equity," he said in an interview later. "And the first thing the market said was, 'Gee, that's good.' The second thing they said was, 'My gosh, we're not going to buy any equity until we know the terms the government's going to come in with.' So the last thing in the world I wanted to do was to start talking publicly about putting equity in the banks."

Paulson even discouraged internal conversations about buying shares in the banks. At one Sunday session, Treasury and Fed officials gathered in a Treasury conference room to discuss options for dealing with the deterioration of the banking industry. Midlevel Treasury officials had prepared a series of slides, a few of which weighed the pros and cons of injecting capital, but one of Paulson's Goldman Sachs crowd, Ed Forst, told them to skip those slides. "Hank doesn't want to talk about capital injections," he said. With so many people in the room, Paulson reasoned, word that the Treasury was talking about putting capital into the banks would almost surely leak.

Bernanke knew the government eventually would put capital into the banks; that had happened in every significant banking crisis in history. However, he saw no reason to challenge Paulson's public statements and focused instead on making sure that the legislation was flexible enough to permit government purchases of bank stock.

Paulson, though, botched the theater. He, and the reputation of the entire bank rescue initiative, never recovered even though Congress did okay the money. Responding to advice from congressional leaders, who told Paulson to let them write the details, the Treasury offered a bare-bones, three-page draft of the proposed legislation. It sought to give the Treasury secretary the unlimited power to buy "mortgage-related assets" and defined the term "mortgage-related assets" broadly as "any securities, obligations, or other instruments" that are "based on or related to" residential or commercial mortgages. Treasury's general counsel, Bob Hoyt, assured colleagues that the phrase was broad enough to cover buying bank shares. But Paulson wasn't contemplating large-scale purchases of bank shares at that point.

Indeed, Paulson was so determined to avoid hurting bank stock prices or scaring off any outside investors in banks that he left himself no wiggle room in congressional testimony. "There were some that said we should just go and stick capital in the banks, preferred stock," he told the Senate Banking Committee. "And that's what you do when you have failures. You know, that's what happened in Japan. That's what happened in other spots. . . . But we said, the right way to do this is not going around and using guarantees or injecting capital." Two days later, he told the House Financial Services Committee the same thing.

The alternative, he said, was to use the money to buy "toxic assets" — mainly securities linked to mortgages that weren't worth anything near their face value — from the banks. But Paulson had a hard time explaining the strategy. Was the game plan to buy these toxic assets from the banks as cheaply as possible so that the banks, freed of this burden, would find it easier to raise capital privately so they could increase lending? Or was the plan to pay more for the assets than the market said they were currently worth, giving the banks some profits they would use to fatten their capital cushions without going to the hostile markets.

The dilemma was obvious to those who knew anything about banking. "If you end up paying too little . . . you're not giving them the support that they need," Senator Bennett, the Utah Republican who was a senior member of the Senate Banking Committee, told Paulson and Bernanke when they testified on the request. "If you end up paying too much, then there's no upside potential for the taxpayer, when the time comes for you to liquidate these."

"You're right," Paulson told him. "The problem is easier to define than to solve. And we believe that we're going to get the right group of experts, and we're going to come up with a solution, and it will be different with different asset classes and in different situations."

It was a tension that Paulson would never be able to resolve to the satisfaction of either the politicians in Congress or the public. A few months after leaving the Treasury, Paulson reflected on lessons he had learned while on the job. "It's difficult," he said, "to get the politics, the policy, and the market reaction all right at any one point in time. It's virtually impossible to get all three of them right, but if you get any one of them very wrong, then you're not going to succeed."

CRACKED-BLOCK ECONOMICS

In any event, House Republicans were not buying Paulson's argument. To quell the rebellion, Vice President Dick Cheney and the Fed's Kevin Warsh—in his role as the Fed's liaison to Republicans—went to Capitol Hill to try to persuade them on Tuesday morning, September 23, accompanied by Keith Hennessey of the White House staff. Hennessey tried Great Panic 101: "Our entire banking system is dramatically undercapitalized. They bought mortgages and complex securities they didn't understand, and they didn't check to see if the mortgages were any good," he said, according to a copy of his presentation. "While the core of the problem was mortgages... and the purchase of overvalued mortgage-backed securities, the underlying problem is that banks don't have enough capital."

Referring to the post-Lehman fallout, Hennessey said, "The really scary thing is what happened in the second half of last week. Investors had been losing confidence in individual institutions. Investors began to lose confidence in the entire financial industry.

"If Ben Bernanke hadn't dumped tons of liquidity on the market, we would have been in a financial meltdown," he told them. Hennessey had a metaphor ready that he didn't use: it's like losing a quart of oil every mile you drive down the highway. If you don't fix it, the engine block will crack.

BERNANKE'S PITCH: CHANGEUPS AND SOFTBALLS

The night before Bernanke and Paulson were to testify before the Senate Banking Committee, a copy of Bernanke's testimony was provided to congressional committees. That's routine. The leak that followed was less routine. Well before morning, the *New York Times*'s Web site posted a story describing what the Fed chairman was going to say—except that Bernanke had decided to do a changeup.

Shortly before 8 A.M., he showed his staff a handwritten alternative to the remarks they had vetted and distributed. "I'm not going to be talked out of this," he said. His staff was uneasy. Any switch in text was bound to provoke confusion, since copies of his prepared testimony now had been distributed to the press as well. And the argument he was making was hard even for some Fed staffers to follow. Bernanke went ahead anyhow.

To bolster Paulson's case for buying assets, Bernanke turned professorial. "I'd like to ask you for a moment to think of these securities as having two different prices," he said to the committee. "The first of these is the fire-sale price. That's the price a security would fetch today if sold quickly into an illiquid market. The second price is the hold-to-maturity price. That's what the security would be worth eventually, when the income from the security was received over time." One could almost see him writing on the blackboard at Princeton as he spoke.

"If the Treasury bids for and then buys assets at a price close to the hold-to-maturity price, there will be substantial benefits. First, banks will have a basis for valuing those assets and will not have to use fire-sale prices. Their capital will not be unreasonably marked down."

It sounded as if Bernanke was suggesting the Treasury buy the assets from banks at an inflated price to pump up their profits and thus their capital. What he meant, he explained later, was that the presence of the Treasury as a buyer would push up the price of the assets closer to their long-run value. But even sophisticated observers misunderstood him.

At an early-morning Fed staff meeting the next day, September 24, a staffer unfamiliar with the snafu lauded the chairman's comments. "Well, Michelle didn't like it," Bernanke said, referring to Michelle Smith, his chief spokeswoman. "Don't worry," Bernanke said, "I'm going to fix it."

The next morning, Paulson had been asked to meet with the rebellious House Republicans who had been so hostile the day before to Cheney, Warsh, and Hennessey. His staff told him that Bernanke couldn't make it.

Paulson knew he needed Bernanke's calm credibility and pleaded with Bernanke to join him. Bernanke changed his plans and showed up to bolster Paulson. The House Republicans listened but were not persuaded.

After that closed-door meeting, Bernanke appeared before the Joint Economic Committee of Congress and said his previous day's comments "might have been slightly misunderstood."

He tried again: "Many of these assets are now currently being sold only under distressed circumstances to illiquid markets. And that leads to very low pricing, pricing which I refer to as fire-sale pricing. It's that fire-sale pricing and the markdowns that it creates for banks that is one of the sources of why capital is being reduced and why banks are unable to expand credit."

If the Treasury began bidding for these assets, the price would rise above the fire-sale price, he argued. "However, I am not advocating that the government intentionally overpay for these assets. Rather, what I'm saying is that it's possible for the government to buy these assets, to raise prices, to benefit the system, to reduce the complexity, to introduce liquidity and transparency into these markets, and still acquire assets which are not being overpaid for in the sense that under more normal market conditions, and if the economy does well, most all of the value can be recouped by the taxpayer."

That hearing was followed by another, this one in the cavernous chamber of Barney Frank's House Financial Services Committee, where an even more serious weakness of the Bernanke-Paulson road show was exposed: Wall Street was in a panic, and both men knew the rest of the economy would suffer unless the government acted swiftly and forcefully. But the voters hadn't felt the pain yet and concluded that the banks, not the rest of the country, were being bailed out. Sympathetic congressmen served up softball questions so Bernanke and Paulson could use the televised hearing to reach beyond the Beltway.

But Walter Jones, a Republican, read a letter from a $40,000-a-year worker from eastern North Carolina: "These bailouts should be about as welcome as malaria. I've read the Constitution. Nowhere does it say that taxpayers are the default dumping ground for mortgages made to people who cannot afford them."

To which Jones added: "They do not see why we have to be bailing out those people whose greed quite frankly got them into trouble."

Bernanke acknowledged the "communications" issue and tried his best to sway the hearts and minds of the voters: "People are saying, Wall Street, what has that got to do with me? That's the way they're thinking about it. Unfortunately, it has a lot to do with them. It will affect their company. It will affect their job. It will affect their economy. That affects their own lives, affects their ability to borrow and to save and to save for retirement, and so on. So it's really a question of saying, there's a hole in the boat. You did it. Why should I help you? Well, there's a hole in our boat. We need to fix it, and then we need to figure out how to make sure it doesn't happen again."

During a break in that hearing, Bernanke's spokeswoman, Michelle Smith, told him that Bush had scheduled a television address to the nation on the financial crisis for 9 P.M. She knew that Bernanke, a fan of Washington's sorry baseball team, the Nationals, shared season tickets with White House Chief of Staff Josh Bolten and had plans to go to that night's game.

"You can't go to the baseball game," Smith said.

"It's my last game [of the season]," he protested.

"You can't go," she insisted.

"I know," he said, with resignation.

The Nationals lost to the Marlins, 9-4.

The next day, Thursday, September 25, Bernanke again accepted some of Smith's advice.

Presidential candidate Barack Obama had called opponent John McCain about issuing a joint set of principles, hoping that such an extraordinary move would help avoid a meltdown. McCain took the call, countering with a suggestion that the two suspend campaigning. Before Obama got back to him, McCain announced unilaterally that he was leaving the campaign trail and flying to Washington to help break the stalemate. The two candidates ended up at the White House Thursday afternoon with Bush and the bipartisan leadership of Congress.

The event turned into a PR disaster for everyone—a partisan free-for-all that tarnished the reputations of nearly everyone in the room. After the meeting disintegrated, Democrats caucused to consider whether to go before the waiting cameras. Paulson walked in and begged them: "Don't blow this up, please." The Democrats shouted back that his fellow Republicans were the problem. In what became one of the most celebrated — though, alas, unphotographed — moments of Washington's response to the Great Panic, Paulson dropped down to one knee, as if in prayer. "Hank," said Pelosi, "I didn't know you were Catholic."

Wisely, Bernanke wasn't there. He had taken Smith's advice to stay away. And as Paulson went back to Capitol Hill to negotiate what eventually became the $700 billion Troubled Asset Relief Program (TARP), Bernanke stayed away. It was time to leave politics to the politicians.

Chapter 12

"SOCIALISM WITH AMERICAN CHARACTERISTICS"

While Congress bickered, the Four Musketeers were struggling to prevent the American financial system from going under. With no master plan, the Fed—assisted by the Treasury and bank regulators—continued to administer emergency, experimental medicine to failing banks and desperate markets. *Whatever it takes.*

In a little more than a week in mid-September, the nation's banking landscape had been radically transformed: Lehman had collapsed, and Bank of America had bought Merrill, leaving only two big investment banks—Morgan Stanley and Paulson's Goldman Sachs. Then, on September 21, the Sunday following Lehman's bankruptcy, the Fed turned these last two investment banks into bank-holding companies, a power granted by Congress that the Fed had used sparingly in the past. The change in legal status seemed a technicality to most people, and the news was overwhelmed by headlines about the chaos on Capitol Hill. But Morgan Stanley's and Goldman Sachs's makeover gave them the Fed's public promise of protection and a permanent source of lending in a crisis—unlike the supposedly "temporary" lending access they had been granted post–Bear Stearns. In exchange, the companies had to submit to Fed oversight and limits on how much they could borrow. (Before the Great Panic was over, American Express and GMAC, the auto-finance arm of General Motors, also would become bank-holding companies, further extending the Fed's reach.)

The change for Morgan Stanley and Goldman Sachs marked the end of a business model: lucrative, lightly regulated investment banks that borrowed far more heavily than commercial banks and did lots of trading for their own accounts as well as for clients. Now, as bank-holding companies, the firms would become less leveraged, less profitable, and more regulated. For the Fed, the change made official what was already becoming apparent: it was the overseer of all of Wall Street now, a fact that Congress would later be asked to ratify by designating the Fed as the nation's "financial stability regulator."

Morgan Stanley and Goldman Sachs further insulated themselves from the ongoing turmoil by raising additional capital on their own, as Paulson had hoped they would. With assurances from Paulson that the U.S. government wouldn't screw them later, Japan's Mitsubishi UFJ Financial Group proceeded with a previously planned, though renegotiated, $9 billion investment in Morgan Stanley, giving Mitsubishi a 21 percent interest in the venerable firm. Goldman Sachs quickly raised $5 billion in capital from legendary investor Warren Buffett and another $5 billion from others.

Next up was Washington Mutual, known as WaMu, an aggressive Seattle mortgage lender whose roots dated to 1889. In 2003, WaMu's chief executive, Kerry Killinger, famously boasted, "We hope to do to this industry what Wal-Mart did to theirs, Starbucks did to theirs, Costco did to theirs, and Lowe's–Home Depot did to their industry." But the subprime loans that WaMu executives pressed their loan officers to make, it turned out, weren't as profitable as lattes and sixty-roll cartons of toilet paper — particularly when the housing bust arrived.

On September 25, after a spectacular run that saw 9 percent of WaMu's deposits flee in ten days, the federal Office of Thrift Supervision seized the bank and its two thousand branches, and turned the whole sinking mess over to the FDIC. That agency, created in the Depression to cope with bank failures just like this, found a ready buyer for the bulk of WaMu's business: JPMorgan Chase, the savior of Bear Stearns, which had been wooing WaMu for months. It paid $1.9 billion for all WaMu branches, deposits, and loans, and agreed to stand behind its financial contracts — $40 billion less than the lender was worth at the peak of market value in late 2003. Shareholders, however, were wiped out, including private-equity investors who had sunk $7 billion into WaMu shares back in April.

From the outside, the financial rescue looked efficient if somewhat brutal. But inside government, debate erupted over whether to protect the holders of WaMu's debt. With Bear Stearns, the Fed had provided that protection. At Fannie Mae and Freddie Mac, the Treasury had done the same. WaMu, though, fell within the jurisdiction of the FDIC, whose strong-willed chairman, Sheila Bair, vowed this one would be different.

BAIR BAITING

A lawyer from Kansas who got her start in Washington with Senator Bob Dole, Bair worked at the Treasury early in the Bush administration, then took a teaching job at the University of Massachusetts at Amherst. She was called back to Washington — by then–White House aide Kevin Warsh, among others — to take over the FDIC in an only-in-Washington saga.

Bush's initial choice for the top FDIC job, Diana Taylor, a New York state bank regulator and companion of New York mayor Michael Bloomberg, was thought to have been shot down because the National Rifle Association objected to Bloomberg's gun-control stance — an accusation the NRA denies. Whatever the reason, the job was then offered to Bair. Senate Democrats investigating Bair were advised by a former Clinton aide to whisk her through before the administration caught on to her views. In fact, Bair turned out to be a far more assertive regulator than the Bush White House had anticipated.

Early in his term as chairman, Bernanke had courted Bair, once going to her office and sitting next to her at a computer keyboard to fashion a compromise on a prolonged argument over the U.S. government's implementation of an international agreement on bank capital. But during the Great Panic, Bernanke, Paulson, and Geithner found her stubborn and myopic. They grew impatient with her staff, and they envied the political agility that made her a hero on Capitol Hill as an advocate for beleaguered homeowners. Bair was also a fierce and relentless defender of the FDIC fund, putting protection of that bank-funded kitty above all else, frustrating Bernanke, Geithner, and Paulson, who saw preventing the collapse of the American financial system and economy as a greater goal. After all, the Fed was stretching its legal mandate almost daily to save the economy while Bair was arguing legal technicalities and institutional self-interest. More than once, Paulson had met one-on-one with Bair and, with the single-minded focus on the client that had made him a success at Goldman Sachs, had pushed her to alter her position.

At WaMu, neither insured depositors — those with $100,000 or less in the bank — nor the FDIC insurance fund would take a hit. Instead, Bair insisted that holders of WaMu debt would suffer along with WaMu shareholders. She had a good argument for this: the law required FDIC to find the "least-cost" solution to any failing bank in all but extraordinary circumstances. Letting WaMu debt holders feel the pain would save the FDIC money — and ultimately protect taxpayers, since they stand behind the deposit-insurance fund — while reminding investors that they should scrutinize banks before buying their bonds, the sort of "market discipline" that was supposed to keep bank managers from taking foolish risks.

Geithner strongly objected to Bair's reasoning. Yes, he said, investors needed a reminder not to expect a government bailout, but pursuing that objective at a moment of intense financial panic was somewhere between imprudent and dangerous. And there was a way out: a 1991 law said that the least-cost rule could be waived for a "systemically important" institution if the FDIC, Fed, and Treasury, in consultation with the president, agreed.

Geithner first complained directly to Bair, who would not be moved. He then called Don Kohn, who had been mediating between the FDIC and the Office of Thrift Supervision. And he lobbied John Dugan, the comptroller of the currency and regulator of national banks, the ones most vulnerable if the terms of the WaMu deal undermined investor confidence. Geithner was beginning to sound like a shill for the banks. He knew that. But in the midst of the Great Panic, the government couldn't sweat such details.

Bernanke, on the other hand, wasn't as worried as Geithner. He was reluctant to pull the "systemic risk" emergency cord — especially since JPMorgan Chase was willing to take over all of WaMu's operations and stand behind all the bets it had made in financial markets. Ultimately, Geithner and WaMu debt holders lost. The latter group was left waiting to see if any money would fall their way in a bankruptcy proceeding against WaMu's parent, but there wasn't much.

The reaction to whacking the bondholders in the middle of the Great Panic instead of bailing them out was much as Geithner feared. "This is an unprecedented destruction of senior bondholders such that bank bond investors may be thinking to themselves 'why bother?'" analysts at Royal Bank of Scotland screamed. "There is now a precedent set which is taxpayer friendly and 100 percent risk asset hostile" — that is, hostile to private investors who had bought bank stock or debt. The move raised big questions that the Fed, Treasury, and FDIC didn't answer, questions that lingered well into 2009: Which investors in banks are to be protected, and which are not? Who is going to bear the losses — the shareholders? The bondholders? The other bank creditors? The investors and institutions who sold insurance to the creditors in the credit default swaps markets? The taxpayers?

NOT SO GOLDEN WEST

Close behind WaMu was Wachovia, a big North Carolina bank that had gambled — and lost — on the real estate market when it bought Golden West, a California mortgage powerhouse. In July, Wachovia, the nation's fourth-largest bank — more than twice as large as WaMu — had hired Bob Steel from Paulson's Treasury to be its chief executive and rescuer. Steel initially hadn't intended to sell the bank, but in the wake of Lehman's bankruptcy, he found it impossible to raise the capital needed to maintain Wachovia's independence. He shopped the bank to Goldman Sachs and Morgan Stanley without success, and talked with Spain's Santander and San Francisco's Wells Fargo. Meanwhile, Vikram Pandit, Citigroup's CEO, was aggressively pursuing Wachovia as a way to expand the deposits that Citigroup desperately needed. On Wednesday, September 24, Steel stopped playing hard to get and tried to reach Pandit to begin takeover talks; they finally connected by e-mail at 4:27 A.M. on Friday, September 26.

By the end of Friday, it was clear to Wachovia and its regulators that the bank would not be able to open Monday without a new owner or massive federal lending. The reaction to the WaMu deal and the uproar in Congress over the

Paulson-Bernanke bank-rescue plan had hit Wachovia hard. As September began, its stock sat at nearly $17, but by Thursday morning, it was down to $14.57, and at the end of trading on Friday, it had fallen to $8.02. The cost of buying insurance on its debt—known as the credit default swaps—soared. Steel intensified his talks with both Citigroup and, particularly, Wells Fargo.

On Saturday, the twenty-seventh, Dick Kovacevich, chairman of Wells Fargo, told Steel and federal regulators that he was contemplating making an offer for all of Wachovia's shares, an offer that wouldn't require any government assistance—far more generous than anything Citigroup was contemplating. Warsh stayed in touch with Kovacevich from the Fed, while Geithner was handling Citigroup's Pandit from New York.

The next day, on a Sunday-morning conference call that began around 11 A.M., Warsh, Geithner, Richmond Fed president Jeff Lacker (in whose turf Wachovia fell), and federal bank regulators listened to Wells Fargo's offer. It was notably lacking in the generosity of a day earlier. Kovacevich said that his bank might still be willing to buy Wachovia without government aid, but not if he had to move immediately. If the Fed wanted a deal done Sunday, then he wanted an assist from the government. Kovacevich told Steel as much early Sunday evening. By then, the Four Musketeers were trying to find a way to make sure the nation's fourth-largest bank would open for business when the sun rose the next day.

The Fed contemplated but ultimately rejected making an "unusual and exigent" loan. Wachovia was a bank, and the law provided a road map for coping with the collapse of a big bank. The only rub was that it meant dealing with Sheila Bair. They decided to do it anyhow.

Bair wanted to do to Wachovia what she'd done to WaMu—take it over, sell the pieces, and wipe out stockholders and bondholders. After all, any losses that the FDIC had to swallow to rescue Wachovia would have to be assessed across the entire banking system in higher premiums on FDIC deposit insurance. "I don't think that the small banks should have to pay for the sins of the big banks," she said.

Geithner blew up. Wachovia has to open on Monday, he argued. It must be sold this weekend, the buyer needs government assistance, and the debt holders need to be protected. "It has to be this way," he said. "We just went to Congress for $700 billion. The policy of the U.S. government is that there will be no more WaMu's."

Don Kohn, the calm, straight shooter who was the Fed's vice chairman, mediated. Eventually, Bair acquiesced; and the Fed, the Treasury, and the FDIC declared Wachovia to be "systemically important," the first such declaration since Congress legislated the notion in 1991. Wachovia was, after all, the fourth-largest bank in the country, and if that didn't make it systemically important, then what did? The officials agreed to provide "open bank assistance" — subsidizing the takeover of a bank before it formally failed — for the first time since 1992. Bair called Wachovia's Steel to tell him that the FDIC would be auctioning off his company that night.

An on-again, off-again conference call among government officials was convened around 8 P.M. On the line: Bernanke, Kohn, and Warsh at the Fed in Washington; Geithner in New York; Bair in her office a few blocks away from the Fed headquarters; John Dugan, the comptroller of the currency and Wachovia's chief regulator; and David Nason, the assistant secretary for financial institutions at Treasury. The call stretched into the night. Because Wachovia's Steel was his former lieutenant, Paulson stayed away from the deliberations, but he asked to be called when there was a resolution. He kept waking up and wondering why the call hadn't come. Shortly after midnight, Wachovia made a last-ditch attempt to remain independent by offering the FDIC a stake in the bank in exchange for government aid. The bid was rejected.

In the end, Bair had to choose between Citigroup and Wells Fargo — an unhappy choice as far as she was concerned because both offers could drain the insurance fund she protected vigorously. She and the other officials kept talking, breaking off the call for her staff to do more number crunching, and then resuming the conversation.

STOCKING THE FRIDGE

The Fed — unaccustomed to all-night meetings — didn't have a twenty-four-hour cafeteria or an all-night diner nearby. One long, late Sunday of the

Great Panic, Michelle Smith, the Fed's chief spokeswoman, called her hus-band and asked him to pick up sandwiches from a Panera near their house in Virginia and deliver them to the Fed headquarters. Early in September, as the crises continued, the Fed made a deal with a nearby Subway to stock a refrig-erator on the governors' corridor with turkey and ham sandwiches—each with an individual expiration date. The emergency rations came in handy that night.

Finally, the Fed officials conducted a Socratic dialogue—via telephone—with Bair and her staff to speed up the decision.

"Has your staff told you what the [FDIC fund's] expected loss is with Citi?" they asked.

"We think it is zero," said Bair. In other words, the most likely scenario wouldn't require the FDIC to absorb any losses.

And Wells?

"We think it is positive," she answered, meaning the FDIC would have to come up with money eventually. That made the call easier.

Around 4 A.M., Bair finally picked a winner: Citigroup. It would acquire the bulk of Wachovia's assets and cover all the deposits and *all* its debt. Wachovia shareholders would get the leftovers that Citi didn't want. Some $312 billion worth of loans—mainly Wachovia's, but some Citi's—would be put in a pot. Citi would eat the first $42 billion in losses, and the FDIC would be stuck with any losses greater than that. Citigroup executives were elated. Not only did they get a sorely needed source of ordinary deposits, but Citi's balance sheet also would be strengthened by absorbing Wachovia's assets.

"You're Not Going to Believe This"

The Wachovia-Citigroup deal was announced first thing Monday morning. To keep customers—and other banks—from immediately fleeing Wacho-via, the Richmond Fed issued an unusual public vow that it stood "ready to provide liquidity as needed" to Wachovia through the Fed's discount win-dow. But the marriage was not to be. Final negotiations on the terms of the

Citigroup-Wachovia deal dragged on. Steel described them as "extremely complicated and difficult," partly because Citigroup wanted to buy some but not all of the company's operations.

On Tuesday evening, Kevin Warsh, the bankers' go-to guy at the Fed, got a call from Wells Fargo's Kovacevich. "I've got great news," said Kovacevich. "I'd love to buy Wachovia…and without government help." What had changed? For one thing, a long-discussed revision to tax rules governing bank mergers had been announced by the Internal Revenue Service on Tuesday, September 30, making Wachovia a lot more attractive to Wells Fargo.

Warsh walked down the hallway to Bernanke's office, where he found the chairman talking to Kohn. "You're not going to believe this," he said. They summoned Scott Alvarez, the Fed's general counsel, and alerted Geithner. They all agreed they couldn't take the baton back from Bair. It would have to be her call.

Meanwhile, Kovacevich called Treasury with the same message he had given Warsh. Although some of his advisers didn't want to tell Bair, Paulson called to alert her.

At 7:15 P.M. Thursday, Wachovia's CEO Bob Steel was on a plane about to take off from New York for Charlotte when his cell phone rang. It was Sheila Bair.

"Have you heard from Kovacevich?" she asked.

No, Steel said.

Well, you will, she told him. He's going to offer you $7 a share, and you should give it serious consideration. Steel asked Bair to call Wachovia's general counsel, Jane Sherburne, with the details. Seared by Wells Fargo's back-and-forth earlier, she insisted on an agreement signed by Wells Fargo. At 9:04 P.M., Steel got an e-mail with a formal, signed offer. At 11 P.M. the Wachovia board met and, after an hour's discussion, decided to jilt Citigroup and go with Wells Fargo. Bair was thrilled: the FDIC was off the hook. Steel, though facing a lawsuit from Citigroup, was thrilled, too: his shareholders, who would have received next to nothing from the Citigroup deal, were getting $7 a share — and, unlike Citi, Wells Fargo would take the entire company.

The Wachovia–Wells Fargo deal was announced the next day, Friday, at 7 A.M. — only four days after the Wachovia-Citigroup union had been announced. Shortly afterward, the Fed, the FDIC, and other government players convened by conference call—again.

Geithner was ballistic over the about-face. This was bad for Citigroup, a big and troubled bank that was hugely important to the system. Though his detractors saw protecting Citi as his main concern, Geithner argued that the switch to Wells Fargo would destroy the government's credibility in cutting Sunday-night deals to sell failing institutions. "You cannot run a government in a financial crisis like this," said Geithner. "You can't let people rebid every time the world changes."

Bair, though, stuck with Wells Fargo, and other Fed officials were reluctant—having turned Wachovia over to her—to try to take it back. Citi executives were understandably livid. Pandit called Geithner, who got Warsh on the phone; a couple of Pandit's top lieutenants joined the call. Not only had they lost Wachovia, but they also now looked like bank executives who couldn't negotiate an airtight merger agreement.

Nonetheless, Fed officials finally agreed not to try to undo Bair's decision. Instead, Warsh—working the phone from his apartment in New York and later from his office in Washington—spent days trying to get the two would-be buyers to divide the Wachovia business between them. Warsh failed in that, but he did win Citigroup's agreement not to try to block the deal—a development the Fed feared would have been extremely unsettling to markets and bank customers.

CONGRESSIONAL STICKER SHOCK

While Fed officials were sorting out Wachovia, the House of Representatives rejected the Bush administration's bank rescue plan on Monday, September 29, by a vote of 228 to 205. The opposition came from both the right and the left in the House, and reflected a groundswell of outrage from voters who saw Wall Street getting bailed out while homeowners were getting forced out. The looming November election was a factor: of the twenty-one most vulnerable Republicans, eighteen voted against the bill; of the fifteen most vulnerable Democrats, ten voted against it.

The vote was a stunning rebuke of Bernanke and Paulson, who had told everyone that the economy as we knew it would end if Congress rejected the proposal. The markets believed the prediction, even if a majority of Congress didn't. The Dow Jones Industrial Average fell by 778.68 points: a 7 percent drop. In all, the stock market lost $1.2 trillion that day—nearly twice the $700 billion price tag on the bailout bill, which had created the Troubled Asset Relief Program, or TARP.

The next morning, Paulson ran into Michele Davis, his spokeswoman and policy coordinator, in the Treasury building. "I think we're going to have to put equity into the banks," he said. Despite what Paulson had told Congress, buying toxic assets was going to take too long. Davis gave him a blank stare. "We haven't even gotten the bill through Congress," she remembered thinking. "How are we going to explain this?" She told her boss: "We can't say that *now.*" He took the advice.

The Senate passed the bill on Wednesday, October 1, and the House, on a second try, passed it on Friday. At the end of that week, the Dow Jones Industrial Average was down 1,096 points, or nearly 10 percent, since Lehman's demise. It would lose another 1,874 points the following week.

Even after Bear Stearns, Lehman Brothers, AIG, WaMu, Wachovia, the sinking stock market, and all the other raging symptoms of widespread distress, getting the $700 billion rescue bill through Congress was difficult. Bernanke took a small measure of comfort in that. It suggested that Congress wouldn't have acted, even if he and Paulson had made an earlier attempt.

Now Paulson, realizing that taking bad loans off the banks' books would not suffice, told his staff to work with the Fed on a plan to put capital into the banks, the option Bernanke had long favored. "It became increasingly clear"—to everyone, including Paulson—"as the crisis got very severe that we needed something quick, and capital injection was quicker than asset purchases," Bernanke said. The Treasury couldn't buy a large enough quantity of toxic assets quickly enough to have any big impact on the banks. Even after Congress had given Treasury hundreds of billions to spend, the Fed still couldn't escape its role as first responder.

THE FED'S NEW TRICK

Meanwhile, money market funds and other investors were still reluctant to buy commercial paper, or IOUs, from big companies — particularly from financial outfits such as General Electric's GE Capital. Though the Fed and Treasury had stemmed the run on money market funds, commercial paper markets continued to worsen. As the Fed explained: "The volume of outstanding commercial paper has shrunk, interest rates on longer-term commercial paper have increased significantly, and an increasingly high percentage of outstanding paper must now be refinanced each day." This was the sort of liquidity issue the Fed existed to solve, but the problem — once again — wasn't in the Fed's traditional banking territory but in the shadow banking system.

Bernanke and Kohn talked to Paulson about tapping the TARP to provide liquidity to the commercial paper market, particularly the commercial paper that was not backed by any collateral. The Treasury balked. Only a month earlier, the Fed had cited the lack of any collateral in refusing to make a loan to a dying Lehman. Yet it was now looking for a way to make loans to GE Capital and others that were backed only by the corporations' promise to pay. No collateral or asset would protect the Fed if the borrower went bust. (During the Depression, Congress had given the Fed the power to make such unsecured loans, but that law had been repealed in the 1950s.)

This time, the Fed wasn't looking for a legal reason to say no. It wanted to find a way to get to yes. Don Kohn in Washington and Bill Dudley in New York — working with Bill Nelson, a forty-something Yale Ph.D. in the monetary affairs unit, among others — found a solution so clever that even some within the Fed wondered if the "unusual and exigent circumstances" statute had been stretched too far.

The idea, announced October 7, was to borrow a trick from the financial engineers: create a "special purpose vehicle," a custom-made financial entity; require companies that want to borrow to pay a fee up front; and set aside this money to create a cushion to protect the Fed if any company didn't pay the money back. Fed lawyers swallowed hard, essentially relying on Fed economists' arguments that the loan was, as the law required, secured and had very little risk of losing money. The Fed was inventing new tools on the fly. "Aggressive surgery for aggressive cancer" is how Bernanke put it. *Whatever it takes.*

Within a week, the Fed was lending more than $225 billion through what it called the Commercial Paper Funding Facility. By January 2009, borrowing was up to $350 billion. Through the end of May, none of the borrowers had defaulted — and the size of the CPFF was shrinking as this part of the market began to function more normally. But Fed officials quietly acknowledged that the deteriorating economy raised the odds that it would someday take a loss on these loans.

Avoiding "Depression 2.0"

By early October, the Great Panic had gone global. Iceland imploded, unable to carry the weight of the foreign debt that its banks had taken on during the euphoria of the boom. The U.K. government, using a provision of a law passed to fight terrorism, seized Icelandic assets in Britain to guarantee the deposits that British savers had made in Icelandic banks. European governments rushed to rescue their banks. Ireland stunned other countries by unilaterally guaranteeing the previously uninsured deposits of its six largest banks and their debts, pressuring other countries to do the same, lest deposits flee their banks for Ireland. Germany followed a week later. The British government one-upped everybody by putting £50 billion of capital into its banks, winning plaudits for doing what Paulson and Bernanke had not yet done. Stock prices were falling around the world, and the manifestations of stress in credit markets — the gap between yields on government securities and everything else — were worsening. Oil prices were falling, but even that had a troubling aspect: it showed a weakening of demand around the world.

"October was critical," Bernanke said. "We came very close in October to Depression 2.0."

Bernanke saw both a need and an opportunity for a show of force by the world's major central banks. He had been talking regularly by phone with Bank of England governor Mervyn King, his friend from their days at MIT. Until September, the British central bank had been worried that the sinking British pound posed an inflation threat. Since the beginning of the Great Panic in August 2007, the Bank of England had shaved rates by only three-quarters of a percentage point, while the Fed had axed them by 3.25 percentage points. Bernanke argued that a global crisis demanded a global response and suggested that perhaps the Fed could cut rates together with other central banks. King was sympathetic.

The European Central Bank also was ready to cut rates, finally. In July, the ECB had been so preoccupied with inflation that it had actually *raised* interest rates by a quarter percentage point. But now all the schadenfreude about the mess made in America gave way to anxiety about Europe's banks and its economy. At a press conference on Thursday, October 2, ECB president Jean-Claude Trichet had — for the first time — hinted that the Europeans were prepared to reverse field. He reinforced that message in a phone conversation the following Monday with Bernanke. The Fed chairman, in turn, signaled the depth of his concern in a speech later that afternoon to the National Association for Business Economics: "Severe financial instability, together with the associated declines in asset prices and disruptions in credit markets, can take a heavy toll on the broader economy if left unchecked."

BERNANKE'S DASHBOARD
October 3, 2008

		Change from August 7, 2007
Dow Jones Industrial Average:	10,325	down 23.5%
Market Cap of Citigroup:	$99.9 billion	down 58.7%
Price of Oil (per barrel):	$93.89	up 29.6%
Unemployment Rate:	6.2%	up 1.5 pp
Fed Funds Interest Rate:	2.0%	down 3.25 pp
Financial Stress Indicator:	2.88 pp	up 2.76 pp

As the British and European central bankers mulled Bernanke's suggestion of a unified show of force, he got a call from Mark Carney, the Canadian central banker, who was definitely interested. Economies and financial markets were far worse than the central bankers had anticipated. Financial markets were, reasonably, anticipating more rate cuts. Moving in unison, Bernanke argued, could bring economic benefits greater than moving separately. It was an act of global theater, to be sure, but the very act of coordination—which had been sorely lacking in the Great Panic until then—could bolster consumer and business confidence, he figured.

After a series of one-on-one phone chats with other central bankers, Bernanke sensed something close to a consensus emerging. With that, he proposed a conference call early Tuesday morning, Washington time, to include himself, Britain's King, Europe's Trichet, and Canada's Carney. Japan's central banker was invited to listen in, even though rates there were already so low he couldn't join the rate cutting. Everyone agreed on a one-half percentage point cut and on the wording of a 141-word statement that each would issue. The central bankers then turned to the formality of getting the consent of their separate committees. To fulfill his end of the bargain, Bernanke convened the FOMC by videoconference around 5:30 P.M., and they voted to drop the federal funds rate target to 1.5 percent.

At 7 A.M. Washington time the next day, October 8, the central banks Bernanke had convened, plus the Swiss and the Swedes, simultaneously announced the cut in rates and released the negotiated statement. Although heavy on the anti-inflation rhetoric favored by central bankers, particularly Europeans, the main message was that the "recent intensification of the financial crisis" was increasing the risks of recession and decreasing the risks that inflation would take off.

The markets didn't cheer this time. The Dow Jones Industrial Average lost another 189 points, or 2 percent, to close 9258.10—down 14.6 percent in six days, while investors continued to move massive sums of money to supersafe U.S. Treasury bills, and away from riskier debt securities. "It obviously didn't calm the markets," Bernanke said with resignation a week later. "The markets were still very stressed about the view that the financial system had a significant chance of collapsing. What it told me was that monetary policy wasn't the only tool. Credit market conditions were so frozen and stress on banks and some specific institutions so intense. And monetary policy works with a lag."

BEN, SHEILA, AND THE GUARANTEE

The economy and the markets couldn't wait. Though the number of untried items on Bernanke's "blue sky" list was getting shorter, a few novelties remained. Hours after the internationally coordinated rate cut was announced, Paulson's office summoned Sheila Bair of the FDIC to meet with him and Bernanke. He refused to tell her the subject of the meeting and told her not to bring any staff. Bernanke and Paulson were determined to persuade her to take an extraordinary step: to declare that the banking system was at risk—the whole thing, not a particular institution—and to offer an FDIC guarantee not just of deposits, but also of all new borrowing that banks did on financial markets. Even though TV cameras weren't showing depositors lining up outside bank doors, money was fleeing the vaults. The government had to stop the run to save the system, Bernanke said. This would be the ultimate repudiation of the WaMu deal: now, the government would guarantee that investors who lent money to banks would be paid back.

A government guarantee is just as much a taxpayer subsidy to banks and the investors who lend to them as low-cost government loans. Heads, private investors win; tails, taxpayers lose. A blanket guarantee was an extraordinary move, but Bernanke and Paulson saw an extraordinary threat—the possibility of a run on the entire American banking system. They proposed that she join them in an extraordinary declaration: "In light of current conditions, the FDIC, with the full support of the Fed and the Treasury will use its authority and resources to protect depositors, protect unsecured claims, guarantee liabilities and adopt other measures to support the banking system."

Bair balked. The FDIC traditionally rescued banks one at a time, not en masse. Guaranteeing all the existing debt of the banking system would be a windfall for bondholders. And the FDIC had little information about the parent companies and affiliates of banks that it was being asked to back. Unlike the Fed it couldn't print money and unlike the Treasury it couldn't borrow vast sums cheaply; except in extremis, the FDIC is funded by premiums paid by the banking industry. Confidence in the banking system would not be helped if the FDIC insurance fund was depleted, she said. Bernanke and Paulson pushed hard. A day or two later, she came back with a memo outlining what the FDIC was prepared to do. It would offer ten-year guarantees—but only for 90 percent, not 100 percent of the money that an investor had put in. And it would guarantee debt of the banks—the units that took deposits—but not of their parent companies. Bernanke and Paulson rejected both conditions, and Bernanke offered an opinion by the Fed's lawyers to support the broader approach.

In the end, Bair acquiesced. The FDIC, for a fee, agreed to guarantee promissory notes, commercial paper, bank-to-bank loans, and other unsecured lending for up to three years—but only for newly issued debt. In return, she won a few concessions: FDIC deposit insurance would cover all checking accounts, even if they had more than $250,000 in them, which was important to nonprofits and municipalities and helped small and midsized banks withstand the runs they were facing as money moved to big banks now widely perceived as too big to fail. Still, Bair did not sound happy. "Why there's been such a political focus on making sure we're not unduly helping borrowers but then we're providing all this massive assistance at the institutional level, I don't understand it," she said a few days later. "It's been a frustration for me." Bernanke, though often impatient with Bair, agreed on the wisdom of a more muscular government effort to avoid foreclosures. But that would have to wait until the Obama administration was in power.

THE G7 SINGS BEN'S SONG

Press accounts tend to paint meetings of finance ministers and central bankers from the Group of Seven — the United States, Britain, France, Germany, Canada, Italy, and Japan — as suspenseful and decisive affairs, akin to a conclave of cardinals selecting a new pope. In reality, G7 gatherings are mostly ritualized recitations of positions already expressed publicly. Four or five hours of predictable statements read by officials are typically followed by a communiqué — negotiated in advance by designated staffers — touching on fourteen points, ranging from a vow to promote economic stability to a promise to crack down on money laundering.

Not this time, though, with all the world watching. For the first time in the Great Panic, national governments were making self-protective moves that threatened to make their neighbors worse off, the sort of bad behavior that worsened the Great Depression. The Irish government's unilateral guarantee of all bank deposits — and the way other European nations had scrambled to catch up — was an early foreshadowing of what could be even worse troubles to come. European prime ministers had met in Europe the Sunday before the G7 finance ministers gathered in Washington, but were unable to agree on anything. The British had announced plans to do what Paulson had been working on privately with Bernanke but was resisting publicly: using taxpayer money to buy stakes in banks.

The October 10 G7 meeting preceded by a day, as it always does in the fall, the annual meetings of the International Monetary Fund and the World Bank. Scores of other finance ministers and central bankers would be in Washington, D.C., raising the visibility of the G7 meeting, which sets the agenda and tone for the assemblies that follow — and also raising the risk of an anti-American backlash prompted by the bankruptcy of Lehman.

With such prospects in mind, Bernanke concluded that a conventional G7 communiqué would do little to reassure anyone that the leaders of the global economy had a game plan for avoiding another Depression. Early Thursday morning, he spent about half an hour typing up principles that he thought the G7 should embrace.

Labeled "very preliminary," Bernanke's nine points amounted to an outline of his "whatever it takes" strategy. Among other things, he proposed that all G7 countries:

- "ensure that domestic and other major financial intermediaries have access to capital from public as well as private sources"
- "restart and reliquefy the secondary markets for mortgages and other assets"

- take "all efforts to prevent the failure of any systemically important financial institutions" and, when failures were "unavoidable," to protect "all creditors and counterparties, both secured and unsecured," an explicit vow not to repeat Lehman Brothers or WaMu

- "unfreeze the interbank market, the commercial paper market, and other money markets" with "guarantees, backstop facilities to purchase short-term paper or other methods"

Bernanke showed his draft to Paulson when the two met for a previously scheduled breakfast on Thursday morning at the Fed. Paulson, who found G7 meetings tedious and unproductive, generally used the term "G7" as an epithet, but he told Bernanke that he liked these suggestions and took the draft Bernanke gave him back to Treasury. Later that day, Nathan Sheets, the Fed's top international hand and another of its army of MIT Ph.D.'s, checked in with his Treasury counterpart, David McCormick, a West Point grad, Princeton Ph.D., and veteran of the first Gulf War, and Mark Sobel, a veteran civil servant on the Treasury's international staff.

By the end of the day Thursday, McCormick and his counterparts from the other six countries had negotiated a communiqué to which a modified annex of Bernanke's points was attached. The G7 convened the next day, Friday, at 2 P.M. in the Treasury's gilded Cash Room, where the U.S. Treasury once had conducted banking business with the public. Bernanke sat to Paulson's right, McCormick to his left. Flags of the participating countries stood behind them.

The German finance minister delivered the usual German "I told you so" speech, warning this crisis would change capitalism forever. But much of the discussion was pragmatic and unscripted. There was consensus the public statement should be terse, direct, and convincing. Countries differed more on *when* rather than *whether* they would take the actions anticipated.

At one point, McCormick leaned to his left and whispered to Mervyn King, governor of the Bank of England, that the best outcome might be a simple half-page communiqué. McCormick, who had been drafting talking points for Paulson and the other ministers to use after the meeting, passed a note to Paulson with a similar suggestion. Paulson scribbled back: "I like it." McCormick took a draft based on his talking points and the Bernanke-inspired annex and circulated it to other deputies. Each conferred with his boss as the meeting progressed, and the ministers blessed the idea. During a break, the deputies tinkered with the wording.

The final 266-word communiqué incorporated nearly all of Bernanke's points and some of his wording, albeit with less specificity. A few things were dropped. There was, for instance, no hint of guaranteeing interbank lending, because Trichet was resistant. The proposed pledge to protect all creditors and counterparties if a systemically important institution failed — the "no more WaMu's" promise — was dropped in favor of a promise to "prevent their failure." Bernanke hadn't taken control from Paulson, but he had helped Paulson get the all-important theater right.

FORCE-FEEDING CAPITAL

Paulson now started dropping hints in public that the Treasury wasn't going to use the $700 billion just to buy toxic assets from the banks, but was contemplating buying shares directly in the banks, as Bernanke and some of Paulson's staff had favored. At a press conference following the G7 meeting, Paulson made it explicit: like the British, the U.S. government would invest taxpayer money to strengthen U.S. banks' capital footing. The few details offered portrayed the program in as promarket terms as possible. The U.S. government would avoid taking a voting stake in the banks and would design its program "to encourage the raising of new private capital to complement public capital."

Paulson struggled to explain the about-face, telling the *Washington Post* a few days later: "The facts as I know them changed. We got a bigger impact per taxpayer dollar with the equity injection so we went that route.... The philosophy has stayed the same, but the tools we employed changed."

In fact, few details had been settled. Despite the conversations about using taxpayer money to buy stakes in banks to "recapitalize" them, the overworked Treasury staff had been spending nearly all its time on structuring the complicated auctions to buy toxic assets. On Thursday, October 9, Geithner called Paulson to nudge him to move faster on the details of the capital injection initiative. Treasury decided against hiring an investment bank for help; the conflicts of interest would have been unmanageable, since all the big ones would be on the receiving end of the government's money. Instead, on Friday, October 10, the Treasury signed a $300,000 contract with the law firm of Simpson Thacher to handle the legal work.

On Saturday, October 11, Bernanke, Geithner, and Kohn moved into the Treasury building, working through the weekend with Treasury officials. As Paulson had hinted a few days earlier, the hope was to use government money as a lever to get the banks to raise capital privately, a sort of matching program. However, it soon became clear that banks were going to have a very hard time selling their stock in what was already a depressed market.

"Everyone said: you know, that just will not work. The private market for bank stock is essentially closed for business," said David Nason, the Treasury official. "You're going to force a lot of people to try to sell common stock at the same time. There are a limited amount of people who want to participate in that. The weak are not going to get it, and the strong might disappoint as well."

The participants also faced the very tough decision of how to price the dividend rate on the preferred stock the banks would issue the government: it should be low enough to be attractive to banks, yet high enough to avoid sparking populist taxpayer outrage. "The pricing was the hardest thing," said Nason. "You've got two competing concerns: you've got the protection of the taxpayer, and you want people to participate. It can't be too expensive because you want everybody to take it."

The eventual terms were intentionally generous. The plan depended on luring even firms that didn't really need the capital — JPMorgan Chase and Goldman Sachs, for instance — to take the money so that no bank would be stigmatized. The tough approach to AIG, Fannie and Freddie, and WaMu was gone, but the second-guessing wasn't. The Bernanke-Paulson-Geithner approach would later be criticized for allowing banks to continue to pay dividends to common shareholders, for not demanding enough commitment from the banks to increase lending, for not restraining executive compensation more, and for not husbanding scarce taxpayer money needed by weak banks by giving so much of it to stronger banks.

"I Suggest You Come"

The next day, Sunday, October 12, Paulson called the heads of the nation's nine largest banks and "invited" each to appear at Treasury at 3 P.M. the next day, the Columbus Day holiday. The Treasury secretary refused to reveal the agenda, setting off a flurry of calls from the invitees to their Washington lobbyists who, in turn, begged contacts at Treasury for clues. Citigroup's Vikram Pandit said he had other things to do and would send someone else if this was just an update on the markets and a photo op. Merrill's John Thain said he had a previous conflict. Wells Fargo's Dick Kovacevich said he wasn't coming. Paulson told him: Dick, the secretary of the Treasury and the chairman of the Fed have asked you to come to a meeting; I suggest you come. In the end, they all showed up.

Meanwhile, Bernanke, Paulson, and Geithner — along with Sheila Bair of the FDIC; Bob Hoyt, the Treasury's general counsel; and David Nason, the assistant secretary — met a couple of times in Paulson's corner office to rehearse their lines for what they all knew would be a historic meeting.

Monday found the bankers seated on one side of a long, polished, dark wood table, arranged alphabetically by the name of their bank. That conveniently put the antagonists in the continuing Wachovia dispute — Pandit of Citi and Kovacevich of Wells — at opposite ends of the table. Paulson, Bernanke, Geithner, and other government officials sat on the other side. Paulson went first, facing men who had once been his peers. His tone conveyed the message: This isn't a take-it-or-leave-it offer. This is a take-it offer. Bernanke talked about the Fed's plans to buy commercial paper. Bair outlined the new guarantee of bank debts and fielded questions. Geithner then detailed the terms of the government's capital injections and how much money each bank was being asked, or told, to take.

The banks would have to pay a 5 percent dividend on the preferred shares they would issue to the government. To encourage banks to find private investors to take the government's place, the dividend the banks had to pay to the Treasury climbed to 9 percent after five years. Banks could keep paying dividends to their common stockholders but couldn't raise them (a provision later changed by the Obama administration). The government would get warrants — the right to buy common stock at then depressed prices so taxpayers would benefit if the banks recovered.

The terms were generous. This was deliberate. Paulson, Bernanke, and Geithner had decided to give capital to all the big banks, the healthy and the weak, to avoid "stigmatizing" the weak ones. "The terms had to be attractive, not punitive," Phillip Swagel, the Treasury's economist, argued. Emphasizing the absence of any legal authority to force banks to take government capital, and minimizing the ability that Paulson and Bernanke had to make banks do things they didn't legally have to do, Swagel said, "In a sense, this had to be the opposite of *The Sopranos* — not a threat to intimidate banks but instead a deal so attractive that banks would be unwise to refuse it."

Only after Geithner finished speaking did David Nason walk around the table and distribute pieces of paper with the terms of the deal and a place for each CEO to sign. "The theory," one of the officials put it later, "was get them warmed up before they see the term sheet. It's like with third graders. If you leave the paper on their desks they don't listen to the teacher; they look at the paper. The same rule applies to fifty-five-year-old billionaires."

The numbers were huge: $25 billion each for Citi, JPMorgan Chase, and Wells Fargo; $15 billion for Bank of America; $10 billion each for Merrill Lynch, Goldman Sachs, and Morgan Stanley; $3 billion for Bank of New York Mellon; $2 billion for State Street Corporation.

Wells's Kovacevich was the most animated. His bank already had announced plans to raise $25 billion in new capital. Was this in addition to that?

Yes, Geithner told him.

That's more capital than Wells has ever gotten, Kovacevich protested.

Dick, you have no idea what the market's going to look like in a year, Geithner responded.

Neither do you, Kovacevich shot back.

Paulson told him he could accept the government's money or risk going without. But if the bank needed capital later and couldn't raise it privately, the government offer wouldn't be as generous as this one.

Citigroup's Pandit looked relieved. "This is very cheap capital," he exclaimed. "I just did the numbers on the back of the envelope, and this is very inexpensive capital." It wasn't clear, though, what numbers he was actually doing, since there wasn't much to calculate. Citi was, by far, the weakest of the big banks in the room — and it was getting taxpayer capital on the same terms as the stronger banks.

Merrill Lynch's Thain asked how taking this money would affect government controls on executive compensation. Someone wanted to know if a bank could take the FDIC guarantee but not the capital. "No way" was the reply. A few of the bankers — the heads of Wells Fargo, Bank of New York Mellon, and Citigroup — began peppering the officials about the restrictions on raising dividends to common shareholders.

Bernanke intervened. "I don't really understand why this needs to be confrontational," he said, his preternatural calm a contrast to Paulson's constant agitation. The paralysis in financial markets was doing great harm to the banks represented in the room. This is in your interest, he told them. This is in the interest of the financial markets. This is in the interest of the economy. This is in the interest of the government.

Morgan Stanley's John Mack was the first to start to sign the paper when one of his fellow CEOs interjected: Don't you have to go to your board?

JPMorgan Chase's Jamie Dimon said he didn't need the capital, but joked if he was in for $25 billion, he was in for $50 billion. Once he had to accept the intervention of the government in his business, the more money the better. Goldman's Lloyd Blankfein said much the same thing. Finally, Bank of America's Ken Lewis ended the banter. "Why are we debating this? We're all going to do this. Let's just get it done," he said, according to participants. "Any one of us who doesn't have a healthy fear of the unknown isn't paying attention."

The meeting broke up after an hour or so with a plan to reconvene at 6:30 P.M. Each CEO retreated to an office assigned to him at the Treasury or to a corporate or law firm office not far away. Regulators wandered from office to office, fielding questions in person or by phone. Before 6:30 P.M., each of the CEOs had signed. The meeting never reconvened.

Even putting $125 billion of taxpayer money into the nine big banks wouldn't suffice, it turned out. Citigroup would be back for more in November — another $20 billion in capital from TARP and a deal with the Treasury, FDIC, and Fed to limit its losses on a $306 billion pool of loans and securities — and still more in February 2009; in June 2009 it would be the one big bank about which officials were most worried. Bank of America would be back for more, too. And the Fed deal with AIG would be redone, redone again, and redone again. Kevin Warsh dubbed them "the proper nouns," the institutions that would pose problems for months to come.

But there was no doubt that on Columbus Day 2008, a Treasury secretary and a Fed chairman appointed by a Republican, self-described conservative president had been forced to cross a line that would have seemed impenetrable a year earlier. The government of the United States, champion of free markets and victor of the cold war, was buying stakes in the banks.

Gao Xiqing, the president of China Investment Corporation, saw the irony. His company manages about $200 billion of Chinese foreign assets, including most of the high-visibility investments such as stakes in private-equity firm Blackstone and investment banker Morgan Stanley. In an interview with James Fallows of *The Atlantic*, Gao said, "Finally, after months and months of struggling with your own ideology, with your own pride, your self-righteousness... finally [the U.S. applied] one of the great gifts of Americans, which is that you're pragmatic."

Alluding to Chinese leaders' description of their tentative embrace of markets as "socialism with Chinese characteristics," Gao said, "Now our people are joking that we look at the U.S. and see 'socialism with American characteristics.'"

Chapter 13

WORLD OF ZIRP

As Fed officials prepared for mid-December's FOMC meeting, none doubted how weak the economy was. Surveys of businesses conducted by the twelve regional Fed banks were unambiguously gloomy: "Overall economic activity weakened across all Federal Reserve districts," the summary said. Tourism spending was "subdued." Factory orders were "soft." The job market was "weakening." Retail and auto dealer sales were down. Prices of energy and food were falling; the pace of other price increases was slowing.

The Green Book—an internal Fed forecast named for the color of its cover—expanded on this darkening outlook. The economy in the fourth quarter was even worse than anticipated just a few weeks earlier. The outlook for 2009 was poor, too. Unemployment, then at 6.8 percent, would rise through 2009, climbing higher than previously predicted. Inflation was a waning worry, but a "moderate recovery" would not arrive until 2010, more than a year away. With such a bleak outlook, President-elect Obama, with Bernanke's strong encouragement, was preparing a huge package of spending increases and tax cuts to stimulate the economy.

BERNANKE'S DASHBOARD
December 11, 2008

		Change from August 7, 2007
Dow Jones Industrial Average:	8,824	down 34.7%
Market Cap of Citigroup:	$44.8 billion	down 81.5%
Price of Oil (per barrel):	$43.60	down 39.8%
Unemployment Rate:	6.8%	up 2.1 pp
Fed Funds Interest Rate:	0% to 0.25%	down 5 to 5.25 pp
Financial Stress Indicator:	1.69 pp	up 1.57 pp

The markets provided no relief: a situation that was unsettled at best had received another blow from Paulson's bumbled communications. A week after the presidential election, Paulson delivered a speech to a few dozen reporters and a half dozen television cameras in the Treasury's fourth-floor "media room." Swigging from a bottle of Dasani water while on live television, Paulson once again screwed up the theater. He made explicit that he was abandoning the very strategy he had used to sell Congress on approving his request for $700 billion: The Treasury wouldn't be buying toxic mortgage assets from the banks because that was no longer "the most effective way" to use the money. That had become obvious to many in the press and the markets, but Paulson feared the mortgage markets were frozen as investors and traders waited for the Treasury to show up with lots of money. Instead, he said, the Treasury planned to use nearly all the money to shore up the capital foundation of the nation's banks and to try to get consumer lending going again. Paulson didn't add that the volume of toxic assets on the banks' books had, in fact, grown so large that $700 billion was no longer enough to buy them all, even at currently depressed prices.

But it wasn't the *substance* of the decision that hurt; there were, after all, arguments for and against buying assets. As Paulson put it later, there was virtue in being "pragmatic enough to change plans when facts and conditions change." Instead the speech was another one in a series of Paulson's abrupt changes in course. This appearance of inconsistency destroyed any lingering credibility Paulson had. The final impression he would leave is of the balding former college football player lurching from one approach to another without a game plan.

With all this dismal economic news on their minds as they gathered around the Fed's board table on December 15 and 16, officials didn't spend much time debating the wisdom of cutting the Fed's target for its key short-term interest rate. This, in itself, was unusual. For decades, each FOMC meeting had one overarching — and sometimes divisive — objective: to decide whether and how much to move interest rates up or down. What's more, since the end of October, the rate had already been sitting at 1 percent, as low as Greenspan had taken it in his nearly nineteen years as Fed chairman. But sixteen months into the Great Panic, everyone in the Fed boardroom realized Greenspan had never faced a downturn this severe.

These historic circumstances made for an unconventional FOMC meeting: longtime roles were reversed, and discussion ranged into previously unexplored territory. Neither the high stakes nor the relatively easy agreement over interest rates signaled a broader harmony within the group; rather, interest rates became a sideshow as arguments roared on about nearly everything else. Before the meeting had even begun, an internal debate erupted over whether the Fed was actually making the financial crisis worse. Many Fed officials argued that, while imperfect, the Fed's interventions had arrested the economy's free fall. But several regional bank presidents insisted that the Fed's inconsistent stance on bank rescues was further destabilizing the economy. Other tensions of the previous eighteen months — the simmering disagreements about the fundamental nature of the Great Panic and the resentment of flyover-state Fed bank presidents toward the power of Washington and New York — boiled over behind closed doors.

CALMING THE STORM

Perhaps fortuitously, one antagonist was missing: Tim Geithner, who had become a target for the dissenting bank presidents. The Four Musketeers now numbered three. Geithner had been plucked from the New York Fed job (2008 salary: $411,200) to be Obama's Treasury secretary (salary: $191,300).

In a face-to-face meeting with Obama in Chicago, Geithner won over the president-elect in characteristic Geithner fashion: he gave the president-elect a list of reasons why he should *not* be chosen. Among them was the obvious fact that he was inextricably intertwined with the politically unpopular Paulson-Bernanke approach to banks and hardly represented the change Obama had promised.

Geithner recommended Larry Summers for the job. Obama instead installed Summers in the White House as chief economic policy coordinator and nominated Geithner to succeed Paulson at Treasury. After a contentious public dissection of his failure to pay all the taxes he owed while working at the IMF, Geithner was confirmed by the Senate, 60–34. Bernanke, for his part, was pleased by Obama's choice: he trusted Geithner and knew they could work well together. He also welcomed the prospect of an administration prepared to be more aggressive and to spend more money to fight the Great Panic. Fiscal policy — spending taxpayer money — was increasingly important because the Fed was entering territory that it had only ruminated about in the Greenspan era: zero interest rate policy, or ZIRP in Fedspeak.

Bernanke knew that Geithner's absence alone wouldn't ensure peace among the various FOMC factions. For weeks, he had been laboring to make the twelve regional Fed presidents feel more involved in decision making. One-at-a-time phone calls from Bernanke and Kohn clearly couldn't keep up with the pace of developments, so Bernanke had begun convening biweekly videoconference staff "briefings" for the entire FOMC. Because no decisions were made, the meetings weren't announced and no minutes or transcripts were kept.

In another gesture toward the presidents, Bernanke convened the December meeting on Monday afternoon, a day earlier than planned, to allow for extra questioning and argument. The Fed staff distributed in advance twenty-one separate memos on topics, from the side effects of cutting Fed rates to zero to alternative ways the Fed could sustain the economy once rates were at zero. Bernanke moved the usual Monday-morning staff briefing for Fed governors to Monday afternoon so the presidents could participate. He circulated questions that he wanted the presidents to address in Monday afternoon's discussion. It was the academic's approach to monetary policy: a seminar first, then a decision on what to do.

GETTING TO ZERO, QUICKLY

Sentiment among Fed officials to cut rates was strong. Although markets were betting the Fed would cut the key rate by one-half percentage point to 0.5 percent, six of the twelve Fed regional banks used their discount-rate petitions to signal support for dropping the Fed's key rate target by a larger than anticipated three-quarters of a percentage point to just 0.25 percent—even hard-liner Jeff Lacker's Richmond Fed joined the parade. Three other banks indicated they favored lowering rates to one-half percentage point. And even the three regional Feds that didn't want any rate cut—St. Louis, Kansas City, and Dallas—weren't optimistic about the economy; they just "preferred for now" to use ways other than interest-rate cuts "to stimulate the economy," according to a Fed summary of their views.

The huge sums the Fed already had pumped into the economy had diluted the importance of the FOMC's target for the federal funds rate. In ordinary times, the trading desk at the New York Fed could keep the rate close to the committee's goal. By buying Treasury securities, the New York Fed put money into the market and pushed the rate down; by selling securities and draining money, it pushed the rate up. Early in the Great Panic, when the Fed lent banks money through the traditional discount window or the new Term Auction Facility, it had drained an equivalent amount elsewhere. But these were not ordinary times. Since September, the Fed had been lending so much in so many different ways—through its alphabet soup of initiatives—that it couldn't drain enough money elsewhere to offset the added credit. Ultimately the Fed stopped trying, leaving banks and traders to push the *actual* market federal funds rate toward zero, well below the Fed's stated target.

Since the key short-term interest rate appeared headed to zero anyhow, Fed officials reasoned, why not let it get there quickly? So the FOMC agreed to cut the target for the federal funds rate to a range of between zero and 0.25 percentage point—effectively to zero, a milestone in monetary policy. *Whatever it takes.*

Making Sure "It" Doesn't Happen Here

Once the federal funds rate was at zero, then what? The Fed's models of the economy suggested that, with unemployment rising and inflation quiescent, the federal funds rate should be three or four percentage points *below* the inflation rate. However, with an underlying inflation rate of roughly 2 percent, it was impossible for the Fed to get its interest rate low enough — even zero was too high. The Fed was forced to confront one of the few immutable facts of monetary policy: a central bank cannot easily cut the sticker price for money below 0 percent, a circumstance the Bank of Japan had confronted in the 1990s. Though the Fed had contemplated this possibility during the U.S. deflation scare of the early 2000s, it was now a living reality. Before the Fed shot the last bullet in its interest-rate gun, it needed to figure out what it could do next — and how to explain this new approach.

The intellectual foundations of the discussion were already laid. Bernanke and the Fed staff had been contemplating ZIRP for years. Brian Madigan, the top Fed monetary staffer, had written about monetary policy in a world of zero interest rates as early as 1994. An influential 1999 research paper by two respected Fed economists, David Reifschneider and John C. Williams, had offered an aggressive prescription for this circumstance: cut the federal funds rate early and sharply to give the economy an early push to compensate for times when the rate will be higher than warranted (because it cannot fall below zero). In his 2002 speech "Deflation: Making Sure 'It' Doesn't Happen Here," Bernanke himself had previewed many of the options that were now on the table in 2008. "A central bank whose accustomed policy rate has been forced down to zero has most definitely *not* run out of ammunition," he said then. He believed it still.

But all this theoretical talk of zero interest rates was akin to physicists plotting the course of an as-yet-unbuilt rocket on a computer screen. "Such episodes are fairly rare," Reifschneider and Williams had observed accurately — "about once every 100 years." When they briefed the FOMC in person in January 2002 — while the federal funds rate was at 1.75 percent and falling—Reifschneider had confessed that much was still unknown: "We did the best we could, though we're extremely uncertain about what would actually take place. The only real guide is to look back at either the Great Depression of the United States or at the more recent experience of Japan."

In a transcript of the same meeting, Greenspan described the discussion as "a rather interesting conversation, and I trust an academic one." No longer: the Fed was like a team of rocket scientists poised to push the launch button, uncertain whether the weather, sunspots, or some undiagnosed mechanical malfunction might divert the rocket from its computer-plotted course.

Developing monetary policy for a weakened economy while the federal funds rate hovered in ZIRP territory raised two distinct sets of issues. One knot of questions clustered at the intersection of ideology, economic theory, and practicality: How best to use the Fed's ability to print unlimited amounts of money to compensate for the private players' unwillingness or inability to provide credit? How best to calibrate what the Fed was doing?

The second issue was turf, which, in Fed deliberations, went by the more dignified term "governance." Would big decisions be made by the Fed governors in Washington or by the entire committee, which included the regional bank presidents? Given the peculiarities of the Federal Reserve Act, the answer depended crucially on how the Fed described what it was doing.

The menu of monetary policy options was laid out, as always, in the Blue Book prepared before every FOMC meeting by Brian Madigan. The custom had been to offer three alternative interest-rate options to the FOMC on late Thursday before the meeting. At times of economic weakness, for instance, the choices usually were (a) cut interest rates a lot, (b) cut them a little, or (c) don't cut them at all. Insiders joked that the *right* answer, the one the chairman favored, was usually (b), the middle answer and the middle ground. The Blue Book also offered alternative wording for the Fed's end-of-meeting statement, a couple of paragraphs that were scrutinized by traders, economists, Fed watchers, and the financial press with the devotion of Talmudic scholars.

This Blue Book was different. Working even more closely with Bernanke than usual, Madigan offered *four* options, none of which resembled anything the FOMC had said before. One option dropped even a mention of a federal funds rate, the Fed's primary lever for decades and the centerpiece of every communiqué it had been issuing since 1994 — a clear indication of how unusual this moment was.

Breaking with his own tradition of speaking last at FOMC meetings, Bernanke spoke first — for about fifteen minutes, according to participants. He talked about issues of substance and questions of "governance." Bernanke also talked a lot about harmony, trying to set a tone for what he knew threatened to be a divisive discussion. "We need to collaborate, work together, and do things in good faith," he said. He was clear that he wanted the Fed to continue aggressive lending targeted at markets that weren't functioning. But he gave few hints as to what he wanted the Fed to say. He sought consensus and was prepared to rewrite the statement at the meeting if necessary. With these unusual efforts, Bernanke attempted to start — productively — confronting a question simpler to state than answer: What else can the Fed do once it has bottomed out its short-term interest rate?

TALK THERAPY

One device was rhetorical: be explicit about the Fed's intent to hold short-term interest rates low for a long time in the hope of influencing longer-term rates. The rates on five- and ten-year Treasury securities are, in part, a bet on where the Fed will set short-term rates over that period. So, by promising to keep short-term rates low, the Fed hoped the bond market would pull down longer-term rates, key numbers for the interest rates that companies and home buyers pay.

However, some FOMC members had misgivings about making this promise. The conventional wisdom, both in and out of the Fed, was that Greenspan had held interest rates too low for too long earlier in the decade, a policy embodied in the Fed's August 2003 promise to keep rates low for a "considerable period." Several Fed officials wanted to be sure the Fed would raise rates promptly when the day for that came.

A few members of the FOMC argued for eliminating any reference to the federal funds rate. They said this would "focus attention" on the shift in Fed policy away from targeting interest rates toward directly expanding the amount of credit in the economy. This option had one side effect that appealed to a few of the regional Fed bank presidents: it might help struggling small banks in their districts that tended to link rates they charged on loans to the Fed-set rates. If the Fed didn't have any explicit target for the federal funds rate, they reasoned, the banks could charge higher rates on loans, fatten their profits, and rebuild their capital cushions. It wasn't a winning argument. Others countered that the goal was helping the economy, not bank profits. In the end, the FOMC's statement made what was, for the Fed, a strong promise about the future: "The committee anticipates that weak economic conditions are likely to warrant exceptionally low levels of the federal funds rate for some time."

It was a remarkable example of the Fed using words as a substitute for action. The Fed couldn't make credit any cheaper to banks than 0 percent, but instead, with a few carefully selected phrases, it was trying to *talk down* interest rates it didn't directly control.

THE RETURN OF THE INFLATION TARGET

A second device was to set a public target for the inflation rate and then vow to do whatever it took to achieve it. This wasn't a new idea, of course. Bernanke had been advocating an inflation target for years. But it took on a different cast at a time when the inflation rate was falling and the conversation crackled with fear about deflation, a widespread decline in prices and wages. At earlier discussions, advocates of an inflation target were the inflation hard-liners, the hawks; their opponents tended to be those who worried more about unemployment. But now, some of the doves found a target appealing: the Fed would be promising to keep inflation from falling too low, even to push up prices if necessary.

There was also talk at the meeting of publicly promising to avoid "an unwelcome decline" in inflation, one of the options in Madigan's Blue Book. But setting a specific target raised thorny issues, not the least of which was exactly what number to pick as the target. One camp favored a target for the

Fed's favorite inflation gauge close to 1.5 percent a year; another 2 percent. The committee, unable to find a consensus, punted. The result: the FOMC statement vowed to "preserve price stability," a phrase meant to convey a determination to avoid too much and too little inflation, and the inflation target discussion was deferred. (In January 2009, the FOMC decided against an explicit target to avoid an unwelcome political debate, but it provided something very close: each member of the committee offered a forecast for inflation five or six years in the future, which was basically his or her inflation target. Most put the inflation goal at between 1.9 percent and 2 percent. A minority wanted it a lower 1.75 percent or even 1.5 percent.)

WHO CONTROLS THE PRINTING PRESS?

Ultimately, the Fed's most powerful weapon was to simply lend more — to run the electronic printing press overtime and expand the amount of credit in the economy, or "expand the balance sheet" in Fedspeak. That balance sheet, the sum of all the loans the Fed made and securities it held, already had ballooned from about $940 billion just before Lehman collapsed to more than $2.3 trillion at the time of the December meeting. The Fed had lent more than $675 billion to commercial banks, another $50 billion to securities dealers, more than $300 billion to companies that issued commercial paper, $540 billion to foreign central banks — plus the loans to Bear Stearns and AIG.

It wouldn't stop there, though. Fed governors in Washington had moved to lend even more in the future, including buying up to $500 billion in mortgage-backed securities and lending perhaps an additional $100 billion to government-sponsored — and now government-controlled — mortgage companies, Fannie Mae and Freddie Mac. In an attempt to reduce mortgage rates and buoy house prices, these expenditures were publicly announced. For once, something worked as planned: mortgage rates fell even before the Fed bought its first Fannie or Freddie security.

Even though the printing press had been running overtime for months, the issue of who controlled it was still contentious. In central-bank accounting terms, the FOMC, which included the regional bank presidents, managed the size of the Fed's *liabilities*, the sum of bank reserves and currency in the economy. The Fed board in Washington controlled the *asset* side of the Fed balance sheet, the loans it made to specific banks or the lending it did in various markets. The two were linked: assets always equal liabilities. The question was which came first: if it was the liability side — the amount of reserves the Fed put into the banking system — then the FOMC had legal authority, and the presidents had a vote. If it was the asset side — the loans that the Fed was making and securities it was buying — then Bernanke and the Fed board had legal authority, while the Fed bank presidents were bystanders.

Up to this point in the Great Panic, Bernanke had been practicing what one aide labeled "pragmatic judgmentalism," an almost Greenspan-like approach that relied less on predictability and more on case-by-case decisions — not exactly what Bernanke had in mind when he came to the Fed. (About the only borrowers Bernanke turned away were state and local governments, because the law didn't permit the Fed to lend to them, and the auto companies, because he said he didn't want the Fed to be the appeals court for loans Congress initially refused to grant. The auto companies later won loans from the Treasury without Fed participation.)

This approach gave Bernanke greater discretion than the presidents wanted him to have. To bolster their case against "pragmatic judgmentalism," the presidents pulled out their economics textbooks: the Fed creates money that it uses to buy government securities from the banking system in open market operations. That, in turn, increases the reserves in the banking system: the more reserves, the more banks can lend. The Federal Reserve Act gave the entire Federal Open Market Committee — hence the FOMC's name — the authority to decide how much to increase or decrease the reserves the Fed supplies to the banking system through open market operations. Instead of lending that is targeted at any particular market, the dissenting presidents wanted the Fed to simply use U.S. Treasury bonds to put reserves into the system and let the money flow to where it was needed.

It was an approach similar to one developed during the previous decade in Japan. To resuscitate the economy and fight deflation, the Bank of Japan had first dropped interest rates to zero and then, with mixed results, increased the supply of reserves. This policy, called "quantitative easing"—because it emphasized the quantity rather than the price (interest rates) of money—suited the ideology of several Fed presidents. The Fed would control how much money was in the financial system but wouldn't influence where it went and for what it was used—that would be up to the markets. It also gave the presidents a say: they wanted a vote on how much credit the Fed was pumping into the economy.

A few presidents even wanted to set a numerical limit on the growth of overall Fed lending. Bernanke objected. A preordained limit on the growth of the Fed's lending would be a huge mistake. It could prevent the Fed from lending heavily at a moment when the economy was most in need of its largesse. San Francisco's Janet Yellen sided with him: "The impact of the totality of Fed programs should not be judged by the overall size of the Fed's balance sheet," she said a few weeks later. "Rather, it will be necessary to evaluate the success of each individual program improving market function and facilitating the flow of credit." *Whatever it takes.*

Bernanke didn't think—at least in December—that flooding the system with more money would work. No matter how much money the Fed pumped into the banking system, the banks were reluctant to lend. Indeed, the banks were depositing the money back at the Fed nearly as fast as the Fed put it out. In September 2008, before Lehman, banks were parking less than $10 billion in reserves at the Fed; by mid-December, bank reserves were close to $800 billion. The credit channel that Bernanke had written about for decades was clogged: banks weren't lending, and Japan was *not* the model. "Credit spreads"—the difference between yields on safe government debt and riskier corporate debt—"are much wider and credit markets more dysfunctional in the United States than they were during the Japanese experiment with quantitative easing," Bernanke said.

Bernanke wanted to continue to bypass the banking system and lend directly in markets—mortgages, commercial paper, student loans—where usually high interest rates indicated the supply of credit was inadequate to meet the demand. To distinguish the Fed's approach from the Bank of Japan's, he wanted to call it something other than "quantitative easing." He and the other Musketeers bandied about alternatives. Warsh offered "qualitative easing," but that didn't fly. In the end, they embraced "credit easing," a phrase Bernanke introduced into the jargon of monetary policy in his first major speech following the December FOMC meeting.

The phrase was a nice try, but it didn't stick.

"MONDUSTRIAL POLICY"

The FOMC dissenters weren't arguing over turf alone. Targeted lending meant deciding in which markets the Fed would be intervening, a practice that ran up against the hard-line ideologies of some regional presidents. Bernanke's critics—Philadelphia's Plosser, Richmond's Lacker, Kansas City's Thomas Hoenig, and St. Louis's Bullard—didn't think the Fed should be picking winners and losers, for instance, deciding to buy residential mortgages but not commercial mortgages. This, they sniffed, was "industrial policy," an epithet that conservatives use to criticize government aid to particular industries and companies.

This group drew intellectual sustenance from John Taylor, the Stanford University economist. Taylor had taken to calling Bernanke's approach "mondustrial policy." It was not a compliment. "What justification is there for an independent government agency to engage in such industrial policy?" Taylor asked. "Will such interventions only take place in recessions, or will Fed officials use them in the future to try to make economic expansions stronger or to assist certain sectors and industries for other reasons?"

In fact, though, the Fed was already far down the road to picking winners and losers. Bernanke and Paulson had negotiated a novel approach that turned auto, student, credit card, and small-business loans into securities. Paulson was so enthusiastic about the innovation that he publicly announced it before the Treasury and the Fed had agreed on details.

Called TALF, for Term Asset-Backed Securities Loan Facility, the program was targeted at the 40 percent of all U.S. consumer lending that didn't stay on the books of banks—the shadow banking system, again. Before the Great Panic, outfits like Ford Motor Credit turned consumer loans for cars and trucks into securities that it then sold to investors. By the fall of 2008, the market for those securities had disappeared, apparently because investors feared a recession so deep that more than the usual number of consumers wouldn't be able to pay back their loans. No securitization equaled no loans, a formula that threatened to further depress consumer spending. In an economy in which banks were important, but no longer the only important channel for lending, the Fed had to broaden its reach, Bernanke figured. *Whatever it takes.*

To nourish this starved market, the Fed combined its unlimited lending with the Treasury's new ability to put up taxpayer cash, making the Fed more comfortable with the risks it was taking. After much back-and-forth between the two institutions, the Treasury agreed to kick in $20 billion of taxpayer money from TARP to be a cushion to absorb losses. The Fed agreed to put up $180 billion, giving the TALF a total of $200 billion in loans at very sweet terms to offer hedge funds and other big investors to buy securitized consumer loans. The beauty of it was that the Treasury needed only $20 billion from its $700 billion congressionally authorized TARP to get $200 billion into the economy. "TALF shows us there are two sides to creative finance," wrote Nobel Prize winner George Akerlof along with Robert Shiller, the Yale economist who had predicted the housing bust. "It may have gotten us into this crisis. But its genius may also get us out of it."

The Fed and the Treasury offered investors an additional carrot to borrow this money to buy auto or credit card loans packaged into securities. If the ultimate consumer didn't pay back the loans, then the big-money investors wouldn't have to pay back the Fed. (The investors weren't completely off the hook, though. To borrow $100 million to buy, say, credit card loans, investors had to post $105 million in collateral with the Fed; in a worst-case scenario, they'd lose that $5 million.)

TALF reflected Bernanke's view of the Fed's role in a panic: assuring consumers, businesses, and investors that it would bear the risk of possible economic catastrophe in the hope that markets would resume normal operations. As he saw it, the alternative—consumers and investors so worried about the worst-case scenario that they all hunkered down, refusing to buy or lend—was bound to make that imagined disaster a reality.

The Treasury and the Fed took months to work through all the technical and legal details and get the TALF operating. Unveiled in late November, it wasn't even close to making its first loan when the FOMC met in December. (Even before it lent its first dollar in March 2009, the ceiling on the TALF was lifted up to $1 trillion by the Fed and the Geithner Treasury, and its scope expanded beyond consumer loans to business loans and, as Paulson had initially wanted, to commercial mortgages.)

PRINCIPLES, PLEASE

The several Fed presidents who strongly disagreed with Bernanke's market-by-market approach to the crisis accused the Fed of contributing to the turmoil by creating uncertainty and confusion about government policy and complained that the Fed didn't have any "exit strategy" — a way to return to normal central banking when the Great Panic had subsided. Among them was Philadelphia Fed president Charles Plosser, who had been lecturing Bernanke privately and publicly that the Fed needed principles, not ad hoc solutions. Of all Bernanke's ideological critics at the December meeting, Bernanke was most worried about Plosser, the only one of his ideological bent who had a vote on monetary policy in 2008. Bernanke didn't want any dissents, and Plosser was clearly skeptical of his programs.

If the Fed was buying mortgage-backed or credit card–backed securities to lower interest rates now, asked Plosser, wouldn't it be accused of raising interest rates when it sold the securities in the future? "Will we face challenges when we attempt to liquidate these longer-term assets from our portfolio?" Plosser continued. "Will there be pressure from various interest groups to retain certain assets? Will there be pressure to extend some of these programs by observers who feel terminating the programs might disrupt 'fragile' markets or that the economy's 'headwinds' are too strong? Such pressures could threaten the Fed's independence to control its balance sheet and monetary policy. We will need to have the fortitude to make some difficult decisions about when our policies must be reversed or unwound."

Bernanke leaned on Plosser, making clear to him before and during the meeting that the Fed needed to be united, given the fragility of the markets and the economy. Fortunately for Bernanke, though Plosser was in the same ideological camp as presidents like the Richmond Fed's Lacker, he was also a more respectful debater and team player. Lacker was antagonistic and more inclined to make a public statement. (When Lacker got a chance to vote on a similar issue at the FOMC's January 2009 meeting, he dissented, arguing that the Fed should avoid lending in particular markets and instead buy long-term Treasury debt to put more credit into the economy.)

As the Fed approached a vote, it became clear that this already unconventional meeting would run well past the normally reliable 1:15 P.M. ending time. Usually, Fed staff have a solid hour after FOMC meetings to get the end-of-meeting statement prepared for worldwide transmission by wire services, Web sites, and business cable TV channels at *exactly* 2:15 P.M. Washington time.

Merely not meeting this self-imposed schedule could shake markets globally, but as 2 P.M. neared, consensus on the wording was anything but certain. Some of the presidents wanted language that asserted the FOMC's role in deciding the scale of Fed lending. There was talk of including a phrase in the statement that the Fed would "use its balance sheet," but that didn't say anything about size and composition. Finally, Christine Cumming, a twenty-year veteran of the New York Fed who was standing in for Geithner, offered a winning compromise: a vague reference in which the committee agreed to "sustain the size of the Federal Reserve's balance sheet at a high level." It was an artful phrase that gave the FOMC a role at least in choosing adjectives without constraining Bernanke.

The discussion ended at 2 P.M., and when the roll was called, Plosser voted with Bernanke. The initial vote, though, was not unanimous. Richard Fisher, president of the Dallas Fed, cast a no ballot. The dissenter's role was hardly new for Fisher. "In a committee such as the FOMC," he said in a September speech, "the best service a member can render is to show his or her affection for the institution... by calling it as he or she sees it." Fisher had objected formally to the majority's decisions in January, March, April, and August. When the Fed had kept interest rates steady at 2 percent in August, before the Lehman fiasco, Fisher had argued, with little prescience, that it should *raise* rates "to help restrain inflation." This time, he fretted that another move down in the Fed-controlled rates wouldn't help the economy much and could hurt banks struggling to make a profit and people who lived on interest on their savings. Still, if Fisher's vote was predictable, it damaged the united front Bernanke had hoped to present to the world.

The FOMC took a break after the vote. While the staff typed the statement, the officials wandered into the adjacent room to grab sandwiches. Suddenly, Fisher had second thoughts about dissenting. He approached Bernanke and told him that he wanted to change his vote. His dissent was erased from the record. Fisher himself didn't inform his colleagues; Bernanke simply announced it. Months later, Fisher explained: "I felt after going for a walk down the hall that I didn't want to pull the legs out from under Ben, and I didn't want to be perceived as not being a team player."

When the unusual Fed statement was issued several minutes later than 2:15 P.M., it recorded the vote as unanimous. Bernanke had his harmony. He also had flexibility. The FOMC statement promised that the Fed would employ "all available tools to promote the resumption of sustainable economic growth." Even better, no one outside the Fed noticed that the statement was tardy. The markets cheered. Laurence Meyer, the former Fed governor who had a consulting business focused on the Fed, e-mailed clients: "The FOMC pulled out all the stops today."

When the FOMC meeting reconvened after lunch, Bernanke promised "continued close cooperation and consultation" with the presidents and adjourned the meeting around 3 P.M. Fisher, in a speech in Dallas that Thursday, offered a full-throated endorsement of the Fed's decision with his usual rhetorical flourishes and quotes from everyone from Washington Irving to Walter Bagehot. "My colleagues at the Federal Reserve and I are red-blooded Americans. We refuse to be fatalistic....," Fisher said. "And though in normal times, central bankers appear to be the most laconic genus of the human species, in times of distress, we believe in the monetary equivalent of the [Gen. Colin] Powell Doctrine. We believe that good ideas, properly vetted and appropriately directed with an exit strategy in mind, can and should be brought to bear with overwhelming force to defeat threats to economic stability." He didn't hint that he had, briefly, objected.

BUYER'S REMORSE

The December 16 FOMC meeting had been both a marathon and, for Ben Bernanke, a triumph. But the Fed chairman wasn't allowed time to ponder the milestone of zero interest rates or what constituted "overwhelming force." That afternoon, Bank of America sent up a flare. The bank's chief financial officer, Joe Price, called Kevin Warsh while the bank's outside lawyer — Ed Herlihy of Wachtell, Lipton, Rosen & Katz — called Ken Wilson, one of Paulson's advisers and another former Goldman executive.

Their message was unwelcome and dire: the big bank was getting cold feet about completing the acquisition of Merrill Lynch, about the only thing that had gone right during that terrible week in September. Merrill was sitting on losses far greater than Bank of America had anticipated.

Wilson, stunned, told the lawyer to have Bank of America's CEO Ken Lewis call Paulson. He did, and Bernanke as well, asking to meet with the two officials in Washington late in the day on Wednesday. Bernanke and Warsh were suspicious. "My first instinct was: they see we're in the candy business, and they want candy," Warsh said. Bernanke had similar sentiments. Bernanke, Warsh, and Don Kohn huddled on the stance Bernanke should take. At 6 P.M. Wednesday, Lewis, flanked by his chief financial officer and general counsel, sat down with Paulson, Bernanke, and their lieutenants in the anteroom off the Fed boardroom. Warsh listened by phone, as did the New York Fed.

The Bank of America executives persuaded most top Fed officials that they had been stunned to discover the size of Merrill's losses—which made the Fed officials wonder about Lewis's competence. "Some of our analysis suggests that Lewis should have been aware of the problem with ML earlier (perhaps as early as mid-November) and not caught be surprise," the Fed's general counsel, Scott Alvarez, wrote in a December 23 e-mail. And some of the troublesome loans and securities weren't Merrill's, but had been made by Bank of America.

The Bank of America executives said they were considering invoking a "material adverse change" clause in the contract to buy Merrill, essentially to cancel the deal. The Fed officials were surprised, though, that Bank of America didn't have anything specific to request. The Fed also was embarrassed that the examiners it had working inside both Bank of America and Merrill Lynch hadn't a clue that Merrill had such big unreported losses.

Bernanke and Paulson were sure of one thing: the markets were unprepared for Bank of America to abandon Merrill Lynch, a deal that already had been approved by shareholders. Not only would Merrill be orphaned, but Bank of America's reputation for competence would be damaged catastrophically. The federal government might end up nursing two more gigantic but critically ill financial institutions.

Bernanke and Paulson listened, sent Lewis away without promising anything, and asked their bank supervisors and lawyers to scrutinize the companies' books and the Bank of America–Merrill contract. Fed lawyers came to one quick conclusion: if Bank of America walked away from Merrill, it would be sued and probably lose. The "material adverse change" clause gave Bank of America very little wiggle room.

Two days later, around 3:30 P.M. on Friday, Bernanke, Paulson, and Bank of America executives talked again, this time by telephone. Bernanke and Paulson emphasized how completing the deal was important not only to Bank of America itself, but also to the overall financial system. They told Lewis what the Fed lawyers had said. Without being specific, they vowed the government would work with Bank of America to find a solution that would allow the merger to go through and produce a stable merged company. Bernanke asked Warsh to be the Fed's point person, coordinating with Fed banking supervisors in New York, Washington, and Richmond — which oversaw Bank of America because it was based in North Carolina. The only good thing was that *this* crisis didn't need to be resolved in a single sleepless weekend.

Bank of America already had received $25 billion in government capital through the TARP program. "[T]hese were funds we did not need and did not seek," Lewis wrote to the bank's employees at the end of November. "At the time the government asked the major banks to accept the injections, we had just completed our own $10 billion capital raise in the market and . . . had more than adequate capital. We accepted the funds from the government as part of a broad plan to stabilize the financial markets generally." That was then. Now he needed more money, a lot more.

Over the weekend, Lewis called Paulson, who was out for a bike ride.

Paulson told him emphatically that the government didn't think it was in Bank of America's "best interest for you to call a MAC" — to trigger the "material adverse change" clause. Then, according to sworn testimony Lewis gave to the attorney general of New York, Paulson threatened to remove the management of the bank and its board and its directors if it tried to back out of the deal. Lewis was stunned. "Hank," he said, "let's deescalate this for a while."

On Monday afternoon, December 22, Lewis briefed Bank of America's board on his conversation with Paulson and Bernanke, and recommended the deal go through. The directors, according to the minutes, said they were "not persuaded or influenced" by Paulson's threat and pressed Lewis to get a firmer commitment from the Treasury and the Fed that the government would help Bank of America absorb Merrill Lynch's losses with money or guarantees.

Paulson and Bernanke didn't explicitly promise anything. They made clear to Lewis that the government saw the survival of Bank of America as critical to the entire economy and pointedly reminded him of what they already had done for Citigroup. "Although we did not order Lewis to go forward," Bernanke said in an e-mail to the Fed's general counsel, Scott Alvarez, that week, "we did indicate that we believed that [not] going forward would be a detriment to the health . . . of his company." In the e-mail, a copy of which was subpoenaed and released by a House committee looking into the episode six months later, Bernanke asked if—should Bank of America be sued—the Fed could offer a letter explaining why it had encouraged Lewis to consummate the deal.

Alvarez rejected the chairman's notion. "Making hard decisions is what he [Lewis] gets paid for," the general counsel e-mailed back. "We shouldn't take him off the hook by appearing to take the decision off his hands."

Lewis pleaded for a letter from the Treasury to reassure his board. Paulson refused. "A vague letter reiterating Treasury's public commitment to prevent systemically important institutions from failing would not help Bank of America but would instead rattle markets by creating more questions than it answered," Paulson's spokeswoman explained later.

Lewis told his board as much at 4:58 P.M. that Monday: "He said there was no way the Federal Reserve and the Treasury could send us a letter of any substance without public disclosure, which, of course, we do not want."

After ten days of back-and-forth — much of it between Lewis and his chief financial officer, Joe Price, and the Fed's Kevin Warsh—on the nature of the aid the government might provide Bank of America and the conditions, the bank closed the deal with Merrill Lynch on January 1. There was no hint in public, by the bank or by the government, that anything was amiss. Bank of America disclosed none of its misgivings about Merrill nor anything about its conversations with Bernanke and Paulson. In an interview with New York's attorney general, Lewis suggested he kept quiet because that's what Paulson and Bernanke wanted. That assertion stirred controversy and, eventually, congressional hearings that publicly dissected the tense conversations that Lewis had with Bernanke and Paulson in December 2008.

BAD TIMING

A few weeks later, just four days before Obama's inauguration, the Treasury—with the Fed's support—agreed to invest another $20 billion of taxpayer money in Bank of America and limit the losses on $118 billion in toxic loans, roughly three-quarters of that from Merrill and the rest from loans Bank of America itself had made. The terms were similar to those agreed to with Citigroup in November. Bank of America agreed to swallow the first $10 billion in losses on that $118 billion portfolio and 10 percent of all losses after that. The Treasury's TARP and the Federal Deposit Insurance Corporation agreed to take the next $20 billion. And if the losses were even bigger than that, well, the Fed would eat them.

Bank of America had planned to release its first-quarter earnings—and news of the government support—on January 20, Inauguration Day. Bad timing, Kevin Warsh told them—very bad. Bank of America relented and moved the announcement to 7 A.M. the Friday before Obama's inauguration. Lewis desperately hoped his bank could avoid being lumped with Citigroup, which was seen by the markets as a ward of the state after its November rescue. The gambit didn't work. Bank of America was widely seen as another Citigroup. Its stock, which had been trading at $14.50 when Lewis came to see Bernanke and Paulson, closed at $7.18 after the Friday, January 16, announcement. Four months later, in early May, the Treasury and the Fed told Bank of America it needed to raise $33.9 million in capital to withstand a severe recession — either privately or from the government. On the day after that sum became public, Bank of America shares closed at $13.55.

GEITHNERISMS

On January 26, a week after Obama's inauguration, the FOMC gathered for dinner on the top floor of the William McChesney Martin Jr. Building, a 1974 structure named for the Fed's longest-serving chairman that stands across the street from Fed headquarters. The occasion was the send-off of Tim Geithner, then struggling to win Senate confirmation as Treasury secretary amid criticism for his failure to pay all the taxes he owed earlier in the decade.

The Fed tradition is that the toast is done by the regional Fed bank president who chairs the Conference of Presidents; that post had just been assumed by Jeff Lacker, the Richmond Fed president who had been Geithner's nemesis. Lacker avoided the temptation to needle Geithner about his tax problems. He presented one of the traditional gifts — a frame holding dollar bills from each of the twelve Fed bank districts — and offered a little insider's humor: "Get used to the fact that at Treasury you don't have the ability to print and circulate money. That's our job."

He told Geithner that his former colleagues had considered giving him one of the newly chartered companies that the Fed had created to hold Bear Stearns or AIG assets. After all, Lacker quipped, they were worth so little that they wouldn't exceed the Fed's $20 ceiling on gifts.

And then Lacker offered a litany of Geithnerisms, words that he used to excess, with a sentence accompanying each — words like "dimension," which Geithner commonly used as a verb. "If you need some people to help *dimension* the losses at Citi, you can have a few from the task force." Geithner, blushing, laughed at the jokes, as did the assembled governors and district bank presidents.

Few, if any, of them envied the task that Geithner had been given. The Fed had cut interest rates to zero. It had more than doubled the size of its balance sheet. It had rushed to the rescue of some of the nation's largest financial institutions. It had done nearly everything it could, and now it was going to be up to the new president — and his new Treasury secretary — to take charge of the battle to arrest the recession and repair the banking system before the Great Panic turned into another Great Depression.

"IT WILL NOT FIX ITSELF"

A few weeks later, Bernanke reflected on the Bank of America rescue, the disintegration of one of the few things that had seemed to go well during one of the worst weeks of the Great Panic. "It was disheartening," he said.

He looked back to the beginning of 2008. "We hoped by stabilizing Bear Stearns, and by stepping up our provision of liquidity to the financial system, that we would give the economy and the financial system time to try to find its feet," he said. "And that seemed to be the case for about three or four months. We hoped that the injections of TARP capital in the fall would give the banking system the breathing space it needed. But then the economy and financial markets deteriorated sharply, and more banking problems continued to surface."

Without prompting, Bernanke recited the criticism he took for rescuing Bear Stearns and then the criticism he took for not rescuing Lehman Brothers. "The people who were initially saying, 'You should just let these guys fail' have turned their complaint to, 'Well, the government's inconsistent responses have been a problem and have prevented recovery.'" He didn't say to whom he was referring, but he didn't have to: it was the argument that, among others, Richmond's Jeff Lacker and Philadelphia's Charles Plosser were making.

"My reply to that is twofold," he said. "First, we did the best we could with the powers we had. Perfect consistency simply wasn't possible given our limited powers and the differences in the various circumstances. If we had a clear legal framework for resolving big financial institutions other than banks, that would have been a different matter. We didn't have one. Second, the dominant cause of the crisis was not what the Fed did or what other parts of the government did. It was the losses that followed the collapse of the credit boom. When losses pass $1 trillion and continue to rise, one can hardly expect anything other than a worsening situation."

"It has to be fixed," he said soberly. "It will not fix itself."

Chapter 14

DID BERNANKE KEEP HIS PROMISE
TO MILTON FRIEDMAN?

More than eighteen months after the Great Panic began, more than a year after Bear Stearns was rescued, more than six months after Lehman collapsed and AIG became a ward of the state, more than a hundred days into the Obama presidency, it was still not entirely clear that Ben Bernanke and his allies at the U.S. Treasury, Hank Paulson and then Tim Geithner, had succeeded at preventing what Bernanke called Depression 2.0.

Given all that the Fed and the rest of the government had done, this fact alone was stark testimony to the severity of the financial crisis that provoked what the International Monetary Fund declared to be "by far the deepest global recession since the Great Depression." After all, the Bernanke Fed had not repeated the mistakes of the 1920s and 1930s; it had been neither passive nor stingy with credit. The Fed had decided to do *whatever it takes.* It had cut interest rates from 5.25 percent to 3 percent by the end of January 2008 and then to zero in December 2008, and promised to keep them there for a long time. It had force-fed more than $2 trillion of credit into the economy and promised as much as $1 trillion more lending for everything from cars to mortgages to the debt of the U.S. government itself. The Fed had begged Congress to spend $700 billion in taxpayer money to rebuild the foundations of the banking system and leveraged that with hundreds of billions of Fed-created money. It had endorsed and welcomed the Obama-backed $787 billion package of tax cuts and spending increases to offset weak demand from consumers, companies, and overseas markets.

But history is a harsh judge. Fed officials and sympathetic academics frame the question reasonably, but narrowly: How well did Bernanke and his fellow Musketeers do, given the information and authority they had at the time? To nearly everyone else, outcomes matter, not intentions. It may someday be said, with substantial accuracy, that after some initial hesitation, Ben Bernanke and his team did all they could to defeat the Great Panic. But if the ultimate result is years of painfully slow economic growth and widespread unemployment, they will be judged by many Americans to have failed. Earning an A for effort is not enough. As Paulson put it a few months after leaving office: "We succeeded in keeping the financial system from collapse, but people were unhappy that we didn't prevent a recession. It's hard to get kudos for what didn't happen."

To be told that the Fed did what it could isn't much comfort to a family who loses its house to foreclosure, a businessman forced into bankruptcy, a sixty-five-year-old whose retirement fund is devastated, a would-be borrower turned away by a beleaguered bank, a new college grad who can't find a job, any job. For those victims and all the others, a final verdict on the Fed's response to the Great Panic must await the health of the U.S. economy in 2010 and 2011 and beyond.

By early summer 2009, the economy still appeared to be in recession and the unemployment rate was still rising.

Tim Geithner was still trying to find his footing at the U.S. Treasury, demonstrating that years of whispering in the ear of the Treasury secretary doesn't fully prepare anyone for assuming the role himself. It turned out looks do matter. Appearing younger than his forty-seven years, just two weeks younger than Obama, made it hard for Geithner to project wisdom and experience, and difficult for him to calm the fears of the people and the markets. His habit of answering questions in public as if he were giving a deposition didn't help. Geithner found himself ridiculed on *Saturday Night Live,* mocked on YouTube videos, lampooned in political cartoons. The *Indianapolis Star's* Gary Varvel showed Geithner as an airline pilot, poking his head through the cockpit door and telling alarmed passengers: "I'm Captain Geithner. We're going to have to try things we've never tried before. We will make mistakes." Mike Luckovich's take in the *Atlanta Journal-Constitution* was a bit more sympathetic: "Now, girls," Michelle Obama tells her daughters, "you know who'll be in charge of cleaning up the new puppy's messes, don't you?" Their reply: "Yes, Mommy. Tim Geithner."

Though Geithner's headline-making mistakes on his tax returns didn't block his confirmation by the Senate, they had lasting effects. They forced extraordinary scrutiny of every potential nominee for a Treasury job, disqualifying some able people with minor blemishes and leading to months of delay in staffing Treasury's top ranks. AIG was a continuing nightmare. The retention bonuses it paid its executives stirred a massive political uproar, and the complexity of overseeing its business was a constant struggle. Given his initial role in the takeover of the firm and his current role as steward of taxpayers' investment in the company, Geithner couldn't escape the AIG cloud. Yet, in private, he exuded impressive calm and self-confidence, and, importantly, appeared to hold on to the president's confidence.

Paulson, meanwhile, occupied a spacious, plain office at Johns Hopkins University's School of Advanced International Studies, about a mile from the Treasury building. With hours and hours of help from his former Treasury staff, he was writing his own account of the Great Panic. He took silent satisfaction from watching Obama and his economic team, which had been so harshly critical of his strategy during the campaign, struggling to do better and, in many cases, relying on people he had hired and tactics he had adopted. Paulson had gained back some of the weight he lost during the most stressful weeks of the Great Panic. And he was, slowly, gaining perspective. Paulson remained grateful to Bernanke for consistently putting the country's interests ahead of the Fed's institutional interests, even though that sometimes made Bernanke appear weak or politically naïve. Paulson was, still, an unabashed Geithner admirer. In a characteristic locker-room compliment, he said of Geithner: "I've been in the trenches with him. He can take a punch."

At the New York Fed, Bill Dudley, the former Goldman Sachs economist who had run the New York Fed's markets desk, was establishing himself as Geithner's successor as president of the New York Fed. He was determined to do better than Geithner at explaining what the Fed was doing and why. To take his place on the markets desk, Dudley hired rising star Brian Sack, thirty-eight, an MIT-trained economist with long-standing ties to the Fed. As a Fed staff economist, Sack had worked closely with then-governor Bernanke before leaving to work for former Fed governor Larry Meyer's consulting firm in 2004.

In fact, the only top-tier economic actor whose job title hadn't changed was Bernanke himself. But Bernanke had changed in one very visible way. The man who arrived at the Fed determined to be the un-Greenspan was going beyond anything Greenspan ever did to raise his public profile and establish himself as the symbol and voice of the Fed. Bernanke was reaching beyond bond traders and financial journalists to the broader public. Shattering tradition, he spoke to the National Press Club and took questions from reporters. He went to Morehouse College and fielded questions on live TV from economics majors. And he went on CBS's popular *60 Minutes* in what he described as a "chance to talk to America directly."

The new Bernanke served both personal and institutional purposes.

Bernanke's four-year term as Fed chairman expires January 31, 2010, and though he was reluctant to admit it, even privately, he hoped Obama would reappoint him for a second four years. That depended on much that was beyond Bernanke's control: the health of the economy in late 2009 when the president would make a decision and the president's opinion of Larry Summers, the smart but self-centered former Treasury secretary who was working in the White House and eyeing Bernanke's chair. The more Bernanke is seen by the public as being calm, competent, and seasoned, the more likely that Obama will reappoint him. But if the economic news gets worse and Summers can maintain rapport with the president, the more likely that Obama will replace Bernanke with Summers. Bernanke insisted in April 2009 he wasn't thinking about reappointment. That was the prudent if unconvincing thing to say. Instead, he said, he was focused on "the best possible outcome for the U.S. economy. Everything I do is with that in mind."

Bernanke's institutional purposes were twofold. The Fed and the Treasury had not succeeded in building public and investor confidence in their efforts to restart the economy, to reignite securitization markets where consumer and business loans were traded, and to shore up the banks so they could and would lend more. Bernanke easily dismissed some of the criticism, particularly attacks from those who hadn't been on the battlefield when he'd had to make instant decisions about Bear Stearns, Lehman Brothers, and AIG. But even sophisticated people were having trouble deducing a game plan from the Fed's and the Treasury's actions and the proliferation of acronym-labeled initiatives. Bernanke knew that if business executives, consumers, and investors around the world were confused, they would hesitate in ways that diluted the Fed's efforts. His 1979 Ph.D. dissertation at MIT, after all, had argued that "increased uncertainty provides an incentive to defer investments in order to wait for new information."

"I think it is important for the public to understand what is going on and to know that the government is trying to solve the problem," he explained later. "They should know we have a plan and we have a strategy."

But that wasn't the whole story. The Fed's aggressive response to the Great Panic had called unwelcome attention to its enormous power and to its capacity to act as the fourth branch of government. Its willingness to come up with money for Bear Stearns and AIG when the Treasury and the president couldn't and its ability to create trillions of dollars in credit surprised many members of Congress. The Fed, it was increasingly clear, could and would act when the political system was frozen. Even in the face of strong political resistance to more taxpayer money to rebuild the banking system, Bernanke demonstrated that the Fed was neither paralyzed nor out of ammunition: he pressed the FOMC, the committee of Fed governors and regional Fed bank presidents, to increase the cap on Fed purchases of mortgage-backed securities from $500 billion to $1.25 trillion and, for the first time in the Great Panic, to okay the purchase of $300 billion of longer-term Treasury debt securities.

Buying Treasury bonds was a step that Bernanke had resisted earlier, but circumstances had changed. The economy and banking system were still struggling. The Treasury's huge borrowing was beginning to push up interest rates on long-term Treasury debt, a development that the Fed found unwelcome because those rates filter through to corporate and consumer borrowing rates. And Congress was hardly rushing to offer assistance. Instead, it was putting conditions on Fed and Treasury aid to banks that Bernanke and Geithner feared would be counterproductive, and showing no interest in approving more money. As Bernanke told the *60 Minutes* interviewer: "The biggest risk is that we don't have the political will, that we don't have the commitment to solve this problem, and that we let it just continue. In which case, we can't count on recovery." Buying enough Treasury debt to finance two months' worth of the federal government's budget deficit at that point showed that the Fed could still act when politicians wouldn't.

By early summer 2009, the Fed had purchased more than $550 billion of mortgage-backed securities and more than $150 billion in U.S. Treasury bonds. But the bond market pushed up interest rates anyhow, prompting tension inside the Fed. Some wanted to step up the bond-buying to help the economy. Others worried the more bonds the Fed bought, the more difficult it would find "the exit strategy," the timely retreat from intervention.

The Fed's actions may have saved the U.S. economy from catastrophe but an increasingly vocal band in Congress found it uncomfortably undemocratic to head off future crises by making the Fed the overarching overseer of financial stability and monitor of the nation's biggest financial companies, as Obama proposed in June 2009. "We should not ignore that the Fed has had some responsibility for systemic risk regulation under the current structure" and thus the current crisis, said Senator Mark Warner, Democrat of Virginia, on the Senate floor, making a case heard with growing frequency at the time. The Fed and the Treasury, he complained, had struck "private deals" that put "smaller, less powerful but often better run institutions at a competitive disadvantage." The answer to the Great Panic, he said, was not to make the Fed more powerful, but to diffuse its regulatory powers in a grand council of regulators. Geithner thought that a dangerous idea, akin to running a firehouse by committee and calling meetings before responding to alarms. But Obama did propose amending the law to require the Fed to get the Treasury secretary's written approval before exercising its authority to lend to nearly anyone in "unusual and exigent circumstances." The Democratic and Republican leaders of the Senate Banking Committee sponsored a nonbinding resolution calling for "an evaluation of the appropriate number and the associated costs of Federal Reserve banks," a flare across the bow of the Fed and regional Fed presidents who are neither appointed by the president nor confirmed by Congress. Even if those efforts fizzled, Congress was likely to reopen the Federal Reserve Act as it renovated the financial regulatory apparatus. As Greenspan had warned privately for years, once the law was reexamined, the Fed was vulnerable to changes that it might not welcome.

Bernanke, like Greenspan and Volcker before him, subscribed to the view that the best way to protect a democratic society from undesirable rates of inflation was to keep control of interest rates and the supply of money away from elected politicians. Politicians need the frequent approval of voters and are naturally tempted to settle for a little more economic growth today and defer the fight against inflation until after the next election; the only case for an independent central bank in a democracy is that it can take a longer-term view and do what is in the interest of the people in ways that elected politicians cannot. By going directly to the politicians' constituents, the voters, through the nonfinancial press, Bernanke was seeking to build public support to resist any changes to the Federal Reserve Act that would curtail the Fed's ability to fight inflation.

Sitting on a bench on Main Street in Dillon, South Carolina, Bernanke made a pitch that would have done a congressional candidate proud. "I come from Main Street. That's my background," he told *60 Minutes*. "I've never been on Wall Street. And I care about Wall Street for one reason and one reason only: because what happens on Wall Street matters to Main Street."

BERNANKE'S DASHBOARD
June 12, 2009

		Change from August 7, 2007
Dow Jones Industrial Average:	8,799	down 34.8%
Market Cap of Citigroup:	$18.9 billion	down 92.2%
Price of Oil (per barrel):	$72.68	up 0.3%
Unemployment Rate:	9.4%	up 4.7 pp
Fed Funds Interest Rate	0%–0.25%	down 5 to 5.25 pp
Financial Stress Indicator	0.43 pp	up 0.31 pp

* * *

So, with the benefit of a bit of hindsight, what did the Bernanke Fed get right and what did it get wrong? What lessons have been learned so far?

The Fed failed to see the problems percolating under the surface of a prospering economy. Once the housing bubble and credit bubble began to burst, the Fed's diagnosis was wrong. It saw risks, but not their full dimensions. It thought the housing bust would be "contained," and it wasn't. The Fed was hardly alone; plenty of others made the same mistakes. But as Congress moves toward designating the Fed to be the guardian of the nation's financial stability, the Fed's inability to see the Great Panic coming is worrisome. Unless it understands what it failed to see then, it will not be any better at seeing the approach of the next crisis in time to avoid it. Bernanke himself remains reluctant to criticize Greenspan publicly. He continues to argue that the single most important factor in creating the credit bubble was something over which the Fed had no control: an inflow of foreigners' savings to the United States that led banks and other financial institutions to compete aggressively for borrowers, which in turn led to increasingly lax lending standards.

"Regulators," he said at Morehouse College in April 2009, "did not do enough to prevent poor lending, in part because many of the worst loans were made by firms subject to little or no federal regulation." Yes, but by using the Fed's existing authority to put new restrictions on subprime mortgages, Bernanke demonstrated that the Fed could have done more than it did and earlier. And the absence of full-throated warnings in the years just before the housing and credit bubbles burst undercuts the argument that the Fed did all that it could.

All that was largely history by the time Bernanke took over as Fed chairman in February 2006. While every one of Bernanke's subsequent decisions can be second-guessed and criticized, and most have been, he cannot be fairly criticized for not anticipating every bizarre turn that the crisis took. Or the bad luck that led nearly everything that could go wrong to go wrong. Or the shortcomings of a U.S. financial regulatory regime woefully ill equipped for a crisis like the Great Panic. Or the unpopularity of a lame-duck president or the missteps of a new Treasury secretary or the shortsightedness of some high-profile actors on Wall Street who badly mis-read the public mood.

All decisions aren't created equal. The fair question is whether Bernanke got the big ones right.

By August 2007, Bernanke understood that the economy was at risk, yet from today's perspective his initial efforts seemed timid. It wasn't until December 2007 that the Fed began experimenting with new ways to lend to banks, and not until January 2008 did the Fed get serious about cutting interest rates aggressively. But once Bernanke and the other Musketeers real-ized the risks, they were creative and bold. To his credit, Bernanke managed to hold the FOMC together as he pushed the Fed to places it had never gone before, or at least to places it hadn't visited since the Great Depression.

Bear Stearns was a shock to the Fed. Helping JPMorgan Chase buy the failing investment bank was prudent. But the Fed's response immediately afterward was flawed. It was clear at the time that Bear Stearns was a big deal. "The past ten days will be remembered as the time the U.S. govern-ment discarded a half-century of rules to save American financial capitalism from collapse," I wrote in the *Wall Street Journal* of March 28, 2008. "On the Richter scale of government activism, the government's recent actions don't (yet) register at FDR levels. They are shrouded in technicalities and buried in a pile of new acronyms. But something big just happened. It happened without an explicit vote by Congress. And though the Treasury hasn't cut any checks for housing or Wall Street rescues, billions of dollars of taxpayer money were put at risk. A Republican administration, not eager to be viewed as the second coming of the Hoover administration, showed it no longer believes the market can sort out the mess."

Yet neither Bernanke, nor Geithner, nor Paulson took the six months between Bear Stearns and Lehman to prepare adequately. They did not use Bear Stearns as a lever to try to get Congress to act quickly to provide emer-gency authority, even if temporary, to handle the collapse of a major finan-cial institution. They did not hint that they anticipated that taxpayer money would be needed to shore up the banking system. They did not turn the bare-bones April 2008 "break the glass" plan into a contingency plan ready to be implemented if needed. Bernanke and Paulson argue that Congress wouldn't have acted in the spring and summer of 2008 because members didn't perceive the Main Street economy to be at risk. Perhaps. But Bernanke and Paulson didn't *try*. Had they done so, they might have had more credibility later when they needed it. If the two men had a game plan, they didn't explain it.

When Lehman weekend arrived, the Fed had left itself only two options, or allowed the Treasury to narrow its options to two: either sell Lehman as Bear Stearns had been sold, or let it go into bankruptcy. Bernanke and Paulson convinced themselves the system could withstand the latter course because the warning signs had been so many and so visible. They were wrong about that. They didn't realize the lesson that many people had drawn from Bear Stearns: the Fed would somehow find a way to keep Lehman going. They didn't appreciate the tidal wave that a Lehman bankruptcy would cause. Had they realized how much damage Lehman's bankruptcy would wreak, they might have had a third option ready, one that showed some of the same creativity they exercised at other points in the crisis as they stretched law to do *whatever it takes* to protect the system from clear and present danger. Whether AIG's collapse was caused by Lehman's or whether it was inevitable is a question that defies a simple answer. The reaction to Lehman's collapse reasonably led Bernanke and Paulson to rush to keep AIG from following Lehman into bankruptcy. But the form it took was flawed, unsuccessful, and expensive in taxpayer dollars and in damage to the Fed's reputation.

Paulson and Bernanke did seize that September 2008 moment to get Congress to come up with $700 billion, even though getting the legislation through Congress proved so tortuous that it undermined confidence in the ability of American democracy to cope with a major financial crisis. (At the Fed, there was more than one conversation about the advantages of parliamentary systems, where the prime minister can count on his party to do whatever he deems necessary at the darkest hour.) But in the weeks and months that followed, neither Paulson nor Bernanke nor Geithner laid out a coherent plan for using the $700 billion to restore the banking system to health. They made mistakes of substance and mistakes of communications. Their plan was seen as, and may have been in retrospect, too generous to Wall

Street and the banks, Citibank in particular. That perception contributed to an uncomfortable political reality in the spring of 2009: Congress appeared unwilling to approve more taxpayer money for the banks, even though Bernanke, Geithner, and White House economist Larry Summers all knew that it probably would take more than the $700 billion already approved to repair or, as they put it, "recapitalize" the banking system.

Professors make the what-if game respectable by calling it "counterfactual." It is tempting. What if Bernanke had moved more swiftly to attack the Great Panic in August 2007? What if Bear Stearns had become the catalyst that generated legislation focused on coping with the collapse of a big financial institution? What if Congress had approved more money sooner to recapitalize the banks? What if the initial bank rescue plan had been more coherently structured, implemented, and explained? What if Geithner had stayed at the New York Fed, his tax returns sheltered by scrutiny and his stature undiminished, and someone with more gravitas had been installed at Treasury? What if someone in the Treasury or the Fed had persuaded AIG not to pay those retention bonuses before they became so public? Things might have been better, of course. It's hard to know for sure.

But there is another side to the what-if game. What if Ben Bernanke had not been a student of the Great Depression? What if he had not resolved to do *whatever it takes* to prevent a second Great Depression? What if he had been timid or cowed by the resistance inside the Fed? Those questions are easier to answer: the economy would have been even worse than it is now, and this book would have been an account of how the Fed had dithered and delayed, as an earlier generation of central bankers had. It would have been a book about Ben Bernanke's failure to keep his November 2002 vow to Milton Friedman: "Regarding the Great Depression. You're right, we did it. We're very sorry. But thanks to you, we won't do it again."

IT COULD HAVE BEEN WORSE

I f Ben Bernanke had hung a banner from the Fed's headquarters early in the spring of 2010, the honest slogan would have read: "It could have been worse."

The U.S. economy was far from healthy. The unemployment rate remained painfully high, and the Fed and the White House expected unemployment to remain above 9 percent into 2011 even if all the policies they advocated were pursued. Huge swaths of the U.S. economy still were addicted to taxpayer support, including the bulk of the American home-mortgage business and much of the auto industry. Small banks, many crippled by commercial real estate losses, were failing at a rate of two or three a week. A $787 billion package of tax cuts and spending increases enacted a month into Obama's presidency was sustaining the economy at the cost of a widening federal budget deficit. The Fed was continuing to give away money for next to nothing in its quest to keep the economy from doing even worse, holding the federal funds rate near zero as it had been since December 2008.

But by spring 2010, it was clear that the actions of Bernanke's Fed and the Bush and Obama administrations had averted a repeat of the Great Depression — no small accomplishment. The worst financial crisis in modern history — those were Bernanke's words — provoked a recession deeper and longer than any since World War II. After contracting for a year and a half, the U.S. economy began expanding in mid-2009 and enjoyed a welcome growth spurt at the end of that year. But that didn't mark a return to consumers and businesses spending as usual. It was, instead, the result of a mix of insulin (the fiscal stimulus) and sugar (businesses rushing to rebuild inventories that had been depleted when many simply stopped producing and buying). Although the risk that the economy would stumble back into recession abated, growth was much too slow to replace quickly the stunning 8.4 million jobs lost during the recession, let alone the 2.2 million additional jobs needed to provide work for newcomers to the job market. Congressional Budget Office economists forecast that the unemployment rate wouldn't return to 5 percent — the lowest level they thought it could go — until 2016! Neither White House nor private economic forecasters surveyed by the *Wall Street Journal* were much more optimistic.

Wall Street looked a lot rosier than Main Street. The Dow Jones Industrial Average hit a low of 6,547 on March 9, 2009. A year later it was up 60 percent (though still well shy of the October 2007 peak of 14,164.) The Fed allowed the emergency-lending programs it had initiated during the crisis to lapse — the unusual offers to lend to blue-chip industrial companies, money market funds, and primary dealers and investors in packages of auto or credit-card loans. And on the afternoon of February 18, 2010, the Fed passed a minor milestone. Two and a half years after its very first reaction to the Great Panic, the August 2007 cut in the discount rate — the price it charges cash-short banks that borrow directly from the Fed — the Fed lifted that rate by a quarter of a percentage point to 0.75 percent. The dollars-and-cents impact was small because banks were no longer borrowing heavily from the Fed. Loans through the Fed discount window had fallen from above $100 billion during the worst of the crisis to below $15 billion. The Fed labored to convince the markets and the press that the rate increase wasn't a signal that it was moving to raise the cost of borrowing throughout the economy. Still, it was a signpost along the Fed's very gradual move toward normal monetary policy.

THE STRESSFUL STRESS TESTS

Bernanke and Geithner, as important an ally for Bernanke as Treasury secretary as he had been as president of the New York Fed, were increasingly confident that they had accomplished one of their top objectives: saving the nation's big banks from a devastating collapse without nationalizing them. For good reason. The survival of the nation's remaining big banks was no longer in doubt. The Fed and the Treasury had prodded banks to raise $112 billion by selling shares to private investors to bolster capital cushions, and most big ones had paid back the taxpayer money that they had taken. Everyone understood — for better or worse — that the U.S. government wouldn't permit the failure of any really big bank or any globally interconnected one, at least for now. That posed huge problems for the future, a government blessing that allowed big banks regarded as "too big to fail" to borrow cheaply and thus encouraged them to take bigger risks. But for now, it was reassuring.

Bernanke, Geithner, and their collaborators in the White House and Congress had written a new chapter in the handbook for government responses to major financial crises. Part of it drew from the lesson that Geithner and Summers drew from the Asian financial crisis of the 1990s: Respond with overwhelming force and make massive amounts of money available. The resulting boost to confidence will reduce the ultimate cost of any rescue. Part of it drew from the seventy-five-year-old teachings of John Maynard Keynes, the British economist whose remedies for the Great Depression had been embraced by government policy makers and academic economists for decades after World War II. Keynes taught that the solution to an economy in which spending and borrowing were weak despite very low interest rates was to increase government spending and cut taxes. But later in the twentieth century, the Keynesian model was undermined by the inflation of the 1970s and critiques from a younger generation of economists. During the Great Panic, Keynes became newly relevant.

In February 2010, Washington fired what Geithner called "the fiscal cannon," Obama's Keynesian-style fiscal stimulus. The Fed was glad for the help. With the benefit of a year's hindsight, the Obama-backed stimulus was an economic success and a political failure. To get Congress to act quickly, Obama and his chief of staff, Rahm Emanuel, the former Chicago congressman, basically let legislators fill in the details. That stamped the stimulus not with the popular Obama brand, but with that of Nancy Pelosi, the not-so-popular Speaker of the House. The wisdom of the components of the stimulus was and will continue to be debated: Was the mix of tax cuts versus spending right? Would bigger tax cuts for families have boosted their spending or their saving? Was the right balance struck between spending on benefits quickly paid to individuals and longer-lagging infrastructure spending that would be useful for years in the future? Would giving employers a tax break for hiring workers have prompted more of them to hire more readily? Did too much or too little money flow to strapped state and local governments? Was the total package too small or too big? But most economists, at the Fed and outside, thought the stimulus had helped prevent an even deeper recession. A survey of fifty-four Wall Street and business economists by the *Wall Street Journal* in March 2010 found that, on average, they said the stimulus added nearly a percentage point to growth in 2009 and reduced unemployment by more than 1 million workers. The Congressional Budget Office, relying on standard economic models, said that there were between 1.4 million and 3 million more jobs in the closing months of 2009 than there would have been without the fiscal stimulus.

Inside the Fed and the Treasury, there was substantial pride in the success of a less conventional, riskier move: the "stress tests" conducted of the nation's nineteen largest financial institutions in 2009. Obama's election provoked a reexamination of the Bernanke-Paulson-Geithner approach to the banks by the new administration. Geithner, working with Bernanke and with Larry Summers in the White House, among others, sought a modern-day analog to FDR's bank holiday, some way to restore public and market confidence in the nation's banks so they could borrow and lend again.

Roosevelt was inaugurated on Saturday, March 4, 1933, after a month-long bank run in which millions of Americans withdrew cash from their banks. Depositors, with good reason, feared their banks might shut their doors. Because federal deposit insurance didn't yet exist, when a bank closed, its customers often lost their savings. Several states already had shuttered their banks. Standing in line to pull out one's cash was a reasonable, even prudent, thing to do. On Sunday, March 5, the new president proclaimed a four-day national bank holiday. On Thursday, March 9, Congress ratified that action and gave FDR extraordinary emergency power over the banks. He promptly extended the bank holiday for the rest of the week, and summoned Americans to their radios on Sunday night, March 12, to hear the first of his famous fireside chats. Only "banks which on first examination by the Treasury have already been found to be all right" would reopen, he said. He instructed the Fed to provide enough cash to cover the deposits in any bank that was allowed to resume business. "I can assure you that it is safer to keep your money in a reopened bank than under the mattress," he said. Americans trusted him. Within two weeks, Americans returned to the banks more than half the cash they had withdrawn in panic.

Three-quarters of a century later, Bernanke again found himself drawing from his academic study of the Great Depression. Despite all that had been done — the TARP investment in banks, the federal guarantee of all new bank borrowing, the Fed's emergency lending — there remained a huge amount of anxiety that the banks might be broke — *insolvent* is the technical term — and that a deepening recession would make them even sicker. Pressure from the left and some on the right to nationalize the big banks was strong. Take them over, cleanse them of bad loans and unattractive assets, and sell them back to investors, Bernanke, Geithner, and Obama were publicly advised. Even in Obama's inner circle, some advisers thought nationalization prudent or inevitable. But Bernanke and Geithner did not, and they prevailed. Banks weren't confronting a 1930s-style run by ordinary depositors as they had in the 1930s. This time, the aim was to reassure more sophisticated investors — the ones who controlled millions, sometimes billions, of dollars that they lent for short spans of time or invested for longer-run profits.

CASH ROOM CATASTROPHE

The initiative got off to an inauspicious start on February 10, 2009, with a Geithner speech in the Treasury's ornate Cash Room. With much less detail than the markets and the press had been led to expect, a messaging misstep by the White House, Geithner said that regulators would scrub the banks' books to gauge how much they would lose if the economy proved very weak and then tell banks how much more capital they needed to withstand such losses. And if banks couldn't raise that capital from private investors, then the government would provide it — and take a bigger ownership stake. He called this approach "a stress test," using a phrase well understood inside financial firms as a technique to examine the consequences of various bad-news scenarios. But for the public, the phrase conjured up images of Citibank on a treadmill, collapsing in heart failure.

While Geithner spoke, his head awkwardly moving from right to left to read from Teleprompters to which he wasn't accustomed, the Dow Jones Industrial Average lost nearly 400 points. "If Geithner's hotly anticipated financial rescue plan . . . were a movie, it would be headed for a short run," a *Philadelphia Inquirer* columnist wrote. Critics — and there were few defenders — decided that the whole operation was going to be either a whitewash of the banks' books or an excuse for nationalization. Indeed, from London a columnist for the Reuters wire service predicted the United States would "nationalize big swaths of its banking system by the time the leaves fall from the trees."

The concept was much simpler to describe than to execute. Bank supervisors traditionally inspect bank books one bank at a time. This time, the plan was to compare and contrast the big banks, and to force them to use the same scenario for the economy, real estate prices, and the like — one devised by Fed economists. A newcomer to the Fed board played a major role: Daniel Tarullo, a lawyer who had been an adviser on economic and banking issues to the Obama campaign. Tarullo had worked closely with Summers as coordinator of international economic policy in the Clinton White House and then took a teaching post at Georgetown University law school. He had been a critic of the government's supervision of the banks before the crisis and authored a book scolding the Fed for being too gentle with banks in international negotiations over how much capital banks had to hold. At the same postelection press conference at which Obama picked Geithner for Treasury and Summers to be the White House economic policy coordinator, the president-elect announced that Tarullo would be his first nominee to the Fed board, taking Bernanke by surprise. Given the speculation that Summers was eyeing the Fed chairman's job, there was whispering that Tarullo would be a Summers spy in the Bernanke camp. But Tarullo focused almost exclusively on the Fed's role in supervising banks. He dug into the stress tests with his characteristic assertiveness and energy, clashing occasionally with Fed staff and the presidents of the regional Fed banks.

In the fall of 2008, Paulson's strategy had been to force capital into all the banks and to avoid singling out the weak ones. With changing circumstances and a change in the cast of strategists, the game plan changed. This time, the goal was to distinguish the weak banks from the strong. The stronger banks, the thinking went, would then be better able to raise capital from private investors and, if needed, the government would provide capital to strengthen weaker ones.

The nineteen big banks were given two economic scenarios. One reflected the consensus of private forecasters that the economy was soon to recover. The other was dubbed "severe but plausible"; that is, a bad economy but not another Depression. Using 2008 year-end financial statements as a starting point, each bank was told to project losses, category by category, for the next two years. The approach drew very little applause. Some predicted the stress tests would be a whitewash of bank books that relied on an overly optimistic outlook for the economy. Others saw them as a justification for the inevitable nationalization of the banks. For months, the stress tests proved, well, stressful to the banking system. Teams of Fed, Treasury, FDIC, and other bank supervisors pushed the banks for information, demanded more information, argued with bank management about questions big and small, used Fed economists to devise statistical formulas to compare the losses different banks anticipated on similar loans, and finally negotiated over just how much capital each bank would be told to raise.

The discoveries and recommendations of government bank supervisors almost always are closely guarded secrets, shared only with bank executives. Grades that supervisors give bank managements on a five-point scale aren't disclosed. Indeed, about the only public notice of furrowed regulatory brows comes when a bank is forced to sign a formal promise to change its ways.

Bank supervisors and bank executives say that public discussion of the government's concerns about a bank's shortcomings could provoke a destabilizing run, effectively turning a mild illness into a fatal one. But these were not ordinary times — and the whole point of the exercise was to rebuild confidence in the banking system.

Behind the scenes, top Treasury, Fed, and bank-supervisory officials argued over how much of the stress-test information should be made public, particularly how much detail to provide on each bank. "Some feared that weaker banks might be significantly harmed by the disclosures," Tarullo recalled. They lost. The results were made very public at a May 9, 2010, press conference starring Geithner, Bernanke, and top bank regulators.

If the economy followed the adverse scenario, they said, the bank losses would come to a whopping $600 billion, a bleak picture that assumed banks would take bigger hits percentage-wise than they did during the Great Depression. Of the nineteen banks, they judged nine had enough capital to meet the thresholds the government had set to withstand the adverse economic scenario. The other ten needed a total of $85 billion to build sufficient capital buffers. In a 38-page document, the government listed the losses they projected for each of the nineteen banks.

Making the results public proved a huge success, vindicating those who had argued for doing so. Tarullo later offered three explanations: One, investors deemed the results credible, because the government shared the assumptions it used and because it distinguished between weak and strong banks. Two, he said, "the results were released at a time when uncertainty about bank conditions was very high, and some market participants feared the worst." The results "helped reassure market participants that, under a severe but plausible scenario, the capital needs of the largest U.S. banks were manageable." And, three, the Treasury made clear that it would use taxpayer money to fill the capital hole for any bank unable to raise money privately.

In the end, only one of the nineteen institutions got more government money — GMAC, which had been the finance arm of General Motors. All the rest raised capital privately. None of the banks were nationalized, although taxpayers still had a 27 percent stake in Citigroup well into 2010.

"I don't understand why people were so persuaded by these stress tests," said Anil Kashyap, the University of Chicago economist who was among the many who were skeptical that the results would be accepted as credible by financial markets. "But they provided a decisive moment." In short, they accomplished what Roosevelt's bank holiday had: they restored confidence in the U.S. banking system.

FOUR MORE YEARS

Barney Frank, the source of almost all the great laughs about the financial crisis, quipped in August 2009: "Not for the first time, as an elected official, I envy economists. Economists have available to them, in an analytical approach, the counterfactual. Economists can explain that a given decision was the best one that could be made, because they can show what would have happened in the counterfactual situation. They can contrast what happened to what would have happened. No one has ever gotten reelected where the bumper sticker said, 'It would have been worse without me.' You probably can get tenure with that. But you can't win office."

Nor can a Fed chairman win a popularity contest. A July 2009 Gallup poll asked Americans to rate the quality of various government agencies. Only 30 percent said the Fed was doing an excellent or good job, down from 53 percent in 2003. Even the Internal Revenue Service did better, with 40 percent rating it good or excellent. The CIA, FBI, and Homeland Security did better still.

The same month, Geithner called Bernanke and asked if he was interested in staying on as Fed chairman after his first four-year term expired in January 2010. He toyed with not staying on. "The main thing I thought about," he said months later, "was unfinished business." Recalling that the economy still looked seriously ill in July 2009, he said, "I felt it was important that there be some continuity in monetary policy to help stabilize the economy, and then to at least get us going on 'the exit,' Fed shorthand for the delicate process of weaning the U.S. economy from the unusual support the Fed had been providing. The other unfinished business was the refashioning of the financial regulatory system to reduce the odds of another crisis like the Great Panic. "I wanted to be part of 'reg reform.' Given my experience of the past couple of years, I felt I had something to bring to the table."

Surely, he figured, the next four years couldn't possibly be as intense as the previous four. "Clearly things were better than they had been earlier," he added. "It didn't seem like it was going to be as draining a job." Bernanke warned his wife, Anna, that he might be offered another term. She wasn't enthusiastic. "Her attitude was stoic," Bernanke said. "She basically said: 'You have to do what you have to do. I'll support you.'"

Bernanke told Geithner he was willing to reenlist. But in the press and in the markets, speculation grew about whether Obama would reappoint Bernanke or turn to someone else, perhaps Summers or Janet Yellen at the San Francisco Fed, or Roger Ferguson, the former Fed vice chairman who was running TIAA-CREF, the big pension and money management firm. Inside the White House, Summers was an obvious alternative. But Geithner and Emanuel, among others in the small circle advising Obama, leaned toward reappointing Bernanke. It seemed foolish to fire one of the top generals at the moment when the president was trying to argue that we were winning the war.

One summer day, Geithner came to Bernanke's office to tell him that he would be offered a second term. Weeks passed and Bernanke heard nothing more. Then late on Wednesday, August 19, Geithner called and asked Bernanke to meet with the president at the White House at 8 P.M. It was a short conversation, no more than fifteen minutes. "He asked me if I would do it, and I said yes," Bernanke recalled later. "And he told me he thought we'd done a great job and that we had saved the economy." Bernanke then flew off to Jackson Hole, Wyoming, for the Kansas City Fed's annual conclave. On Friday, he mounted a defense of his policies. "History is full of examples in which the policy responses to financial crises have been slow and inadequate, often resulting ultimately in greater economic damage and increased fiscal costs," he said. "In this episode, by contrast, policy makers in the United States and around the globe responded with speed and force to arrest a rapidly deteriorating and dangerous situation." After that he went horseback riding — not his forte, friends say — with former Princeton colleague Alan Blinder, sharing the news with almost no one.

Before he flew back to Washington on Saturday, Bernanke got word from the White House that the president planned to announce the decision early the following week while vacationing on Martha's Vineyard off Cape Cod. The White House tipped off a handful of reporters Monday night, and early Tuesday morning, on August 25, Bernanke flew from Andrews Air Force Base to Martha's Vineyard on a military Gulfstream jet. White House staffers had alerted Bernanke's aides that the president would wear slacks and a blazer but no tie. Bernanke dressed accordingly, but brought a tie just in case. First thing that morning, the two men stood before a blue curtain on a stage set up at the Oak Bluffs School for the battalion of reporters who accompany the president. "As an expert on the causes of the Great Depression, I'm sure Ben never imagined that he would be part of a team responsible for preventing another," Obama said. "But because of his background, his temperament, his courage, and his creativity, that's exactly what he has helped to achieve." Mr. Bernanke spoke briefly, thanked the president politely, flew back to Washington, and was at his desk by 11 A.M. Obama went to play golf.

President Obama's decision, more than five months before Bernanke's four-year term expired, appeared to be a firm pat on the back from the nation's political leadership. At the time, few inside the White House or the Fed thought Senate confirmation was in doubt. The Senate Banking Committee hearing in early December was uncomfortable but predictable.

The senior committee Republican, Richard Shelby of Alabama, threw Bernanke's own reassuring words from earlier in the decade at him, indicting the Fed for its failure to see the crisis coming and to adequately supervise the banks.

Bernanke replied, "If you fight a battle and you lose the battle, does that mean you never use an army again?" Using the forum not only to defend himself but to plead with senators not to pursue their plan to shift oversight of the big banks away from the Fed to another agency, he added, "You have to improve and fix the situation. You don't have to necessarily eliminate the institution."

That argument didn't satisfy Jim Bunning, the Kentucky Republican and former baseball pitcher who had opposed Bernanke's initial nomination because he expected him to continue Greenspan's policies. "Where I come from, we punish failure, not reward it. That is certainly the way it was when I played baseball, and it is the way across all America presently," he said. "Judging by the current Treasury secretary, some may think Washington does reward failure, but that should not be the case. I will do everything I can to stop your nomination and drag out this process as long as I can. We must put an end to your and the Fed's failure, and there is no better time than now."

Firmly planting himself as the latest in a long line of those who distrusted the Fed, Bunning concluded: "Your Fed has become the creature from Jekyll Island," a reference to the 1910 meeting at the Georgia resort where bankers met secretly to outline their plan for a central bank. (See page 37 for an account of that meeting.)

Two weeks later, the committee voted 16-7 to recommend that the full Senate confirm Bernanke for a second term. Shelby and the majority of the Republicans, joined by a single Democrat, Jeff Merkley of Oregon, voted against him. But neither the White House nor the Fed anticipated serious trouble on the Senate floor.

A month later, Massachusetts voters elected Republican Scott Brown to take the seat vacated by the death of Teddy Kennedy, stunning Democrats and offering the most tangible evidence to date of the public's antipathy toward incumbents and anger toward the bailout. The day after that election, Wednesday, January 20, several Senate Democrats revealed at a closed-door caucus that they were considering voting no. On Thursday, Senate Majority Leader Harry Reid, who was facing a tough fight for reelection in Nevada, issued a brief statement after meeting with Bernanke. It emphasized the need to pressure banks to lend more, and said nothing about support for a second term — unnerving the Fed and the White House.

It had been clear for some time that the public and many of its elected representatives thought Bernanke and his allies in the Treasury had saved Wall Street but hadn't saved Main Street. Bernanke struggled to make the case that saving Wall Street and the banks was the only way to protect Main Street, but he didn't have much success. Geithner captured the problem succinctly: "My basic view is that we did a pretty successful job of putting out a severe financial crisis and avoiding a Great Depression or Great Deflation type of thing," he said. "We saved the economy, but we kind of lost the public doing it."

Bernanke's reappointment was becoming a lightning rod for widespread public resentment of the bailout. A Wall Street Journal/NBC News poll conducted in late January asked whether Bernanke should get a second four-year term as Fed chairman; 37 percent said no and 34 percent yes. The remaining 29 percent were unsure. In contrast, when the poll asked the same question about Alan Greenspan in 1999, the tally was 61 percent to 16 percent in favor of reappointment. Bunning and a few other senators objected to putting the confirmation to a vote, a parliamentary move that required the votes of 60 senators to overcome. Senate Republican leaders, emboldened that Brown's victory had given them 41 votes, saw every reason to make life difficult for Democrats and were cagey about how many of their side would vote no. Suddenly aware that Bernanke was in trouble, Rahm Emanuel, Tim Geithner, and other top administration officials began calling individual senators. Bankers and businessmen did the same, fearful that rejecting Bernanke would roil markets. On CBNC, Warren Buffett, the legendary investor from Omaha, was asked what would happen if the Senate rejected Bernanke. "Well, just tell me a day ahead of time so I can sell some stocks," he said. Privately, he helped persuade Nebraska Democrat Ben Nelson to side with Bernanke.

Inside the Fed, Bernanke and his closest aides were in shock. At one point, he asked aloud if he should withdraw his name to protect the larger interest of the institution. His colleagues were horrified at the thought. "Your brand is better than our brand," one top aide told him. By the weekend, the tide was turning in Bernanke's favor. Pressured by Emanuel, Reid issued another statement, this time indicating he *would* vote for a second term. On Sunday's *Meet the Press*, Republican leader Mitch McConnell predicted Bernanke would prevail. From his perch on the *New York Times* op-ed page, Paul Krugman gave his former colleague a less than ringing endorsement. Bernanke failed to heed warnings about subprime lending, he said, and wasn't doing enough to bring down unemployment. But, he added, "Replacing him with someone less established, with less ability to sway the internal discussion, could end up strengthening the hands of the inflation hawks and doing even more damage to job creation." The *Wall Street Journal* editorialized against him, saying he was "far too susceptible to political pressure."

By the time the Senate turned to the issue on Thursday, January 28, the ultimate outcome was no longer in doubt. Reid wouldn't have scheduled a vote without the 60 votes needed to prevail. But Bernanke's critics pressed their indictment. Rhode Island's Sheldon Whitehouse recited a litany of the embarrassingly reassuring statements Bernanke had offered in 2007 and early 2008 about the state of the U.S. economy. (Among them was Bernanke's reassuring, and ultimately inaccurate, commentary on February 28, 2008: "Among the largest banks, the capital ratios remain good and I don't expect any serious problems.") Merkley described Bernanke as "calm and unassuming, responsible and thorough in his explanations, and very likeable," but said he had "helped set the fire that destroyed our economy." Chuck Grassley of Iowa said Bernanke's "lack of foresight makes me wonder if he is ready to lead our economy."

Bernanke's backers fought back rhetorically. Judd Gregg, the New Hampshire Republican, lauded his "strong, definitive leadership at a moment of acute crisis." But even some of those who favored confirmation diluted their support with criticism, not so much of the bailout — though there was some of that — but of the Fed's failure to prevent the crisis. "Mr. Bernanke kept our nation out of a depression and has kept inflation in check," said Tim Johnson, the South Dakota Democrat who was in line to succeed the retiring Chris Dodd as chairman of the Senate Banking Committee, which oversees the Fed. "But it cannot be business as usual for the Fed. . . . The status quo at the Fed is not acceptable."

In the end, the vote to end debate was 77-23. A few minutes later, the Senate voted 70-30 to confirm him for a second term. Seven senators succumbed to pressure to provide the votes needed to overcome parliamentary hurdles, and then cast what they figured would be a politically popular vote against him. It was a comfortable majority, but there were nearly twice as many no votes as the 16 that Paul Volcker got in 1983 after pushing interest rates into double digits. Bernanke didn't throw a party. He went home for a quiet evening with his wife.

From the vantage point of early 2010, the bank rescue looked far less expensive than had been feared a year earlier. In March 2009, the Congressional

Budget Office had pegged the ultimate cost of TARP at $356 billion, taking account of the money taxpayers invested in the banks and the money that would flow back to the Treasury later. A year later, CBO said the cost — including investments, grants, and loans that were completed, outstanding, or anticipated — would be $109 billion, the bulk of that attributed to AIG and the auto companies. The much maligned bank bailout, it said, was likely to produce "a very small net gain to the government." In March, as the Treasury began to plan the sale of its Citi shares, it stood to turn a $7.19 billion profit on its $25 billion investment. Outside of TARP, though, the losses on Fannie Mae and Freddie Mac continued to mount as the housing market languished — and the portfolio the Fed bought from Bear Stearns was worth about $3 billion less than the $30 billion it had paid for it.

The Fed crossed another milestone at the end of March 2010 when the Fed completed the truly extraordinary purchase of $1.7 trillion in mortgage-backed securities and long-term debt of the U.S. Treasury, Fannie Mae, and Freddie Mac. That portfolio amounted to 22 percent of all such securities in existence when it began buying them in January 2009 to help the economy by reducing longer-term mortgage and other interest rates because the Fed already has pushed short-term rates as low as it could. "No investor — public or private — has ever accumulated such a large amount of securities in such a short period of time," the New York Fed's market chief, Brian Sack, and colleagues said in a retrospective that pronounced the experiment a success.

Sack and his colleagues calculated the Fed maneuvering not only revived an important and troubled market at a time of stress but reduced the rate markets set on ten-year debt securities by between a third of a percentage point and a full percentage point, a significant amount. Bernanke argued that the Fed's purchases — initially announced in November 2008 and expanded in 2009 — had two salient effects: One, they greased the wheels of banking, putting more money — *liquidity,* as economists call it — into the banking system, reducing the reliance of the financial system on the Fed's emergency lending programs. Two, the purchases took huge quantities of mortgage-linked securities off the hands of investors, prompting them to put the proceeds into bonds issued by companies, municipalities, and others.

That made it easier, and cheaper, for those organizations to borrow. Not everyone saw it that way, though. For instance, Stanford economist John Taylor attacked the Bernanke analysis with the same vigor that he criticized nearly everything Bernanke had done. The Fed purchases hadn't done much, he insisted. And even some Fed insiders wondered whether the purchases had reduced interest rates as much as Sack estimated.

Although unemployment remained high and, by some measures, the inflation rate was falling in the spring of 2010, the Fed's internal discussions turned to when and how to reduce the size of the Fed's $2.3 trillion portfolio. Bernanke, despite the impatience of some regional Fed bank presidents, put off the "when" decision to see how the economy performed. Instead, he and Fed staff focused on the technicalities of the exit, devising and publicizing ways the Fed would withdraw its unusually generous support without overturning the economy. It was both prudent preparation for the monetary technicians who had to implement the eventual exit and a deliberate effort to persuade financial markets that the Fed did actually see a way out.

While Bernanke had reupped, some of his partners were beginning to disperse. Paulson published his book, revealing, among other things, how much of a physical toll the crisis took on him. Ever since high school, he wrote, he had had occasional bouts of "dry heaves" at moments of exhaustion, of which there were many during the Great Panic. In one of the most poignant scenes, he described the sleepless nights over Lehman Brothers during the weekend in September 2008 and how close he came to taking sleeping pills despite his Christian Scientist aversion to medication. "I stood under the harsh bathroom lights, staring at the small pill in the palm of my hand. Then I flushed it — and the contents of the entire bottle — down the toilet. I longed for a good night's rest. For that, I decided, I would rely on prayer, placing my trust in a Higher Power."

In June, Don Kohn retired as Fed vice chairman after forty years at the institution. Along with the three other vacancies that Bush had bequeathed Obama — including the one that Tarullo filled — that retirement gave the president an unusual opportunity to remake the Fed. To succeed Kohn, Obama nominated Janet Yellen, the San Francisco Fed president who had been a member of Greenspan's Fed board and chairman of the White House

Council of Economic Advisers. To fill the other empty seats, he picked Peter Diamond, an MIT economist, and Sarah Bloom Raskin, the Maryland state bank commissioner. In contrast to their predecessors, the Obama appointees, if confirmed by the Senate, were certain to be more activist in regulatory matters. They also were likely to serve as counterweights to the increasingly vocal band of regional Fed presidents who were more eager than Bernanke to raise short-term interest rates and reduce the Fed's portfolio of mortgages.

With his job secure, Bernanke turned to protecting the Fed's institutional interests as Congress lurched toward the most sweeping changes to financial regulation since the 1930s. The Fed's reluctance to share information with Congress and the press — the names, for instance, of the big U.S. and European banks whose bets with AIG had been paid off at 100 cents on the dollar after the Fed rescue — reinforced its image as excessively secretive and too protective of the interests of big financial firms. Anger at the Fed's failure to prevent the crisis and a widespread sense that it had bailed out Wall Street prompted more than a few members of Congress to contemplate proposals that alarmed Bernanke. The full House approved a proposal by Representative Ron Paul, the Republican libertarian from Texas who bluntly titled his book *End the Fed,* to force the Fed to submit to audits of monetary policy decisions by the congressional Government Accountability Office. Bernanke saw that as a threat to the Fed's independence on monetary policy. Several influential senators, backed by some usually Fed-friendly economists, sought to shift oversight of banks from the Fed to a new agency, arguing that the Fed was too soft on banks and should concentrate on monetary policy. Bernanke, the scars of managing the crisis still fresh, insisted that that would cripple the Fed in future crises. With Geithner's strong backing, though, the Fed appeared in the spring of 2010 to be winning most major battles.

"Once your near-death experience has passed and people are contemplating what a terrible event this was, the natural question is who to blame," Bernanke said in an interview. "I think any fair assessment would say that the Fed, like other regulators, made some mistakes," he said. In short, the Fed had failed as a regulator.

On monetary policy, though, he was unrepentant. In interviews and speeches, he insisted that the evidence didn't support the charge that he and

Greenspan had contributed to inflating the housing bubble by keeping rates too low earlier in the 2000s. "House prices began to rise in the late 1990s, and although the most rapid price increases occurred when short-term interest rates were at their lowest levels, the magnitude of house-price gains seems too large to be readily explainable by the stance of monetary policy alone," he told fellow economists in a detailed defense delivered at the annual meetings of the American Economic Association in January. Housing bubbles emerged in other countries, too, he noted, and it's hard to find a link between their monetary policies and the pace house prices increased there. Greenspan made similar arguments. Critics say that argument evades at least one big factor: That by reducing short-term rates and promising to keep them low for a long time, the Fed had played a role in prompting investors seeking higher returns to take ever-greater risks — helping to fuel the subprime mortgage boom.

Looking back on two and a half years of financial firestorm, Bernanke was quietly proud of what he had done and what he had helped avoid. "In terms of the actual policies," he said, "I don't have any significant regrets. We're all disappointed that the economy isn't growing faster than it is, but I think the policies have worked pretty well.

"One thing I've learned now, a very painful lesson, is that sometimes the politics and the appearance is more important than the substance," he added. "Obviously, I wish I'd had more foresight on some things that happened. It would have helped my reputation. Whether it would have changed the outcome, though, is less clear." He laughed.

NOTES

INTRODUCTION: WHATEVER IT TAKES

3 **AIG shares:** Michael Grynbaum, "Wall St.'s Turmoil Sends Stocks Reeling," *New York Times*, September 9, 2008. http://www.nytimes.com/2008/09/16/business/worldbusiness/16markets.html?hp

3 **"We came very, very close":** House Financial Services Committee, February 25, 2009.

4 **"It is either our curse":** Bradford DeLong, "Republic of the Central Banker," *The American Prospect*, October 27, 2008. http://www.prospect.org/cs/articles?article=republic_of_the_central_banker

5 **"the dernier resort":** Glenn Stevens, "Liquidity and the Lender of Last Resort," Reserve Bank of Australia, April 15, 2008. http://www.rba.gov.au/Speeches/2008/sp_gov_150408.html

6 **"the pawnbroker of last resort":** Yves Smith, "Covert Nationalization of the Banking System," *naked capitalism*, August 3, 2008. http://www.nakedcapitalism.com/2008/03/covert-nationalization-of-banking.html

7 **"I think highly of":** Federal News Service, "The Foreclosure Crisis and Older Americans," from AARP Solutions Forum Web site, September 19, 2008. http://assets.aarp.org/rgcenter/ppi/foreclosure_transcript.pdf

7 **"No one in a democracy":** Brian Blackstone and Patrick Yoest, "Bailouts

Turn Up Heat on Fed Chief," *Wall Street Journal,* September 19, 2008.
http://online.wsj.com/article/SB122176444088253287.html

8 **"Perhaps it's time":** Ben S. Bernanke, "Japanese Monetary Policy: A
Case of Self-Induced Paralysis?" in Adam Posen and Ryoichi Mikitani,
eds., *Japan's Financial Crisis and Its Parallels to US Experience,* Special
Report 13, Institute for International Economics, Washington, D.C.,
2000, 149–166.

CHAPTER 1: LET OL' LEHMAN GO

9 **"luxurious and lavish":** "MAKES NEW ATTACK ON RESERVE BANK; Building
Here, to Cost $25,000,000, a Waste of Public Funds, Says J.S. William's.
COMPARES IT TO TWEED DAYS Cites Architects' and Engineers' Fees of
$1,106,000—Suggests Gov. Strong's Resignation" *New York Times,*
December 17, 1921, 25. http://query.nytimes.com/gst/abstract.html?res=9
C02E2DA113EEE3ABC4F52DFB467838A639EDE

10 **"Everyone out there knew":** Interview, Henry Paulson.

13 **Between 1986 and 1995:** Timothy Curry and Lynn Shibut, "The
Cost of the Savings and Loan Crisis: Truth and Consequences," *FDIC
Banking Review,* December 2000. http://www.fdic.gov/bank/analytical/
banking/2000dec/brv13n2_2.pdf and http://www.fdic.gov/bank/
analytical/banking/2000dec/brv13n2_2.pdf

15 **"U.S. Helps Lehman":** David Cho, Heather Landy, and Neil Irwin,
"U.S. Helps Lehman Go Up for Sale; Regulators Are Seeking a
Weekend Deal Not Involving Public Money," *Washington Post,*
September 12, 2008, A1.

15 **"For market discipline":** Henry Paulson, "Remarks on the U.S., the World
Economy and Markets before the Chatham House," London, July 2,
2008. http://treas.gov/press/releases/hp1064.htm

18 **"If we're going to do":** Susanne Craig, Jeffrey McCracken, Aaron
Lucchetti, and Kate Kelly, "The Weekend That Wall Street Died—Ties
That Long United Strongest Firms Unraveled as Lehman Sank Toward
Failure," *Wall Street Journal,* December 29, 2008, A1.

18 **Thain tried:** Bank of America Corp, Form DEFM14A, November 3,
2008.

19 **"We are not going":** Interviews, Treasury staff.

20 **Barclays later bought:** http://www.barcap.com/static/BarCap/Press%20 office/Attached%20Document/Lehman_Press_Release_170908.pdf _acquisition.pdf

20 **On Sunday afternoon:** Henry M. Paulson Jr., *On the Brink* (New York: Hachette Book Group, 2010), p. 216.

23 **"I never once considered":** Transcript at http://georgewbush-whitehouse. archives.gov/news/releases/2008/09/20080915-8.html

23 **Paulson said months later:** Interview, Henry Paulson.

23 **"In the case of Lehman Brothers":** House Financial Services Committee, hearing, September 24, 2008.

23 **"Everything fell apart":** Alan Blinder, "Six Errors on the Path to the Financial Crisis," *New York Times*, January 25, 2009. http://www.nytimes. com/2009/01/25/business/economy/25view.html?ref=business

24 **"You don't want to say":** Interview, Henry Paulson.

25 **"We could have saved it":** Interview, October 2008.

26 **"A disorderly failure of AIG":** House Committee on Financial Services, hearing, September 24, 2008. www.house.gov/financialservices/ hearing110/hr092408.shtml

26 **"The national commitment":** Damian Paletta, "Barney Frank Celebrates Free Market Day," *Real Time Economics*, September 17, 2008. http://blogs.wsj.com/ economics/2008/09/17/barney-frank-celebrates-free-market-day

Chapter 2: "Periodical Financial Debauches"

28 **The opening years:** John Steele Gordon, *An Empire of Wealth: The Epic History of American Economic Power* (New York: HarperCollins, 2004), 277.

28 **Campaigning to end:** Robert F. Bruner and Sean D. Carr, *The Panic of 1907: Lessons Learned from the Market's Perfect Storm* (Hoboken, N.J.: John Wiley & Sons, 2007), 9.

28 **"God made the world":** Gordon, 262.

28 **"War was fresh in mind":** Bruner and Carr, *The Panic of 1907*, 13.

29 **"the idle holders":** William Jennings Bryan, "Bryan's 'Cross of Gold' Speech: Mesmerizing the Masses," July 9, 1896, from History Matters Web site http://historymatters.gmu.edu/d/5354

30 **"agrarian antipathy for city":** Bray Hammond, *Banks and Politics in*

America from the Revolution to the Civl War (Princeton, N.J.: Princeton University Press, 1957), 33.

30 **"I sincerely believe":** Thomas Jefferson, "Money & Banking," 1816, from Thomas Jefferson on Politics & Government Web site http://etext .virginia.edu/jefferson/quotations/jeff1325.htm

30 **more than one a decade:** Charles W. Calomiris and Gary Gorton, "The Origins of Banking Panics: Models, Facts, and Bank Regulation," in R. Glenn Hubbard, ed., *Financial Markets and Financial Crises*, 1991, Table 4.1, 114. http://www.nber.org/chapters/c11484.pdf

30 **an elaborate allegory:** Ranjit S. Dighne, *The Historian's Wizard of Oz: Reading L. Frank Baum's Classic as a Political and Monetary Allegory* (New York: Praeger, 2002).

31 **Never mind that:** Bruner and Carr, 84.

32 **JP Morgan Chase's decision:** Carrick Mollenkamp et al., "The Two Faces of Lehman's Fall—Private Talks of Raising Capital Belied Firm's Public Optimism," *Wall Street Journal*, October 6, 2008, A1.

32 **On Monday, October 21:** Federal Reserve Bank of Boston, "Panic of 1907," 12. http://www.bos.frb.org/about/pubs/panicof1.pdf

32 **"he had added several":** Bruner and Carr, 109, citing *New York Times*, October 24, 1907.

33 **"I remember Mr. Morgan"** Bruner and Carr, 87–88, from Strong 1924 letter to Thomas W. Lamont (see reference on p. 222 of Bruner and Carr).

33 **"what was probably the most extensive":** Quoted in Gary Gorton, "The Panic of 2007," 2. Federal Reserve Bank of Kansas City, Jackson Hole Conference, August 2008. http://www.kc.frb.org/PUBLICAT/ SYMPOS/2008/gorton.08.04.08.pdf

34 **Commodity prices fell:** Bruner and Carr, 142.

34 **Some 240 banks failed:** Allan H. Meltzer, *A History of the Federal Reserve, Volume 1: 1913–1951* (Chicago: University of Chicago Press, 2004), 65.

34 **"Crowds cheered when":** Howard Means, *Money & Power: The History of Business* (Hoboken, N.J.: John Wiley & Sons, 2001), 142.

34 **"Something has got to be done":** Andrew Sinclair, *Corsair: The Life of J. Pierpont Morgan*, 1981, 226, cited in Ron Chernow, *House of Morgan* (New York: Grove Press, 2001), 128.

35 **"What is wanted":** Walter Bagehot, *Lombard Street* (Homewood, Ill.: Richard D. Irwin, 1962), 31–32.

37 **"The Panic of 1907"**: William Greider, *Secrets of the Temple* (New York: Simon & Schuster, 1987), 274.

37 **"While most bankers"**: Roger T. Johnson, *Historical Beginnings . . . The Federal Reserve*, Federal Reserve Bank of Boston, 18. http://www.bos.frb .org/about/pubs/begin.pdf

37 **"The whole world is united"**: Bruner and Carr, 145.

38 **"in complete control of everything"**: Johnson, 19.

38 **"a great and growing concentration"**: Bruner and Carr, 148.

38 **"impossible another panic"**: Howard M. Hackley, *Lending Functions of the Federal Reserve Banks: A History*, Board of Governors of the Federal Reserve System, 1973, 10.

39 **"Americans still maintain"**: Hammond, 122

40 **"He regarded the twelve"**: Meltzer, 76.

40 **"an incredibly dramatic"**: Ben S. Bernanke, *Essays on the Great Depression* (Princeton, N.J.: Princeton University Press, 2004), viii, 8.

41 **"That went on for three"**: "Fed Chairman's Q&A on Financial Crisis," *Wall Street Journal*, October 16, 2008. http://online.wsj.com/article/ SB122409761899937343.html

41 **"To understand the Great Depression"**: Bernanke, *Essays*, 5.

41 **"Not only have we"**: Quoted in Greider, 298.

42 **He prevailed**: Ben Bernanke, "On Milton Friedman's Ninetieth Birthday," Federal Reserve Board, November 8, 2002. http://www.federalreserve .gov/boarddocs/speeches/2002/20021108/default.htm

42 **"The monetary policy"**: "Fed Chairman's Q&A."

42 **"important not primarily"**: Milton Friedman and Anna Jacobson Schwartz, *A Monetary History of the United States* (Princeton, N.J.: Princeton University Press, 1963), 352.

43 **"expensive and difficult to obtain"**: Bernanke, *Essays*, 42.

43 **Nearly half the banks**: Ibid., 44.

43 **"Thus, expectation of failure"**: Ibid., 45.

44 **"The widespread banking panics"**: Ben S. Bernanke, "The Financial Accelerator and the Credit Channel," from Board of Governors of the Federal Reserve System Web site, June 5, 2007. http://www.federalreserve .gov/newsevents/speech/Bernanke20070615a.htm

45 **That was more than double**: Bernanke, *Essays*, 54.

45 **Exactly the same**: Comparison of Ten-Year Treasury to Moody's

Seasoned Baa Corporate Bond Yield, from http://research.stlouisfed
.org/fred2

46 **$185 billion of which:** Douglas W. Elmendorf, Congressional Budget
Office, March 2, 2009. http://www.cbo.gov/ftpdocs/100xx/doc10008/
03-02-Macro_Effects_of_ARRA.pdf

46 **"In one camp":** Lawrence H. White, "Did Hayek and Robbins Deepen the
Great Depression?" *Journal of Money, Credit and Banking* 40(4), 751–768.
http://economics.sbs.ohio-state.edu/jmcb/jmcb/07056/07056.pdf

47 **"with the operation":** Jeremy Atack and Peter Passel, *A New Economic
View of American History from Colonial Times to 1940* (New York:
W. W. Norton & Company, 1994), 614.

47 **Only a minority of Fed:** David M. Kennedy, *Freedom from Fear: The
American People in Depression and War, 1929–1945* (New York: Oxford
University Press, 1999), 70–104.

47 **"believed with me":** Herbert Hoover, *The Memoirs of Herbert Hoover: The
Great Depression, 1929–1941* (New York: Macmillan, 1952), 31–32.

48 **"After Strong's death":** Bernanke, "On Milton Friedman's Ninetieth
Birthday."

48 **"a weak reed":** Meltzer, 413.

48 **"I optimistically think that":** Randall Parker, *The Economics of the Great
Depression: A Twenty-First Century Look Back at Economics of the Interwar
Era* (Northampton, Mass.: Edward Elgar, 2007), 67. http://www.ecu
.edu/cs-educ/econ/upload/Ben_Bernanke.pdf

48 **"Regarding the Great Depression":** Bernanke, "On Milton Friedman's
Ninetieth Birthday."

48 **"We may look":** "A Great Financier," *New York Times*, April 1, 1913, 10.
http://query.nytimes.com/gst/abstract.html?res=9807E1DD1F3AE633A2
5752C0A9629C946296D6CF

CHAPTER 3: AGE OF DELUSION

50 **only the third time:** Press release, Board of Governors of the Federal
Reserve System, February 3, 2006. http://www.federalreserve.gov/
newsevents/press/other/20060203b.htm

50 **"Alan Greenspan is perhaps":** The White House, "President Attends
Swearing-In Ceremony for Federal Reserve Chairman Ben Bernanke,"

February 6, 2006. http://georgewbush-whitehouse.archives.gov/news/releases/2006/02/20060206.html

51 **Bernanke's Dashboard:** From publicly available sources. Price of oil is spot price for West Texas Intermediate Crude. Unemployment is latest available on date shown. Financial stress indicator is spread between London Interbank Offered Rate (LIBOR) and overnight indexed swaps.

51 **During the 2000:** Joshua Cooper Ramo, "After Greenspan: The Taylor Rule?" *Time*, February 26, 2001. http://www.time.com/time/magazine/article/0,9171,999303,00.html

51 **Richard Fisher:** Personal communication, Richard Fisher.

52 **"Jim Baker didn't":** Bob Woodward, *Maestro* (New York: Simon & Schuster, 2000), 19.

52 **"How did my Jewish uncle":** Robert B. Reich, *Locked in the Cabinet* (New York: Alfred A. Knopf, 1997), 80.

53 **"No one has yet":** Alan Blinder and Ricardo Reis, "Understanding the Greenspan Standard," Federal Reserve Bank of Kansas City, Jackson Hole Conference, August 2005. www.kc.frb.org/PUBLICAT/SYMPOS/2005/pdf/BlinderReis.paper.0804.pdf

55 **A week after Hurricane Katrina:** Greg Ip and Mark Whitehouse, "Awash in Cash: Cheap Money, Growing Risks—Stash Flow: Huge Flood of Capital to Invest Spurs World-Wide Risk Taking—Corporate and Foreign Savings Chase Assets, Driving Prices Up, Keeping Returns Low—'A Global Game of Chicken,'" *Wall Street Journal*, November 3, 2005, A1.

56 **Australia's biggest homegrown:** Patrick Barta and Mary Kissel, "Awash in Cash: Cheap Money, Growing Risks—Buying Bridges: From Australia, Money Chases Roads, Airports Around Globe—Forced-Savings Plan Creates Big War Chest That Banks Match Up with Projects—Macquarie Bails Out Chicago," *Wall Street Journal*, December 6, 2005, A1.

56 **An investment partnership:** E. S. Browning, "Awash in Cash: Cheap Money, Growing Risks—Woodland Haven: U.S. Timberland Gets Pricey as Big Money Seeks Shelter—Rush Reflects Glut of Capital, Low Payoff on Other Assets; Sold: 5% of State of Maine—But Do Trees Grow to the Sky?" *Wall Street Journal*, November 4, 2005, A1.

56 **"The most severe":** Charles W. Calomiris, "The Subprime Turmoil: What's Old, What's New and What's Next," Jackson Hole, Wyoming,

October 2, 2008. http://www.kc.frb.org/publicat/sympos/2008/
Calomiris.08.20.08.pdf

57 **"make sense tactically"**: Transcript, FOMC meeting, June 24–25, 2003.
http://www.federalreserve.gov/monetarypolicy/fomchistorical2003.htm

57 **"It was like someone"**: "Outspoken: A Conversation with Nassim
Nicholas Taleb," *Washington Post*, March 15, 2009, B2.

58 **"an eventual crisis"**: William R. White, "Is Price Stability Enough?"
Bank for International Settlements, April 2006. http://www.bis.org/publ/
work205.pdf

58 **"We tried in 2004"**: Greg Ip and Jon Hilsenrath, "Debt Bomb: Inside the
Subprime Mortgage Debacle," *Wall Street Journal*, August 7, 2007, A1.

58 **"I will stipulate"**: Transcript, FOMC meeting, August 12, 2003. http://
www.federalreserve.gov/monetarypolicy/fomchistorical2003.htm

59 the *Wall Street Journal:* "WSJ Forecasting Survey—March 2008,"
Wall Street Journal. http://online.wsj.com/public/resources/documents/
wsjecon0308.xls

59 **A 2004 Fed working paper:** Joshua Gallin, "The Long-Run Relationship
between House Prices and Rents," Board of Governors of Federal
Reserve System, September 2004. http://www.federalreserve.gov/pubs/
feds/2004/200450/200450pap.pdf

59 **"I would tell audiences"**: Alan Greenspan, *The Age of Turbulence:
Adventures in a New World* (New York: Penguin Press, 2007), 232.

60 **"We cannot practice"**: Transcript, Federal Reserve Bank of Kansas
City, Jackson Hole Conference, August 2008. http://www.kc.frb.org/
PUBLICAT/SYMPOS/1999/sym99prg.htm

61 **"He didn't say anything"**: John Cassidy, "Anatomy of a Meltdown,"
The New Yorker, December 1, 2008. http://www.newyorker.com/
reporting/2008/12/01/081201fa_fact_cassidy?currentPage=all

61 **"The biggest bubble"**: Alan S. Blinder and Ricardo Reis, "Understanding
the Greenspan Standard," Federal Reserve Bank of Kansas City, Jackson
Hole Conference, August 2005. http://www.kc.frb.org/publicat/
sympos/2005/pdf/blinderreis.paper.0804.pdf

61 **"persistent and ultimately"**: Phil Izzo, "Volcker Supports Popping
Bubbles, Regulating Hedge Funds," *Real Time Economics*, February 26,
2009. http://blogs.wsj.com/economics/2009/02/26/volcker-supports-
popping-bubbles-regulating-hedge-funds

61 **"Mopping up after"**: John Gieve, "Seven Lessons from the Last Three Years," speech delivered February 19, 2009.

62 **"In the subprime market"**: Edward M. Gramlich, "Booms and Busts: The Case of Subprime Mortgages," Federal Reserve Bank of Kansas City, Jackson Hole Conference, August 2007. http://www.kc.frb.org/publicat/sympos/2007/pdf/Gramlich_0415.pdf

63 **"He was opposed to it"**: Greg Ip, "Did Greenspan Add to Subprime Woes? Gramlich Says Ex-Colleague Blocked Crackdown on Predatory Lenders Despite Growing Concerns," *Wall Street Journal*, June 9, 2007, B1.

63 **"I told him"**: "'The Impact Was Larger Than I Expected': Greenspan's Chats with the Journal,'" *Wall Street Journal*, April 8, 2008. http://online.wsj.com/article/SB120759233667695449.html#

64 **"planned to be largely passive"**: Greenspan, *Turbulence*, 373.

64 **"It is effective"**: Alan Greenspan, letter to John J. LaFalce, May 30, 2002.

65 **"I made a mistake"**: House Committee on Oversight and Government Reform, hearing, October 23, 2008. http://oversight.house.gov/story.asp?id=2256

CHAPTER 4: THERE ARE JEWS IN BOSTON, TOO

68 **"The Fed needs"**: Ben S. Bernanke, Frederic S. Mishkin, and Adam S. Posen, "What Happens When Greenspan Is Gone?" *Wall Street Journal*, January 5, 2000, A22.

68 **"That's the one thing"**: Interview, Ben Bernanke.

68 **Bernanke was a clue**: *New York Times* crossword puzzle, November 12, 2008, 21-Across. Personal communication with Bob Klahn.

68 **"Cause of difficulty"**: "Shuffled Cards," *New York Sun*, August 24, 2007, 34-Across. http://www.nysun.com/crosswords/subscriber_puzzle.php

69 **tobacco town of 6,400**: S.C. Budget and Control Board, "Office of Research & Statistics, Population 1950–2000 Cherokee, Chester, Chesterfield, Clarendon, Colleton, Darlington, Dillon," from South Carolina Population Reports Web site http://www.ors2.state.sc.us/population/pop03c.asp

69 **"In Dillon"**: Ben S. Bernanke, "Chairman Ben S. Bernanke National and Regional Economic Overview at the Presentation of the Citizen of the Carolinas Award," from Board of Governors of the Federal Reserve System

Web site, November 29, 2007. http://www.federalreserve.gov/newsevents/speech/bernanke20071129a.htm

69 **the comic book section:** Ben S. Bernanke, "Chairman Ben S. Bernanke at the Presentation of the Order of the Palmetto, Dillon, South Carolina," from Board of Governors of the Federal Reserve System Web site, September 1, 2006. http://www.federalreserve.gov/newsevents/speech/Bernanke20060901a.htm

69 **"Grandma, why don't you teach":** Phil Izzo, "Bernanke Advises Going Long on Blintzes," *Real Time Economics*, December 3, 2007. http://blogs.wsj.com/economics/2007/12/03/bernanke-advises-going-long-on-blintzes

70 **"One of his teachers":** Greg Ip, "Banker in Chief: Bernanke Is Named to Lead the Fed—Ex-Academic Is Expected to Focus on Inflation, Not on 'Asset Bubbles'—Stock Investors Cheer the Pick," *Wall Street Journal*, October 25, 2005.

70 **"UNC-Chapel Hill":** Interview, Ben Bernanke.

70 **"I assured them":** Interview, Kenneth Manning.

71 **"was the superstar":** Michael M. Grynbaum, "At Harvard, They Hail a Fed Chief," *New York Times*, June 5, 2008, 1.

71 **Pedro's South of the Border:** Bernanke, "Chairman Ben S. Bernanke at the Presentation of the Order of the Palmetto."

71 **"Ben Bernanke Interchange":** H. 4600, South Carolina General Assembly, 117th session. www.scstatehouse.gov/sess117_2007-2008/bills/4600.doc

72 **"It's just a great sense":** Michael Phillips, "Fed Chief's Boyhood Home Is Sold after Foreclosure," *Wall Street Journal*, February 15, 2009, A1.

72 **"He wasn't a prima donna":** Interview, Stanley Fischer.

72 **"My first reaction":** Interview, Mark Gertler.

75 **how the trio:** *Time*, February 15, 1999. http://www.time.com/time/covers/0,16641,19990215,00.html

76 **"Fix the roof":** Bernanke et al. "What Happens When . . ."

76 **"All I had in mind":** Interview, Ben Bernanke.

76 **Research Papers in Economics database:** University of Connecticut: IDEAS Repec. "Top 5% Authors as of December 2008," December 2008. http://ideas.repec.org/top/top.person.nbcites.html

76 **"On the administrative side":** Ben S. Bernanke, "Remarks by Governor Ben S. Bernanke at the Annual Meeting of the American Economic Association, Philadelphia, Pennsylvania: The Transition from Academic to

Policymaker," January 7, 2005. http://www.federalreserve.gov/boarddocs/speeches/2005/20050107/default.htm

77 **"We were always pessimistic":** Federal Reserve Board of Governors, "Meeting of the Federal Open Market Committee," August 13, 2002. http://www.federalreserve.gov/monetarypolicy/files/FOMC20020813meeting.pdf

77 **"I support your recommendation":** Federal Reserve Board of Governors, "Meeting of the Federal Open Market Committee," December 10, 2002. http://www.federalreserve.gov/monetarypolicy/files/FOMC20021210meeting.pdf

78 **He lamented:** Bernanke, "The Transition from Academic to Policymaker," American Economic Association, January 7, 2005. www.federalreserve.gov/BOARDDOCS/SPEECHES/2005/20050107/default.htm

78 **"essentially equivalent":** Ben S. Bernanke, "Deflation: Making Sure 'It' Doesn't Happen Here," Federal Reserve Board, November 21, 2002. http://www.federalreserve.gov./BOARDDOCS/SPEECHES/2002/20021121/default.htm

79 **"Now YOU can drop":** David Beckworth, "'Helicopter Ben' Pictures," *Macro and Other Market Musings*, September 19, 2007. http://macromarketmusings.blogspot.com/2007/09/helicopter-ben-pictures.html

79 **"Big Ben Fires Up":** Joshua Zumbrun, "Big Ben Fires Up the Chopper," *Forbes*, December 8, 2008. http://www.forbes.com/businessinthebeltway/2008/12/06/bernanke-fed-recession-biz-beltway-cx_jz_1208interest.html

79 **"A part of monetary policymaking":** Bernanke, "Transition from Academic . . ."

81 **"I came to trust":** The White House, "President Attends Swearing-In Ceremony for Federal Reserve Chairman Ben Bernanke," February 6, 2006. http://georgewbush-whitehouse.archives.gov/news/releases/2006/02/20060206.html

81 **When the time came:** Interviews with Ben Bernanke, Keith Hennessy, and Allan Hubbard.

82 **"While speculative behavior":** Ben S. Bernanke, "Skills, Ownership, and Economic Security," July 12, 2005. http://georgewbush-whitehouse.archives.gov/cea/20050712.html

84 **"embarked on a fundamentally"**: Vincent Reinhart, "The Governance, Communication and Conduction of the Federal Reserve's Monetary Policy," February 29, 2008. http://research.chicagogsb.edu/igm/events/docs/Reinhart-SecondMonetaryPolicyForum.pdf

86 **"I will tell you that"**: Transcript, FOMC, July 2–3, 1996. http://www.federalreserve.gov/monetarypolicy/files/FOMC20020319meeting.pdf

87 **"Mr. Inflation"**: Interview, Alan Blinder.

88 **"Changes in the structure"**: Lawrence Summers, "A Lack of Fear Is Cause for Concern," *Financial Times*, December 27, 2006, 13.

89 **"housing activity appears"**: Henry M. Paulson, "Statement by U.S. Treasury Secretary Henry M. Paulson following the Meeting of the G7 Finance Ministers and Central Bank Governors Essen, Germany," February 10, 2007. http://www.ustreas.gov/press/releases/hp255.htm

89 **"At this juncture"**: Ben S. Bernanke, "Chairman Ben S. Bernanke, the Economic Outlook before the Joint Economic Committee, U.S. Congress," from Board of Governors of the Federal Reserve System Web site, March 28, 2007. http://www.federalreserve.gov/newsevents/testimony/bernanke20070328a.htm

89 **The Fed created**: Greg Ip, "Bernanke, in First Crisis, Rewrites Fed Playbook," *Wall Street Journal*, October 31, 2007, A1.

91 **"We are in the midst"**: Timothy F. Geithner, "Perspectives on U.S. Monetary Policy," from Federal Reserve Bank of New York Web site, April 1, 2005. http://www.newyorkfed.org/newsevents/speeches/2005/gei050404.html

92 **"Economics policy makers"**: Lawrence Summers, "As America Falters, Policy Makers Must Look Ahead," *Financial Times*, March 26, 2007, 17.

92 **One of them**: Kate Kelly, "A 'Subprime' Fund Is on the Brink," *Wall Street Journal*, June 16, 2007, B1.

92 **"near the low end"**: Ben Bernanke, "Semiannual Monetary Policy Report to the Congress," House Financial Services Committee, July 18, 2007. http://www.federalreserve.gov/newsevents/testimony/bernanke20070718a.htm

93 **"fairly significant"**: Senate Banking Committee, hearing, July 19, 2007.

93 **In April 2009**: International Monetary Fund, *Global Financial Stability Report*, April 2009, xi. qwqwimf.org/external/pubs/ft/gfsr/2009/01/index.htm

93 **On the last day of July**: http://timeline.stlouisfed.org

94 **"believes that there is always"**: "JIM CRAMER: 'Mad Money w/ Jim Cramer.'" http://www.cnbc.com/id/15838187

CHAPTER 5: PAS DE DEUX

97 **"normalization of the assessment"**: Greg Ip and Joellen Perry, "Credit Turmoil Tests Central Banks—As Market Losses Spread, Policy Makers Grapple with Hard-Line Stance," *Wall Street Journal*, August 10, 2007, A3.

97 **The ECB officials:** Joellen Perry, "ECB, After Hard Birth, Comes of Age in Crisis," *Wall Street Journal*, November 6, 2007, A1.

99 **"There was an appreciation"**: Interview, Eric Rosengren.

100 **"Sometimes the role"**: Vincent Reinhart, "The Governance, Communication and Conduction of the Federal Reserve's Monetary Policy," February 29, 2008. http://research.chicagogsb.edu/igm/events/docs/Reinhart-SecondMonetaryPolicyForum.pdf

100 **"the complete evaporation"**: "BNP Paribas Investment Partners temporarily suspends the calculation of the Net Asset Value of the following funds: Parvest Dynamic ABS, BNP Paribas ABS EURIBOR and BNP Paribas ABS EONIA," August 9, 2007.

101 **"We were the first"**: Interview with Jean-Claude Trichet, president of the European Central Bank, and *Le Figaro* magazine conducted by Ghislain de Montalembert, from European Central Bank Web site, January 23, 2009. http://www.ecb.int/press/key/date/2009/html/sp090123.en.html

102 **That morning:** Federal Reserve Bank of New York, "Temporary Open Market Operations" Web site http://www.newyorkfed.org/markets/omo/dmm/historical/tomo/search.cfm

103 **"The lack of a spare tire"**: Alan Greenspan, "Do Efficient Financial Markets Mitigate Financial Crises? Before the 1999 Financial Markets Conference of the Federal Reserve Bank of Atlanta," from the Federal Reserve Board Web site, October 19, 1999. http://www.federalreserve.gov/boarddocs/speeches/1999/19991019.htm

103 **"enable risk and return"**: Donald L. Kohn, "Commentary: Has Financial Development Made the World Riskier?" from Federal Reserve Bank of Kansas City Web site, August 2005. http://www.kc.frb.org/publicat/sympos/2005/PDF/Kohn2005.pdf

104 **"All of a sudden"**: Interview.

104 **In 2006:** Olivier Blanchard, "The Crisis: Basic Mechanisms and Appropriate Policies," International Monetary Fund, April 2009. www .imf.org/external/pubs/ft/wp/2009/wp0908.pdf

105 **"When the music stops":** Michiyo Nakamoto and David Wighton, "Bullish Citigroup Is 'Still Dancing' to the Beat of the Buy-out Boom," *Financial Times*, July 10, 2007, 1.

CHAPTER 6: THE FOUR MUSKETEERS:
BERNANKE'S BRAIN TRUST

106 **"Since 1945":** Frederic Mishkin, "Asymetrical Information and Financial Crises: A Historical Perspective," National Bureau of Economic Research, Working Papers 3400, July 1990, 29.

107 **"always calm and thoughtful":** Laurence Meyer, *A Term at the Fed: An Insider's View* (New York: HarperBusiness, 2004), 45.

108 **"It is just not credible":** Alan Greenspan, "Remarks by Chairman Alan Greenspan at the Haas Annual Business Faculty Research Dialogue, University of California," from the Federal Reserve Board Web site, September 4, 1998. http://www.federalreserve.gov/boarddocs/ speeches/1998/19980904.htm

108 **That's what he was doing:** Interview, Don Kohn.

109 **Before Bernanke ascended:** "Panel Discussion," Federal Reserve Bank of St. Louis, October 13, 2003. http://research.stlouisfed.org/publications/ review/04/07/PanelDisc.pdf

110 **"This is the most":** Interview, John Cogan.

110 **The couple has a penthouse:** William Neuman, "A Board Turndown, and Then a Buyer with Board Ties," *New York Times*, April 24, 2005. Also, District of Columbia property records.

113 **"I told Larry":** Noam Scheiber, "Obama's Choice," *The New Republic*, November 5, 2008. http://www.tnr.com/politics/story.html?id=c85b418- b-5237-4f54-891f-8385243162bd

CHAPTER 7: RE: RE: RE: RE: RE: RE: BLUE SKY

116 **In the same way:** Stephen Cecchetti, "Federal Reserve Policy Actions in August 2007: Frequently Asked Questions," *Vox*, August 13, 2007. http:// www.voxeu.org/index.php?q=node/460

117 **The "tri-party" term:** Kenneth D. Garbade, "The Evolution of Repo Contracting Conventions in the 1980s." *Economic Policy Review*, Federal Reserve Bank of New York, May 2006. http://www.newyorkfed.org/research/epr/06v12n1/0605garb.pdf

117 **"The structure of the financial system":** Timothy F. Geithner, "Reducing Systemic Risk in a Dynamic Financial System," Economic Club of New York, New York City, June 9, 2008. http://www.ny.frb.org/newsevents/speeches/2008/tfg080609.html

117 **In June 2009:** Securities and Exchange Commission, "SEC Charges Former Countrywide Executives with Fraud," June 4, 2009. http://www.sec.gov/news/press/2009/2009-129.htm

118 **"We worked it out":** Greg Ip, "Bernanke, in First Crisis, Rewrites Fed Playbook," *Wall Street Journal*, October 31, 2007, A1.

121 **He no longer:** Ibid.

123 **"I generally do not place":** Frederic S. Mishkin, "Housing and the Monetary Transmission Mechanism," Federal Reserve Bank of Kansas, Jackson Hole Conference, August 2007. http://www.kc.frb.org/Publicat/Sympos/2007/PDF/Mishkin_0415.pdf

123 **"The problem this time":** Lawrence Summers, "This Is Where Fannie and Freddie Step In," *Financial Times*, August 27, 2007. http://blogs.ft.com/wolfforum/2007/08/this-is-where-fhtml

CHAPTER 8: RUNNING FROM BEHIND

125 **The Federal Open Market Committee:** Vincent Reinhardt, "The Outlook for Federal Reserve Policy," American Enterprise Institute, www.aei.org, April 21, 2010.

125 **"You challenge Greenspan":** Interview.

125 **"influenced by his own":** Vincent Reinhart, "The Governance, Communication and Conduction of the Federal Reserve's Monetary Policy," February 29, 2008. http://research.chicagogsb.edu/igm/events/docs/Reinhart-SecondMonetaryPolicyForum.pdf

127 **"The Federal Reserve needs":** Greg Ip, "Rate Cut Has Foes on Main Street—Some Americans Think Fed Should Avoid the 'Hazard' of Bailing Out Speculators," *Wall Street Journal*, September 18, 2007, A2.

128 **At a closed-door:** Personal communication.

128 **"The mistake I made"**: Interview, Ben Bernanke.

129 **"scant evidence"**: FOMC minutes, October 31, 2007. http://www.federalreserve.gov/monetarypolicy/files/fomcminutes20071031.pdf

130 **"The hawks are very passionate"**: Laurence Meyer, "Hawks Are from Mars/Doves Are from Venus," *Monetary Policy Insights: Policy Focus*, Macroeconomic Advisers LLC, August 26, 2008.

131 **"Putting the 'shm' "**: Frederic S. Mishkin, "Sandridge Lecture of the Virginia Association of Economists and the H. Parker Willis Lecture of Washington and Lee University, Lexington, Virginia," March 27, 2008. http://www.federalreserve.gov/newsevents/speech/mishkin20080327a.htm

132 **After he dropped**: Frederic S. Mishkin, "Risk USA 2007 Conference," November 5, 2007. http://www.federalreserve.gov/newsevents/speech/mishkin20071105a.htm

132 **"quite unlikely"**: Dennis P. Lockhart, "On Rocket Science," November 7, 2007. http://www.frbatlanta.org/invoke.cfm?objectid=1B1B8CE2-5056-9F12-127409C441EFE60F&method=display

132 **A few months later**: Dennis P. Lockhart, "Thoughts on the Future of Credit Markets," February 7, 2008. http://www.frbatlanta.org/invoke.cfm?objectid=F400D2BA-5056-9F12-12C1F5156DCBB7A3&method=display

132 **Janet Yellen**: Janet L. Yellen, "Risks and Prospects for the U.S. Economy," July 10, 2008. http://www.frbsf.org/news/speeches/2008/0710.pdf

132 **"a worrisome possibility"**: FOMC Minutes, June 24–25, 2008. http://www.federalreserve.gov/monetarypolicy/fomcminutes20080625ep.htm

133 **"The public should understand"**: Donald L. Kohn, "National Association for Business Economics Session, Allied Social Science Associations Annual Meeting," New Orleans, Louisiana, January 5, 2008. http://www.federalreserve.gov/newsevents/speech/kohn20080105a.htm

133 **Bernanke's speeches**: Brian Blackstone, "Bernanke Reasserts Dominance over Wall Street," *Real Time Economics*, July 22, 2008. http://blogs.wsj.com/economics/2008/07/22/bernanke-reasserts-dominance-over-wall-street

134 **Several Fed officials**: FOMC minutes, December 11, 2007. http://www.federalreserve.gov/monetarypolicy/fomcminutes20071211.htm

134 **"Underpinning this story"**: Lockhart, "On Rocket Science."

134 **"When I'm out there"**: Interview, Dennis Lockhart.

134 **"monetary policy that is appropriate"**: Frederic S. Mishkin,

"Monetary Policy Flexibility, Risk Management, and Financial Disruptions," January 11, 2008. http://www.federalreserve.gov/newsevents/speech/mishkin20080111a.htm

135 **"Democracy is a good thing"**: Ethan S. Harris, *Ben Bernanke's Fed: The Federal Reserve after Greenspan* (Cambridge, Mass.: Harvard Business School Publishing, 2008), 195.

135 **"a deteriorating housing sector"**: Minutes of FOMC, December 10, 2007. http://www.federalreserve.gov/monetarypolicy/files/fomcminutes20071211.pdf

135 **"From talking to clients"**: Greg Ip, "Rate Cut Fails to Cheer Market; Fed Sifts Options," *Wall Street Journal*, December 12, 2007, A1.

137 **"Central banks have great"**: Stephen Cecchetti, "The Art of Crisis Management: Auctions and Swaps," *Vox*, December 16, 2007. http://www.voxeu.org/index.php?q=node/814

139 **"a more effective"**: Timothy Geithner, "Restoring Market Liquidity in a Financial Crisis," December 13, 2007. http://www.newyorkfed.org/newsevents/speeches_archive/2007/gei071213.html

140 **That 134 percent increase**: European Central Bank, "The International Role of the Euro," July 2008, 16. http://www.ecb.int/pub/pdf/other/euro-international-role200807en.pdf

142 **By the end of December 2008**: Data at http://www.ustreas.gov/press/international-reserve-position.html, Table 2

142 **"Central banks have been"**: Barry Eichengreen, "The Global Credit Crisis as History," December 2008. http://www.econ.berkeley.edu/~eichengr/global_credit_crisis_history_12-3-08.pdf

146 **"It does look like"**: Greg Ip, "Criticism of Rate Cut Mounts: Société Générale Issue Prompts Question of Possible False Alarm," *Wall Street Journal*, January 25, 2008, A2.

CHAPTER 9: "UNUSUAL AND EXIGENT"

148 **"I would be very cautious"**: Senate Committee on Banking, hearing, March 4, 2008.

148 **"Central banks typically"**: Charles Kindleberger and Robert Aliber, *Manias, Panics and Crashes*, 5th ed. (Hoboken, N.J.: John Wiley & Sons, 2005), 237.

149 **in normal times:** Brad DeLong, "Republic of the Central Banker," *The American Prospect*, October 27, 2008. http://www.prospect.org/cs/articles?article=republic_of_the_central_banker

150 **"The bottom line is simple":** Paul McCulley, "The Paradox of Deleveraging Will Be Broken," November 2008. http://www.pimco.com/LeftNav/Featured+Market+Commentary/FF/2008/Global+Central+Bank+Focus+11-08+McCulley+Paradox+of+Deleveraging+Will+Be+Broken.htm

151 **"They've got a month or so":** Interview, Treasury staff.

153 **"I think I've been around":** Interview, Treasury staff.

154 **"I just never, frankly":** Senate Banking Committee, hearing, April 3, 2008.

154 **Months later:** Interview, Kevin Warsh.

154 **$2 billion in cash:** Securities and Exchange Commission, "Chairman Cox Letter to Basel Committee in Support of New Guidance on Liquidity Management," March 20, 2008. http://www.sec.gov/news/press/2008/2008-48.htm

154 **The company asked Gary Parr:** Bryan Burrough, "Bringing Down Bear Stearns," *Vanity Fair*, August 2008. http://www.vanityfair.com/politics/features/2008/08/bear_stearns200808

154 **Schwartz followed up:** Form S-4, JPMorgan Chase.

154 **"Tim, look":** Interview, Timothy Geithner.

155 **quietly gave Friedman:** Kate Kelly and John Hilsenrath, "New York Fed Chairman's Ties to Goldman Raise Questions," *Wall Street Journal*, May 4, 2009.

156 **"So what can taxpayers expect":** Allan H. Meltzer, "Keep the Fed Away from Investment Bank," *Wall Street Journal*, July 16, 2008, A17.

157 **The SEC was legally:** Kara Scannell and Susanne Craig, "SEC Chief under Fire as Fed Seeks Bigger Wall Street Role—Cox Draws Criticism for Low-Key Leadership during Bear Crisis," *Wall Street Journal*, June 23, 2008, A1.

158 **"We've got to make":** Greg Ip, "Crisis Management: Fed's Fireman on Wall Street Feels Some Heat," *Wall Street Journal*, May 30, 2008, A1.

158 **"Things happened very quickly":** Senate Banking Committee, hearing, April 3, 2008.

159 **"Everybody on the phone":** Interview, Donald Kohn.

159 **Bear Stearns had:** Harvey Rosenbloom, et al., "Fed Interview: Managing

Moral Hazard in Financial Crisis," *Economic Letter*, Federal Reserve Bank of Dallas, October 2008.

160 **"a gigantic centralization":** Herbert Hoover, "Herbert Hoover: 1932–33," from the Public Papers of the Presidents of the United States Web site, 1932, 308. http://quod.lib.umich.edu/cgi/t/text/pageviewer-idx?c=ppotpus;cc=ppotpus;rgn=full%20text;idno=4731694.1932.001;didno=4731694.1932.001;view=image;seq=00000364

160 **After the 1932 law passed:** Howard H. Hackley, *Lending Functions of the Federal Reserve Banks: A History* (Washington, D.C.: Federal Reserve Board of Governors, 1973), 130.

160 **"guiding monetary policy":** David Fettig, "Lender of More Than Last Resort," Federal Reserve Bank of Minneapolis, December 2002. http://www.minneapolisfed.org/publications_papers/pub_display.cfm?id=3392

162 **"We recognized, of course,":** Senate Banking Committee, hearing, April 3, 2008.

163 **"It seems like I showed up":** Transcript posted at http://georgewbush-whitehouse.archives.gov/news/releases/2008/03/20080314-5.html

164 **"It was just clear":** Robin Sidel et al., "The Week That Shook Wall Street: Inside the Demise of Bear Stearns," *Wall Street Journal*, March 18, 2008, A1.

167 **"It became clear that":** Senate Banking Committee, hearing, April 3, 2008.

168 **"My question then was":** Interview, Kevin Warsh.

168 **"The only feasible option":** Senate Banking Committee, hearing, April 3, 2008.

169 **"It took some time":** Phillip Swagel, "The Financial Crisis: An Inside View," *Brookings Papers on Economic Activity*, April 3, 2009, 24. http://www.brookings.edu/economics/bpea/~/media/Files/Programs/ES/BPEA/2009_spring_bpea_papers/2

170 **"The Primary Dealer Credit Facility":** William C. Dudley, "May You Live in Interesting Times: The Sequel," Federal Reserve Bank of Chicago, May 15, 2008. http://www.newyorkfed.org/newsevents/speeches/2008/dud080515.html

173 **"This cost . . . must be":** Senate Banking Committee, hearing, April 3, 2008.

173 **"Did the Federal Reserve":** Video posted at http://www.charlierose.com/guest/view/420

174 **"a rogue operation"**: Craig Torres, "Fed 'Rogue Operation' Spurs Further Bailout Calls," Bloomberg, May 2, 2008. http://www.bloomberg.com/apps/news?pid=20601109&sid=a1ctn1Xfq5Do&refer=home

174 **"There is no question"**: Interview, Frederic Mishkin.

CHAPTER 10: FANNIE, FREDDIE, AND "FEDDIE"

179 **"The chance"**: Interview, Henry Paulson.

179 **"The more complex issues"**: House Financial Services Committee, hearing, July 10, 2008.

179 **"[R]egulators are working together"**: Ibid.

180 **"Financial crises are extremely difficult"**: Ben Bernanke, "GSE Portfolios, Systemic Risk and Affordable Housing, March 6, 2007. http://www.federalreserve.gov/newsevents/speech/Bernanke20070306a.htm

183 **"If you're not used"**: Senate Banking Committee, hearing, July 15, 2008.

183 *Fortune* **magazine**: "21 Dumbest Moments in Business," *Fortune*, http://money.cnn.com/galleries/2008/fortune/0812/gallery.dumbest_moments_2009.fortune/7.html

184 **"They should have wiped"**: David Wessel, "Greenspan Sees Bottom in Housing, Criticizes Bailout," *Wall Street Journal*, August 14, 2008, A1.

184 **"Although it is widely described"**: Stanley Fischer, "Concluding Comments," Federal Reserve Bank of Kansas City, Jackson Hole Conference, August 2008. http://www.kc.frb.org/publicat/sympos/2008/fischer.09.28.08.pdf

185 **While his wife rode**: David Cho and Neil Irwin, "In Crucible of Crisis, Paulson, Bernanke and Geithner Forge a Committee of Three," *Washington Post*, September 19, 2008, A1.

187 **"The troops got to Falluja"**: James R. Hagerty and Damian Paletta, "Red Ink Clouds Role of Fannie, Freddie," *Wall Street Journal*, February 27, 2009, A2.

CHAPTER 11: BREAKING THE GLASS

188 **The dealers jumped**: Fed's H 4.1 report, September 10, 2008, September 27, 2008.

189 **"That weekend really hit home"**: Interview, Ben Bernanke.

190 **"I left expecting the markets"**: Interview, Henry Paulson.

191 **"I just changed my mind"**: Interview, Timothy Geithner.

192 **AIG disclosed in early 2009**: "Attachment A—Collateral Postings Under AIGFP CDS," http://www.aig.com/aigweb/internet/en/files/CounterpartyAttachments031809_tcm385-155645.pdf

194 **"We did this very unhappily"**: Interview.

196 **"If you are comfortable"**: Interview.

196 **At 4:50 P.M.**: Monica Langley, Deborah Solomon, and Matthew Karnitschnig, "Bad Bets and Cash Crunch Pushed Ailing AIG to Brink," *Wall Street Journal*, September 18, 2008, A1.

197 **At 7:50 P.M.**: Ibid.

197 **Fed officials were stunned**: American International Group, Inc., Form 10-Q, September 30, 2008. http://media.corporate-ir.net/media_files/irol/76/76115/reports/Q308_10Q.pdf

197 **At one point, Barney Frank recalled**: House Financial Services Committee, hearing, February 10, 2009.

199 **The Dow Jones Industrial Average**: Tom Lauricella, Liz Rappaport, and Annelena Lobb, "Mounting Fears Shake World Markets as Banking Giants Rush to Raise Capital," *Wall Street Journal*, September 18, 2008, A1.

199 **"It was becoming clear"**: Interview.

200 **When asked by CBS's *60 Minutes***: "Paulson Warns of 'Fragile' Economy," *60 Minutes*, aired September 28, 2008; taped September 26, 2008. www.cbsnews.com/stories/2008/09/28/60minutes/main4483612.shtml

202 **"I remember sitting"**: "Transcript: Charlie Gibson Interviews President Bush," *ABC News*, December 1, 2008. http://abcnews.go.com/WN/Politics/Story?id=6356046

204 **"I kind of scared them"**: Interview, Ben Bernanke, October 14, 2008.

205 **"Our political calculation"**: Interview, Ben Bernanke.

207 **The news triggered**: Documents released by the Massachusetts secretary of state.

207 **Bruce Bent**: *Securities and Exchange Commission v. Reserve Management Company, Inc, Resrv Partners, Inc., Bruce Bent Sr. and Bruce Bent II*, Civil Action No. 09-CV-4346 (S.D.N.Y. May 5, 2009). http://www.sec.gov/litigation/litreleases/2009/lr21025.htm

212 **A few months after leaving:** David Wessel, "Capital," *Wall Street Journal*, March 28, 2009.

213 **"I'd like to ask you":** Senate Banking Committee, hearing, September 23, 2008.

213 **At an early-morning:** Interviews with participants.

214 **"Many of these assets":** Joint Economic Committee, hearing, September 24, 2008.

215 **McCain took the call:** Jonathan Weisman, "How McCain Stirred a Simmering Pot," *Washington Post*, September 27, 2008, A1.

CHAPTER 12: "SOCIALISM WITH AMERICAN CHARACTERISTICS"

218 **In 2003, WaMu's chief executive:** Peter S. Goodman and Gretchen Morgenson, "Saying Yes, WaMu Built Empire on Shaky Loans," *New York Times*, December 27, 2008. http://www.nytimes.com/2008/12/28/business/28wamu.html?pagewanted=2

219 **Bush's initial choice:** Jim Rutenberg and Raymond Hernandez, "F.D.I.C. Post Seems Unlikely for New York Banking Chief," *New York Times*, February 2, 2006, B4. http://www.nytimes.com/2006/02/02/nyregion/02diana.html

221 **"This is an unprecedented":** Sam Jones, "The WaMu Wipeout: Who Gets Hit?" *Financial Times*, September 26, 2008. http://ftalphaville.ft.com/blog/2008/09/26/16384/the-wamu-wipeout-who-gets-hit

221 **On Wednesday:** Affidavit of Robert K. Steel, http://www.scribd.com/doc/6403234/Affidavit-of-Robert-K-Steel. Also, Wells Fargo Form S-4.

225 **For one thing:** Stephen L. Feldman, "Notice 2008-83: The IRS Offers Reassurance to Troubled Banks," from Morrison Foerster Web site, October 2008. http://www.mofo.com/news/updates/files/14544.html

226 **"You cannot":** Interview, Timothy Geithner.

226 **The looming November election:** June Kronholz, Sarah Lueck, and Greg Hitt, "The Financial Crisis: 'No' Votes Came from All Directions," *Wall Street Journal*, September 30, 2008, A3.

227 **"It became increasingly clear":** Interview, Ben Bernanke.

229 **"Aggressive surgery":** Interview.

230 **"Severe financial instability":** Ben S. Bernanke, "Current Economic and

Financial Conditions," October 7, 2008. http://www.federalreserve.gov/
newsevents/speech/bernanke20081007a.htm

231 **Although heavy on the:** "Joint Statement by Central Banks,"
October 8, 2008. http://www.federalreserve.gov/newsevents/press/
monetary/20081008a.htm

233 **"Why there's been":** Damian Paletta, "FDIC Chief Raps Rescue for Helping
Banks over Homeowners," *Wall Street Journal*, October 16, 2008, A1.

233 **Four or five:** See the June 14, 2008, communiqué. http://www
.g8.utoronto.ca/finance/fm080614-statement.pdf

235 **At one point:** Interview, David McCormick, other participants.

236 **"The facts":** Neil Irwin and David Cho, "Paulson's Change in Rescue
Tactics: Plans Revamped After Scope of Bad Assets Became Clear, Stocks
Plunged," *Washington Post,* October 15, 2008, D1.

237 **"Everyone said":** Interview, David Nason.

238 **The next day:** Interview, Kevin Warsh, David Nason, other participants.

239 **"The terms had to be":** Swagel, 39. http://www.brookings.edu/
economics/bpea/~/media/Files/Programs/ES/BPEA/2009_spring_bpea
_papers/2009_spring_bpea_swagel.pdf

241 **In an interview:** James Fallows, "Be Nice to the Countries That Lend
You Money," *The Atlantic*, December 2008. http://www.theatlantic.com/
doc/200812/fallows-chinese-banker

CHAPTER 13: WORLD OF ZIRP

242 **Surveys of businesses:** Federal Reserve, "The Beige Book
Summary," January 14, 2009. http://www.federalreserve.gov/fomc/
beigebook/2009/20090114/default.htm

243 **"pragmatic enough":** "Remarks by Secretary Henry M. Paulson Jr. at the
Ronald Reagan Presidential Library," November 20, 2008. http://www
.treas.gov/press/releases/hp1285.htm

246 **six of the twelve:** Federal Reserve, discount-rate meeting minutes.
http://www.federalreserve.gov/newsevents/press/monetary/
monetary20081125b1.pdf

247 **Brian Madigan:** Jeffrey Fuhrer and Brian Madigan, "Monetary Policy
When Interest Rates Are Bounded at Zero," Working Paper 94-1, Federal
Reserve Bank of Boston, 1994.

247 **"A central bank"**: FOMC minutes, January 29–30, 2002. http://www
.federalreserve.gov/boarddocs/speeches/2002/20021121/default.htm

247 **When they briefed the FOMC**: Transcript, http://www.federalreserve
.gov/monetarypolicy/files/FOMC20020130meeting.pdf

251 **That balance sheet**: From U.S. Treasury, "U.S. International
Reserve Position," January 5, 2009, http://www.treas.gov/press/
releases/200915163047912.htm; and Federal Reserve, "Factors Affecting
Reserve Balances," December 18, 2008, http://www.federalreserve.gov/
releases/h41/20081218

253 **"The impact of the totality"**: Janet Yellen, "U.S. Monetary Policy
Objectives in the Short and Long Run," Federal Reserve Bank
of San Francisco, January 4, 2009. http://www.frbsf.org/news/
speeches/2009/0104b.html

253 **In September 2008:** Fed H.3 release.

254 **"credit easing"**: Ben S. Bernanke, "The Crisis and the Policy Response,"
Federal Reserve Board, January 13, 2009. http://www.federalreserve.gov/
newsevents/speech/bernanke20090113a.htm

254 **"What justification is there"**: John B. Taylor, "The Need to Return to a
Monetary Framework," January 2009. http://www.stanford.edu/~johntayl/
NABE%20Business%20Economics%20Article%20-%20Taylor.pdf

255 **"TALF shows us"**: George A. Akerlof and Robert J. Shiller, *Animal Spirits*
(Princeton, N.J.: Princeton University Press, 2009), 92.

256 **"Will we face challenges"**: Charles I. Plosser, "The Economic Outlook
and Some Challenges Facing the Federal Reserve," Federal Reserve Bank
of Philadelphia, January 14, 2009. http://www.philadelphiafed.org/
publications/speeches/plosser/2009/01-14-09_university-of-delaware.cfm

257 **"In a committee such as the FOMC"**: Richard W. Fisher, "Responding
to Turbulence (with Reference to Bob Dylan, Alan Brooke, Washington
Irving, Anna Fisher and Marcus Nadler)," Federal Reserve Bank of
Dallas, September 25, 2008. http://www.dallasfed.org/news/speeches/
fisher/2008/fs080925.cfm

258 **"I felt after"**: Interview, Richard Fisher.

258 **"My colleagues"**: Richard W. Fisher, "Historical Perspectives on the
Current Economic and Financial Crisis," Federal Reserve Bank of
Dallas, December 18, 2008. http://www.dallasfed.org/news/speeches/
fisher/2008/fs081218.cfm

260 "[T]hese were funds": Kenneth Lewis memo, filed with Securities and Exchange Commission. http://msnmoney.brand.edgar-online.com/EFX_dll/EDGARpro.dll?FetchFilingHTML1?1D=6274964&SessionID=txp3WohEzEop249

260 **Over the weekend:** Testimony of Kenneth Lewis, "In Re: Executive Compensation Investigation, Bank of America–Merrill Lynch," Office of the Attorney General, State of New York, February 26, 2009, p. 52. http://www.oag.state.ny.us/media_center/2009/apr/apr23a_09.html

261 **"A vague letter":** Personal communication with Paulson spokeswoman.

261 **"He said there was no way":** E-mail released by New York attorney general. http://www.oag.state.ny.us/media_center/2009/apr/apr23a_09.html

262 **A few weeks later:** Bank of America Corporation Q4 2008 Earnings Call Transcript, January 16, 2008. http://seekingalpha.com/article/115373-bank-of-america-corporation-q4-2008-earnings-call-transcript?page=-1

264 **A few weeks later, Bernanke reflected:** Interview, Ben Bernanke.

CHAPTER 14: DID BERNANKE KEEP HIS PROMISE TO MILTON FRIEDMAN?

265 **"by far the deepest":** International Monetary Fund, *World Economic Outlook,* April 2009, p. 9. http://www.imf.org/external/pubs/ft/weo/2009/01/index.htm

267 **"I've been in the trenches:"** Interview, Henry Paulson.

268 **"chance to talk":** CBS News, *60 Minutes,* March 15, 2009. http://www.cbsnews.com/stories/2009/03/12/60minutes/main4862191.shtml

268 **"the best possible":** Jon Hilsenrath, "Bernanke's PR Push Rewrites Fed Script," *Wall Street Journal,* April 15, 2009, A1.

269 **"increased uncertainty":** Ben Bernanke, "Long-term commitments, dynamic optimization, and the business cycle," MIT, 1979. http://dspace.mit.edu/handle/1721.1/29839

269 **"I think it is important":** Jon Hilsenrath, "Bernanke's PR Push Rewrites Fed Script," *Wall Street Journal,* April 15, 2009, p. A1.

270 **"The biggest risk":** CBS News, *60 Minutes,* March 15, 2009. http://www.cbsnews.com/stories/2009/03/12/60minutes/main4862191.shtml

270 **"We should not"**: Sen. Mark Warner, "Floor Statement: Systemic Risk Regulation," June 16, 2009.

271 **"I come from Main Street"**: Ibid.

272 **"Regulators"**: Ben S. Bernanke, "Four Questions About the Financial Crisis," Federal Reserve Board, April 14, 2009. http://www.federalreserve.gov/newsevents/speech/bernanke20090414a.htm

275 **"Regarding the Great Depression"**: Ben S. Bernanke, "On Milton Friedman's Ninetieth Birthday," Federal Reserve Board, November 8, 2002. http://www.federalreserve.gov/boarddocs/speeches/2002/20021108/default.htm

EPILOGUE: IT COULD HAVE BEEN WORSE

276 **The worst financial crisis:** Ben S. Bernanke, "Monetary Policy and the Housing Bubble," January 3, 2010. http://www.federalreserve.gov/newsevents/speech/bernanke20100103a.htm

277 **unemployment rate:** Congressional Budget Office. http://www.cbo.gov/ftpdocs/108xx/doc10871/Chapter2.shtml#1096918

277 **private economic forecasters:** Phil Izzo, "Economists Credit Fed for Alleviating Crisis," wsj.com, March 12, 2010. http://online.wsj.com/article/SB10001424052748703625304575115674057260664.html

279 **A survey:** Ibid.

279 **between 1.4 million and 3 million:** Congressional Budget Office, "Reinvestment Act on Employment and Economic Output from October 2009 Through December 2009," February 2010. http://www.cbo.gov/ftpdocs/110xx/doc11044/02-23-ARRA.pdf

279 **Roosevelt was inaugurated:** William L. Silber, "Why Did FDR's Bank Holiday Succeed?" *FRBNY Economic Policy Review,* July 2009, pp. 19–30. http://www.newyorkfed.org/newsevents/news/research/2009/rp090615.html

281 **"If Geithner's"**: Harold Brubaker, "Geithner Flops on Wall Street," *Philadelphia Inquirer,* February 11, 2009, p. C1.

281 **"nationalize big swaths"**: James Saft, "Nationalisation by Autumn, Bank on it," Reuters, February 12, 2009.

283 **"Some feared"**: Daniel K. Tarullo, "Lessons from the Stress Test,"

March 26, 2010. www.federalreserve.gov/newsevents/speech/
tarullo20100326a.htm

283 "the results were released": Ibid.

283 "I don't understand": David Wessel, "Lehman's Legacy: Government's
Trial and Error Helped Stem Panic," *Wall Street Journal,* September 14,
2009, p. 1.

284 "Not for the first time": House Financial Services Committee hearing,
July 21, 2009.

284 A July 2009 Gallup poll: Lydia Sad, "CDC Tops Government
Ratings; Federal Reserve Board Lowest," Gallup, July 27, 2009.
http://www.gallup.com/poll/121886/CDC-Tops-Agency-Ratings
-Federal-Reserve-Board-Lowest.aspx

284 "The main thing": Interview, Bernanke.

285 "History is full": Bernanke, "Reflections on a Year of Crisis, August
21, 2009. http://www.federalreserve.gov/newsevents/speech/
bernanke20090821a.htm

286 Bernanke got word: Jon Hilsenrath, Elizabeth Williamson, and Jonathan
Weisman, "Calm in Crisis Won Fed Job — Obama Sticks with 'Bold,
Persistent' Chief, but Next Term Could Be Tense If Rates Rise," *Wall
Street Journal,* August 26, 2009.

286 "If you fight a battle": Senate Banking Committee hearing, December 9,
2009. http://www.gpo.gov/fdsys/pkg/CHRG-111shrg206/pdf/CHRG
-111shrg206.pdf

287 "My basic view": John Cassidy, "No Credit," *The New Yorker,* March 15,
2010. http://www.newyorker.com/reporting/2010/03/15/100315fa_fact_
cassidy?currentPage=all

288 A Wall Street Journal/NBC News poll: Posted at http://online.wsj.com/
public/resources/documents/WSJ-NBCpoll-01262010.pdf

288 "Well, just tell me": Michael Corkery, "Warren Buffett Predicts Chaos
If Bernanke Is Not Re-Confirmed," Deal Journal, wsj.com, January 22,
2010. http://blogs.wsj.com/deals/2010/01/22/buffett-predicts-chaos-if-
bernanke-is-not-re-confirmed/tab/article/

288 "Replacing him": Paul Krugman, "The Bernanke Conundrum," *New
York Times,* January 24, 2010, p. A17.

288 "far too susceptible": "The Bernanke Nomination," *Wall Street Journal,*
January 25, 2009, p. A18.

290 **$109 billion:** Congressional Budget Office, Report on the Troubled Asset Relief Program, March 2010. www.cbo.gov/ftpdocs/112xx/doc11227/03 -17-TARP.pdf

290 **$1.7 trillion:** Joseph Gagnon et. al, "Large Scale Asset Purchases by the Federal Reserve: Did They Work?" Federal Reserve Bank of New York, March 2010.

291 **Stanford economist John Taylor:** Johannes Stroebel and John Taylor, "Estimated Impact of the Fed's Mortgage-Backed Securities Purchase Program," National Bureau of Economic Research, Working Paper No. 15626, December 2009.

291 **Paulson published his book:** Henry M. Paulson Jr., *On the Brink* (New York: Hachett Book Group, 2010), pp. 241, 290, 313.

291 **"I stood under the harsh":** Ibid., p. 206.

292 **"Once your near-death":** Interview, Bernanke.

293 **"House prices began to rise":** Bernanke, "Monetary Policy and the Housing Bubble," January 3, 2010. http://www.federalreserve.gov/ newsevents/speech/bernanke20100103a.htm

GLOSSARY

Bank of England

The Fed's counterpart in the United Kingdom.

central bank

An institution, such as the Fed, that controls the supply of credit in an economy.

collateral

Property pledged by a borrower to pay off a loan if the borrower can't come up with the money. When a lender holds collateral, a loan is said to be secured; when it doesn't, a loan is unsecured.

discount rate

Rate at which the Fed lends directly to banks, set by the Federal Reserve Board of Governors and based on recommendations from district Fed banks.

discount window

Nickname for the Fed's direct lending to banks.

European Central Bank

The Fed's counterpart for the sixteen countries that share the euro.

Exchange Stabilization Fund

Created in 1932 to give the Treasury money to buy gold, currencies, and other securities to influence exchange rates; used to backstop money market mutual funds in 2008.

federal funds interest rate

Rate at which banks lend to each other overnight; largely controlled by the Fed.

Federal Open Market Committee (FOMC)

Monetary policy committee composed of the seven governors plus the twelve presidents, five of whom have a vote at any one time.

Federal Reserve Board of Governors

Seven members, known as governors, each appointed by the president and confirmed by the Senate. Based in Washington.

Federal Reserve Bank of New York

Most important of the twelve regional or district Fed banks, each with its own president and private-sector board of directors.

lender of last resort

The entity, usually the central bank, that can lend to banks and others who cannot get loans elsewhere.

Maiden Lane

Special corporations created by the Fed (named for a street that goes by the New York Fed headquarters) to hold assets the Fed bought from Bear Stearns and American International Group.

money market mutual funds

Investment vehicles that take money from investors large and small and buy short-term government and corporate securities.

mortgage-backed securities

Widely held financial instrument composed of large numbers of mortgages or pieces of mortgages.

primary dealers

Sixteen banks and securities firms with which the New York Fed trades securities.

Primary Dealer Credit Facility

Created by the Fed in March 2008 to expand the discount window to provide loans to securities firms, not only banks.

repurchase agreement

Loan in which one side agrees to buy a security from the other and sell it back at a fixed date and a fixed price. Known as "repo."

securitization

Practice of turning loans made by banks and others into securities that can be held and traded by investors.

Term Asset-Backed Securities Loan Facility (TALF)

Launched In March 2008 by the Fed and Treasury to lend to investors who buy securities backed by loans to consumers and businesses.

Term Auction Facility (TAF)

Created by the Fed in December 2008 for banks to borrow from the Fed as an alternative to the discount window; rate set in auctions.

tri-party repo

Loan—or repurchase agreement—in which a bank serves as a middleman between the borrower and lender.

Treasury Securities Lending Facility

Created by the Fed in March 2008 to lend easily sold Treasury securities to Wall Street firms in exchange for less easily sold securities.

Troubled Assets Relief Fund

Created by Congress in October 2008 to provide $700 billion to Treasury to buy assets from and invest in banks.

unusual and exigent

Circumstances, under federal law, in which the Fed can lend to nearly anyone.

yield

Interest rate that the market sets on government and private debt securities.

SELECTED BIBLIOGRAPHY

In addition to newspaper, magazine, and wire service accounts and academic papers, the following books provided useful perspective.

Ahamed, Liaquat. *Lords of Finance: The Bankers Who Broker the World,* New York: Penguin Press, 2009.

Atack, Jeremy, and Peter Passell. *A New Economic View of American History,* New York: W. W. Norton & Co., 1979.

Bagehot, Walter. *Lombard Street: A Description of the Money Market,* New York: Armstrong & Co., 1873.

Bernanke, Ben S. *Essays on the Great Depression,* Princeton, N.J.: Princeton University Press, 2000.

Blinder, Alan S. *Central Banking in Theory and Practice,* Cambridge, Mass.: MIT Press, 1998.

Carr, Sean D., and Robert F. Bruner. *The Panic of 1907: Lessons Learned from the Market's Perfect Storm,* Hoboken, N.J.: John Wiley & Son, 2007.

Dighe, Ranjit S. *The Historian's Wizard of Oz: Reading L. Frank Baum's Classic as a Political and Monetary Allegory,* Westport, Conn.: Praeger, 2002.

Frank, Robert, and Ben S. Bernanke, *Principles of Economics,* New York: McGraw Hill, 2001.

Friedman, Milton, and Anna Jacobson Schwartz, *A Monetary History of the United States, 1867–1960,* Princeton, N.J.: Princeton University Press, 1963.

Glass, Carter. *An Adventure in Constructive Finance,* Garden City, N.Y.: Doubleday Page & Company, 1927.

Gordon, John Steele. *An Empire of Wealth: The Epic History of American Economic Power,* New York: HarperCollins Publishers, 2004.

Gramlich, Edward M. *Subprime Mortgages: America's Latest Boom and Bust,* Washington, D.C.: Urban Institute Press, 2007.

Greenspan, Alan. *The Age of Turbulence: Adventure in a New World,* New York: Penguin Press, 2007.

Greider, William. *Secrets of the Temple,* New York: Simon & Schuster, 1987.

Hackley, Howard H. *Lending Functions of the Federal Reserve Banks: A History,* Washington, D.C.: Federal Reserve Board of Governors, 1973.

Hammond, Bray. *Banks and Politics in America from the Revolution to the Civil War,* Princeton, N.J.: Princeton University Press, 1957.

Kelly, Kate. *Street Fighters,* New York: Penguin Press, 2009.

Kindleberger, Charles P., and Robert Aliber, *Manias, Panics, and Crashes,* Hoboken, N.J.: John Wiley & Sons, 2005.

Meltzer, Allan H. *A History of the Federal Reserve, Volume 1: 1913–1952,* Chicago: University of Chicago Press, 2003.

Meyer, Laurence H. *A Term at the Fed: An Insider's View,* New York: HarperCollins Publishers, 2004.

Mishkin, Frederic S. *The Economics of Money, Banking, and Financial Markets,* Boston, Mass.: Addison Wesley, 2007

Tarullo, Daniel K. *Banking on Basel: The Future of International Financial Regulation,* Washington, D.C.: Peterson Institute for International Economics, August 2008.

Taylor, John B. *Getting Off Track,* Stanford, Calif.: Hoover Institution Press, 2009.

Woodward, Bob. *Maestro: Greenspan's Fed and the American Boom,* New York: Simon & Schuster, 2000.

ACKNOWLEDGMENTS

This book was possible only because of the cooperation of Federal Reserve officials willing to spend time talking candidly to a reporter even while the Great Panic raged. I'm particularly grateful to Ben Bernanke, Don Kohn, Kevin Warsh, Tim Geithner, and Rick Mishkin and their public relations staff, Michelle Smith and David Skidmore in Washington and Calvin Mitchell in New York. At the Treasury, Hank Paulson, Bob Steel, Phillip Swagel, David Nason, David McCormick, Neel Kashkari, and public relations staff Michele Davis and Jennifer Zuccarelli all were helpful, as were Keith Hennessey and Tony Fratto at the White House. Several other Fed and Treasury staff helped me piece together the story. Their careers would not be enhanced by mentioning their names, so I thank them anonymously. Alan Greenspan was generous with his insights. Anil Kashyap of the University of Chicago and Damian Paletta of the *Wall Street Journal* read early drafts and offered useful advice. The Woodrow Wilson International Center for Scholars gave me a quiet place to think and write.

At a time of turmoil in the newspaper industry, the *Wall Street Journal* remains the best place in America to practice journalism. I relied heavily on the reporting of my colleagues there, especially Greg Ip, Jon Hilsenrath, Kate Kelly, Sara Murray, Damian Paletta, Joellen Perry, Sudeep Reddy, and

Deborah Solomon. Bob Davis, Laurie McGinley, Brenda Cronin, and Mitra Kalita kept the paper's economics bureau going while I was away. Jerry Seib was always available to listen and dispense his sage advice.

Raphael Sagalyn, my agent, began encouraging me to consider a book about the Fed long before the Great Panic, and provided wise and patient counsel from conception to completion. John Mahaney at Crown offered both welcome enthusiasm and acute editing. Howard and Nathan Means strengthened the manuscript with efficiency and skill. Shelly Perron delivered meticulous copyediting.

Most of all, I'm grateful to my wife, Naomi Karp, who never once complained as this book preoccupied me, and instead offered unflagging support and love.

INDEX

ABOUT THE AUTHOR

David Wessel is economics editor of *The Wall Street Journal* and writes the Capital column, a weekly look at forces shaping living standards around the world. A native of New Haven, Connecticut, and a 1975 graduate of Haverford College, David joined *The Wall Street Journal* in 1983 after working at the *Middletown (Conn.) Press,* the *Hartford Courant,* and the *Boston Globe.* He was a Knight-Bagehot Fellow in business and economics journalism at Columbia University in 1980–81, and has shared two Pulitzer Prizes. David and his wife, Naomi Karp, live in Washington, D.C. They have two children, Julia and Ben.